Representations of Swift

"Commemorative" pastel portrait of Swift, with *Verses on the Death of Dr. Swift*, by Rupert Barber. Reproduced by kind permission of Robert and Vivian Folkenflik.

Representations of Swift

Edited by

Brian A. Connery

DELAWARE
Newark: University of Delaware Press
London: Associated University Presses

Associated University Presses
2010 Eastpark Boulevard
Cranbury, NJ 08512

Associated University Presses
16 Barter Street
London WC1A 2AH, England

Associated University Presses
P.O. Box 338, Port Credit
Mississauga, Ontario
Canada L5G 4L8

The paper used in this publication meets the requirements of the American National Standard for Permanence of Paper for Printed Library Materials Z39.48-1984.

Library of Congress Cataloging-in-Publication Data

Representations of Swift / edited by Brian A. Connery.
    p. cm.
Includes bibliographical references and index.
ISBN 0-87413-797-7 (alk. paper)
    1. Swift, Jonathan, 1667–1745—Criticism and interpretation. I. Connery, Brian A.

PR3727 .R45 2002
828′.509—dc21

    2002021765

For Andrew Carpenter, scholar and host, without whose hospitable genius this work could never have been collected.

Contents

Illustrations   9
Introduction   11
  BRIAN A. CONNERY

Part I: A Tale of a Tub

The *Tale,* Temple, and Swift's Irish Aesthetic   25
  DAVID DEEMING
"This Way of Printing Bits of Books": The Fiction of Incompletion
in *A Tale of a Tub*   41
  NICK RUSHWORTH
Swift's *Tale,* the Renaissance Anatomy, and Humanist Polemic   57
  W. SCOTT BLANCHARD

Part II: "Swift"

The Authorial Strategies of Swift's *Verses on the Death*   77
  STEPHEN KARIAN
"He Hates Much Trouble": Johnson's *Life of Swift* and the Contours
of Biographical Inheritance in Late Eighteenth-Century England   99
  J. T. SCANLAN
The Rupert Barber Portraits of Jonathan Swift   117
  ROBERT FOLKENFLIK
Swift's Mythopoeic Authority   150
  ANN CLINE KELLY

Part III: Gender, Class, Swift

Hints Toward Authoritative Conversation: Swift's Dialogical
Strategies in the Letters and the Life   159
  BRIAN A. CONNERY
Swift, Women, and Women Readers: A Feminist Perspective on
Swift's Life   181
  LOUISE BARNETT
Swift, Reynolds, and the Lower Orders   195
  SEAN SHESGREEN

Part IV: Swift and Ireland

Swift, Postcolonialism, and Irish Studies: The Valence of
Ambivalence   217
  ROBERT MAHONY

Speaking for the Irish Nation: The Drapier, the Bishop, and the
Problems of Colonial Representation   236
  CAROLE FABRICANT

Part V: Coda: Swift Today

Swift's Satiric Authority: Prospects from a Late Twentieth-
Century Perspective   269
  KENNETH CRAVEN

Select Bibliography   286
Notes on Contributors   300
Index   303

List of Illustrations

"Commemorative" pastel portrait of Swift, with *Verses on the
Death of Dr. Swift,* by Rupert Barber. 2

Tale of a Tub. 42

Verses on the Death of Dr. Swift, Faulkner, fourth edition. 85

Frontispiece engraving to Orrery's *Remarks,* by Benjamin Wilson. 118

"LeFanu" pastel portrait by Rupert Barber. 119

"Bryn Mawr" pastel portrait. 120

Miniature portrait by Rupert Barber. 121

Watercolor after Francis Bindon. 122

Etched self-portrait by Rembrandt. 130

Engraved portrait of Alexander Pope by Jonathan Richardson. 131

"Commemorative" framed portrait by Rupert Barber. 134

Portrait of William Thompson by Rupert Barber. 136

Miniature portrait of William Thompson by Rupert Barber. 137

Portrait of Swift, attributed to Francis Bindon. 139

Mezzotint portrait by Andrew Miller, after Francis Bindon. 141

Introduction

Brian A. Connery

IN LATE JULY 1999, STUDENTS OF THE EIGHTEENTH-CENTURY THRONGED to University College, Dublin, for the Tenth International Congress on the Enlightenment, sponsored by the International Society for Eighteenth-Century Studies (ISECS) and organized and hosted by Dr. Andrew Carpenter of UCD, a prodigious student of eighteenth-century Irish literature and an eminent Swiftian. Four years of publicity had ensured that scholars worldwide had long known of the conference to be held in the city where Jonathan Swift held sway in his latter years as Dean of St. Patrick's Cathedral and Drapier, as well as "absolute Monarch in the *Liberties,* and King of the Mob."[1] As added attractions to Prestophiles, Bruce Arnold, the literary editor of the *Irish Independent,* had organized an exhibition of Swift-related eighteenth-century art at the National Library of Ireland, and Andrew Carpenter arranged a meeting room in Marsh's Library, adjacent to St. Patrick's Cathedral, for sessions devoted to Swift's life, associates, and work.

The consequences of such a propitious location and magnanimous hospitality were seven panels devoted exclusively to Swift, as well as frequent papers on Swift sprinkled throughout other sessions. Many scholars whose research has routinely focused upon issues tangential to the works of Swift were moved to consider his life and his writings in papers specifically for this occasion, offering a myriad of new and exciting perspectives. In the tradition of ISECS, many papers were interdisciplinary, combining literature, history, art history, and cultural studies. These sessions and papers, as well as the many opportunities for Swiftians to meet and talk, laid the groundwork for what should be a burgeoning production of new and insightful work on the Dean. This volume, collecting some of the very best work presented at the congress, represents only the very first fruits.

This collection, like many of Swift's own productions, may thus be considered an "occasional" publication. As such, it offers not only the "representations of Swift" to which its title refers, but also a representation of Swift scholarship at the close of the twentieth century. It is worthy to note, in this light, that these essays consistently strike a note of cautious reconsideration. Subsequent to the nineteenth-century disdain for Swift, to his recuperation and defense in the twentieth century, including the revaluing from the 1950s to the '70s of much of his poetry; after the poststructuralist musings on his always already deconstructed satires and the feminist examination of his seeming misogyny in the 1970s and '80s; and following the magisterial biography by Irvin Ehrenpreis completed in 1983, these essays return to fundamental questions about the life, writing, and views of Swift, issues raised in part by literary scholarship's return to historicism but most powerfully suggestive of a return to biography: What was his attitude toward and relation with Ireland? What was the nature of his relationships with the women in his life? What were his literary goals? His literary disappointments? What was his relation with the poor in the Liberties of St. Patrick's? What does his work say to us about the present moment? Such, of course, might be expected in any project organized under the name of an author. Nonetheless, these essays are remarkable in their almost universal and relentless curiosity about the man who produced the work.

Both the curiosity about the author and his meaning and the caution with which it is satisfied are provoked by Swift's works themselves. A recurrent theme in the essays is Swift's deliberate withholding of information, his teasing of readers with gaps and fragments, his playful and serious disguises, his rampant ironies that direct us away from wrong answers but point only tentatively toward right ones. Several essays lament the paucity of supplementary evidence that would allow us conclusively to fill in gaping holes in Swift's biography: the missing letters of Esther Johnson and Esther Vanhomrigh, the absence of accounts of Swift's conversation, the questionable authorship of many works attributed to Swift. The cautious tone of many of the commentators herein is, no doubt, a product of the self-consciousness that any writer on Swift feels as a consequence of Swift's own characterizations of critics. Two of the essays here cite the following ironic passage from *A Tale of a Tub:*

> I do here humbly propose for an Experiment, that every Prince in Christendom will take seven of the deepest Scholars in his Dominions, and shut them up close for seven Years in seven chambers, with a Command to write seven ample Commentaries on this comprehensive Discourse. I shall venture to affirm, that whatever Difference may be found in their several conjectures, they will be all, without the least Distortion, manifestly deduceable from the Text.[2]

The Tale-Teller's vaunting of the polysemic quality of his text calls attention to the *Tale*'s textual instability even as Swift's ironic disguise suggests the dangers of critical reading. Twenty-two years later, Gulliver's account of his encounters with the ghosts of the commentators on Homer and Aristotle suggest that Swift's view of the "true Critick" had not changed:

"these commentators always kept in the most distant quarters from their principals in the lower world, through a consciousness of shame and guilt, because they had so horribly misrepresented the meaning of those authors to posterity."[3]

Four of the essays in this volume react to Swift's admonitions, his teasings, and our critical heritage by offering histories of Swiftian biography: reading earlier biographies both appreciatively and skeptically, aiming to discover not only what the biographies tell us about Swift but what they tell us about the biographers—and what *that* tells us about Swift. Another essay, similarly, offers a history of Swiftian portraiture, suggestively linking different artists and portraits with different popular images of Swift. All of the essays are characterized by a resistance to oversimplification, a resistance that is itself emerging as a Swiftian characteristic. Whereas earlier critics, commentators, and biographers have most frequently raised and sought to resolve, on one side or the other, questions of the either/or sort, which Swift's own texts seem to invite (Whig or Tory? Houyhnhnm or Yahoo? Ancient or Modern? Misogynist or feminist? British colonist or Irish nationalist?), the writers in this volume are more likely to respond to these questions with "both/and" or "neither/nor" answers.

It was to be expected that at an international conference in Dublin in the late twentieth century, with plentiful plenary sessions on eighteenth-century Ireland, the question of Swift's Irishness would be thoroughly discussed. One of the liveliest roundtable discussions of the conference, organized by Robert Mahony under the relatively innocuous banner of "The Emergence of Ireland in Eighteenth-Century Studies," swerved early toward and lingered long on the question of the applicability of postcolonial theory to Ireland. The implications of such an application for the study of Swift are explored in essays in this volume by Mahony, David Deeming, and Carole Fabricant. But again and again, the issues of Swift's self-identification with Ireland and England; Ireland's cultural influence on his worldview and on his writing, both early and late in his career; and the relative importance in his life of Irish friends, institutions, and landscapes, were raised and investigated.

This volume begins with three new essays on *The Tale of a Tub,* a work that appears now to be eclipsing the *Travels* in the amount of extended critical exploration it receives. David Deeming's contribution to the exploration of the *Tale,* as mentioned above, initiates the theme of the significance in his work of Swift's Irish background. Placing the *Tale*'s textual fragmentariness in the context of the emergence of modern subjectivity, especially as delineated in John Locke's *Treatise on Humane Understanding,* Deeming selectively and precisely deploys both postcolonial and psychoanalytic theory in order to investigate the vexed question of Swift's Irishness as it is manifest in the *Tale* and proposes that the text's self-division reflects the self-division of Ireland itself. Applying Harold Bloom's model of the anxiety of influence to the relationship between Swift and his mentor, Sir William Temple, Deeming finds Temple to be representative of English nationalism and colonialism, while Swift's "self-transcending excesses of wit" are manifestations of Ireland, its resentments, and its self-division. Moreover, in the *Tale*'s teller, we hear the voice of exclusion and exile, which Deeming tentatively identifies with that of Swift. Arguing that the wit of the *Tale* is un-English (and thus un-Templesque), Deeming suggests that Irish wit, exuberance, and excess are deployed throughout the *Tale* to expose English sublimations.

In a feat of historical imagination of a different sort, Nick Rushworth attempts to see the *Tale* as many of its original readers might have, assuming its apparent incompleteness as a fact rather than a fiction, a fact easily explainable within the context of the early eighteenth-century book trade. After exploring the ways in which a naive eighteenth-century reader might approach the text's fragmentation and paratext, especially its annotations, Rushworth turns to the contemporary philological approach to fragmented texts and their challenges in order to explore the ways in which the *fiction* of its fragmentariness, once perceived, underwrites the satire of the *Tale*. In particular, Rushworth offers as a backdrop for the *Tale,* the work of Richard Bentley, one of the satire's primary targets, and his approach to fragmented texts. While many critics have looked upon Bentley's work on the epistles of Phalaris as both the target and the instigation for the *Tale,* Rushworth looks to two earlier works, *Epistolar ad Millium* (1691) and *Notes on Callimachus* (1697) as representative of Bentley's method and as possible sources for Swift's method and possibly thus as the objects of his parody.

W. Scott Blanchard, a scholar of Renaissance Menippea, draws our attention to the ways in which *The Tale* is situated in the tradition of the Menippean satire—not the Menippea of Rabelais, which have received so much attention as a consequence of the work of Mikhail Bakhtin (and with which Swift was intimately familiar), or of Erasmus, or even of Robert Burton, but the Italian Menippean tradition. Specifically, Blanchard calls our attention to works that he characterizes as the products of philological squabbles, works that are more likely to be characterized by polemic and invective than the anatomies more widely known in Swift scholarship. Just as the *Tale* works with the oppositions between traditional but dilettantish scholarship of Temple and Boyle and the emerging philological professionalism of Bentley and Wotton, so, as Blanchard illustrates, the Menippea of Justus Lipsius and Angelo Poliziano, to which Swift had access, had done so before and may have provided Swift with appropriate examples of both vehicle and style. In exploring Swift within this larger context,

Blanchard suggestively situates Swift's work historically in the emergence of modernity and gestures toward a manifestation of the "public sphere" hitherto unremarked in Swift's work.

The Swift of this collection's second section—"Swift"— appears in scare quotes, following the usage of Ann Cline Kelly's essay, to suggest that even with Swift's semirehabilitation in the twentieth century, the painstaking research of Ehrenpreis's biography, and the ongoing work at the Ehrenpreis Institute, Swift scholarship proceeds in something like a textual hall of mirrors, with many representations of Swift that cannot be traced directly, unambiguously, finally, or definitively to the man himself. As Kelly suggests, in the introduction of her essay, "fundamental questions about the man are still unanswered. Were his allegiances to England or to Ireland? Was he ever married? Was he frigid or libidinous? What was the nature of his religious belief? Was he a Jacobite? How far did his sympathy with the underclass extend?" Swift scholarship seeks simultaneously to demythologize, that is to pare away apocrypha that have adhered to the "author function" of Swift; to definitively eliminate misattributed work that has accrued in the Swift canon; and to rebuild Swift from the ground up, ever self-conscious of the constructedness of the Swift that emerges from this process, as well as increasingly self-conscious about the process itself.

One of the most vexing foci for attempts to reconstruct Swift, to find and delineate the Swift who constructs representations of himself, is the late great poem, *Verses on the Death of Dr. Swift*. Controversy about the editing of the poem has been continuous since its first publication, and the degree of Swift's self-ironizing in the poem has also been subject to lively debate. In an important essay here, incorporating and applying recent work and theory on print culture, Stephen Karian examines the poem both as text and as publishing event, finding corresponding strategies employed by Swift as both writer and author. In an analysis of the voice, character, and function of the speaker at the Rose Tavern, to whom Swift gives the bulk of the poem, Karian finds Swift's acknowledgment of the author's ultimately incomplete control of both his text and his author-function, while also tracing his rhetorical efforts to maintain as much control as possible. Like so many of his texts, *Verses* delineates a double-bind, according to Karian: Swift wants to escape the vagaries of the book trade in order to represent himself definitively yet remains dependent upon it for the dissemination of his self-representation.

Another notoriously problematic representation of Swift is Samuel Johnson's *Life of Swift*. Long the cause of dissension between Swift scholars (who sometimes maintain that the biography says more about Johnson than Swift) and Johnson scholars (who sometimes admit misjudgments on Johnson's part but maintain his overall acuity), the *Life* has borne considerable influence over representations of Swift since its publication. In "He Hates Much Trouble," Johnson scholar J. T. Scanlan attempts to bridge the gulf between Johnsonians and Swiftians, offering an overview of Johnson's working approach to the project, an analysis of Johnson's use of his sources, an appreciation for the conditions under which Johnson worked, and an examination of the ways in which the methods, habits, and insights with which Johnson routinely worked proved less insightful when applied to Swift.

Robert Folkenflik introduces his essay on "The Rupert Barber Portraits of Jonathan Swift" by tracing the genealogy of "a series of problematic engravings . . . that disseminated Swift's image through Europe and America," perhaps contributing to the conception, supported by Johnson's *Life,* of a mad Swift. To balance these representations, Folkenflik offers the portraits by the son of a Dublin draper, artist Rupert Barber, including the one gracing the cover and frontispiece of this volume. In the course of the essay, Folkenflik, in the spirit of the true scholar-adventurer, methodically gathers and evaluates biographical information on Barber, correcting along the way many inaccuracies recorded in Swift scholarship, and provides data regarding the provenances of a variety of Swift portraits. In sum, the essay powerfully suggests the variety of extant visual representations of Swift and argues that Barber's work offers a "melancholy dignity" that needs to be incorporated, along with the wittiness of the more famous Charles Jervas portraits and the severity of the Francis Bindon portraits, into our imaging of Swift.

Ann Cline Kelly's essay, "Swift's Mythopoeic Authority," broadly addresses the complicated scene of Swift studies, detailing the many obstacles between a twenty-first century reader and a definitive representation or construction of Swift. Swift's unstable irony, his self-conscious and sometimes self-ironizing representations of a character called "Swift," the many textual impersonations of Swift, Swift's own impersonations of others, the seeming contradictions within his work, and the self-interested or politically motivated representations of Swift by others—all produce a very "enigmatic Dean." Kelly suggests that the very inconsistency among the various representations of Swift in his lifetime—indeed, the construction of a "Swift" as a sign for inconsistency—induced a process of mythopoesis, a mythologizing of Swift, begun in his lifetime and continuing today. Kelly argues that generic patterns, as well as details about Swift's life, have helped to determine the stories that have been told about him—and have thus produced a variety of Swifts. To this extent, Kelly suggests, the authority of Swift today is as much or more the authority of the mythic Swifts as it is of "Swift" himself.

A similar sense of the way in which a Swiftian nothing becomes a reader's something underlies my own essay on Swift's "authoritative conversation," proposing an authority derived as much from silence as from pronouncement, an authority that is the product of the auditor's conferral rather than the speaker's claim. The evidence for examination in a study of Swift's talk is scant, with gaps and silences more apparent than extended illustrations of conversation. But the essay argues that the gaps and silences are significant, that they are, in fact, Swiftian characteristics, just as anonymity has become recognized as a Swiftian signature. Of some note, within the context of this section on gender and class, is Swift's repeated assertion, explored within the essay, of the desirability of conversation unimpaired by considerations of class or gender distinctions—and the occasional instances of his own practice deviating from this principle.

Louise Barnett emphasizes the latter, focusing in particular upon Swift's relationship with Esther Johnson (Stella) and suggesting that Swift's conversational principles of silence and restraint were articulated primarily for the adoption of others, particularly women, for whom, Barnett suggests, silence constituted Swift's ideal. Barnett begins with a survey of previous constructions and representations of Swift. In particular, she sorts out the different Swifts constructed by male and female biographers, especially in their handling of his relationship with Johnson, on the principle that gender difference can be significant in the evaluation of some data. Barnett herself explores in some detail Swift's representations of Johnson in the birthday poems, in which she finds the same aversion to female physicality, albeit muted, as others have remarked in his scatological poems, and comments on Swift's remarkable *nonrepresentation* of Stella after her death. Barnett focuses on Johnson's requesting a memorial marker, and she reads Swift's negligence in this regard as both a literal and metaphorical denial of female will. She suggests, with the example of Daniel Defoe, that empowered femininity was not unthinkable for men in the early eighteenth century, and she finds, in the absence of any evidence in Swift's writing of his having considered it, matter for serious reflection.

In "Swift, Reynolds, and the Lower Orders," Sean Shesgreen places Swift in juxtaposition with Joshua Reynolds, in order to explore the ways in which they represent the poor, as well as their relative attitudes toward the poor. While Reynolds routinely used the poor for models, he most often and most famously transformed them into representatives of the higher orders. Swift, on the other hand, whose work is suffused with the poor and the common, characteristically represents them as he finds them, unflinchingly, though sometimes, as Shesgreen suggests, transforming them from individuals into types. Shesgreen demonstrates that Swift's manifest attitudes toward the poor are multiple: jocular, compassionate, punitive. In some works, he impersonates them good-naturedly; in others, he sternly proposes disciplining them. This multiplicity, Shesgreen finds, resists the oversimplification of current theory.

One of the most powerful "Swifts" constructed over the past 250 years, as Robert Mahony has shown in his volume, *Jonathan Swift: The Irish Identity,* is the Irish patriot, the rhetorical founder of Irish nationalism through his campaign as the Drapier. In his essay in this volume, "Swift, Postcolonialism, and Irish Studies: The Valence of Ambivalence," Mahony discusses the ways in which the construction of Swift as patriot has come under attack, how Swift's not infrequent anti-Irish remarks have been construed as evidence for deeply biased views against Ireland and the Irish, revealing him as an opportunist who seized upon an Irish issue in order to exact his revenge upon the England with which he identified but by which he felt badly treated. Some of this critique has been launched from the precincts of Irish studies, and Mahony offers an overview of the emergence of this multidisciplinary project with particular attention to its receptivity (or, more frequently, nonreceptivity) to postcolonial theory. The applicability of postcolonial theory to Ireland, as the essay suggests, is inexact. And the application of such theory to Swift is similarly and consequently imprecise. Nonetheless, Mahony argues that Swift's ambiguous relationships with Ireland and England seem more consistent with those typical of the "dissenting subaltern" proposed by postcolonial theory than with the character of a venal hypocrite.

Carole Fabricant's "Speaking for the Irish Nation: The Drapier, the Bishop, and the Problems of Colonial Representation" extends further the exploration of the difficulties of hyphenated identities. Focusing upon the Drapier's Fourth Letter, addressed to the Whole People of Ireland, Fabricant wonders who this Whole People might be, and who might be qualified to represent them or speak for them: Can an Anglo-Irish Protestant, like Swift, speak for the Whole People of Ireland? Fabricant assembles a variety of historical contingencies that render the question more pragmatic than ethical by demonstrating the conditions that militated against Irish Catholics speaking for themselves or being heard if they did. The Declaratory Act, which in effect rendered the Irish Parliament silent, had already created a situation in which the English Parliament spoke for Ireland. The example of George Berkeley is examined as a demonstration of the capacity of writing by the colonizer, in spite of overt racialism, to open an opportunity for the colonized to speak. Fabricant's close reading of the Fourth Letter demonstrates Swift's rhetorical deftness and acuity, as he simultaneously excludes the Irish Catholics on sectarian grounds yet includes them in the conflict of class into which he renders the Wood controversy. Fabricant concludes with a consideration of another problem of representation, shifting from the problem of representing the silent and/ or silenced to that of representing the unspeakable.

It is, perhaps, in his attempts to speak of that which is unspeakable, the thing that truly is, rather than the thing that is not, that accounts for our sense of Swift's continuing pertinence to our world. In the volume's final essay, Kenneth Craven, whose book *Jonathan Swift and the Millennium of Madness* explored the *Tale*'s peculiar resonances for the end of the twentieth-century, looks again at the ways in which Swift's work pertains today and reflects on the ways in which our culture resists what Swift has to tell us. Well-suited to his task, a business consultant and a former avatar of the information age, as well as a student of the eighteenth-century, Craven includes a brief account of his own momentarily blind eye to Swift's acute insight and foresight.

In toto, these essays reflect the seriousness with which Swift's work continues to be read, now in the twenty-first century, as well as the ways in which both the man and the work continue to tease us out of complacency and into unease. Swift's work raises questions—biographical, textual, psychological, social, political, ethical, and moral—in ways that delight, perplex, and, of course, vex us. The essays collected here consider these questions with seriousness and high purpose.

I am grateful to Johns Hopkins University Press for permission to reprint Carole Fabricant's essay, "Speaking for the Irish Nation," which originally appeared in *English Literary History* 66 (1999), 337–72, and to *Swift Studies,* edited by Hermann Real, for agreeing to the publication here of Scott Blanchard's "Swift's *Tale,* the Renaissance Anatomy, and Humanist Polemic." For permission to publish the many images in this volume, I am grateful to the Rare Books and Special Collections Library of the University of Sydney, Plate 1; to the Teerink Collection, Annenberg Rare Book and Manuscript Library, at the University of Pennsylvania, Plate 2; to Robert and Vivian Folkenflik, the frontispiece and Plates 3, 8, 9, and 10; the Lefanu family, Plate 4; Bryn Mawr College, Plate 5; the National Gallery of Ireland, Plates 7, 11, 13, and 14; and the New Orleans Museum of Art, Plate 12.

I am grateful to Donald Mell, of the University of Delaware Press, for organizing this project and for his oversight throughout; to Dean David Downing of the College of Arts and Sciences at Oakland University for his generosity and support; to my colleagues in the Department of English at Oakland for support and advice, and especially to June Fisher, Nola Puvalowski, Dawn Deitsch, and Rosemary Aiello for their many assistances, without which this project could never have been completed. Stephanie Howse, graduate assistant, has been invaluable as quote-checker, documentation-fixer, and copyeditor. And, finally, I thank my family—Marlene Mears, Carina, and Brendan—for the time they've afforded me and the encouragement they've given me to complete this work.

NOTES

1. Laetitia Pilkington, *The Memoirs of Laetitia Pilkington,* ed. A. C. Elias Jr., 2 vols., (Athens: University of Georgia Press, 1997), 1: 35.

2. Jonathan Swift, *A Tale of a Tub,* ed. A. C. Guthkelch and D. Nichol Smith, 2nd ed. (Oxford: Clarendon Press, 1958), 185.

3. Jonathan Swift, *Gulliver's Travels,* vol. 11 of *The Prose Works of Jonathan Swift,* ed. Herbert Davis et al. (Oxford: Basil Blackwell, 1939–68), 197.

Representations of Swift

Part I
A Tale of a Tub

The *Tale,* Temple, and Swift's Irish Aesthetic

David Deeming

SIR WILLIAM TEMPLE, AT THE MOMENT OF JONATHAN SWIFT'S FIRST meeting with him, had already retired from public life following a long, distinguished career as diplomat and as confidant of William of Orange. He retained, nevertheless, a position of considerable eminence; not least in the world of learning and letters, where he devoted himself in the tradition of the Renaissance gentleman to the exaltation of the ancients, whose peerless example the moderns were enjoined to follow. Swift, in contrast to Temple, lacked any substantial independent means, had almost failed his degree at Trinity College, Dublin, and had recently become, to all intents and purposes, a refugee: a product of the sectarian conflict that arose in Ireland following the Williamite succession in England. It is in the light of such profound discrepancies in status and background between patron and protégé, I shall be arguing, that we can better understand the extraordinary rhetorical strategies to be found in certain texts written by Swift during his prolonged stay with Temple during the 1690s: namely, the satires *A Tale of a Tub* and *The Battle of the Books.* For if, as I shall go on to illustrate, Temple's own ideas on culture were the corollary of an essentially English nationalist and colonialist mentality, especially as regarded Ireland, then the self-transcending excesses of wit in Swift's books can also be said to signify impulses that are social and political, and not merely literary, in origin. In fact, Swift's relationship with Temple might be said to constitute a most profound exemplification of Harold Bloom's "anxiety of influence." For to have merely enacted a bland aping of Temple and his cultural precepts, instead of trying to exceed or depart from them in some way, would not only have been a betrayal of Swift's own highly distinctive literary gift, it would also have constituted a profound self-betrayal for a man whose country of origin appeared to Temple (as will be illustrated later) as a scene of civil chaos that left the stigmata of barbarism on all of its children.[1]

This can only have contributed toward a rather pronounced inner contradictoriness in the younger Swift. John Traugott speaks of a proud yet self-loathing person who "smarted under his patron's cold looks" and who

25

felt as a result "a life-long distrust of [his own] Irish character, by his own lights only a servile imitation of the English oppressor" (Traugott 83). Such remarks recall William Empson's description of Swift's doubled, self-contradictory style in the *Tale:* "What Swift was trying to say was a minor matter; he was rightly accused of blasphemy for what he said; his own strength made his instrument too strong for him." Empson points out how a kind of "strange metamorphosis takes place in Swift's mind," discernible in the way his books came to produce the *contradiction* of their ostensible thematic (that is, Templarian) purpose.[2] Hence, in *The Battle,* the bee of antiquity's "sweetness and light" is quite obviously being compared very favorably at one level with the loathsome, dirty, foul-mouthed spider of modernity. And yet we cannot ignore the fact that at the same time it is the "high blood" and "energy" of the spider, the mode of the "radical individualist," that the satirist is himself adopting as his own:

> The satire—a satire fit for gentlemen—turns from the vulgarian back upon the "Christian humanist" with his smug assumptions of reason and order. The provincial Irishman in England, the psychological bastard triumphs. The nihilist asserts his rights against the imitator of Temple, the present snob, the Establishmentarian apologist to be. Self-hate becomes hate; posture becomes art. (Traugott 88)

Irvin Ehrenpreis also directs our attention to the connections that exist between the nature of Swift's writings and his Irish origins. "The meaning of Swift's work," Ehrenpreis states at the outset of his biography, "will escape anybody who forgets that his English career, long and important as it was, only interrupted an Irish life." In terms of the composition of the *Tale* in particular, Ehrenpreis makes suggestive comments as to the kind of cultural choices that would have divided Temple and Swift.[3] Temple felt "distrust of the comic and the satirical," dismissed "Swift's adored Rabelais," judged mock-epic "pernicious to poetry and virtue alike," and "detested the raillery and witticisms in which Swift rejoiced." In addition:

> the puns and word games which Swift loved held small appeal for Temple; in fact, his [Temple's] difficulties as a diplomatist were sometimes aggravated by his distaste for codes: "God almighty has given it to other men to make cyphers and to flie, but to me to walk only upon plain ground and to read plain hands."

Swift, then, would have been circumspect in how much he revealed to Temple of his early satires. In fact: "If Swift had such works under way when he came to Moor Park, he probably tabled them. Returning to Ireland in 1694, he might well have felt emancipated enough to let his instincts have their way" (Ehrenpreis 1: 8; 1: 110–11; 1: 186–87). And indeed, Swift's decision to defer publication of these works until 1704, five years after Temple's death, also indicates a wariness on Swift's part as to the possible reaction of his sponsor. Importantly then, Ireland became that location, either literally or as a source of an imaginative license, where Swift's literary predilections could be exercised, a place to which those cultural expectations existing in Temple's England did not fully extend.

The dominant feature of the *Tale* and the *Battle,* obvious even to the most casual reader, is their attempt to present an extraordinary degree of fragmentariness. Their continual digressions, various prefatory sections, footnotes, lists, and the occasional collapsing of meaning into, literally, an empty space on the page such as the one marked *"Hiatus in MS,"* are all manifestations within the body of these texts of an analogous chaos, schism and dissension that the individualizing, atomizing forces of modern life were wreaking upon the body of the state and society.[4] From this perspective, Swift replicates Temple's own position with regard to the seventeenth-century *bataille des anciens et modernes.* By questioning the destabilizing contingency of the modern, a result of individualism's tendency to set up a proliferation of competing, innovative worldviews, a traditionalist emphasis on the virtues and values of antiquity sees common sense as available only to those who are prepared to nurture the claims of continuity.[5] Perhaps the most famous distillation of this position in Swift appears in the allegory of the spider and the bee already mentioned. Whereas the foul modern spider spins materials "out of . . . [his] own Entrails," the bee of antiquity humbly sips from a variety of fixed sources "thro' every Corner of Nature" in order to produce "Sweetness and Light" (234–35). But what if, in fact, the notions of the "ancients" were really just another version of the modern, ideologically dressed up so as not to appear too radical or disruptive?

In this context, it is Locke's *Essay concerning Human Understanding* (1690) that proves a valuable point of contextualization and illumination; particularly as its author not only was the contemporary of Temple, but also shared the political outlook of the latter. The *Essay* enjoyed an immediate success after its publication, providing as it did in England a philosophical analogue to the postrevolutionary *Zeitgeist* of the 1690s, the decade during which Swift composed his early satires. The *Essay* constitutes a pivotal moment in the ongoing definition of an individual subject or personality; describing how that personality is formed through the imaginative and idiosyncratic combining of simple into complex ideas. As such, it is a preeminently *modern* text. However, it also warns against taking such imaginative associations to too great an extremity, so that the individual begins to disregard the shared norms of society in order to inhabit a deluded realm where all reality conforms to his or her own desires. The faculty through which otherwise incongruous ideas are put "together with quickness and variety, wherein can be found resemblance or congruity, thereby to make up pleasant Pictures, and agreeable Visions in the Fancy" is identified by Locke as "Wit." Such a tendency, moreover, fancifully to conflate ideas into elaborate conceits is compared unfavorably with a discerning and sober "Judgment," whose task involves "separating carefully, one from the other, *Ideas.*" Ultimately, said Locke, excessive wit results in madness:

> *mad Men* . . . have joined together some *Ideas* very wrongly, they mistake them for Truths . . . by the violence of their Imaginations, having taken their Fancies for Realities, they make right deductions from them. Thus you will find a distracted Man fancying himself a King [and] . . . a Man, who is very sober, and of a right Understanding in all things, may in one particular be as frantick as any in *Bedlam.*[6]

There is little need to force a comparison here with the "Digression on Madness" in the *Tale,* whose satirical title at once echoes and inverts Locke's own title: *An Essay Concerning Understanding.* Bedlam in the *Tale,* as in Locke, becomes the analogue for processes of disintegration in society generally. However when, in the *Tale,* Swift comes to describe that moment when "a Man's Fancy gets *astride* on his Reason, when Imagination is at Cuffs with the Senses," Bedlam becomes conjured for the reader in all its lurid detail in a way foreign to Locke. It is "the Hole of another Kennel [where, on] first stopping your Nose, you will behold a surley, gloomy, nasty, slovenly, Mortal, raking in his own Dung, and dabling in his Urine" (178). Additionally, such scenes of excremental excess, in helping to convey the experience of one inhabiting Bedlam, become wittily interwoven into the fabric of the text as a way of reinforcing our impression of the narrator's egomaniacal derangement. As a (wrongheaded) proponent of modern scholarship's tendency to consult an index rather than reading a book in its entirety, the narrator of the *Tale* comes to describe the index, with his customary (that is, mad, Bedlam-inhabiting) excremental emphasis as "the *Posteriors* of a book" (145). Essentially disparate phenomena are thereby endlessly associated and conflated: a symptom of the narrator's too subjectivized imaginative vision. Given such an intensity of presentation, it seems pertinent to ask whether Swift's text is merely the enactment of Locke's position in a satiric, ironized form, or does it produce something else as well: a surplus that actually turns in on itself in order to reinforce what it is attacking?

What it is important to remember about the witty associations and conjunctions of ideas, made at a *subjective* level in the head of the too intensely self-absorbed and self-legitimating consciousness of the *Tale*'s narrator, is that these can become the cause, at an *objective* level, of dissensions and disagreements in the actual social world. In this, the *Tale* has perhaps been too effective a demonstration of that which it is supposedly out to condemn. In other words, the form of the *Tale,* meant satirically to reflect social fragmentation, actually ends by exacerbating that fragmentation in reality because of the way the text's ambiguities provoked (and continue to provoke) such violently different reactions in its readership.[7] Swift's narrator himself speaks, with typical self-reflexivity and uncanny accuracy, on this very topic:

> I do here humbly propose for an Experiment, that every Prince in *Christendom* will take seven of the *deepest Scholars* in his Dominions, and shut them up close for *seven* Years, in *seven* Chambers, with a Command to write *seven* ample Commentaries on this comprehensive Discourse. I shall venture to affirm that whatever Difference may be found in their several Conjectures, they will be all, without the least Distortion, manifestly deducible from the Text. (185)

Locke thought that such epistemological ruptures and fissures in the social whole could be limited through the employment of a plain, straightforward language where the possibility of the individual mind's ideas becoming too caught up in fancy and imagination—and so wrenched from a connection to actual, empirical and essentially *shared* reality—was minimized: a position echoed by Temple in his desire to "walk upon plain ground, and read plain hands." Paul de Man's cleverly argued point is that Locke's writings possess a metaphoricity—a store of literary fancy—paradoxical in the light of their attempts to enact the ideology of a linguistic transparency between word and idea.[8] However, the self-conscious rhetorical excesses of the *Tale* and their effects are surely of a qualitatively different order from the largely unintended and strictly limited flourishes of Locke and Temple.

Locke's own diagnosis concerning the diametrically opposed qualities of an associative wit and a discriminating judgment becomes itself here a useful tool in examining the *Tale.* For even though the *Tale* attempts to critique excesses of wit by way of satiric example, the fact remains that it is in the very nature of wit, as the medium in which the *Tale* exists, continually to collapse all kinds of vital distinctions. This effectively means that the reader is forever losing his or her moral and ideological bearings. A good illustration occurs when Swift's narrator pulls the three allegorical brothers of the Christian Church into the vortex of his witty conceits. All three brothers are shown in Section Two of the text to become engaged in the kind of debauched, dissipated, and thoroughly silly existence that was also meant simultaneously to depict the life of the modern coffeehouse Whiffler or *beau* (see 74–75). However, by allowing the witty logic of the narrator (or, rather, his lack of judgment) to collapse the distinction between the satire on religious malpractice and the satire on modern urban life, Swift loses control of one of his objects: the defense of the Church of England as the rational median point between Catholicism and Dissent. His description of the three brothers' life of youthful sin and folly fails to distinguish or exempt the character who would later be named as Martin: the allegorical embodiment of Anglicanism. Such effects led Swift to be severely criticized in the immediate wake of the book's publication, prompting him to compose his "Apology" to the *Tale* for the fifth edition of 1710. It was here that a rather older Swift, anxious to prove himself loyal, consistent, and reliable enough for a position of high responsibility in England, attempted to ameliorate the ambiguities raised in the original text. He states that "[the *Tale*] Celebrates the Church of *England* as the most perfect of all others in Discipline and Doctrine, it advances no Opinion they reject, nor condemns any they receive" (5). Any malicious misreadings, moreover, are produced by those lacking in the "Tast" and "Judgment" (4) the author claims he had been exercising all the time.

Of course, the text's actual self-subverting energy is much more powerful than the apologist's excuse of a youthful height of invention would account for (4). Indeed, the *Tale* can be read as a kind of wholesale undermining of a distinctively new emphasis on the aesthetic as a socially unifying force that came into being in late seventeenth-century England. Hence, the bourgeois individual, striding toward a social preeminence that was underpinned theoretically by the modern epistemology of Locke's *Essay,* was also encouraged to see a particular version of the simplified, rational whole as beautiful; so engendering the consensus of individuals to which Swift appeals in his "Apology" when he invokes gentlemanly "Tast" in order to guarantee the ideological legitimacy of his text. Such a consensus accords, moreover, with the image of the ancients' bee, described earlier, making its judgments of taste as an individual but taking its sustenance from shared, communal points in nature and tradition, rather than the wholly subjectivized, antisocial tendencies of the modern spider. But if, as Adorno notes, the original "truth content of art" resided in the "organon of integration,"[9] then such a model of "integration," had comparatively little truth value for late seventeenth-century Ireland: a country deeply divided according to religious affiliation into three communities of Catholics, Dissenters, and Anglicans. The latter constituted the colonial minority who maintained their rule and privileges by continually having to accentuate their utter *difference* from the other communities, notably in their vehement support of the Penal Laws restricting Catholic rights and for the Test Act restricting the Dissenters' participation in public life. Despite his own position within this Irish ruling elite, however, Swift's writings bespeak the trauma of inhabiting such a radically self-divided place. As mentioned earlier, Swift had been forced into exile by the Jacobite coup of 1689. He can also be said to have suffered a kind of internal exile when he accepted the parish of Kilroot in 1694 and went for some months to live among a community the majority of whom were Ulster Dissenters (Ehrenpreis 1: 157-59). Do not, then, these conditions of mutual exclusion also emerge symptomatically in the *Tale*'s fragmentations and digressions?

In one passage in particular, the form of a book becomes directly analogized with the conditions prevailing "in a *State*":

> They tell us, that the Fashion of jumbling fifty Things together in a Dish, was at first introduced in Compliance to a depraved and *debauched Appetite,* as well as to a *crazy Constitution*. . . . Farther, they affirm, that *Digressions* in a Book, are like *Forein Troops* in a *State,* which argue the Nation to want a *Heart* and *Hands* of its own, and often, either *subdue* the *Natives,* or drive them into the most *unfruitful Corners.* (144)

Swift was surely thinking of Ireland when he spoke of the "*crazy Constitution*" and "digressive" state here. The "Nation" wanting "a *Heart* and *Hands* of its own" connotes the way the three different major communities fought for preeminence in Ireland, each finding its source of support and identity in other countries: those of English descent looking for support from England, the Ulster Presbyterians looking to Scotland, and the Catholics looking to France. If the image of "subdued natives" being driven into the "most unfruitful corners" by a foreign power suggests too disinterested a sympathy for the subordinated communities of Ireland by a Swift who would, later in his career, often be vociferous in his support of continued Anglican supremacy, it is also worth remembering the sense of subordination felt by the Anglicans themselves; their frustration in the face of those forces of colonial exploitation emanating from England during the 1690s, the period of the *Tale*'s composition. In this context, the voice of the insecure Irish Anglican might actually come to be seen as synecdochic of a more general Irish sense of oppression.

Patrick Kelly has described how the final years of the seventeenth century saw in England an increasing antipathy toward Ireland's right to trade free of English interference. This antipathy was finally embodied in the English Parliament's restrictive and thoroughly colonialist Irish Woollen Export Prohibition Act of 1699.[10] The campaigning by English trading interests that eventually engendered this legislation and its like was not passively ignored by the Irish Anglican ruling elite, the most famous response being William Molyneux's *The Case of Ireland's Being Bound* . . . (1698). Another, much less well-known Irish intervention from the same year, though, is worth examining here for the way in which it seems to be a kind of rational transcription of the concerns the *Tale* articulates in so oblique and demented a fashion. Attributed to the Irish politician and economist Sir Francis Brewster, the *Discourse Concerning Ireland* fought for the trading rights of an Irish wool industry controlled overwhelmingly by the Anglican Protestant community in an Ireland composed of "three several types of people whose interests and dependencies are different from each other." In order to accentuate these differences, Brewster resorts to some traditional stereotyping of the French-oriented Catholics as indolent, archaic, impoverished; while the Presbyterians in Ulster are depicted as violently intolerant zealots. Brewster's main point, however, is that English legislation concerning the Irish wool trade will only act to the detriment of their English brethren in Ireland (the latter being described by Brewster in relation to the former as "flesh of their flesh and bone of their bone"). With the Catholic gentry and poor remaining largely outside of the cycles of trade and economic activity, and with the Ulster Dissenters reliant on linen rather than wool, Brewster's text highlights the fact that, far from there being a special bond between the English and their "brethren" in Ireland, the relationship was instead becoming one of colonial subordination by the home country of its colonial progeny.[11] In depicting the intense internal antipathies of Ireland, Brewster's concerns mirror a logic that emerges in the *Tale* and its own exploration of the processes of ejection and rejection. Additionally germane in this regard is the description of the two Protestant brothers in the *Tale* as "the two Exiles, so nearly united in Fortune and Interest" (133), a phrase that again resonates beyond the general meaning of diverse forms of Protestantism coming into existence after the Reformation and suggests a much more historically specific event. For just as all the Protestants of Ireland became united for a while during the Williamite war, so the eventual separation of the brothers into the specific designations of "Martin" and "Jack" becomes emblematic of the postrevolution splitting of Irish Protestants; one based, as J. C. Beckett has argued, on "a struggle . . . between the Established Church and the Presbyterians over the spoils secured by the revolution."[12]

The sensibility of the English in Ireland during the late 1690s became increasingly conditioned, then, by a growing sense of abandonment by England and by their sense of isolation in a country where they were greatly outnumbered and resented by two other distinct communities. For while in England those sections of society represented by the Established Church enjoyed a largely unrivaled preeminence, flanked only by relatively small Jacobite and Dissenting blocks, Irish Anglicans experienced an intense communal paranoia at being closely encircled by alien forces that, in the *Tale,* come to appear as the same irrational thing:

> . . . the Phrenzy and Spleen of both, having the same Foundation, we may look upon them as two Pair of Compasses, equally extended, and the fixed Foot of each remaining in the same Center; which, tho' moving contrary Ways at first, will be sure to encounter somewhere or other in the Circumference. (199)

Hence, the point of (Anglican) reason in the *Tale*—the allegorical Martin—assumes only a very minor role within the text: one that seems approximate to the proportion of Anglicans in Ireland compared to the population as a whole. That which looks like substantial satirical exaggeration when reading the *Tale* in a purely English context was actually rather closer to the Irish Anglican's sense of reality in Ireland.

At this point it is appropriate that we return to a consideration of Traugott's insight that, in the *Tale,* "self-hate becomes hate, posture becomes art." His well-argued contention is that Swift developed a style in the *Tale* whose "crazy, catachrestical images" allow for his feelings of antagonism toward Temple to emerge simultaneously with his need to produce a suitable, and, in many ways, undoubtedly sincere homage (Traugott 89). In other words, the *Tale* was written in order to name Temple's ideas but, in the manner of a catachresis, also constituted a productive *mis*naming. Swift articulated thereby certain aspects of his Irish background and experience, aspects that went against the grain of those cultural ideas that Temple viewed as an important method of upholding the civilized unity of England, and from which a decidedly disunited Ireland was excluded. There is, in fact, little need to *construct* a picture of Temple's anti-Irish sentiments—one of his early tracts on Ireland (dated 1667-68) articulates such sentiments with chilling explicitness. Some twenty years before meeting Swift, Temple had suggested that the English of Ireland, contaminated by their birth and upbringing in an essentially barbaric land, lacked sufficient civility or trustworthiness to be able to run Ireland with properly English levels of rigor. According to Temple, there had to be:

> an uninterrupted Pursuit of the old Maxim, to supply all the vacant Charges of great importance there [in Ireland], either civil or military, with persons of *English Birth and Breeding.* . . [.] To *own and support* on all Occasions, that which is *a loyal English Protestant Interest.* . . [,] *to keep a constant and severe Hand in Government* of a Kingdom, composed of three several nations. . . . [F]or *to think of governing that Kingdom by a sweet and obliging Temper, is to think of putting four wild Horses into a Coach and driving them without Whip or Reins.*[13]

Such a view, with its disturbingly violent language, indicates an indisputable contempt for *all* the communities of Ireland, including an Anglican Protestant community that was itself supposed to embody by proxy the "loyal Protestant Interest." Something of the same attitude remains in a letter Temple wrote to Sir Robert Southwell concerning Swift just after the latter had first arrived at Moor Park: "This afternoon I hear . . . that you are going over into Ireland . . . upon wch I venture to make you the offer of a servant. . . . He was born and bred there (though of a good family in Herefordshire) and was neer seven years in the colledge of Dublin."[14]

Obviously a need is felt here to qualify the "born and bred" in Ireland with assurances of Swift's recent English ancestry, while the overall tone is one of condescension toward someone whose Irish birth and breeding seems to mark him out as a "servant."[15]

It is as a response to such attitudes, therefore, that "posture becomes art" in the *Tale*. Swift's own aesthetic and artistic strategies differ from those of the new social order in England, whose own self-image was being galvanized through a particularly effective ideology of the aesthetic. Terry Eagleton, in his recent survey of this phenomenon, draws our attention to an aesthetic that is, like the work and attitude of Traugott's young Swift, "a contradictory, self-undoing sort of project [which, u]nderstood in a certain sense, [. . .] provides an unusually powerful challenge and alternative to . . . dominant ideological forms."[16] Adorno in *Aesthetic Theory,* as we have already seen, talks of the "organon of integration" as an aesthetic function but also draws our attention, elsewhere in his study, to the function of "the subject . . . [as] the organon of art" (Adorno 45). We can say, then, that if the aesthetic functions ideologically in the kind of modern society that began to emerge in the late seventeenth-century England as a way of integrating the emergent, individualized subject into a social whole, there also existed the possibility (as Locke well knew) that a shift toward a more thoroughly subjectivist mode might actually come to scupper the socially integrationist function of the aesthetic. And would not this be best achieved by an Irishman like Swift, whose experiences told him that there were places and people subject to English power where such a vision of social integration was substantially false? Such is the "art" that Swift conjures in the *Tale* out of his "hate" toward Temple's English, Augustan hauteur. Another way of terming this is to state that Swift employs an aesthetic whose essentially subjective content is foregrounded, so that the satire on oversubjectivized, essentially fragmenting forces in society actually becomes grasped as the *assertion* of those forces. Brewster, by contrast, is less bold, his formulation more unimaginatively conformist and unwittingly self-defeating. He describes an Irish situation of extreme civil disunity and compensates by stressing the consanguine unity of the English in Ireland with England itself. In continually arguing the English community's nonparticipation with the other communities of Ireland, however, Brewster succeeds only in *accentuating* the perception of Ireland as possessing a barbarity the source of which is its chaotic fragmentariness: the very argument made by Temple twenty years earlier in which the English of Ireland became seen as conditioned by such barbarity rather than existing, serenely, above it. In the *Tale,* by contrast, the intensely realized deployment of wit becomes, as it were, almost defiantly Irish. For if, according to orthodox Lockeanism, the function of wit is to make connections at the subjective level but to fragment at the social, objective level, Swift's formal and rhetorical strategies actually succeed in representing the (internally divided) situation of Ireland. In enacting and presenting such extremes of division and fragmentation in the *Tale,* Swift comes thereby to create something that approaches a truthful, and notably anti-English, vision of the *whole* of Ireland.

That Swift was developing an art or an aesthetic logic can be further illustrated through an examination of the following passage from the *Tale,* in which wit becomes both subject and method:

> nothing is so tender as a *Modern* piece of Wit, and which is apt to suffer so much in the Carriage. Some things are extremely witty *to day,* or *fasting,* or *in this place,* or *at eight a clock,* or *over a Bottle,* or *spoke by Mr.* What d'y'call'm, or *in a Summer's Morning:* Any of which, by the smallest Transposal or Misapplication, is utterly annihilate. Thus, *Wit* has its walks and Purlieus, out of which it may not stray the breadth of a Hair, upon peril of being lost. The *Moderns* have artfully fixed this *Mercury,* and reduced it to the Circumstances of Time, Place and Person. Such a Jest there is, that will not pass out of *Covent-Garden;* and such a one, that is no where intelligible but at *Hide-Park* Corner. (43)

At one level, the (broadly Lockean) strategy here is to reinforce the idea of the fragility, the ludicrously narrow specificity of modern wit; its connecting and associating of ideas in an incongruous and irrational way. Such self-amusing devices, it implies, can have no meaning outside of very limited constituencies: those of the new, urban coffeehouses (in "Covent-Garden" and "Hide-Park Corner"), gatherings as restricted and exclusive as the world of the individual imagination itself. Once again, the *Tale*'s acute self-reflexivity, displayed through the text's description of its own "witty" processes, acts to accentuate a characteristic absorption with the processes of the interior (both for the individual and the self-enclosed clique). But the text, in conveying the chaotic irrationality of modernity, itself comes simultaneously to possess quite the opposite quality. For it also has its own carefully arranged, literary character grounded in the endlessly associative, allusive wit of which it provides so brilliant an exposition. An example of this, at the level of the text as a whole, has already been illustrated: the excremental jokes and allusions that infuse the text and imbue it with a kind of consistency and continuity despite itself. What we see in the short extract just quoted, though, is the way in which wit really is made to look deliciously attractive and liberating through the exercising, paradoxically, of a superb rhetorical and syntactical control. Thus, a clause such as: "Any of which, by the smallest Transposal or Misapplication, is utterly annihilate," is actually poised and balanced perfectly, expertly deploying its subclause so as to ensure that the dark extremity of "annihilate" is reserved until the end. Equally, the mercurial wit of modernity abides happily in a prose that conveys in so accomplished a way the effect of formlessness, of evaporating upon contact; particularly in the series of utterly disparate phenomena, "today," "fasting," "eight o'clock" etc., that succeed one another with an almost incantatory, mesmeric power. The ultimate irony, of course, is that the *Tale has* lasted in its appeal and fascination for posterity. The witty processes that it was intended we mock as utterly hollow and transient have taken on the mantle of *real* artistry, lending its satirized object a powerful, poetic legitimacy. Nobody, in fact, "artfully fixed" the fluid, unstable "Mercury" of the modern better than Swift himself, provocatively inhabiting a domain that was so mistrusted by his English contemporaries.

Ireland, it has been argued, constituted the "other" of England—that which in psychoanalytical terms rendered it, in Declan Kiberd's words, "England's unconscious."[17] This being the case, then the aesthetic strategies of the *Tale* itself disclose an English "subject" replete with denials, repressions, and sublimations. Freud argues that in order to imagine we have secured a certain level of "civilization" we become dependent upon "mental forces which are later to impede the course of the sexual instinct and, like dams, restrict its flow—disgust, feelings of shame and the claims of the aesthetic and moral ideas." Thus, his work also identifies the importance for such a culture of an aesthetic ideology reliant upon the beauty, unity and virtue of the whole:

> The progressive concealment of the body which goes along with civilization keeps sexual curiosity awake. This curiosity seeks to complete the sexual object by revealing its hidden parts. It can, however, be diverted (sublimated) in the direction of art, if its interest can be shifted away from the genitals on to the body as a whole.[18]

The aesthetic became the means by which modern England could develop, as it were, an ego, a sense of stable, self-consistent identity. However, just as the products of the selective conscious mind do not tell the whole story about a personality, so the ideological narratives emanating from English culture, with their foregrounding of the civilized virtues of taste and politeness, do not reveal the truth about the expropriating commercial and colonizing forces on which the polished, elegant world of the elite was founded.

As opposed to such a civilized and civilizing self-image, the *Tale,* for Norman O. Brown, represents the "intoxicated overflow of youthful genius and fountainhead of the entire Swiftian apocalypse." And part of this "apocalyptic" effect is the way wit is exercised in so profound and impressive a manner in the *Tale,* hence utilizing to maximum effect the means by which Swift investigated certain "unconscious" processes. As Brown goes on to point out: "Swiftian psychoanalysis differs from the Freudian in that the vehicle for the exploration of the unconscious is not psychoanalysis but wit."[19] Such insights, of course, are themselves thoroughly Freudian in provenance. For while there exists a sublimated aesthetic of the ego that correlates with the emergence of modern national self-consciousness, there is also an aesthetic of the unconscious that Freud himself linked to "*der Witz*" (jokes or wit).[20] If it is *this* (unconscious) aesthetic—like the inner world of the *Tale*'s narrator constructed completely around a principle of metaphoric substitutions and the associating of dissimilar elements—that emanates from an unconscious realm, then it is unsurprising that it should have affronted the likes of Temple and Locke (guarantors of the new national identity) with their desire to fix "plain" linguistic meanings and curtail metaphor. Despite its satirical intent, the strategies of wit and wordplay in the *Tale* come ultimately to confront the view that language can be reduced to fixed and transparent meanings (a view that Swift himself would openly endorse on behalf of Robert Harley some years later in the *Proposal for the Correction of the English Tongue*). It is here, moreover, that we recall Jacques Lacan's description of the unconscious as being "structured like a language": that domain in which there takes place an "incessant sliding of the signified under the signifier." The fragmented textual "body" of the *Tale,* in which there also appear more literal scenes of bodily dissection, is also a feature that resonates in the light of Lacan's work. The cutting up of "the Outward of Bodies," says the narrator of the *Tale,* is that process in which "Reason" comes "officiously, with Tools for cutting, and opening, and mangling, and piercing," and leads in turn to the spectacle of the "*flay'd*" woman and the dismembered "*Beau*," whose "*Brain . . . Heart . . .* and *. . . Spleen*" are all "laid open" (173). Lacan's writings, likewise, abound with the notion of the fragmented body. In his celebrated paper "The mirror stage" (with its uncannily similar imagery of inside/ outside to the one used by Swift) we read how there is "usually manifested in dreams . . . a certain level of disintegration in the individual. It then appears in the form of disjointed limbs, or of those organs represented in exoscopy." Hence, the fragmented body of the (Irish) unconscious returns to undermine "the synthesizing functions of the ego" endorsed in Temple's (and Locke's) vision of English national identity.[21]

Psychoanalysis provides a tool through which we may see how Swift, in the *Tale,* enacted an Irish aesthetic of wit negatively, as a way of undermining and exposing English aesthetic sublimations. However, it is also worth pointing out by way of a final remark that such strategies, as Vivian Mercier contends, are also what might be termed *positively* Irish in origin. Mercier himself refers thoughtfully to Freud's work in his study, pointing out the seemingly anomalous nature of wit as that which has an "irrational element" at the same time as it "is so closely related to the intellect." His central argument, however, emerges out of his insights into the way Irish writers in English came to adopt the modes of Irish-language literature, through a kind of cultural osmosis. Mercier's book is divided into four sections entitled, respectively, "Humour," "Wit," "Satire," and "Parody." And if it was indeed these specifically Irish literary features that became absorbed by English-language culture in Ireland, then it can also be argued that the *Tale* provides the ultimate exemplification in Anglo-Irish literature of Mercier's thesis, given that the *Tale* appears to be structured solely around his four main principles. Particularly striking is Mercier's description of Irish literary humor as containing elements of "the fantastic . . . , macabre [and] grotesque," mirrored perfectly in the *Tale*'s scenes of degradation and dissection already quoted here:[22] scabrous, energizing strategies that formed the early, if somewhat elliptical, manifestation of the more explicitly articulated rage against the injustices of colonialism that a thwarted and disillusioned Swift would pour forth decades later.[23]

NOTES

Based upon a paper given at the Tenth International Congress on the Enlightenment entitled "Swift, Ireland and The Aesthetic Critique of Modernity." The altered title reflects the more modest scope of this essay.

1. I should acknowledge near the outset that this piece by no means represents the first attempt to describe the ways in which the respective characters and backgrounds of Temple and Swift produced elements of difference and subversion in the work of the latter. John Traugott's stylish and erudite account of the *Tale*, and Irvin Ehrenpreis's sections on Temple and the early work of Swift in the first volume of his celebrated biography, moreover, are both highly suggestive with regard to the effect that an Irish provenance had on Swift and his early writings. Both studies will be drawn upon and discussed in the present piece: John Traugott, "*A Tale of A Tub* in *Focus: Swift,* ed. C. J. Rawson (London: Sphere Books, 1971), 76–120; Irvin Ehrenpreis, *Swift: The Man, His Works and the Age,* 3 vols. (New York: Methuen, 1959–83), 1: 91–264. A valuable and scrupulously researched book-length study of Swift's years with Temple is A. C. Elias, Jr.'s *Swift at Moor Park: Problems in Biography and Criticism* (Philadelphia: University of Pennsylvania Press, 1982). As in the earlier studies, Elias also concludes that various "tensions and anomalies" obtrude when trying to reconcile the strategies and effects of the *Tale* and the *Battle* with Temple's aesthetic tenets. He dismisses, however, all attempts to account for these inconsistencies by any means other than those of "careful inductive analysis," while any speculative efforts are perceived merely as "brief conjectural forays in armchair psychology" (155). The result of such a relentlessly empiricist method, however, is the very impasse that Elias himself describes with admirable, if rather self-defeating, candor in the foreword to his book. Here, Elias voices the hope that his study will provide a "foundation" for "further work" on the topic. However, if his own rigorously empirical and archival research has only served to complicate and fragment the sense we have of Swift and his world—things that Elias now feels *less* able "to answer for in a positive sense"—then how, exactly, will "further research . . . help to narrow the possibilities" (ix) when it is his own (unmediated)

accumulation of findings that has caused such a *widening* of the "possibilities" in the first place? My own contention, put into practice most evidently in the latter half of the present essay, is that theory and informed speculation are not necessarily the signs of intellectual laziness that Elias seems to suggest they are, as anyone who has read a paragraph by G. W. F. Hegel will attest. The positivist fetishization of factuality in which the testimony of the text and the archive is seen as being the *only* source of truth, together with a pathological fear of making any generalizing or conceptualizing gesture at all, tends to produce in the end merely the pale reproduction of the object in question, so failing to analyze and penetrate it adequately.

2. William Empson, *Some Versions of Pastoral* (Harmondsworth: Penguin, 1995), 56.

3. See Ehrenpreis, *Swift,* 1: 92: "The profundity of Temple's effect on Swift has always been underestimated." This does not mean, of course, that Swift always reacted positively to that "effect."

4. Jonathan Swift, *A Tale of a Tub,* ed. A. C. Guthkelch and D. Nichol Smith, 2nd ed. (Oxford: Clarendon, 1958), 62.

5. The fullest recent account of this debate is Joseph M Levine, *The Battle of the Books: History and Literature in the Augustan Age* (Ithaca: Cornell University Press, 1991). According to Levine, Swift's *Battle* is "the true culmination of the ancients' defense of antiquity" (115). Although I shall be complicating such a judgment here, it is obviously the case that Swift wished to appear at one level to endorse a Temple who had claimed, in his *Ancient and Modern Learning* (ed. 1696), that the writers of antiquity were fixed "models of form and content till the end of time" (267).

6. John Locke, *An Essay Concerning Human Understanding,* ed. Peter H. Nidditch (Oxford: Clarendon, 1975), 156–57, 161.

7. See, for example, Ehrenpreis, *Swift,* 2: 328–29.

8. See Paul de Man, "The Epistemology of Metaphor" in *Aesthetic Ideology,"* ed. Andrzej Warminski (Minneapolis: University of Minnesota Press, 1996), 34–50.

9. Theodor W. Adorno, *Aesthetic Theory,* ed. Gretel Adorno and Ralph Tiedemann, trans. Robert Hullot-Kentor (Minnapolis: University of Minnesota Press, 1997), 45. Hence, the emergence of those patriotic early eighteenth-century writers who proselytised on behalf of the tasteful gentleman and polite, civil society. See, in particular, Addison's *Spectator* (1710–12) and Shaftesbury's *Characteristicks* (1714). The notions Locke and Temple had about the imposition of plain language and the reining in of wit were part of a broader project to consolidate national identity and cohesion. While this was in one sense an epistemological project from which would emerge a uniformity of understanding and interpretation in the community at large, it also took on a moral character inasmuch as the model being presented was one of *virtuous* simplicity. For a longer discussion of the ideology of virtue in Enlightenment thought, paying particular attention to Swift's works, see Seamus Deane, "Swift, Virtue, Travel and The Enlightenment," *Walking Naboth's Vineyard,* ed. Christopher Fox and Brenda Tooley (Notre Dame: University of Notre Dame Press, 1994), 17–39. As Deane puts it: "The simplicity of the virtuous person is both the source and symptom of his or her moral stability. The vicious person, on the other hand, is characterized by waywardness, fragmentation, disloyalty, political and social volatility" (32–33).

10. Patrick Kelly, "The Irish Woollen Export Prohibition Act of 1699: Kearney Revisited," *Irish Economic and Social History,* 7 (1980): 22–44.

11. Sir Francis Brewster, *A discourse concerning Ireland and the different interests thereof: In answer to the Exon and Barnstable petitions; shewing that if a law were enacted to prevent the exportation of woollen manufactures from Ireland to foreign parts, what the consequences would be for both England and Ireland* (London: 1698), 13, 18–20, 28–33, 50.

12. J. C. Beckett, *Protestant Dissent in Ireland: 1687–1780* (London: Faber and Faber, 1948), 16.

13. Sir William Temple, *Essay upon the Present State and Settlement of Ireland, Select Letters to the Prince of Orange* (London: 1701), 213–14.

14. Sir Harold Williams, ed., *The Correspondence of Jonathan Swift,* 5 vols. (Oxford: Clarendon, 1963–65), 1: 1.

15. Significantly enough, Temple was himself of an Anglo-Irish family, or rather, of a family who helped to rule Ireland and who had property there. If, as Roy Foster has written, "those of [eighteenth-century] Anglo-Irish stock who lived largely in England tended to compensate by anti-Irishness," then this would help to account for the rather extreme nature of Temple's views (R. F. Foster, *Modern Ireland: 1687–1780* [Harmondsworth: Allen Lane, 1988], 178). Such stridency can, at the same time, also be seen as possessing a certain clarity in terms of the way it presents a particular version of English nationalist identity as dependent upon the denigration of the colonial "other."

16. Terry Eagleton, *The Ideology of the Aesthetic* (Oxford: Basil Blackwell, 1990), 2, 3.

17. See the prefatory section entitled "England's Unconscious?" in Declan Kiberd, *Inventing Ireland* (London: Jonathan Cape, 1995).

18. Sigmund Freud, *On Sexuality,* trans. James Strachey (Harmondsworth: Penguin, 1991), 93, 69.

19. Norman O. Brown, *Life Against Death: The Psychoanalytical Meaning of History,* 2nd ed. (Hanover, N.H.: Weslyan University Press, 1985), 179, 186.

20. See Sigmund Freud, *Jokes and Their Relation to the Unconscious,* trans. James Strachey (Harmondsworth: Penguin, 1991).

21. Jacques Lacan, *Écrits: A Selection,* trans. Alan Sheridan (London: Routledge, 1977), 147, 154, 4, 138.

22. Vivian Mercier, *The Irish Comic Tradition* (Oxford: Clarendon, 1962), 5, 1.

23. For a recent discussion of the way Swift's later writings spoke in defense of Irish rights in the face of English colonial practises, see Carole Fabricant, "Speaking for the Irish Nation: The Drapier, The Bishop, and the Problems of Colonial Representation," elsewhere in this volume.

"This Way of Printing Bits of Books": The Fiction of Incompletion in *A Tale of a Tub*

Nick Rushworth

TO THE FIRST OF ITS ELEVEN LACUNAE, THE FIFTH EDITION OF THE *TALE* has this unattributed note:

> Here is pretended a Defect in the Manuscript, and this is very frequent with our Author, either when he thinks he cannot say any thing worth Reading, or when he has no mind to enter on the Subject, or when it is a Matter of little Moment, or perhaps to amuse his Reader (whereof he is frequently very fond) or lastly, with some Satyrical Intention.[1]

This essay is about the last of these intentions. What could be the satirical point of the *Tale*'s pretended incompletion? We have the complete texts. Why the fiction? What I intend to do is take at face value, as some or most readers of its earliest editions would have, the story that the *Tale* tells about how it came to be in the physical state that it is in.

On face value a lot really is missing from the printed *Tale*. Gather together the various details provided by the narrator and the bookseller, and the *Tale* that finally makes it into print—the "surreptitious Copy, which a certain great Wit had new polish'd and refin'd" (29), not the "Authors Original Copy" (17) nor his "blotted Copy . . . which he intended to have writ over, with many Alterations" (16)—amounts to an unfinished fragment of an expurgated, retrenched, finally malformed copy of an original defective copy of a set of manuscripts.

As soon as critics realized that the *Tale*'s incompletion was a fiction, the need to know about these different versions and their transmission was obviated, as was the need to study the apparatus. There was only one text for 1704, there was no unauthorized interference with it by "those who had the Papers in their Power"—those who "blotted out" the description of the fourth machine (8), the "Friend of the Author" who took "no other Liberties besides that of expunging certain Passages where now the Chasms appear under the Name of Desiderata" (21)—and all its lacunae, marginalia, footnotes, and prefatory material were Swift's doing.

41

42 INTRODUCTION.

of Worms: which is a * Type with a Pair of Handles, having a Refpect to the two principal Qualifications of the Orator, and the two different Fates attending upon his Works.

THE *Ladder* is an adequate Symbol of *Faction* and of *Poetry*, to both of which fo noble a Number of Authors are indebted for their Fame. * Of *Faction*, becaufe * * * * * * * *
* * * * * * * *

Hiatus in * * * * * * * *
MS. * * * * * * *

* * * * Of *Poetry*, becaufe its Orators do *perorare* with a Song ; and becaufe climbing up by flow Degrees, Fate

---

* *The Two Principal Qualifications of a Phanatick Preacher are, his Inward Light, and his Head full of Maggots, and the Two different Fates of his Writings are, to be burnt or Worm eaten.*
* *Here is pretended a Defect in the Manufcript, and this is very frequent with our Author, either when he thinks he cannot fay any thing worth Reading, or when he has no mind to enter on the Subject, or when it is a Matter of little Moment, or perhaps to amufe his Reader (whereof he is frequently very fond) or laftly, with fome Satyrical Intention.*

is

Tale of a Tub, fifth edition, 1710. Reproduced by kind permission of the University of Sydney Rare Books and Special Collections.

As a result, what has been lost to criticism of the *Tale* is an appreciation of the precariousness of its physical form commensurate with the appreciation of the general uncertainty of the *Tale*'s meaning. The *Tale* looks odder than has been noticed by critics. And therefore two potentially fruitful lines of inquiry that derive from its pseudo-fragmentation—into the *Tale*'s choice of satiric targets and its satiric method—have yet to be fully explored.

In its pseudo-fragmentation, the *Tale* is engaged with the work of the classical scholar, Richard Bentley, but work completed prior to what has been accepted as the primary impetus for the side the *Tale* takes in the Ancients-Moderns controversy: his enlarged 1699 *Dissertation Upon the Epistles of Phalaris*. Instead, the *Tale*'s hiatuses point at Bentley's earlier work of conjectural emendation: his performances at countering centuries' worth of editorial and scribal error by rewriting what he imagined to be the lost parts of the classics—on obscure and fragmentary Greek texts, in particular Callimachus—that is, "the Art of Exposing weak Sides, and publishing Infirmities" (172).

The *Tale* makes much serious play of the inefficacy of satire. It worries that satire never hits its target; that it is "a sort of Glass, wherein Beholders do generally discover every body's Face but their Own; which is the chief Reason for that kind of Reception it meets in the World, and that so very few are offended with it" (215). It is but "a Ball bandied to and fro, and every Man carries a Racket about Him to strike it from himself among the rest of the Company" (52). In hocussing about its textual history the *Tale* is aiming for a satire that will not only foil its targets' attempts at deflection but a satire that will actively implicate some of its chief enemies—the "Learned Reader" (260) like a Bentley or a Wotton—by inviting them to complete its joke; for instance, the Bookseller offers to "gratefully acknowledge" the "Gentleman" who furnishes the *Tale* with a "Key" to its "more difficult Parts" by printing it separately (29). Swift's virtuosic neutralization of Wotton's hostile key, the "Observations Upon the Tale of a Tub," into annotations is precisely such an act of (self-)implication; the name of one of the *Tale*'s chief enemies (but the Author's "ingenious Friend" [128]) is transmitted to posterity as but one of a number of its "learned commentators" assisting in its explanation.[2] Moreover, what if the *Tale*'s eleven interstices had set such critics on a hunt for the *Tale*'s "original manuscripts"—the author's "blotted copy"? Failing discovery, what if the critic conjectured his own version of what the author intended?

But who is this annotator of the 1710 *Tale* and why should its readers have taken any notice of his speculations about the author's intentions, especially when his contention that the defects in the manuscript are "pretended" contradicts the accounts of both the Bookseller and the author of the "Apology"? The notes have many authors. Those ascribed to "W.

Wotton" derive from Swift's editing of the "Observations Upon a Tale of a Tub" appended to the 1705 third edition of Wotton's *Reflections on Ancient and Modern Learning*. One note is attributed to Denys Lambin, a French classical scholar who died in 1572. This and the remaining notes are now known to be Swift's, though the "Apology" attributes them to "several Gentlemen" (20)—the "others" of "W. W——tt——n, B.D. and others" of the fifth edition's title page—prevailed upon by the bookseller "to write some explanatory Notes" (20). The Author claims to have seen none of them and "it is not unlikely he may have the Pleasure to find twenty Meanings, which never enter'd into his Imagination" (20). If the "Apology" and the 1710 *Tale*'s title page are taken at face value—notwithstanding the irony that "generally runs . . . through the Thread of the whole Book" (8) and the fact that the annotators are wise to it in the book's attitude to Wotton; he is at once the Author's "ingenious friend" and someone "to whom our Author never gives any Quarter" (128)—then the authority of what the annotators say about the *Tale* derives from the Bookseller's judgment of them as readers of a stature sufficient to be "prevailed upon" for "explanatory notes" (20) and for those notes to sit alongside Wotton's, the darling son of Momus, the goddess of "True Criticism" (242).

The *Tale* looks like other texts that have notes. A text that has notes is a text that has been edited. To the reader the editor is both a prior reader and an explicator. This reader has made two decisions about the text: it needs editing and it is worth editing. This editor has spent time editing on the basis of these two considerations. The reader reads the text with the aid of that editing.

The text must have been written before it was edited. One of the editor's functions therefore will be to establish when the text was written. The editor will often argue for the need to edit on the basis of the text's age. These arguments will be of three types: that the text comes from an unfamiliar world or time; that it is damaged or fragmentary or corrupt and in need of establishment; or that it contains contexts or references or obscurities the explanation of which only a specialist can supply. All these surface indications point to the character of the text—difficult or exotic in place and time but susceptible of meaning. But they also point to the authority of the editor as a reader of various priorities, a reader one or more editions closer to the date of composition than is the reader of his annotations, and a reader with some special/ specialist knowledge of the text.

That the *Tale* mocks the "True Criticism," that it satirizes any critical practice of the neat intention-colonizing, meaning-delivering kind, that it tricks and toys with readers generally I want to accept as données of the *Tale* well covered by three hundred years of criticism. But a list of probable targets for the *Tale*'s satire on the "True Criticism" always includes

Richard Bentley. And Swift's dislike of Bentleyan critical practice has been sufficiently explained by their respective supposed allegiances in the Ancients-Moderns controversy. Swift is Temple's charge. Bentley attacks Temple. Therefore Swift avenges Temple. But the work of biographers like Ehrenpreis and Elias[3] on the Temple period has complicated this reflexive defense explanation. What can be conjectured about the specifics of Swift's dislike? And what will they deliver in explanation for the *Tale*'s pretended incompletion?

While Swift was at Moor Park writing the earliest portions of the *Tale,* Bentley was at Cambridge working not on editions of Homer or Horace or Cicero but on what the *Tale* terms the "weak sides of the Antients" (96); on Menander, Philemon, Phalaris, Manilius and Callimachus, on the obscure and the fragmentary. Bentley was a one-man industry in the collation and attribution of fragments from classical authors. He had grand plans at Cambridge for a collection of all the fragments of ancient Greek poetry— their arrangement under the titles and the times to which they originally belonged and (most suggestively for the defective *Tale*) the conjecture (*divinatio*)[4] of what originally lay between the *disjecta membra poetae.* Conjecture, according to Bentley, "can cure all . . . [Its] performances are, for the most part, more certain than anything we can exhibit from the manuscripts."[5] The true critic's use of "reason and the subject matter are worth a hundred manuscripts" (Levine 248). Bentley saw himself as undoing the damage inflicted on Greek and Latin texts by successive generations of copyists. The received texts were mongrel, riddled with errors; "all ancient books . . . must now be set aside as uncertain or precarious . . . but so, even now, by a good eye and a skilful person, the old writing might be read under the new."[6]

In 1691, Bentley had produced the *Epistola ad Millium,* observations on "an obscure text of no literary merit" by a writer characterized by L. D. Reynolds and N. G. Wilson as an "obscure and mediocre Byzantine Chronicler of the sixth century," John Malelas of Antioch.[7] Bentley set out to make historical sense of the chapters of ancient Greek literary history that Malelas had mangled and to make classical Greek out of the many fragments that Malelas and similar writers had misquoted. In the estimation of C. O. Brink, in one of the most recent histories of classical scholarship, the *Epistola*'s "learning is so massive and the readiness so complete that the combination may well be unique in the history of classical scholarship, not perhaps equalled by Scaliger and Wilamowitz."[8] Suggestively for Bentley's enterprise in the settlement of the Phalaris question two years later, the *Epistola* disproves Malelas's attribution of a fragment of Greek to the tragedian Sophocles by showing that its language belonged to a "later time" (Brink 45). Individual words thought by earlier commentators to be of Malelas's creation were, to Bentley's eyes, scrambled anagrams mimicked in the *Tale,* perhaps, by the brothers' tortuous readings of their father's will in justification for the wearing of shoulder-knots on their heirloom coats, readings that begin *totidem verbis,* become *totidem syllabis,* then *totidem literis.* Though the word "conjecture" and its permutations occur twenty times in the *Tale,* its use here is pointed at Bentley: "'Tis true,' said he, 'there is nothing here in this Will, *totidem verbis,* making mention of Shoulder-knots, but I dare conjecture, we may find them *inclusive,* or *totidem syllabis'*" (83).

The place of intersection, though, between my own conjectures on the "Satyrical Intention" (62) underlying the *Tale*'s fiction of incompletion and its target in Bentleyan conjectural emendation lies with his 1697 *Notes on Callimachus,* notes on perhaps the most uncertain, the most precarious of the Ancients.[9] Of the six hundred treatises that Swift's contemporaries thought Callimachus had written, mostly fragments remained. Bentley's *Notes* produced a rancorous preliminary *querelle* to the main *querelle* between the Ancients and the Moderns, encapsulated in England by the settlement of the Phalaris question: whether the 148 letters ascribed to the sixth century B.C. Sicilian tyrant (and cited by Temple as proof of the Ancients' superiority over the Moderns) were real or forged. At the request of his Dutch classical scholar and friend, Joannes Graevius (whose son had died leaving behind an unfinished edition of the Greek poet), Bentley drafted a new set of Callimachus's epigrams (some of them published for the first time from a new manuscript) and added notes on Callimachus's hymns. Bentley's *Notes* presented almost twice as many fragments as the previous editor, Thomas Stanley, whose work on Callimachus was unfinished when he died in 1678. Stanley's notes to Callimachus were in manuscript form and held by his friend, the scholar Sir Edward Sherburn. Sherburn lent the manuscript of Stanley's notes to Bentley. *A Short Account of Dr. Bentley's Humanity and Justice, to those Authors who have written before him: With an Honest Vindication of Thomas Stanley, Esquire and his Notes on Callimachus* (attributed to Bentley's Christ Church opponents, including William King) accuses Bentley of having passed off the fragments of Callimachus restored by Stanley as his own and of likewise plundering the conjectures of two earlier Callimachus commentators, Vizzani and Nevelet: "I shall prove that [Stanley's] locks were picked, and his Trunks rifled and that both Dr. Bentley's method, in marshalling his Fragments, a great part of his Notes on Several Heads are taken from that very Learned Gentleman." Bentley is "a Notorious Plagiary . . . an Author who has resolved to run a muck (sic) at all who had written before him, and who, under the covert of some Philological Knowledge, was bent to trample upon all the laws of Decency and good Behaviour, for an air of Pride and Contempt, of scornful Censure and Supercilious Correction." Sherburn "put the [Stanley] manuscript into Dr. Bentley's hands, upon this express condition, that an Honourable mention might be made who first communicated it to him. . . . The Dr. has made great use of it without ever so much as naming his benefactor, or the author of those acute observations. . . . The Dr. has had such a peculiar fondness for this his issue (his fragments and animadversions) that in common conversation himself calls that edition . . . whereas what he has published makes up but a little more than the tenth part of the book"[10]

This "Callimachus controversy" (*A Short Account* 26) was the most arcane of literary-archaeological dogfights about ownership fought on two fronts: naming rights to the fragments of the poems (which scrap of Callimachus belongs to Bentley, which to Stanley, which to Vizzani, and which to Nevelet) and to the conjectures purporting to act as seamless ligaments between the fragments. As he began writing the *Tale,* Swift would have found the controversy a motivation for writing that is not only open and contestable in meaning but physically precarious.

But how widely known was the controversy? *A Short Account* went into two editions in 1699 and was, in turn, answered in the same year by another tract, *An Answer to the Late Book Written Against the Learned Reverend Dr. Bentley,* attributed to Cambridge's Solomon Whately. Furthermore, conjectural emendation like that practiced by Bentley on Callimachus was more widely the stuff of contemporary satire. In the course of "The Imposture," one of William King's eight *Dialogues of the Dead,* Democritus reassures Heraclitus of the antiquarian value of his decaying marble inscription: "it is not a critic's business to read marbles, but out of the broken pieces to guess at them, and then positively to restore them."[11]

Whoever had rightful claim to which fragments of Callimachus and which emendations, the history of classical scholarship has overlooked allegations of plagiarism in favor of assessment of Bentley's pioneering technique. Callimachus's twentieth-century editor, Rudolf Pfeiffer, calls Bentley's *Notes* "the first methodical work in this field; the collection itself was exhaustive for its time, and by attempting to arrange the fragments in the order of the lost works and give some cautious reconstructions he made it exemplary for posterity. . . . Many even of his boldest conjectures have been completely confirmed by the papyri."[12]

Would Swift have come across either the *Notes* or either of the 1699 tracts pro or con Bentley's early work? Swift certainly knew of Graevius; his and Johann Gronovius' twenty-nine volume compilation of classical poetry—"the most expensive works in his library,"[13] a gift from Lord Bolingbroke—was valued by Swift "more than all my books besides" (*Correspondence* 3:330).

But would the *Tale* have had enough in common with the "scraps of Callimachus"[14] to tempt a critic of Bentleyan stripe into conjectural emendation of its hiatuses; of, for instance, why the ladder is an "adequate Symbol [of] "Faction" (62) or "the whole Scheme of spiritual Mechanism . . . deduced and explained, with an Appearance of great reading and observation" (276)? Clearly, the *Tale* is linguistically—and physically—worlds removed from a compilation of the fragments of an Alexandrian poet. The closest the *Tale* comes to a direct plea for the kind of conjectural emendation fit for an infirm classic like Callimachus is "The Bookseller's Advertisement" to *A Discourse Concerning the Mechanical Operation of the Spirit in a Letter to a Friend, a Fragment.* Like a remnant scrap of Callimachus in Bentley's hands, the fragmentary "Discourse" came into the Bookseller's "Hands perfect and entire" (260) though he cannot "conjecture" whether the Author is also responsible for the "two foregoing Pieces" because it was sent to him "at a different Time, and in a different Hand. The Learned Reader will better determine; to whose Judgement I entirely submit it" (260). Bentley, Stanley, Vizzani, and Nevelet had to submit every fragment of the received Callimachus to the test of their forensic chronology and philology; does one fragment's "Hand" match its "Time" and, in turn, belong with another fragment under the same title?

It is because chronology is fundamental to classical scholarship that Swift also makes mischief with the *Tale*'s date of composition. What compelling *terminus ante quem* (admittedly, perhaps for the most "Credulous Reader") could reconcile statements made during "this present Month of August, 1697" (xlv) and references to the "His Majesty" (181) William III, who died in 1702, with the Bookseller's claim that he received "these Papers" (28) in 1698 and then with a footnote, newly added to the fifth edition, attributed to a French classical scholar, Denys Lambin, who died in 1572? In this, I believe that Swift has the extremes of the Ancients-Moderns controversy in his sights; *when* something was written, whether a writer is the first, the last, or the "freshest" (130) matters less than the intrinsic quality of the writing. Swift also has in mind Bentley's demolition of Phalaris; though the critic discovered "the Ass under the skin of the Lion" (*Dissertation* 89) does the timeless quality of the epistles still stand Bentley's test of time?

Do any of the *Tale*'s superficial commonalities with the classics and satiric frictions with the politics of classical scholarship matter when the fifth edition comes complete with a built-in explanation of its own fragmentariness? The writer of the "Apology" repeats the story of the "Papers being out of [the author's] Power" (12) five times. Some of the lacunae are the results of interference by persons unknown to the author, others by a "Friend." Could the most credulous of "True Critical" readers of the earliest editions of the *Tale* have not only accepted the story it tells about its transmission but also have brought to bear the modish conjectural emendation on its completion and so treat the Modern *Tale* like an infirm classic?

The *Tale*, like the *Battle*, the *Discourse*, the *Peri-Bathous* and the *Dunciad*, exploits an analogy to the classics not only by its fragmentariness, but with all its pomp of preface, dedication, and apparatus, resembling a classical text in a Modern edition, like Dryden's 1697 *Virgil* or Bentley's 1713 *Horace*. And like Dante's *Vita Nuova* and *Il Convivio* and Spenser's *Shepheardes Calendar* (dressed up to borrow the status of a Renaissance edition of Virgil's *Eclogues*) the *Tale,* so concerned with matters of surface over depth, style over substance, clothes over bodies, sauce over meat, mocks the extremes of the Ancients-Moderns controversy by conflating the body of a Modern text with an Ancient coating.

The *Tale*'s fragmentation is also suggestive of the text's age. Apart from looking like an Ancient text or an Ancient text in a Modern edition, the *Tale* is actually Ancient by the Modern standards it details. If books are the "Children of the Brain" (71), then the common fate for Modern works is to miscarry; they simply fail to make it into print; like the "universal System in a small portable Volume" written by the "great Philosopher of O. Brazile" (125) or the "compleat and laborious Dissertation upon the prime Productions of our Society" by the author of Reynard The Fox (67). The author prepares a list of Modern titles to present to Prince Posterity. They are "posted fresh upon all Gates and Corners of Streets" but in "a very few Hours . . . all torn down, and fresh ones [put] in their Places" (34). The author has heard of the criticism of Bentley, Rymer, Dennis, and Wotton, the poetry of Nahum Tate and Dryden's Virgil but has yet to see a copy of any of their works (36).

Yet the work of this "Last Writer . . . the freshest Modern" (130), a work "calculated" for tastes of "this present Month of August, 1697" (44) has survived until 1704 and been found worthy to publish. Neither it nor the *Dunciad,* however, have been spared the attentions of edacious Time. Both have been interfered with. Their fragmentariness indicates loss and proscription: "In the Authors Original Copy there were not so many Chasms as appear in the Book; and why some of them were left he knows not; had the Publication been trusted to him, he should have made several Corrections of Passages against which nothing hath been ever objected" (17).

At the end of Pope's four-book *Dunciad* there is a lacuna with an unattributed note: "it is impossible to lament sufficiently the loss of the rest of this poem . . . it is to be hop'd however that the poet compleated it and that it will not be lost to posterity." In the "Advertisement to the First Edition separate of the Fourth Book of the Dunciad" it is stated that the text was found "in so blotted a condition, and in so many detach'd pieces, as plainly shewed it to be not only incorrect but unfinished."[15]

My conviction that in its incompletion the *Tale* is directly engaged with Bentleyan conjectural emendation as a target for satire does not exclude the possibility of other targets. Neither is my preference for the explanation of "some Satyrical Intention" underlying its incompletion meant to exclude the other intentions offered by the annotator: the Author's desire to "amuse his Reader," that the lacunae are the result of the Author thinking "he cannot say any thing worth Reading" (62).

One other immediate impetus for the Tale's pseudo-fragmentation may have come from Swift's work as editor of Temple's *Miscellanea: The Third Part,* published two years after Temple's death in 1701. As in the *Discourse,* where what's missing from it comprises "the whole Scheme of spiritual Mechanism . . . deduced and explained" (276), right at the point in "Some Thoughts Upon Reviewing the Essay of Antient and Modern Learning" where Temple will prove the Ancients "the Foundation of all Modern Learning,"[16] the "Copy fails"[17] and Swift writes: "Here it is supposed, the Knowledge of the Antients and Moderns was to have been compared; But, whether the Author designed to have gone through such a work Himself, or intended these Papers only for Hints to some body else that desired them, is not known" (Temple 230ff.). Furthermore, just as the Bookseller claims to have been forced into publishing the *Tale* "in its Naturals" before "hearing from the Author" by "the Intelligence of a surreptitious Copy" (17), Temple's *Miscellanea: The Third Part* appends his translations from Virgil, Horace, and Tibullus, "not intended to have been made public" until Benjamin Tooke learned of "several copies that were got abroad, and those very imperfect and corrupt" (Temple 99).

"Those who had the Papers in their Power" (8) thought it "neither safe nor Convenient to Print . . . the whole Scheme of spiritual Mechanism . . . deduced and explained, with an Appearance of great reading and observation" (276). The pursuit of safety and convenience are two other motivating factors for the *Tale*'s pseudo-fragmentation. Swift was caught between furtive delight at the *Tale*'s rapid dissemination, private disownment of it as "you know what"[18] or "&c." (*Correspondence* 1:166) and elbowing out pretenders to its authorship.[19] Because he knew the damage the *Tale* could do to his ambitions in the church, Swift wanted to keep this child at arm's length at least. Note that the story of the "Papers being out of [the author's] Power" gains most of its support from the fifth edition as do Swift's attempts to push the date of composition as far back as possible, to 1696; "which is eight Years before it was published. The Author was then young, his Invention at the Height, and his Reading fresh in his Head . . . which might not suit with maturer Years, or graver Characters . . . and which he could have easily corrected with a very few Blots, had he been Master of his Papers for a Year or two before their publication" (4). The Author can hardly be held responsible for what is published when publication is without his knowledge, when what is published has been interfered with and had the work received "his last Hand," he would have both made "more severe Corrections" (10) and restored sections expunged, "never suspecting it possible any wrong Interpretations could be made of them" (17).

Indeed, just as the *Battle* undermines the Modern and Ancient ideals of authorship in the figures of the Spider and the Bee by arguing that all writing is more or less the confection of an author's original genius with his "Common-place-Book" (148), the responsibility for the *Tale*'s final physical form is genuinely multiple: the product of the interaction between the Author, the book machine, "those who had the Papers in their Power," and the "W. W——tt——n, B. D. and others" of the footnotes. What constitutes the modern book is as unlikely to be "entirely of one Hand" (20) as its author's wit is "entirely his own" (13).

The convenience of the *Tale*'s pseudo-fragmentation cuts the other way as well; when the annotator-editor chooses to emphasize the sin of omission—drawing attention more to what has been lost to publication and offering a precis of or presuming what the missing piece of the original text would have said—over the sins of commission, the acts of expungement themselves by "those who had the Papers in their Power." It is Wotton, in his 1705 *Defense of the Reflections upon Ancient and Modern Learning,* who draws the link between the "*Hiatus in Manuscripto*" (45) placed by the "Publisher of the Tale of a Tub" (46) in Temple's "Some Thoughts Upon Reviewing the Essay of Antient and Modern Learning" and "this way of printing Bits of Books that in their Nature are intended for Continued Discourses, and are not loose Apophthegms, Occasional Thoughts, or incoherent Sentences" (47), exemplified by the *Tale.* As rivals in the Ancients-versus-Moderns pamphlet wars, Wotton is forced by Temple (or by Swift, if the hiatus is indeed of his invention) into shadow-boxing with a comparison of Ancient and Modern learning that is missing from the manuscript, a comparison that nevertheless manifests when the essay resumes that: "the Pre-eminence of the Antients in Poetry, Oratory, Painting, Statuary, and Architecture," a preeminence "the Modern Advocates yield, though very unwillingly" (Temple 230).

Even though Guthkelch and Nichol Smith are still raising the question of "how far" Swift was responsible for the "text as it appeared" (xi) in 1958, the fiction of incompletion collapses as soon as authorship of the *Tale* is laid at Swift's door. But in the study of the history of a particular literary work, it can benefit interpretation to imagine how a different set of circumstances might have generated a different criticism; in this case, if the *Tale* had retained its anonymity (or at least the status of a work only commonly attributed to Jonathan Swift) and thus, retained this fictional textual history. For as long as the *Tale* could keep up the fiction, and for as many Bentleyan "True Criticks" as the fiction could dupe, the "Satyrical Intention" behind the *Tale*'s lacunae was not only to compel belief in its incompletion, but to provoke a conjectural emendator into hunting up the *Tale*'s "original manuscripts"—the author's "blotted copy." Failing discovery, the critic can write in his own version of what the author intended, like the blank page in *Tristram Shandy,* as many contemporary readers (and some editions) had filled in the blanked names in Pope's *Dunciad.*[20] Significantly, the spurious 1720 Dutch edition of the *Tale* included a "History of Martin" and "A Digression on the nature usefulness and necessity or Wars and Quarels" precisely because the bookseller had access to the author's "Original Manuscript . . . which contains a great deal more than what is printed" (294).

There's evidence from the "Digression Concerning Criticks" that the *Tale's* defects were pretended to cater to the prevailing critical tastes:

> Pausanias is of Opinion, that the Perfection of Writing correct was entirely owing to the Institution of Criticks. . . . He says, *They were a Race of Men, who delighted to nibble at the Superfluities, and Excrescencies of Books; which the Learned at length observing, took Warning of their own Accord, to lop* the *Luxuriant,* the *Rotten,* the *Dead,* the *Sapless,* the *Overgrown Branches from their Works.* But now, all this he cunningly shades under the following Allegory; *that the Nauplians in Argia, learned the Art of pruning their Vines, by observing, that when an ASS had browsed upon one of them, it thrived the better, and bore fairer Fruit.* (98)

Enlisting a passage such as this as evidence for deliberate fragmentation with a "Satyrical Intention," with any intention of a sacralized author, must come with a rider. The brothers' mercurially adaptable readings of their father's will are the types of the True Critick's willful and self-indulgent readings of the *lectio recepta* of the Ancients and, in turn, that of the happiness-madness of any reader of the *Tale:* the "perpetual Possession of being well Deceived" (171). And one can hardly look to the *Tale's* digressions as a refuge of readily distillable meaning from an aggressively polysemous allegory.

That rider notwithstanding, the "Digression Concerning Criticks" presents to "True Criticks" like Bentley and Wotton "a short Account of themselves and their Art, by looking into the Original and Pedigree of the Word [Critick], as it is generally understood among us, and very briefly considering the antient and present State thereof" (92). The "True Critick" is a "Discoverer and Collector of Writers Faults . . . taken up with the Faults and Blemishes, and Oversights, and Mistakes of other Writers" (95). This is the conjectural critic, the dog at the feast "whose Thoughts and Stomach are wholly set upon what the Guests fling away, and consequently, is apt to Snarl most, when there are the fewest Bones" (103–104). He feeds on literary remains, the scraps of authors. The "True Critick" delights in the study of what outworn critics, the "Restorers of Antient

Learning from the Worms, and Graves, and Dust of Manuscripts" (93) ordinarily rejected; the "Superfluities and Excrescencies of Books" (98).

Like the Ancients, "highly sensible of their many Imperfections," who sought to "soften or divert the Censorious Reader, by Satyr, or Panegyrick upon the True Criticks" (97), whoever designs to be a "perfect Writer, must inspect into the Books of Criticks, and correct his Invention there as in a Mirror" (102–103). Is the *Tale*'s pseudo-fragmentation, while satirizing the criticism of the day, also geared to its tastes? The "Perfection of Writing correct was entirely owing to the Institution of Criticks" (98). Books thrived the better, bore fairer fruit for being "browsed" upon by them (fame, "being a Fruit grafted on the Body" [185]). Writers, observing the kinds and parts of books that critics enjoyed the most, "pruned" and "lopped" from their own.

Are the Tale's hiatuses, then, and the palimpsests that they connote (the author's "blotted copy," the *Tale*'s "original manuscript") the result of Swift's "prunings" and "loppings"? Has he prepared and adjusted his work to cater to the prevailing critical tastes, and hoped it will bear fruit by being browsed upon? To pursue the above analogy, are the annotations and the countless commentaries made on the *Tale* (including this one as well as those to come), the "fruits" of its fame "grafted" onto the "body" of the text? Its openness, its contestability of meaning is not only a feature of the *Tale* that Swift enjoyed but is fundamentally *a* meaning of the *Tale*. The difficulty readers have in delivering stable meaning is not accidental:

> I do here humbly propose for an Experiment, that every Prince in Christen-
> dom will take seven of the deepest Scholars in his Dominions, and shut them up
> close for seven Years in seven chambers, with a Command to write seven
> ample Commentaries on this comprehensive Discourse. I shall venture to af-
> firm, that whatever Difference may be found in their several conjectures, they
> will be all, without the least Distortion, manifestly deduceable from the Text.
> (185)

At the time of the writing of the *Tale* the prevailing tastes of the "deepest Scholars," as much as Bentley reflects them, were for the obscure and the fragmentary. Further, the appeal of the obscure and the fragmentary re-flects the overall charge the *Tale* makes against critics and exegetes, that they value works of literature and the Bible precisely for what is not in them literally, at the surface, but rather for their obscure meaning "darkly and deeply couched" (67) or "prophetically held forth" (147), and for the kinds of meanings the brothers wrench from their father's will *totidem verbis, totidem syllabis,* finally *totidem literis.* This is precisely the way the Author wants readers to understand his own work: "where I am not under-stood, it shall be concluded, that something very useful and profound is couch't underneath" (46).

To a conjectural emendator the fragments, the hiatuses, were sufficient proof of the existence of the perfect text that had left the author's hand, a perfection that he could restore. They offered the critic the chance to ghostwrite the missing bits of the original and to attach explanatory notes, prefaces, appendices, and apocrypha; those "pernicious Kind of Writings, called Second Parts, [which] usually passes under the Name of the Author of The First" (183). Just as the brothers annex a spurious codicil to their father's will in order to justify the wearing of "flame Coloured Sattin" (86) on their coats, the 1720 "Dutch edition" of the *Tale* appends "The History of Martin" just as later in the century, magazines published "missing" chapters from *Tom Jones* and *Amelia* and a third volume to *Tristram Shandy.*

Does it matter that the *Tale*'s intended victim for the hocussing about its "genesis and parturition"[21]—a conjectural emendator, even Bentley himself—did not fall for it, that no trace exists of a conjectural emendation of a description of the *Tale*'s fourth machine (8), for instance?[22] First, the answer begs the question of attribution: How many more readers would have drawn up "Second Parts" (183) like the "History of Martin" had the *Tale* retained its anonymity? Second, it would depend on how broadly acts of completion of the *Tale*'s meaning are defined. The *Tale* is keenly aware that, alongside the hubristic conjectures of the learned, are the more benign interpolations of readers "common," "superficial," "gentle," "cautious," and "impatient." Just as Bentley completes Callimachus by conjecture, makes it his Callimachus, the *Tale*'s pseudo-incompletion, its general uncertainty in meaning makes it plastic, expressly readerly, potentially infinitely extensible. Just as the *Tale*'s final physical form is genuinely multiple, its meaning to me "literally true this Minute I am writing" (36) is a confection of (at least) the anonymous *Tale* with knowledge of Swift's life and his other writings, and with Wotton's and Guthkelch's and Nichol Smith's apparatus.

Though it is unlikely to be the first literary work to have achieved this kind of plasticity, what makes the *Tale*'s contemporary background different is the advent of meaning-delivering professionals like Bentley, whose specialist knowledge intervenes (literally, on the page, in the apparatus, in the footnotes) between the classics and their eighteenth-century readers. While the *Tale* could not claim to have been emended like a Callimachus, Swift benefited from a bemused double delight at the reception that the *Tale* received. The "empty tub" amused and diverted both its friends and detractors. But in "laying violent Hands" (40) on the *Tale,* enemies like Wotton played into its hands; the tub is surrounded with all the trappings of pseudo-scholarship ordinarily accorded a Callimachus. And the fact that Wotton's name is transmitted to posterity as but one of a number of learned commentators honoring the *Tale* completes the joke.

NOTES

The quotation in the title of this article is from William Wotton, "A Defense of the Reflections Upon Ancient and Modern Learning, In Answer to the Objections of Sir W. Temple, and Others, with Observations Upon The Tale of a Tub," London, 1705, 47.

1. Jonathan Swift, *A Tale of a Tub, to Which Is Added the Battle of the Books and the Mechanical Operation of the Spirit,* ed. A. C. Guthkelch and D. Nichol Smith (Oxford: Clarendon Press, 1958), 62. All subsequent pagination for references to the *Tale* comes from this edition.

2. Swift makes much serious play of anxiety about satire delivering the names of its enemies to posterity: "I do here give notice to posterity, that having been the author of severall writings, both in prose and verse, which have passed with good Success, it hath drawn upon me the censure of innumerable attempters and imitators and censurers, many of whose names I know, but in this shall be wiser than Virgil or Horace, by not delivering their names down to future ages; and at the same time disappoint that tribe of writers whose chief end next to getting bread, was an ambition of having their names upon record by answring [sic] or retorting their Scurrilityes. . . . I do therefore charge my Successors in fame, by virtue of being an antient 200 years hence, to follow the same method. Dennis, Blackmore, Bentley and severall others, will reap great advantage by those who have not observed my rule: and heaven forgive Mr. Pope, who hath so grievously transgressed it, by transmitting so many names of forgotten memory, full at length, to be known by Readers in succeeding times. . . . I heartily applaud my own innocency and prudence upon this occasion, who never named above 6 authors of remarkable worthlessness; let the Fame of the rest be upon Mr. Pope and his children ("Holyhead Journal," *The Prose Works of Jonathan Swift,* ed. Herbert Davis [Oxford: Blackwell, 1939–68], 5: 201). Swift had warned Pope in 1725: "Take care the bad poets do not outwit you, as they have served the good ones in every Age, whom they have provoked to transmit their Names to posterity" (Swift to Pope, 26 November 1725, *The Correspondence of Jonathan Swift,* ed. Harold Williams [Oxford: Clarendon Press, 1965], 3: 118). But Swift was happy for the Dunces to be named in full as soon as they were transposed to the apparatus (as with Wotton's "Observations") transforming a detractor into helpmate in the text's explanation. Swift changed his mind about Pope when he saw the Dublin edition of *The Dunciad* in 1728: "The Notes I could wish to be very large, in what relates to the persons concerned; for I have long observed that twenty miles from London no body understands hints, initial letters, or town-facts and passages; and in a few years not even those who live in London. I would have the names of those scriblers printed indexically at the beginning or end of the Poem, with an account of their works, for the reader to refer to. . . . Again I insist, you must have your Asterisks filled up with some real names of real Dunces" (Swift to Pope, 16 July 1728, *Correspondence* 3: 293).

3. Irvin Ehrenpreis, *Swift: The Man, His Works, and the Age* (London: Methuen, 1962–83); A. C. Elias, Jr., *Swift at Moor Park: Problems in Biography and Criticism* (Philadelphia: University of Pennsylvania Press, 1982).

4. "During the Renaissance conjecture meant guesswork; that is, a reading lacking manuscript or independent authority. It was something the editor divined, and *divinatio* was synonymous with *coniectura* [conjecture.] Simple improvement by any means was designated *emendatio* and might or might not encompass *coniectura*" (John F. D'Amico, *Theory and Practice in Renaissance Textual Criticism: Beatus Rhenanus Between Conjecture and History* [Berkeley: University of California Press, 1988], 10).

5. Joseph M. Levine, *The Battle of the Books: History and Literature in the Augustan Age* (Ithaca: Cornell University Press, 1991), 248. These are the author's translations, respectively, of Bentley's Preface to Horace (Amsterdam, 1728), sig. **3v and of Bentley's note to Horace, *Odes,* 3.27.15, in *Q. Horatius Flaccus, ex recensone et cum notis atque.*

6. Richard Bentley, *Remarks Upon a Late Discourse of Free-Thinking in a Letter to F. H. D. D. by Phileleutherus Lipsiensis* (London: Printed for John Morphew and E. Curll, 1713), 359.

7. L. D. Reynolds and N. G. Wilson, *Scribes and Scholars: A Guide to the Transmission of Greek and Latin Literature* (Oxford: Clarendon Press, 1974), 167.

8. C. O. Brink, *English Classical Scholarship: Historical Reflections on Bentley, Porson, and Housman* (Cambridge: Oxford University Press, 1986), 41.

9. Bentley's notes appeared at the end of the first of Joannes Graevius's two-volume *Callimachi Hymni, Epigrammata et Fragmenta, ex recensione Theodori J G F Graevii cum eiusdem Accedunt N. Frischlini, H. Stephani, B. Vulicanii, P. Voetii, A.T.F. Daceriae, R. Bentleii commentarius, et annotationes viri illustrissimi Ezechielis Spanhemii,* 1697.

10. [William King?] *A short account of Dr. Bentley's humanity and justice, to those authors who have written before him : with an honest vindication of Tho. Stanley, Esquire, and his notes on Callimachus : to which are added, some other observations on that poet : in a letter to the Honourable Charles Boyle, Esq. with a postscript, in relation to Dr. Bentley's late book against him: to which is added an appendix, by the bookseller wherein the doctor's mis-representations of all the matters of fact wherein he is concern'd, in his late book about Phalaris's Epistles, are modestly considered : with a letter from the Honourable Charles Boyle, Esq., on that subject* (London: Printed for Thomas Bennet, 1699), 32, 76, 28.

11. William King, John Arbuthnot and other hands, *A Miscellany of the Wits* (London: Scholar's Library, 1920), 65.

12. Rudolf Pfeiffer, *History of Classical Scholarship from 1300 to 1850* (Oxford: Clarendon Press, 1976), 153.

13. Harold Williams, *Dean Swift's Library* (Cambridge: Cambridge University Press, 1932), 46.

14. Charles Boyle, *Dr Bentley's Dissertations on the Epistles of Phalaris, and the Fables of Æsop Examin'd* (London: Printed for Thomas Bennet, 1698), 133.

15. Alexander Pope, *The Poems of Alexander Pope,* ed. John Butt (London: Methuen, 1968), 799.

16. Sir William Temple, *Miscellanea: The Third Part* (Published by Jonathan Swift, London : Printed for Benjamin Tooke, 1701), 204.

17. William Wotton, "A Defense of the Reflections Upon Ancient and Modern Learning," *Swiftiana 1: On The Tale of a Tub, 1704–1712* (New York: Garland Publishing Company, 1975), 46.

18. Jonathan Swift, *Journal to Stella* (Gloucester: Alan Sutton, 1984), 74.

19. Swift's response to Edmund Curll's attribution of the major portions of the *Tale* to Swift's cousin, Thomas, was, "it is strange that there can be no satisfaction against a Bookseller for publishing names in so bold a manner" (Swift to Tooke, 29 June 1710, *Correspondence* 1: 165).

20. David L. Vander Meulen, *Pope's Dunciad of 1728: A History and Facsimile.* (Charlottesville: Published for the Bibliographical Society of the University of Virginia and the New York Public Library by the University Press of Virginia, 1991), 40.

21. Robert Martin Adams, "Jonathan Swift, Thomas Swift and the Authorship of *A Tale of a Tub,*" *Modern Philology* 64 (February 1967): 211.

22. Though the Bookseller of the 1720 Dutch edition is still waiting for Bentley's "Remarks" on the *Tale* to appear: "I am told that this is a Masterpiece of modern Criticism, & that this Prince of Pedants has, with a vast deal of laborious learning, shewn that he can interpret almost nine passages of Antient Authors in a sense different from that which our Author has given them" (293).

Swift's *Tale,* the Renaissance Anatomy, and Humanist Polemic

W. Scott Blanchard

READERS OF SWIFT'S *A TALE OF A TUB* HAVE PUZZLED THEMSELVES OVER its formal characteristics for many years, for just as its ironies tend to lead readers into a hall of mirrors, so also its generic underpinnings finally exasperate even those critics with a very liberal notion of literary norms. The enigma that is Swift's *Tale* is in great part designed to remain an enigma, but part of this enigma can be resolved if we shift our perspective somewhat and account for some of the *Tale*'s formal unruliness by recourse to Renaissance traditions of satire. Since Swift's career has largely remained an object of study for literary historians of the eighteenth century, it is not surprising that the stricter standards of neoclassical criticism have tended to infiltrate, if only unconsciously, critical readings of the *Tale,* thereby reducing it to a somewhat more manageable literary curiosity. But seen from the perspective of several strains of Renaissance satire, Swift's work can appear in a somewhat different, if more refracted, light. A number of scholars have placed its literary pedigree more firmly in the seventeenth century by acknowledging Swift's debts to Burton's *Anatomy of Melancholy,* while others have gone back even further to humanist rhetorical traditions of the sixteenth century to trace Swift's debt to authors like Erasmus and to the playful mock encomia that were part of the Renaissance scholar's repertoire of literary practice and imitation.[1] I would like to add some further influences from the European Renaissance to the already rich grabbag of sources that literary scholarship has surmised to have contributed to Swift's inventive work, and I want to suggest that these sources can help us to sharpen the focus on certain themes that assume a special force when the *Tale* is seen in their light. These more serious issues—issues involving the delineation of professional from amateur intellectual activity, the troublesome proliferation of textual interpretations arising from the pursuit of a more exact philological method, and the emergence of canons of "authenticity" and classicism—were as acute for Swift's age as they are for us today, and in tracing the roots of some of these issues as they appear in satirical works of the Renaissance humanists,

I hope to shed more light on a work that will likely remain enigmatic for some time but that can always be profitably viewed from the vantage point of its literary ancestors.

Swift's work is in the most general sense a Menippean satire, a literary form that was rather narrowly defined in antiquity and whose broad features in postclassical literature were first traced by Mikhail Bakhtin and Northrop Frye.[2] The only truly consistent hallmark of Menippean satire in both the classical and modern periods is its tendency to focus on the world of learning, on intellectuals or more specifically on philosophers, a habit already clearly marked in Lucian and one that we believe was present in the lost writings of its namesake, the Greek cynic Menippus. We might helpfully suggest that the intent of much Menippean satire is to engage in satiric assault upon those reigning conceptions and ideologies that have acquired hegemonic authority in a given culture and that are generally proffered by the most conspicuous intellectuals, whether they be philosophers, theologians, or critics. Such attacks on the status quo would seem to have been an intention of the form even in its origins, when the Greek cynics voiced disenchantment with the idealisms of fifth-century Athenian culture as it devolved into the tyranny and, according to Plato, the aesthetic barbarism of the fourth century. But because like most satire Menippean satire is chameleonic, taking its shape and color from the very specific topical contexts of its construction, it may not be useful to define the Menippean form any further in the present context, but rather to remain satisfied with focusing on its tendency to satirize intellectual life in general.

There are two specific strains of Menippean satire that enjoyed a great deal of popularity among the Renaissance humanists—who incidentally revived interest in classical proponents of the form like Petronius, Apuleius, and Lucian[3]— and that would seem to have left their mark on Swift's *Tale*. The first strain, which arose out of the very specific context of the early humanist criticisms of the medieval university, is the "anatomy," a term that has been applied fruitfully to Swift's work by a number of scholars and that Swift himself also employs (along with the related term "dissection"). As we shall see in a moment, the satirical anatomy has an interesting and revealing history prior to its appearance in the titles of works by the English authors Phillip Stubbes and Robert Burton. The second strain is one that has received less attention from scholars of both the Renaissance and the eighteenth century in great part owing to its very specialized intellectual context. This is a form that I shall denote by the term "philological squabble" but that could more loosely be placed within the tradition of literary invective and polemic. As a form that appeared with the emergence of the increasingly exact and professionalized discipline of classical philology among the Italian humanists of the fifteenth century, the form is better known to historians of classical scholarship and of textual transmission than to students of literature. But inasmuch as the topics of textual interpretation and of textual authenticity provide an important backdrop for Swift's work, it may be profitable to consider the more rarefied genre of the literary invective (whose family resemblance to all forms of satire should be readily apparent), especially as it is used by scholars to attack other scholars. While not perhaps deserving consideration as "Menippean" by virtue of its ad hominem character, its social grounding in the world of learning makes the invective a literary cousin, at the very least, of intellectual satire.

To understand the features of the Renaissance satirical anatomy, we first need to appreciate its cultural origins. Those origins are to be found, in my opinion, in the teaching practices of the late medieval university, where the students' more memorable curricular experiences, those involving both the inception (or *accessus*) to the course of study and the culmination of university studies in ceremonies of laureation, had developed a formulaic character that, not surprisingly, would soon become ripe for parodic treatments. At the beginnings of Renaissance humanism, when educational reforms placed pressure on scholastic methodology and pedagogy, these two liminal experiences of the university student had come to seem especially archaic, and we have examples of academic parody and satire from as early as the 1430s at the University of Pavia, where the playwright Ugolino Pisani mocked the scholastic *repetitio,* a summative demonstration of the student's knowledge conducted prior to laureation.[4] In Pisani's skit, classificatory zeal in the scholastic application of distinctions yields a comical anatomy, so that the profession of cookery becomes the field wherein the cardinal and theological virtues can be elaborated to the best advantage—a rage for order and encyclopedic plenitude turned upside-down. Here the comic effect is achieved by setting an "elite" academic discussion in the popular context of food, an effect that can yield what Ernst Curtius has termed *Küchenhumor,* a linguistic inventiveness and pluralism that has also been noticed by Bakhtin under his terminology of "polyglossia."[5] More important for understanding the traditions out of which Swift wrote is the mockery of systematic procedures: the totalizing methodology of the scholastic *repetitio* appears especially silly when displaced from its learned university contexts. In Pisani's work, the pedantically enumerated "system" of the virtues becomes displaced by an earthy and anarchic festivity rooted in the body and its claims on human experience rather than the intellect.

Of even greater relevance are two works of the late fifteenth century with which Swift may have had at least a passing familiarity. Also deriving from a university setting, two of the inaugural lectures of the Florentine humanist Angelo Poliziano (Politian) were delivered as *praelectiones* (opening lectures or prolusions) to courses on the works of Aristotle that were given at the Studio Fiorentino in the 1490s. The first of these lectures, the *Panepistemon,* inaugurates the study of the *Nicomachean Ethics* and uses that work's systematic attempt at classifying the ethical categories of human experience—and perhaps Aquinas's exhaustive elaboration of that scheme in the *Summa Theologiae*—as an opportunity to engage in a comically prodigious classification of all of the fields of human knowledge. Poliziano was apparently composing his satire with two objects in mind: on the one hand, he was mocking the pretentiousness of university professors, whose inaugural lectures were traditionally opportunities to showboat their talents as they surveyed the special relevance of their discipline within the whole scheme of the liberal arts encyclopedia, and on the other hand he was mocking any and all attempts to treat human experience or knowledge in any kind of systematic way, a presupposition that would seem to lie beneath much of the late medieval cognitive project. (I might add that such antisystematic guerrilla warfare is a constant in the academic world and is very much alive and well in the twentieth and twenty-first centuries, where the adjective "systematic" often signals a pejorative judgment of the critic against "totalizing" structures of knowledge.) In Poliziano's *Panepistemon* we have the first appearance, to my knowledge, of the Greek term "anatomy" as applied metonymically to knowledge and the world of criticism and interpretation, and Poliziano's definition would seem as precisely operative for Swift as it was for its originator.[6]

The tendency for these satires to embrace iconography that is encyclopedic or synthetic (the liberal arts, the virtues) is partly explained by the academic contexts of these satires, but a more important observation can also be made about this feature of the anatomy's object. If the satirist wishes to be true to the medical pedigree of the term "anatomy," he presumably wishes to dissect his subject—the world of learning and of intellectuals—until the etiology or pathology of its illness has been determined. The capacity for satirists to arrive at startling generalizations in their diagnoses gives a justification for such a comprehensive overview of learning. Burton's *Anatomy,* for example, concludes that all of melancholy's forms can be explained by a distortion, excess, or deficiency in the virtue of charity or love, while Swift's *Tale* in a similar manner reduces his culture's maladies to the dangerous and even wild latitude of interpretation that seems to prevail and that is sanctioned by the egoistic moral universe of the modern world, where all opinions count. What we would today call a holistic approach to diagnosis and therapy is just as necessary to the Augustan or Renaissance satirist because whatever vice seems to be most prevalent in the culture has presumably infected all branches of its learning, in each of which symptoms can be discovered. If the entire thought and feeling of a society are thus in the throes of a disease or epidemic, the satirist must anatomize or dissect the corporate body to find the source of the disease that influences all of the intellectual productions of that society. In short, the satirical anatomist is busy tracking down ideology or hegemonic discourses, and a systemic approach that examines the whole body rather than individual organs is therefore necessary. An interesting and late example of this tracking down of a root source for wrongheaded thinking or false consciousness is William Blake's rather obscure satire on science, *An Island in the Moon:* changes in the epistemological foundations of knowledge through the pursuit of an experimental method have invaded all areas of thought and feeling, including literature and the visual arts, or so Blake would seem to insist in his satirical analysis. A later philosopher like Michel Foucault is acting no differently (if much more seriously) when he discovers that all representations are influenced by the ruling *episteme* of the "classical" (Foucault's term) or Enlightenment mentality, a mentality that has displaced the analogical habits of mind of Renaissance thinkers and writers.[7]

Another of Poliziano's lectures, the *Lamia,* enjoyed an even greater fortune than the *Panepistemon* and similarly mocked the university establishment (and especially its philosophical faculty), but I should like to defer treatment of this work for the moment. While I could give more examples of the "anatomical" academic exercise from other Italian university contexts in the period of Renaissance humanism, I think that my two examples are sufficient to demonstrate that the Renaissance anatomy in its origins intended to survey the world of learning first and foremost, and only later developed the more socially oriented perspectives that Frye notes when he describes the anatomy as enumerating occupational types and "professions" (such as the types of beggars surveyed by Stubbes in the *Anatomy of Abuses*).[8] The Renaissance anatomy had what we might most precisely call a goliardic attitude emanating from a context that was in its origins exclusively academic. Its satire gave expression to a ritualistic need to debase and uncrown the intellect along with its professionalizing gestures—whether by mischievous students or clever professors themselves—in order to ground its audience in their shared amateurism, much in the way that a later work like Burton's *Anatomy of Melancholy* forces its readers to acknowledge their own fallen or melancholic human natures. The diagnosis—whether of melancholy, folly, pedantry, or pretentiousness—is of course always pandemic, and so the satirical anatomy succeeds in subverting structures of rank and privilege that prevail in the everyday world, immersing such conceptions in a festive *communitas* that exposes the artificial and contingent character of hierarchy. Of course Erasmus's *Praise of Folly* stands out as the masterpiece of this form and the one that conveys, perhaps, the fullest blending of the goliardic and humanistic strains of this type of academic satire.

We might pause for a moment and reexamine the anatomy's satirical tendency to address the problem of intellectual credibility by opening up the categories of "amateur" and "professional" to analysis, however anachronistic this may sound, since this is clearly an issue of great importance in Swift's work. This polarity coincides with the more manifest categories of "ancient" (learned amateurs like Temple and Swift himself) and "modern" (pedantic, specialist professionals like Wotton and Bentley) in the *Tale of a Tub,* but they also are at the root of the tensions that are played out in the religious allegory of the *Tale.* By the late seventeenth century, the effects of the new philological learning that humanism reintroduced into the West would have been all too apparent to scholars and churchmen, and to many thinkers its consequences for Christendom would not necessarily have seemed beneficial. Humanist scholars like Valla, Poliziano, and Erasmus had begun—through a more critical and specialized form of scholarship that would eventually be termed classical philology—a process of redefining and emending the canonical texts of both classical and Christian culture, a process that continues into the present and one that Bentley was engaged in when he attacked Temple's praise for the pseudepigraphic letters of Phalaris.[9] While the skirmishes and firefights of early philology seem from our vantage point to be minor episodes in a more interesting history of "rationalization" and "disenchantment" as might be described by a sociologist like Max Weber, these somewhat forgotten episodes in the history of scholarship are also concrete expressions of a tension that would only become resolved in the nineteenth century with the emergence of formal "professions" and the attendant processes of credentialization familiar to us today. For a writer like Swift, there was a felt tension and ambiguity between the categories of amateur and professional, just as there had been legitimate fears from the earliest moments in the Protestant Reformation that allowing tinkers and ploughmen to arrive at their own interpretations of scripture would rend the fabric of Catholic Europe. I am quite obviously not the first reader of Swift's work to single out the theme of interpretation as the one that synthesizes many of the otherwise disparate elements of his work, but I think it needs saying that the trenches in which the struggle over interpretive freedom were fought were the technical treatises, scholarly editions, and humanist polemics that define the two centuries of classical and biblical scholarship prior to the *Tale.* And it was the very authors of these learned works who themselves found a need, on occasion, to relieve some of the anxiety that accompanied this competitive process of professionalization by engaging in academic satire of themselves and of the humanist project as a whole.

Even more important in some ways is an implicit distinction that emerges in Swift's work between a "professional" like the critic "in the modern kind" and the more cosmopolitan figure of the intellectual. Edward Said usefully suggests that the term "amateur" in its root sense conveys many of the aspects of the unaffiliated and yet passionately involved intellectual whose allegiances lie only in his claim to represent humanity as a whole rather than a particular party or sphere of interests.[10] Said's notion of the exilic intellectual standing apart from the "corporate ensemble" is one that seems especially applicable to the humanist intellectual in his office as anatomist, for it is precisely the need to step outside of the "system"—whether that system be ethical, cognitive, or social in its descriptive contours—that makes his diagnostic work possible. In an essay entitled "Swift as Intellectual," Said stresses the dual aspect of Swift's ironic stance both inside the "literary system" as the impersonator of a critic, but also as a metacritic outsider capable of unmasking the master ideas out of which the cultural and intellectual life of his age are constructed.[11] What emerges from Swift's portrait of contemporary intellectual life is the detraction, one-upmanship, rivalry, and sectarianism of his society, all of which can be laid at the feet of a competitive ethos engendered by an incipient professionalism. Even Bentley, whose professionalism Swift apparently found distasteful, acknowledged that his peers in the republic of letters were more concerned with their "noble science of detraction" than by any high-minded or disinterested love of learning; the petty "Phalarism" he found himself engaged in was equally distasteful to his sensibilities as well, or so he claimed.[12] In Swift's work the competitive marketplace for the critic and man of letters has produced both a flood of printed matter and a hopeless proliferation of competing or contradictory interpretations. Only a thoroughly critical stance that assumes the possibility of ideological disinterestedness—the anatomist's detached stance as an "amateur" intellectual—can reveal this diseased or fallen condition. While it may be difficult in the age of postmodernism to maintain the credibility of the notion of a disinterested pursuit of "absolute values,"[13] nevertheless Swift's manipulation of personae does provide him with an ironic distancing from a highly partisan debate over ancients and moderns. His assumption of roles both as a contestant in the fray and an outsider helps to explain why it has seemed, at times, difficult to pinpoint his critical allegiance with certainty. Though one suspects that his adoption of the more humanistic role of "ancient" was more congenial to his mind and to his patron's, his satiric method makes explicit identification with Temple's cause difficult to prove unequivocally. Swift's capacity to pose as both an exilic figure pursuing disinterested detachment and as an energetic modern willing to participate in the paper chase that forms the immediate background to the *Tale* exemplifies his versatility, his ability to uphold both universal and local values, to be both a detached "traditional" and a historically rooted "organic" intellectual at one and the same time.[14]

If the satirical traditions of the anatomy help to illuminate Swift's ideal—if not his consistent practice—of disinterested analysis, the more specialized genre of the philological squabble would seem to tend in the opposite direction, toward the aggressive invective and ad hominem attack requisite for participation in the very local and immediate turf wars of historical scholarship. The universalizing diagnostic capacities of the anatomy figure here less explicitly, though it almost goes without saying that the proliferation of competing interpretations, whether in the religious sphere or in the field of classical scholarship, are a presupposition of this humanist form. If we revert to the heyday of humanist invective in the early quattrocento (though the invective can be traced as far back as Petrarch in the fourteenth century), the combative metaphors and the linguistic and philological concerns that permeate the genre make it clear that interpretive contestation is at the soul of this form, however personal and slanderous the attack may seem on the surface.[15] Literary gladiators like Poggio, Valla, Filelfo, and others popularized this mode of assault as much as a means of advancing their own reputations as detracting from that of their enemies. What interests me here, however, is the way in which such squabbles tended to solidify positions on styles of learning and on canonical issues of standards and cultural values. A common topic of the earliest humanist invectives, for example, was an examination of the relative merits of competing discourses such as medicine and law, so that these invectives could quickly escalate into institutional struggles for the definition of cultural values, full-blown *querelles* pitting the ancients (humanist men of letters with their ethical and rhetorical interests rooted in the study of antiquity) against the "moderns" (scholastic natural philosophers and logicians with their obsessive pursuit of Aristotelian method).[16] The personal invectives of the quattrocento were rooted in this larger and more lasting struggle for cultural domination as it was fought over by authors like Petrarch and Coluccio Salutati, even if such central matters later became obscured by the slander and sheer pettiness of fifteenth-century proponents of the form like Poggio, Valla, and Filelfo. In the case of Swift, how did a very local conflict that had arisen out of a misstatement on the part of Temple concerning the authorship of some relatively obscure texts from antiquity come to be a global affair, to engender the friction that would allow it to become magnified into a battle of the books, a struggle for the cultural soul of the Augustan age?

Literary criticism of the *Tale* has made quite apparent that a whole series of momentous issues in the cultural history of the Restoration were absorbed into the Pandora's box that Swift composed: the disturbances that mechanistic views of the universe had generated among the learned community, the troubling persistence of dissenting and heterodox religious views, the explosive force that a volatile and at times sensational press had engendered in England, and finally the presumptuous emergence of a new, Baconian standard by which the ideology of progress came to supplant the reverence for tradition that had characterized so much of the humanist movement in European society. That such a host of important issues should have emerged out of the Temple/Wotton squabble is a singular example of the Freudian concept of overdeterminacy. Latent beneath all of the shoving matches lies, I think, the true cause of all of these symptoms: the troubling corrosion of historical certainties that accompanied the interpretive interventions of classical philology.[17] Just as in the humanist confrontation with scholasticism, methodological and canonical issues were at the core of this conflict as well.

As philosophers and historians of science have reminded us, innovation and novelty arise most often from new interpretations rather than from actual discoveries. Swift's satire therefore isolates interpretation itself as an object of its satire, and his capacity to invert the normal procedures of interpretation, which often involve a distrust in the surfaces of things and in our senses, and a grasping of an inner principle or structural framework to elicit truth, is a masterstroke of his satirical method. It is also a kind of populist challenge to the sort of self-interested mystification of their arts or professions that academics erect to ward off mere amateurs—for if appearances do matter, then anyone can play in the game. If interpretation itself is subject to interpretation, then we really can become victims of what Rabelais termed the "abysme" of knowledge, and the only solution may be to rub our noses in the greasy stuff of the material world. In the period of humanism, scholasticism was most sharply attacked for its recourse to an entire vocabulary of concepts for purely imagined but unobserved qualities in the physical world: quiddities, haecceities, and so forth. Just as humanists could appeal to common sense to awaken the world of learning from the dreams of scholasticism, so also Swift's satire takes on the issue of appearances and realities, of depth and surface. In the context of his work, Swift would seem to be mocking the overdetermined pursuit of arcana, of hidden knowledge, in the face of a common, if less hyperactive and novel, wisdom that the cumulative efforts of centuries of human reflection have amassed. The immediate example is of course Bentley's intervention in the Phalaris affair, where an interpretation has supplanted the literal text's claim for authorship by the ancient king himself. That Bentley had it on good authority from Poliziano himself and other classical scholars does not concern Swift;[18] the example of Bentley is simply the most recent instance of a cultural tendency that has gotten out of hand and that of course includes Martin and Jack as well as their Aeolist followers. All pursue singularity and novelty rather than tradition. The utter topsy-turviness of Swift's work thus supports the following paradox: the "popular" crowd follows doctrines that are mystified and arcane, while the "elite" purveyors of ancient wisdom appeal to common sense and appearances. Interpretive style, of course, is at the heart of these distinctions.

Swift's *Tale* may for this reason derive some of its thrust from Renaissance satires that specifically took upon themselves the topic of the textual critic or philologist's role as a determiner of what is to be considered authentic or truthful. What is especially apparent in Renaissance satires of this type is the satirist's capacity to imagine his work as having a very crowded intellectual marketplace as its backdrop. One of Swift's complaints was of course that virtually any fool could secure himself a reputation by availing himself of the market for productions of wit. The excessive production of books figures in the early pages of Swift's *Tale* as itself a sign of intellectual decadence, and it is no different in the sixteenth-century satire of Justus Lipsius, the *Somnium,* where papers swirl about the ancient Roman forum in his dream vision to form a backdrop for a "fictional" work that mocks the excessive license that textual critics have taken in emending, correcting, or simply mangling classical texts.[19] The crowding of the marketplace for literary productions and the unconstrained freedom that "modern" critics have taken with the precious cargo of antiquity would seem to require the establishment of standards, and it was therefore the task of the most skilled humanists to struggle with defining the office of the critic. Even in its earliest manifestations, this task necessarily involved its authors in debating issues of canonicity as well as professionalism.

The overlapping issues of the *querelle* of the ancients and the moderns and the critique of upstart professionalism emerge in philological squabbles such as Lipsius's. Poliziano's *Lamia* and Lipsius's *Somnium* are not as thoroughly destructive as Swift's *Tale* or Agrippa's *De vanitate* (the latter probably known to Swift), for in them a sane portrait of the responsible "critic" emerges. While Swift's century has often been characterized as the "age of criticism," a definition that is accurate enough given the attention to issues of taste and critical judgment in writers with such strongly neoclassical moorings as Addison, Johnson, Pope, and Dryden, the emergence of the modern concept of the "critic" first arose in the humanistic works of Poliziano, or perhaps even earlier in works like the *Elegantiae* of Lorenzo Valla, both of whose career paths were imitated by later Renaissance humanists like Erasmus and Joseph Scaliger. The office of the "criticus" is made equivalent with that of the "grammaticus" in the *Lamia* in what is to my knowledge the first postclassical instance of the term's use.[20] Interestingly, Poliziano's definition and renewal of the term is made as a countercultural gesture against the traditions of scholastic Aristotelianism and therefore has somewhat of an "amateur" cast when defined in contrast to the narrow philosophical specialization of the schools. On the other hand, while situated outside of traditional conceptions of the university curriculum and professorial functions as these were inherited from the medieval world, the office of critic requires a virtually polymathic training in all of the arts and sciences, not just in philosophy. Poliziano sees his role as a *criticus* as far more demanding of talent and energy than that of a scholastic commentator on Aristotle or Peter Lombard. His sense of the critic's tasks is humanistic in orientation, grounded in classical conceptions of the rhetorician and his training as we might meet these in Cicero's *De Oratore* or Quintilian's *Institutio oratoria*. The nonspecialized mastery of the entire classical heritage, inclusive of legal, medical, and scientific texts, make it encyclopedic, but curiously enough it retains an amateur sensibility for itself, driven more by love of learning than by guild requirements (as in the medieval university) or credentialization (the latter, of course, would only emerge in the very distant future). We might say that Poliziano's text negotiates a redefinition of what "professing" entails, raising the bar, as it were, and necessarily excluding from its charmed circle the scholastic "specialists" in the Aristotelian *Organon*.

This paradigm shift, from "modern" logician and Aristotelian expositor to "ancient" philologist, rhetor, or critic, was played out many times in Renaissance culture. Further refinements—separating out the truly gifted textual scholars from the impetuous neophytes—occurred in the sixteenth century. Lipsius's *Somnium* takes up the issue of professionalism at a more advanced stage of its development, and in his work the "moderns" are the arrogant humanistic editors who, overconfident in their skills as classicists, have gone about mangling the "ancients"—actual ancient authors. The dream vision of the *Somnium* enacts a debate among resurrected classical authors such as Cicero, Ovid, and Varro, all of whom complain about the torture they have suffered at the hands of their modern editors. Only a rare scholar like Joseph Scaliger escapes Lipsius's censure upon the excessive interpretation and emendation to which the classical corpus has been subjected. Interpretive license is explicitly associated with madness by Lipsius, and I am certain that Swift knew this work and that his two digressions (upon critics and "in the modern kind") are partly modeled on Lipsius's work, which was, incidentally, subtitled *Satyra Menippea.*

In the *Tale*'s "Digression on Critics," Swift initially delineates three types of critics, and his first two definitions coincide exactly with the definitions given by Poliziano. The *grammaticus* or *criticus* for Poliziano is responsible both for what we would today call the "judgment" of a work (as in our term "movie critic") and for the textual accuracy or authenticity of the work (closer to our term "editor" or "textual scholar"). Swift's third definition is the one that ridicules moderns: scholars who make it their business to gather up the mistakes of others, to form their own reputations through the compilation of others' mistakes, taking a sadistic pleasure in harming the reputation of others. A product of envy and amour propre in a society where one-upmanship can advance one's reputation in the literary world, this kind of critic is the one ironically delineated as a "true" critic by Swift. (A further irony resides, of course, in Swift's penchant for engaging in such detraction himself.) In Lipsius's satire, one group of scholars is indicted in the underworld for having committed the crime of litigiousness (*prurigo*), as being, that is, especially prone to quarreling and nit-picking, and Swift would appear to have these critics in mind when he enumerates his third type of critic. As "discoverers and collectors of others faults" these "true" critics are revealed in Swift to be petty and mean-spirited, and they are described in the language of monstrosity and grotesquerie as a phenomenon that is "wholly Modern" (96). Whether we appeal to Lipsius's lashing of textual scholars or Poliziano's laying claim to the office of the "critic" in the *Lamia*—a passage dear to the minds of many an Augustan classicist, and a formulation quoted (or plagiarized) with warm approbation by Bentley in his *Dissertations*[21]—both Swift and his Renaissance forebears were struggling to define a new cultural function in the West, a new standard of historical scholarship and critical judgment. Swift's reticence at jumping on the modern bandwagon is more reminiscent of the caution that Lipsius advises than the heady enthusiasm for philological learning we find in Poliziano, but clearly the *Tale* can be helpfully placed within the satirical tradition of the philological squabble.

That these academic satires should concern themselves with a somewhat raucous marketplace that forms the backdrop of the critic and his interpretations reminds us that competition for intellectual mastery was not a new phenomenon of the Augustan age's "public sphere," just as it should remind us that any "anatomy" that examines the state of learning in a culture will naturally focus on the more contested territories within it. What Italian scholars have termed the "*disputà delle arti*" as it occurred in the texts of Renaissance humanism can often escalate into satire or devolve into invective, and there is certainly the suggestion in Swift's satire that an academic rivalry between men of letters, on the one hand, and textual specialists on the other is one of the many tensions behind its composition.[22] Both Swift and his Renaissance counterparts used Menippean satire as a literary instrument for taking the pulse of their cultures, for measuring the spirit of their ages in an astonishingly modern, self-reflexive, and even self-deprecating manner. Such a move toward self-criticism is an important one, for it signals both the possibility of increasing autonomy for intellectuals and also an increasing space for public discourse, and in closing I should like to examine some of the wider implications Swift's satire might have in relation to the debts he may owe to his humanist forebears.

For the past two decades a great deal of attention has been drawn to the concept of the "public sphere" and to the notion of public intellectuals enacting competing discourses in such a sphere, largely from a series of thinkers who align themselves with the school of critical theory represented by Horkheimer, Adorno, Marcuse, and Habermas. These thinkers were strongly influenced by both Weber's and Mannheim's examination of the social function of intellectuals. Weber and especially Mannheim were concerned with describing the more utopian possibility of the classless (or autonomous) intellectual, a notion that postmodern criticism would no longer vouchsafe but that history, which is filled with a host of instances of acts of resistance that were made even in the face of certain death, would seem to verify. I would qualify one assumption that seems to govern the work of Habermas and his followers: the notion that the "public sphere" emerges in the eighteenth century as a byproduct or coterminous development of the European Enlightenment. I would rather like to trace its emergence to the reappearance of the learned symposium as a dialogic literary form in the republican political climate of early fifteenth century Florence in authors like Leonardo Bruni, Matteo Palmieri, Poggio Bracciolini, Lorenzo Valla, and many others, as well as to the less decorous invectives and squabbles that also became popular at this time, not to mention the very public satirical university lectures I discussed at the outset. Emerging just prior to the invention of printing and practiced by scholar-intellectuals whose careers show in many cases a freelance character, the humanist movement was not nearly as elitist at its inception as many historiographical traditions have portrayed it—though it eventually tended toward a more courtly embodiment—and was carried out in certain cases in cultural milieux where literacy rates approached the levels of eighteenth-century London and where civic discourse was highly valued. In these dialogic symposia and literary invectives what is at stake is more than the public reputation of their authors, but rather struggles over defining canonical norms, standards of authenticity, and intellectual style and method during a given historical period. Leonardo Bruni's open-minded *Dialogi* of the early 1400s are in fact the *locus classicus* for the *querelle* over the ancients and the moderns, evidence that such a "public sphere" was emerging in embryonic form, exclaustrated, perhaps, from a more circumscribed habitus in the late medieval university guild, though not as thoroughly "public" and media-saturated as later intellectual contexts such as those we might encounter during the English Civil Wars or in the Augustan age.[23] Nevertheless, the continuity in both theme and imagery that Swift's *Tale* shows with such Renaissance works is testimony of a sensitivity to a wider, more pluralist and more urban audience for the productions of wit, and of a very public struggle for leadership in the cultural brokerage of literature and learning.

The openness, the multiple ironies of Swift's *Tale,* while perhaps only matched in cleverness and caginess in Renaissance culture by authors like

Erasmus and Rabelais, nevertheless have their roots in the dialogic initiatives of Italian humanism. Postmodern criticism, often misconstruing "humanism" through a process of back-formation that entirely excludes the early Italian humanists who invented it, and nostalgically misconstruing the "middle ages" as a world of communal togetherness and guild solidarity, continues to give short shrift to the profoundly critical investigation of the finest humanists, as well as to their capacity for self-reflexive analysis of their own cultural project. Swift learned some of this openness and autonomy from his mentor William Temple, whose humanistic tastes in learning are everywhere apparent. Swift's *Tale,* while hardly an entirely humanistic work in the manner of Renaissance learned symposia (it would need further stuffing with apropos classical citations to achieve that status), nevertheless shares the openness that is characteristic of them—even when we suspect that a party line friendly to Temple's "ancients" is eventually settled on. His debts to such humanistic works helped him to consider the moral implications of an overhasty endorsement of an emerging public sphere where cultural values were capable of contestation, though the moderns, then as now students of their own singularity and of the faulty syllogisms, aporias, and overdetermined metaphors of their textualized universes, would win the struggle for narrow-mindedness.

NOTES

1. For Swift's indebtedness to Burton, see Angus Ross, "*The Anatomy of Melancholy* and Swift," in *Swift and His Contexts,* eds. John Irwin Fischer, Hermann J. Real, and James Woolley (New York: AMS Press, 1989), 133–58. Miriam K. Starkman's *Swift's Satire on Learning in A Tale of a Tub* (Princeton: Princeton University Press, 1950), while less certain of Burton's influence, importantly suggests that the "new criticism" is among the more important themes of Swift's work, part of a larger attack on novelties in the world of learning as a whole. I have generally followed John R. Clark, *Form and Frenzy in Swift's Tale of a Tub* (Ithaca: Cornell University Press, 1970), xii, in considering the three parts of the *Tale* as a single whole (that is, the fable itself, the mock-epic battle of the ancient and modern books, and the letter to a friend concerning the mechanical operation of the spirit). Clark is especially helpful in pursuing the possibility that Swift had traditions of Renaissance mock encomia in mind when he composed the *Tale* (199–200). For citations from Swift's work, I have used the edition of A. C. Guthkelch and D. Nichol Smith, *A Tale of a Tub,* 2nd ed. (Oxford: Clarendon Press, 1958), and give page numbers in parentheses.

2. Northrop Frye, *Anatomy of Criticism* (Princeton: Princeton University Press, 1957), 309–12; Mikhail Bakhtin, *Problems of Dostoevsky's Poetics,* ed. and trans. Caryl Emerson (Minneapolis: University of Minnesota Press, 1984), 106–37; Bakhtin, *The Dialogic Imagination,* ed. Michael Holquist, trans. Caryl Emerson and Michael Holquist (Austin: University of Texas Press, 1985), 21–27; W. Scott Blanchard, *Scholars' Bedlam: Menippean Satire in the Renaissance* (Lewisburg, Pa., and London: Bucknell University Press, 1995); F. Ann Payne, *Chaucer and Menippean Satire* (Madison: University of Wisconsin Press, 1981); Gay Sibley, "*Satura* from Quintilian to Joe Bob Briggs: A New Look at an Old Word," in *Theorizing Satire,* eds. Brian Connery and Kirk Combe (New York: St. Martin's Press, 1995), 57–72.

3. For the inclusion of Apuleius among Menippean authors in the understanding of Renaissance humanists, see Blanchard, *Scholars' Bedlam*, 22ff.

4. Ugolino Pisani's *Repetitio Magistri Zanini Coqui* has been edited by Paolo Viti in *Due commedie umanistiche pavesi* (Padua: Antenore, 1982); its author confesses in the prologue that he is acting in the role of a "rubbish collector" and "mangler" of philosophy and the arts (141: "quisquiliarius et philosophiae et cuiuscumque scientiae lacerator et simulacrum") in expanding upon his theme that "infinite are the kinds of fools" (Eccl. 1:15). Swift apparently had direct contact with a goliardic experience of this kind. Irwin Ehrenpreis, in *Swift: The Man, His Works, and the Age,* 3 vols. (Cambridge: Harvard University Press, 1962–83), 1: 67, records that Swift probably heard a contemporary student at Trinity College, John Jones, give the satirical *tripos* speech at commencement exercises when he was a student.

5. Ernst Robert Curtius, *European Literature and the Latin Middle Ages,* tr. Willard Trask (Princeton: Princeton University Press, 1953), 431–35; Bakhtin, *The Dialogic Imagination,* 61–83.

6. "Imitabor igitur sectiones illas medicorum, quas Anatomas vocant" (Angelo Poliziano, *Opera Omnia,* ed. Ida Maier, 3 vols. [Turin: Bottega d'Erasmo, 1970–71], 1: 462). Swift would seem to have such an anatomical understanding of his own satirical method when he points to a discourse that will be "speedily published" entitled "Lectures upon a Dissection of Human Nature" in a list facing the title-page of the *Tale* (2); when he speaks of his examination of "the Universal Body of all Arts and Sciences" (38) in the dedication; when he promises to "display by Incision" "the most finished and refined Systems of all Sciences and Arts" (67); and when he mocks Wotton's use of the term "anatomy" by suggesting that he has since "dissected the Carcass of *Humane Nature*" and is prepared to "shew a very compleat Anatomy thereof" (123). For the possibility that Swift knew Poliziano's work, see n. 19.

7. Michel Foucault, *The Order of Things: An Archaeology of the Human Sciences,* n.t. (New York: Pantheon, 1971).

8. Frye was probably thinking of Flaubert's *Bouvard et Pécuchet* when he spoke of an "occupational approach to life" in the handling of the Menippean author's canvas of characters (*Anatomy,* 309); he does, however, also stress the Menippean form's "vision of the world in terms of a single intellectual pattern" (310) or what I term below a "pandemic" diagnosis.

9. On historical criticism as a background for the *Tale,* see the study of Joseph Levine, *The Battle of the Books: History and Literature in the Augustan Age* (Ithaca: Cornell University Press, 1991), who is especially concerned to delineate the "ancient" position as deriving from the traditions of Renaissance humanism. For the rise of modern scholarship, see more generally Donald Kelley, *Foundations of Modern Historical Scholarship* (New York: Columbia University Press, 1970); E. J. Kenney, *The Classical Text* (Berkeley: University of California Press, 1974); and Anthony Grafton, *Joseph Scaliger: A Study in the History of Classical Scholarship,* 2 vols. (Oxford: Clarendon Press and New York: Oxford University Press, 1983–).

10. Edward Said, *Representations of the Intellectual* (1994; New York: Pantheon, 1996).

11. Edward Said, "Swift as Intellectual," in *The World, the Text, and the Critic* (Cambridge: Harvard University Press, 1983), 72–89.

12. Richard Bentley, *Dissertations upon the Epistles of Phalaris, Themistocles, Socrates, Euripides, and upon the Fables of Aesop,* ed. Alexander Dyce, 3 vols. (London: F. MacPherson, 1836), 1: xxv–xxvi; xl.

13. Said, "Swift as Intellectual," 80, responding to some of the ideas of Julien Benda's 1928 book, *La trahison des clercs,* would seem to suggest that such "absolute values" are indeed imaginable.

14. In addition to Said's works just cited, see also Carole Fabricant, "Swift in His Own Time and in Ours: Some Reflections on Theory and Practice in the Profession," in *The Profession of Eighteenth-Century Literature,* ed. Leo Damrosch (Madison: University of Wisconsin Press, 1992), 113–34, who expands the notion of Swift as an intellectual beyond the Gramscian typologies of "traditional" and "organic" to include the "specific" and "universal" intellectual (117ff.).

15. On humanist invective and polemic, there are two older studies by Felice Vismara, *L'invettiva, arma preferita dagli umanisti: nelle lotte private, nelle polemiche letterarie, politiche e religiose* (Milan: Umberto Allegretti, 1900) and Charles Nisard, *Les Gladiateurs de La République des Lettres aux XVe, XVIe, et XVIIe Siècles* (1860; rep. Geneva: Slatkine Reprints, 1970). More recently, see Antonio Lanza, *Polemiche e berte letterarie nella Firenze del primo Quattrocento* (Rome: Bulzoni, 1972) and Martin Davies, "An Emperor without Clothes? Niccolò Niccoli under Attack," *Italia medioevale e umanistica* 31 (1988): 94–148.

16. This is the context for Petrarch's *Invective contra medicum* (1352) and Coluccio Salutati's *De nobilitate legum et medicinae* (1399–1400). The bifurcation between humanists and scientists is visible in Temple's *An Essay upon the Ancient and Modern Learning:* "near the age of Socrates, lived their [i.e., the Chinese] great and renowned Confucius, who began the same design of reclaiming men from the useless and endless speculations of nature, to those of morality" (cited from *Five Miscellaneous Essays by Sir William Temple,* ed. Samuel Holt Monk [Ann Arbor: University of Michigan Press, 1963], 46).

17. Dustin Griffin, "Interpretation and Power: Swift's *Tale of a Tub,*" *The Eighteenth Century: Theory and Interpreation* 34 (1993):151–68, has emphasized the very aggressive language Swift uses in the *Tale,* as well as its emphasis on interpretive contestation.

18. Temple disagreed with Poliziano's rejection of Phalaris's authorship in his *Essay* (ed. cit., 64); Bentley, in response, cited a host of authorities including Poliziano in the *Dissertations* (ed. cit., 90).

19. Justus Lipsius, *Somnium. Satyra Menippea,* in *Two Neo-Latin Menippean Satires,* eds. C. Matheeussen and C. L. Heesakkers (Leiden: E.J. Brill, 1980). While my purpose in this essay in not to prove with any great certainty that Swift may have read a particular Renaissance author, I would suggest that it is quite probable that he was familiar with this work of Lipsius. The Stillingfleet collection housed in Archbishop Marsh's Library contains a copy of Lipsius's *Opera* containing this work. Furthermore, Temple's familiarity with Poliziano's judgment on the Phalaris letters suggests that Temple himself probably had copies of the *Opera* of major humanists like Poliziano, Valla, and Lipsius, and so Swift might have encountered Poliziano's satirical *praelectiones* (including the *Lamia* mentioned in the next note) while at Moor Park. I would also argue that Swift's work may have been influenced by the satire of Agrippa von Nettesheim, *De incertitudine et vanitate scientiarum,* which is suggested by Clark, *Form and Frenzy,* 200, as a work available to Swift.

20. There is a modern edition of this important humanist work: *Lamia: Praelectio in Priora Aristotelis Analytica,* ed. Ari Wesseling (Leiden: E.J. Brill, 1986). The relevant passage on "critics" reads: "apud antiquos olim tantum autoritatis hic ordo habuit, ut censores essent, et iudices scriptorum omnium soli grammatici, quos ob id etiam Criticos vocabunt" ("formerly in antiquity this class had such authority that grammarians alone were the evaluators and judges of all writings, and because of this were even called Critics"). For an assessment of this work's importance, see Aldo Scaglione, "The Humanist as Scholar and Politian's Concept of the Grammaticus," *Studies in the Renaissance* 8 (1961): 49–70.

21. Bentley, *Dissertations* (ed. cit., 82) is a direct borrowing from Poliziano's *Lamia.* It should be noted that Poliziano was reacting against Quintilian's attempt to constrain the office of the grammarian in *Institutio oratoria* 2.1.4.

22. Eugenio Garin, *La disputà delle arti nel Quattrocento* (Florence: Vallecchi, 1947) cites fifteenth-century examples, many of which draw on the similar works by Petrarch and Salutati mentioned above, n. 16.

23. While the issue of the genesis of the "public sphere" is a wide-open one, I note that John Bender reflects the tendency to inscribe it within the eighteenth century in "A New History of the Enlightenment?" in *The Profession of Eighteenth-Century Literature,* 62–83, citing Peter Gay and Peter Hohendahl on the Enlightenment as "the founding era of criticism as we know it" (67). In the context of Swift's *Tale,* which registers the profound impact of "modernity" that a critical age must experience in severing itself from past traditions, I note that David Quint has discovered the emergence of a modern sense of belatedness in the face of an accurate and truly historical confrontation with antiquity in Bruni's work ("Humanism and Modernity: A Reconsideration of Bruni's *Dialogues,*" *Renaissance Quarterly* 38 [1985]: 423–45). In Quint's view, it is precisely the "peculiarly modern consciousness of Niccoli" (445) that presides over two dialogues in which the critical reception of modern vernacular authors (Dante, Petrarch, and Boccacio) are weighed against ancients like Cicero and Vergil. Clearly Italian humanism was an intellectual movement that had set its sights on becoming an "age of criticism" *avant la lettre,* and that was therefore an important early stage of an emergent "public sphere." See also Hans Baron, "The *Querelle* of the Ancients and the Moderns as a Problem for Renaissance Scholarship," *Journal of the History of Ideas* 20 (1959): 3–22.

Part II
"Swift"

The Authorial Strategies of Swift's
Verses on the Death

Stephen Karian

OF SWIFT'S POEMS, *VERSES ON THE DEATH OF DR. SWIFT* (1739) HAS RE-
ceived perhaps the most critical attention, though surprisingly little has
focused on the complex publishing history that surrounds its appearance.
Here I refer not to the unauthorized editing of the poem shortly before
publication—discussed by Herbert Davis, Arthur H. Scouten, and Robert
D. Hume—but more specifically to Swift's various stratagems prior to that
event.[1] Before trying to publish the *Verses,* Swift shared his poem with
others, encouraged its oral circulation, and fostered a hoax to capitalize on
this fame. A detailed and complete publishing history of the *Verses* reveals
Swift's efforts to negotiate a tension fundamental to early eighteenth-
century authorship, namely the tension between textual control and the
desire for publicity. In the case of the *Verses,* Swift attempted to maximize
control over his poem's circulation while he also generated a broad public
appetite for his text. His efforts to control the poem were not entirely
successful, however, and this partial failure speaks to larger concerns
about print and authorship during this period.

Before examining this publishing history in the second part of this essay,
I discuss the poem in the first part. I connect the two parts not in terms of a
text/context relationship, but as parallel instances of similar authorial
strategies. That is, Swift's publishing strategies parallel and extend the
rhetorical strategies of his poem. In the *Verses,* Swift attempts to locate a
posthumous public identity outside of the book trade, whose largely un-
scrupulous agents distort or refuse to sell his work. Absent the author and
his devices, textual control is impossible. In response to this imagined
situation, Swift constructs the Rose speaker, who is wholly ignorant of the
trade and serves as a synecdoche for the public. But having chosen to
separate the public from the book trade in such a dichotomous fashion,
Swift presents an assessment of his career largely devoid of reference to
his writings. He constructs a posthumous reputation at the cost of his
authorial identity, just as his publishing strategies help him reach a broad
audience with an unauthorized text.

My essay thus situates Swift's *Verses,* both as text and publishing event, in relation to recent debates about print culture and authorship. These subjects receive a thorough theoretical revaluation in Adrian Johns's *The Nature of the Book,* which reveals that beliefs in print's stability and fixity were rarely taken for granted in seventeenth- and early eighteenth-century England.[2] Instead, piracy, inaccurate attribution, and unauthorized alteration were integral features of the landscape of print. In response to this situation, some authors employed specific strategies, the most well-known being anonymity and pseudonymity, so that they could shield their identities while communicating their authorship to others via unofficial channels. Further strategies might include oral or scribal publication, or even hoaxes on the book trade itself. The *Verses* demonstrates the centrality of these issues for Swift; the poem, after all, covers his life and posthumous reception. The *Verses* also shows the risks and rewards of these strategies, whose extent and depth are perhaps more evident in this instance than anywhere else in Swift's authorial career.

I

Swift's poem reveals his ongoing concern with authorial control and dramatizes how others will ultimately construct his posthumous identity. Indeed, this dramatic aspect is apparent in the poem's formal organization. Critics generally agree that the *Verses* has a tripartite structure, that it is divided into proem (ll. 1–72), a middle section describing others' reactions (ll. 73–298), and the Rose speaker's eulogy (ll. 299–484).[3] However, this rigid view of the poem's form fails to account for the heterogeneity within the "middle section" and more generally neglects the poem's fluid nature. While not dismissing ways in which the *Verses* is structured, I want to emphasize how the poem might be reconceived as a developing dialectic that dramatizes the contestation over Swift's public identity after his death. The specific poetic form that Swift adopts permits us a lens to view the complex status of his posthumous identity.

The poem's dynamic organization is especially evident in the "middle section" which contains a variety of contrasting responses to Swift's death by a variety of people. Friends contrast with enemies, booksellers with a vested interest contrast with the financially disinterested, and Swift's reputation emerges as dependent upon neither enemy, friend, nor bookseller. The dialectic is "progressive" or "developing," because the length and detail of the responses increase as the poem proceeds, adding further emphasis to the concluding speech.

Along these lines, here is a more detailed outline of the poem. Swift's proof of La Rochefoucauld's maxim constitutes the explicitly labeled "proem" (ll. 1–72), which leads Swift to ask how his friends will react to his impending death (ll. 73–146). To answer this, he depicts his own death and then reports the reactions from two contrasting groups of those who knew him: first his enemies (Lady Suffolk, Queen Caroline, Charteris, Walpole, and Curll; ll. 177–204) and then his friends (Pope, Gay, Arbuthnot, Bolingbroke, and the women playing cards; ll. 205–42). The rest of the poem contains two longer and contrasting responses, those of the bookseller Bernard Lintot (ll. 253–98) and of the anonymous speaker at the Rose (ll. 299–484). From a broad perspective, the poem contrasts responses to Swift's death by those who knew him well or had a personal interest in him (such as Lintot's economic interest) against that of the ostensibly impartial Rose speaker. The Rose speaker addresses his eulogy in response to all the preceding respondents.[4]

The poem's organization suggests that Swift's reputation is ultimately based not on his published works, nor on the opinions of those enemies or friends who knew him. Rather it depends on some general public memory, of which the Rose speaker is a synecdoche. Thus the poem moves from Swift as personally known, to Swift as a print author, to Swift as posthumous, public myth.[5] Nonetheless, this transition does not entail an absolute distinction between public memory and published works, for the Rose speaker himself refers to Swift's writings. This slight qualification of the poem's dialectic suggests the difficulty, perhaps impossibility, of authors reaching the public except through the book trade.

Indeed, authors' problematic dependency on the printed book trade concerned Swift throughout his career. Much of the *Verses* reveals Swift's fame as an author to be inextricably bound with the book trade and its sometimes questionable economic practices. Three issues specifically concern Swift here: inaccurate attribution, unauthorized publication, and the corrupt marketplace, the first two represented by Edmund Curll and the third by Bernard Lintot. These negative presentations set the stage for the Rose eulogy.

The depiction of Curll significantly follows the descriptions of Swift's enemies reacting to his death. Lady Suffolk, Queen Caroline, Charteris, and Walpole precede Curll, suggesting that the bookseller is elevated (or degraded) to their level. Curll is the climactic enemy of the poem precisely because of his desire to control Swift's authorial reputation. The other four are powerful figures, and reflect on past experiences with Swift, but Curll looks to a future that the real living Swift cannot affect and that his shade "must bear" (204). The final note on Curll refers to his forgery of peers' letters, reveals his affront to the powerful, and shows him as a danger both to authors and to England.

The first note on Curll describes him as "the most infamous Bookseller of any Age or Country." Swift loathed Curll's publishing practices, and his harsh attitude toward the bookseller was indeed shared by others. Within the poem, Curll's reaction to Swift's death exemplifies his character:

> Now *Curl* his Shop from Rubbish drains;
> Three genuine Tomes of *Swift*'s Remains.
> And then to make them pass the glibber,
> Revis'd by *Tibbalds, Moore, and Cibber.*
> He'll treat me as he does my Betters.
> Publish my Will, my Life, my Letters.
> Revive the Libels born to dye;
> Which Pope must bear, as well as I.
>
> (197–204)

Offenses against Swift compound as the passage proceeds. The falsely attributed works—sarcastically called "genuine Tomes"—derive from "Rubbish." The collection of "*Swift*'s Remains" employs a definition of "remains" common during the period as referring to "unpublished writings."[6] The word also invokes a sense of Swift's status; being physically dead, he exists only as remains but, more importantly, his works are his only remaining traces. His authorial identity is fragile because Curll apparently controls it through volumes revised by three Popean dunces: Lewis Theobald, James Moore Smythe, and Colley Cibber. Further, Curll makes private things public by disseminating Swift's will, life, and letters. This description accurately reflects Curll's mode of piracy, which was more often from private manuscript to print than from print to print.

While emphasizing Swift's distorted reputation, the passage also reveals it as quite prominent. The publication of will, biography, and letters revives "Libels born to dye," and suggests his extensive popularity. Print publication seems to be both effect and cause of Swift's fame. An earlier section of the poem describes some "Grub-Street Wits" "cloying" the town with elegies on Swift "in ev'ry Paper" (165–67). Of course this fame is not gained without a cost; some of these elegies "*curse* the *Dean,*" others "*bless* the *Drapier*" (168). But as with the description of Curll, Swift seems to be pervasive, even after his death. This strong sense of Swift's presence in the passage on Curll is also suggested by the repetition of first person references: "me," "I," and "my" (four times). Swift's presence in both written works and grammatical "I" is strikingly absent in the later scene with Lintot.

The section depicting Lintot contrasts with and extends this brief scene with Curll. Curll was a pirate, Lintot a respectable publisher of Pope, Gay, and others. Curll's assault on Swift's authorial reputation is deliberate and motivated by a desire to profit from the author he also defames. Though Lintot does not attack Swift directly, his speech is far more damaging to Swift than Curll's actions. Furthermore, Lintot's position in the poem parallels that of Curll. The hostility of Swift's enemies culminates in Curll's piratical practices, and the transient grief of Swift's friends finds its analogue in the transient status of Swift's works in Lintot's book shop.

Because few critics analyze the Lintot scene, it is necessary to start with the fundamental question as to why Swift specifically chose Bernard Lintot. An analogous question is not as necessary with Curll, who deliberately manipulated Swift's name and was despised by many other authors, Pope among them. Most authors, on the other hand, highly regarded Lintot, and those he published were among the most distinguished of the day, including Pope. Additionally, Swift himself had hardly any professional relations with the man, and never expressed personal resentment toward him. In contrast with Swift's note on Curll ("the most infamous Bookseller"), Lintot does not receive an epithet, only a factual note referring to Pope's *Dunciad* (1728, 1729), which depicts Lintot briefly.

The reference to *The Dunciad* should not obscure the essential difference between the two works' depictions of Lintot. As with Swift attacking Curll, Pope chastises Lintot for something he in fact did, namely publish James Moore Smythe's *The Rival Modes* (1727). Swift, however, presents Lintot marketing authors he never published, such as the thresher poet Stephen Duck, the Walpole supporter and eccentric preacher John Henley, and the blasphemous yet popular clergyman Thomas Woolston. Swift's depiction of Curll is largely accurate; that of Lintot is intentionally distorted.

This evidence suggests that Swift chose Lintot for his recognizable name and for what he represents within the book trade. Although Lintot is a respectable bookseller who publishes respectable authors, his main concern is financial, and if the economic or political climate demands it, he will adapt to the market rather than resist it. A bookseller, even one with taste, is fundamentally a man of business and willing to debase his stock to serve prevailing trends. Lintot's position in the poem can be summed up in the line: "Your Honour please to buy a Set?" (280). Thus Swift depicts Curll as he already is, but shows Lintot as what he expects him to become.

Throughout this scene, Lintot is gleefully indifferent to Swift's fate. The death of Swift's works comes a year after his imagined death, and indeed the two are closely related: "Where's now this Fav'rite of *Apollo?* / Departed; *and his Works must follow*" (249–50). These lines make explicit the analogy between man and work. When the Country Squire asks for Swift's works, Lintot responds:

> "I sent them with a Load of Books,
> "Last *Monday* to the Pastry-cooks.
> "To fancy they cou'd live a Year!
> "I find you're but a Stranger here.

> (259–62)

Now out of fashion, Swift's works line pies. The material emphasis here exemplifies both the ephemerality of printed texts and the debasement of Swift's works; he implies that his own works are like infant offspring unable to live even a year.[7] The corrupt times reduce Swift to an ephemeral author, much like the narrator of *A Tale of a Tub* (1704). In Swift's place, we have Cibber, Duck, Henley, and, worst of all, Woolston. Each of these authors inversely reflects a different facet of Swift. Together they point to the roles of poet, public intellectual, and clergyman, but each author is "inauthentic" in comparison to Swift. That is, each writer is subservient to corrupt masters or causes; Cibber and Duck flatter the monarchs, Henley serves Walpole through the journal *The Hyp Doctor* (1730–41), and Woolston challenges the historical authenticity of Christ. Nonetheless, each is compensated, unlike Swift.

As bad as Curll's treatment of Swift is, at least there we have a sense that Swift survives as an author beyond his death, albeit in a degraded way, in spurious works. In the scene with Lintot, Swift ceases to exist at all. The scenes of Curll and Lintot together show the range of assault on an author from the book trade—from piracy to neglect. The poem shifts from a situation in which the dead author is worth something however spurious the works, to a situation in which the dead author becomes worthless however authentic the works. The poem's final scene, however, removes Swift from the realm of the book shop, and places him among a public divested of economic interests.

This scene occurs in "the Rose," possibly the Rose Tavern in Covent Garden at the intersection of Bridges and Russell Streets, near Drury-Lane Theater. Perhaps the most famous or infamous memorial of this Rose Tavern appears in Plate III of William Hogarth's *The Rake's Progress* (1735), which depicts the orgy scene of Tom Rakewell's continuing dissipation. On the basis of this image and other contemporary references, Peter J. Schakel concludes that the Rose "was consistently used throughout the Restoration and early eighteenth century as a symbol of disrepute." Other contemporary references, however, are more neutral; more significantly, the *Verses* does not characterize the Rose as a place of drunkenness, lewdness, or violence.[8]

Rather, the Rose of this poem is a place of engaged discussion of various subjects. "Discourse of this and that" directly leads to active debate about Swift: "they toss my Name about, / With Favour some, and some without" (301, 303–304). Swift may in fact be using the Rose to suggest a generic public house. Such a use not only parallels his similar use of Lintot, but it also accounts for his minimal description of the Rose. In addition, Bryant Lillywhite notes that the Rose was one of the most popular signs in London, and he cites multiple establishments identified as "the Rose."[9]

Thus Schakel's particular context probably does not apply to Swift's use of the Rose. What seems more certain is the way in which the Rose speaker contrasts with Lintot. Unlike Lintot, the speaker at the Rose is not part of the book trade:

> "As for his Works in Verse and Prose,
> "I own my self no Judge of those:
> "Nor, can I tell what Criticks thought 'em;
> "But, this I know, all People bought 'em.
>
> (309–12)

Here, the economic fact of bookselling reflects well on Swift; "all People" suggests all types of people, all literate classes. In one sense, however, the speaker does not contradict Lintot; the speaker does not imply that Swift's works are still read, only that they once were.

The Rose setting also contrasts with previous settings. The earlier reactions occur in enclosed, restricted spaces, whether "political" (the Court or Sir Robert's levee) or "private" (the drawing room of the card game). None of these instances is as public as the setting at the Rose. Curll's and Lintot's bookshops are public to a degree, but not in the same way. The mode of communication is a crucial difference between the bookshop and the Rose; in the former, communication depends on a trade subject to corruption, censorship, and financial debasement, and in the latter, it occurs in a relatively public arena, in which opinions can be discussed and debated and Swift himself can exist beyond his death, though only as a disembodied name and subject.

Thus it seems appropriate that this section would be spoken by an anonymous figure in contradistinction to other central figures in the poem, most of whom are named. In this sense, the Rose speaker seems to function as what James Woolley calls "a man-in-the-street," or as Swift terms him, "One quite indiff'rent in the Cause" (305).[10] Swift thus situates this speaker as not only independent of the trade and its economics, but also as representative of the general public. This rhetorical strategy has certain advantages for Swift, for it allows him to locate his posthumous reputation outside the book trade and those who operate in it. He also posits a public removed from the corrupt influences of the trade. Having made this choice, however, Swift has the Rose speaker refer hardly at all to his writings, an omission cited by many critics. Yet the Rose speaker suggests that one aspect of Swift's enduring legacy depends on his published works:

> "Two Kingdoms, just as Faction led,
> "Had set a Price upon his Head;
> "But, not a Traytor cou'd be found,
> "To sell him for Six Hundred Pound.
>
> (351–54)

As the note informs us, the lines refer to *The Public Spirit of the Whigs* (1714) and *The Drapier's Fourth Letter* (1724). In each instance, a reward of three hundred pounds was offered to anyone who would implicate Swift as the author of these works; no one claimed the rewards. Here Swift's identity is an open secret that is not for sale. The passage's economic implications sharply contrast with Lintot's speech.

This contrast is not absolute, for although the Rose speaker is "no Judge" of Swift's works and the setting appears removed from the book trade, the mythologized depiction of Swift directly depends on his status as a print author. The speaker talks not about Swift's writings per se but about the effects of his writings, both on Swift himself and on others. This reading is supported by the passage cited above and others elsewhere: "HAD he but spar'd his Tongue and Pen, / He might have rose like other Men"; "THE Dean did by his Pen defeat / An infamous destructive Cheat" (355–56, 407–8). In these lines, "pen" serves as a synecdoche for the printed book, and these references only slightly obscure the reality that such writings were spread via a printing press and the book trade, as is of course the *Verses* itself.

Thus Swift's celebration as a public hero-author at first seems in opposition to the book trade, but ultimately is an extension of it. This paradox seems to suggest a desire to attain respectable fame as an author and public figure outside the corrupt or utilitarian realm of the printed book trade, and yet the road to fame ultimately follows the same path guarded by Curll and Lintot. As we read the poem in its developing dialectic, we can see the final section as only a partial resolution to the problems posed earlier.

The poem's notes also point to this partial resolution. For while Swift constructs the Rose speaker as "One quite indiff'rent in the Cause," he directly inserts his own particularized commentary through the notes. The most controversial portions were never printed, including the ones blasting the Irish Parliament. The printed notes allow Swift to levy more explicit indictments against, for example, Wood and Whitshed, and to detail his political activities and persecution at the hands of the Whigs. Even more striking is the dominance of these notes at this point in the poem. The only other section of the poem that contains so many notes is that describing Swift's enemies. Through this device, Swift, in the third person, gets the last word, as the poem closes with a gloss on "That Kingdom": "Meaning *Ireland,* where he now lives, and probably may dye." This device perhaps suggests both an unwillingness to allow a fictional character center stage and a general attempt to control readers' reactions.

Because of the rhetorical limitations of the Rose speaker, only Swift can comment on his authorial identity. In the examples cited above, the Rose speaker never refers to a specific work of Swift's. Even the reference to the six hundred pound reward does not explicitly mention Swift's role as an

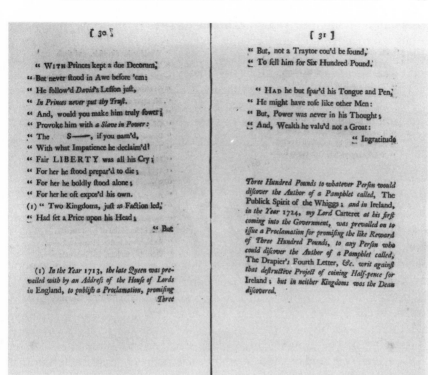

Verses on the Death of Dr. Swift, Faulkner, fourth edition. Reproduced by kind permission of the Teerink Collection, Annenberg Rare Book and Manuscript Library, University of Pennsylvania.

author, and the references to his "pen" remain vague. In the notes, on the other hand, Swift cites *The Public Spirit of the Whigs* and *A Proposal for the Universal Use of Irish Manufacture* (1720) once each and *The Drapier's Letters* three times.

The material text of George Faulkner's separate editions emphasizes the notes' importance. In these editions, the notes appear in the same type size as the poem's lines, and during parts of the Rose speech, they even dominate the page. They thus compete with the lines for the attention of readers. This visual emphasis, absent in most modern editions of the poem, foregrounds the medium of print itself and thus suggests the technology and business of publishing. Though Swift removes the book trade from the Rose speech, it reappears in the content and visual form of his notes.

The Rose episode reveals Swift's desire to escape the book trade and the corruption associated with it, as well as his ultimate need for and dependence on it as a vehicle for fame. Because Swift so clearly recognizes the costs and limitations of either position exclusive of the other, the *Verses* points to an energetic ambivalence that is also evident in the poem's publishing history. For at least four years, Swift publicized the *Verses* while maintaining tight control over his text and, via an elaborate hoax, satirized the entire process of print publication. Swift's publishing strategies extend the situation depicted in the poem; caught in this web of piracy and neglect, he attempts to manipulate it, though without final success.

II

Eleven individual editions of the *Verses* appeared in the eighteenth century, seven of these during 1739, its first year of publication. But Swift probably completed the poem around November or December 1731 and added the notes in the following May (though he may have made minor revisions up until publication).[11] This gap between composition and publication resulted from the concatenation of at least three events, all of which reveal Swift's combined desires to control the work's circulation and arouse the public's interest.

The first of these events involves Swift's private circulation of the poem, which occurred outside the traditional media of script and print. In a letter to Pope, Swift writes: "I never gave a Copy of mine, nor lent it out of my sight, and although I shewed it to all common acquaintance indifferently: & some of them, especially one or two females had got many lines by heart, here & there and repeated them often." To Edward Harley, second Earl of Oxford, he states that "I have often shown [the poem] . . . but I never gave it out of my power." Swift elaborates in a letter to Lord Carteret: "I have suffered all my acquaintance to read it in my presence, but never gave a copy, or sent it out of my sight. all this town had heard of it and some had so good memorys that they could repeat many lines. therefore I have of late been more reserved. I confess my chief aim was to provoke peoples curiosity and a longing they had to see it in print." In the same letter he refers to "at least fourty of both sexes" who saw the poem.[12] Swift's reliance on these private showings ensured that word of the poem would spread, while his possession of the manuscript would help prevent unauthorized printing.

Swift is often deceptive about publishing matters in his letters, so we cannot assume the complete veracity of these statements. Indeed, these comments occur in letters wherein Swift falsely denies authorship of the poem *The Life and Genuine Character of Doctor Swift* (1733), an issue I discuss in more detail below. Swift's statements about the private circulation of the *Verses,* however, are mostly corroborated by a contemporary witness who also reveals that Swift "gave [the poem] out of [his] power" at least once. Laetitia Pilkington is certainly one of the "females" Swift mentions to Pope, and in the first volume of her *Memoirs* (1748), she describes her encounter with Swift's *Verses*. After showing the poem to Pilkington, Swift loaned it to her "on certain Conditions, which were, that I should neither shew it to any body, nor copy it, and that I should send it to him by Eight o'Clock the next Morning, all which I punctually perform'd." Rather than copy the poem, Pilkington memorized it and "could not forbear delighting some particular Friends with a Rehearsal of it." Swift later learned of her recitals and accused her of disobedience. In her defense, Pilkington demonstrated her impressive memory to Swift, who responded in kind by reciting lines from Samuel Butler's *Hudibras* (1663, 1664, 1678).[13]

Pilkington's claim to have memorized the poem is further supported by the lines she quotes in her *Memoirs,* which contain variants not occurring in any printed copy during her lifetime. These variants suggest that she recollects the poem from memory and not from a printed text. Her memory may be faulty in these instances, but it is equally possible that she recalls lines from an early, prepublication manuscript. In one case, she records variants found only in manuscript additions from two printed copies of the poem; since her variants and those in manuscript are strikingly similar though not identical, it is doubtful that either source derives from the other, which further supports her claim about memorizing the poem. These variants also suggest the likelihood that Swift continued to modify his poem between Pilkington's perusal and its later publication by Faulkner.[14]

That Pilkington does not report any further bitterness from Swift suggests that he was not upset at her oral transmission of his poem. Had Swift wished to prevent any public knowledge of the piece, he would have never loaned it to Pilkington in the first place; but his desire to maintain textual control is evidenced by his command against copying. Swift's actions distinguish him from a kind of coterie poet, whose works are meant to remain within the province of select readers. By his own admission, he clearly intended that others learn of the poem and feel a "longing" to see it in print.

The public anticipation of the *Verses* may have led Swift to undertake the second event, an elaborate hoax on his own unpublished poem. In the spring of 1733, a poem appeared in London and then Dublin called *The Life and Genuine Character of Doctor Swift.* Swift's devious strategies with this poem have confused critics for generations, but the accumulation of evidence reveals not only that Swift wrote this poem, but that he did so in part to burlesque the *Verses.*[15] A reconstruction of this complicated hoax reveals Swift exploiting and compounding the publicity surrounding the *Verses.* Through the *Life,* Swift crafts a multifaceted satirical project that indicts a wide range of targets, including disreputable publishers, hack writers, and gullible readers.

Preferring to keep as many people confused as possible, Swift shared his authorship of the *Life* with only a few. He had Matthew Pilkington, the diminutive clergyman and husband of Laetitia, use an intermediary to arrange for Benjamin Motte to publish the poem in London. Recalling this activity over three years later, Motte wrote to Swift that from Matthew Pilkington

> the Life and Character was offered me, though not by his own hands, yet by his means, as I was afterwards convinced by many circumstances: one was, that he corrected the proof sheets with his own hand; and as he said he had seen the original of that piece, I could not imagine he would have suffered your name to be put to it, if it had not been genuine. When I found, by your advertisement, and the letter you were pleased to write to me, that I had been deceived by him, I acted afterwards with more reserve.

Motte's letter indicates that Swift not only never told him about his authorship, but explicitly denied it. George Faulkner, on the other hand, was probably in on the hoax, for he reprinted the poem in Dublin, though not under his own name. This caginess with Motte, with whom Swift was generally on good terms, points to the depth of Swift's maneuvers, which extended even further to include his closest friends.[16]

As the text of the *Life* indicates, Swift wanted some of his readers to think that the poem was a spurious item composed by "some very low writer" who falsely claimed to have acquired a copy of the *Verses*.[17] To accomplish this aim, Swift included a dedication by "L. M.," who describes how the poem was transmitted via Swift's untrustworthy servant. (These initials might refer to "Little Matthew," that is, Pilkington.) L. M. adds that "I have shewn it to very *good Judges,* and *Friends* of the *Dean* . . . who are well acquainted with the *Author*'s *Stile,* and *Manner,* and they all allow it to be *Genuine,* as well as perfectly *finished* and *correct;* his particular *Genius* appearing in every Line, together with his *peculiar* way of *thinking* and *writing*" (*Poems* 2: 544). Here Swift probably mocks both piratical publishers and those readers who presume that they can detect his authorship from style alone.

At the same time, Swift plants seeds of doubt about the poem's authenticity. L. M.'s dedication is dated April first, one of Swift's favorite holidays, suggesting the possibility of a hoax.[18] L. M.'s emphasis on "the Author's Stile and Manner" combined with the dedication's excessive italics should at the very least cause readers to direct their attention to the stylistic features of the poem. Once they do, they would find overused typographic devices atypical of Swift. The *Life* is only 202 lines long, yet it contains 345 italicized words and 52 sets of dashes, devices that Swift later mocks in *On Poetry: A Rapsody* (1733):

> In modern Wit all printed Trash, is
> Set off with num'rous *Breaks*——and *Dashes*—
>
> To Statesmen wou'd you give a Wipe,
> You print it in *Italick Type.*
>
>   (93–96)

The *Life* also has four triplets, which Swift often eschewed, unless he employed it satirically as in "A Description of a City Shower" (1710). Swift once called triplets "a vicious way of rhyming." In a posthumous collection of Swift's *Works,* Faulkner adds further confirmation, for he states that the *Life* "was published with Breaks, Dashes, and Triplets, (which the Author never made use of) to disguise his Manner of Writing."[19]

To further the hoax, Swift places an advertisement in Faulkner's *Dublin Journal* of 15 May 1733 to persuade the public that the *Life* is spurious. Swift does not even spare his friends, for he denies authorship to several of them. Writing to Carteret, Swift remarks about the *Life:* "what I wonder at is how it should come to pass that the Author should not put one original line, or peice [sic] of a line, or one single thought of the true poem in this spurious peice since it plainly appears, that he had often heard of the genuine one and probably some lines of it repeated."[20] As the architect of this entire hoax, Swift had nothing to wonder at, and Carteret's position as a powerful Irish figure and close friend of Swift emphasizes the depth of Swift's efforts to hide his authorship.

These stratagems may well have worked, at least for a time. Writing to Swift shortly after publication, the Duchess of Queensbury says that she "heard severall people talk about it [the *Life*] & the generall opinion was that you had no hand in it, but that the thing happend just as you say." John Boyle, Fifth Earl of Orrery, states that Swift "hoped the public might mistake it for a spurious, or incorrect copy stolen by memory from his original poem. He took great pleasure in this supposition: and I believe it answered his expectation."[21] Pope at least was too acquainted with Swift's strategies to be fooled. Pope's comments on the subject are ambiguous, explicitly accepting Swift's denial, but hinting at his awareness that Swift wrote the *Life.* On 1 September 1733, he writes to Swift that "the man who drew your Character and printed it here, was not much in the wrong in many things he said of you," and on 15 September 1734 he notes that the writer of Swift's *Epistle to a Lady* (1733) "was just the same hand (if I have any judgment in style) which printed your Life and Character before, which you so strongly dis-avow'd in your letters to Lord Carteret, myself and others."[22] Years later, Pope almost certainly knew of Swift's author-ship, for he probably participated with others in borrowing lines from that poem and inserting them into the *Verses.*

Laetitia Pilkington offers a special insight into Swift's attitude toward the *Life.* Having accused her of disobeying his orders about the *Verses,* he claims that she was responsible for the *Life*'s circulation. He does not claim that she wrote the poem, but that she showed the *Verses* around Dublin, and someone consequently composed an "odd Burlesque" on his poem. After Swift asks her to read the *Life* aloud, she writes:

> I did so, and could not forbear laughing, as I plainly perceiv'd, tho' he had endeavour'd to disguise his Stile, that the Dean had burlesqu'd himself; and made no manner of Scruple to tell him so. He pretended to be very angry, ask'd me, did I ever know him write Triplets? and told me, I had neither Taste nor Judgment, and knew no more of Poetry than a Horse. I told him I would confess it, provided he would seriously give me his Word, he did not write that Poem. He said, Pox take me for a Dunce. (*Memoirs* 1: 54–55)

This humorous anecdote shows Pilkington getting the better of Swift. Her challenge that he deny writing the *Life* is answered only by his frustrated "pox take you for a dunce," suggesting that he was annoyed or at least disappointed that she saw through his ruse.

Pilkington's story has additional significance, for it points to different reactions by different audiences of the *Life.* Her position as a Dubliner allows her insight into aspects of the poem that those in London could not have recognized. I say this assuming that Londoners would not have been exposed to the oral circulation of the *Verses* that Swift describes. Swift may have fooled these readers regardless of what they thought about the *Life;* those who doubted Swift's authorship would be wrong, but even those who believed Swift wrote the poem would be taken in, because then they would read it as the "genuine" Rochefoucauld poem, instead of its burlesque. Some Dubliners, however, heard parts of the poem recited, and could have recognized the *Life* as an inept reconstruction of the *Verses.* Swift alludes to this possible reading in the previously quoted letter to Carteret: "it plainly appears, that he [the "low" writer of the *Life*] had often heard of the genuine one and probably some lines of it repeated." To her credit, Pilkington realizes that Swift has burlesqued himself, and her com-ment demands further comparison of the two poems, a comparison that Pilkington herself was in a good position to make, as she had memorized the *Verses.*

Pilkington calls the *Life* a burlesque, though it is perhaps more specifi-cally labeled a travesty, that is, a work that mimics a specific poem by treating its important subject in an undignified style.[23] This aspect is apparent in the early parts of the *Life,* especially in its awkward rhythm and its speaker's harsh attitude. Indeed, the opening of the *Life* reads like a doggerel imitation of the more metrically pleasing *Verses* that opens with these lines:

> As *Rochefoucault* his Maxims drew
> From Nature, I believe 'em true:
> They argue no corrupted Mind
> In him; the Fault is in Mankind.
>
> (*Verses* 1–4)

The *Life* begins as follows:

> WISE *Rochefoucault* a *Maxim* writ,
> Made up of *Malice, Truth,* and *Wit:*
> If, what he says be not a *Joke,*
> We *Mortals* are strange kind of *Folk.*
>
> (*Life* 1–4)

The parallels continue when each poem paraphrases Rochefoucauld's maxim:

> "In all Distresses of our Friends
> "We first consult our private Ends,
> "While Nature kindly bent to ease us,
> "Points out some Circumstance to please us.
>
> (*Verses* 7–10)

The emotional register of the *Life* is quite different:

> He says, "Whenever *Fortune* sends
> "*Disasters,* to our *Dearest Friends,*
> "Although, we *outwardly* may Grieve,
> "We oft, are *Laughing in our Sleeve.*
>
> (*Life* 7–10)

The *Life* shifts from "Distresses" to "Disasters," from an observation about natural instinct to sadistic hypocrisy. Similarly, in the first pair of quotations, we see that in the *Verses* Swift characterizes Rochefoucauld's source as "Nature," whereas in the *Life* he omits this reference and states that the maxim consists of "*Malice, Truth,* and *Wit.*" Elsewhere in the *Verses,* Swift describes the relief that a friend and not oneself is suffering; the *Life,* in contrast, depicts the pleasure derived from witnessing injury:

DEAR honest *Ned* is in the Gout,
Lies rackt with Pain, and you without:
How patiently you hear him groan!
How glad the Case is not your own!

(Verses 27–30)

We see a *Comrade* get a fall,
Yet *laugh* our hearts out, *one* and *all.*

(Life 13–14)[24]

Of course, the *Verses* contains references to cruel impulses, though the context often renders them comical. When addressing the envy a poet feels toward his competitors, Swift writes with exaggeration: "But rather than they should excel, / He'd wish his Rivals all in Hell" (*Verses* 33–34). The main contrast between the early parts of the *Verses* and the *Life* depends on the former's moral insight and the latter's malicious pleasure. This contrast further emphasizes that Swift created these parallels to suggest that the *Life* was not his work but rather a flawed memorial reconstruction of the *Verses.* Consequently, even those who knew the *Verses* might still be fooled into thinking that Swift did not write the *Life.*

Not all of the *Life,* however, fits the travesty genre. Once the dialogue begins at line 68, parallels between the two poems are minimal. The dialogue itself may be part of Swift's travesty, as if the "low writer" of the *Life* has bungled the complimentary monologue of the *Verses* by substituting a dialogue between one man supporting Swift and another attacking him. But I detect no further level of irony by comparing specific lines. I also think that the statements made by the *Life*'s "pro-Swift" speaker are in no way ironic. Although much of his commentary serves the rhetorical purpose of introducing positive statements that are immediately undercut by the other speaker, the antidissenter speech of lines 144–79 resonates with Swift's own views. Pope and others must have recognized the difference between the early and later parts of the *Life,* for when the first London edition of the *Verses* appeared, it contained 62 lines from the *Life,* all from the later section of the poem.[25]

The hoax of the *Life* reveals Swift's shrewd awareness and manipulation of the public. He mocks the system of authorship, including the disreputable element in the book trade, its hack writers, its scheming efforts to circulate works of questionable attribution, and its opportunistic exploitation of an established author's identity. Such activities extend his depiction of Curll in the poem; rather than suffer at the hands of piratical publishers, he beats them at their own game through this multilayered hoax. Swift further adds to the mystique of the *Verses,* controls the text, and even satirizes the idea of pirating his poem.

Swift ultimately sought the broader audience associated with print pub-lication. This third event was difficult to plan, though it need not have been. Swift could have easily arranged for publication in Dublin, but he instead chose to publish the poem in London. This preference corresponds to his general practice, unless the work in question was of primarily Irish concern, and probably stems from a combination of two factors: a cultural snobbery toward his native country and an awareness of the larger au-dience reached by a London publication. In a letter to Motte on 25 May 1736, Swift expresses his preference for London publications: "If I live but a few Years, I believe I shall publish some Things that I think are impor-tant; but, they shall be printed in *London,* although Mr. *Faulkner* were my Brother" (*Corr.* 4: 494). These comments may be misleading because Swift here addresses a London bookseller who was loyal to Swift and involved in a copyright dispute with Faulkner, but Swift's publishing prac-tices support the stated attitudes, as suggested by the examples of both the *Life* and the *Verses,* which were transmitted to London for publication, and shortly thereafter reprinted in Dublin by Faulkner. Other works of "impor-tance" by Swift followed the same pattern. London's position as a cultural capital is dramatized in the *Verses* itself, whose final episode occurs in the Rose, a London public house. That this episode assesses Swift's entire career only underscores London's primacy over Dublin in this regard.

As with the *Life* and other poems during the same year, Swift employed Matthew Pilkington as an agent to arrange publication with a London bookseller. By early 1734, though, many Dubliners saw Pilkington as unreliable, for they suspected him of informing on one of Swift's book-sellers or even on Swift in the political and legal debacle surrounding *On Poetry: A Rapsody* and *An Epistle to a Lady.* Pilkington's guilt was never clearly established, but the controversy resulted in his return to Ireland.[26]

Consequently, Swift needed another agent, and he found one in William King, Jacobite poet and principal of St. Mary Hall, Oxford. Swift's trust is evidenced by his use of King as the agent to arrange publication of the long-awaited *History of the Last Four Years of the Queen,* a work Swift had let him read in manuscript as early as the summer of 1735.[27] But before the manuscript of the *History* was given to King, Swift gave him a copy of the *Verses* to publish. We cannot determine exactly when he did so, but it was probably during the following summer when King was in Dublin. After leaving Dublin, King traveled to Edinburgh and then to Paris before arriving in London in early December 1736.[28] While in Paris, King writes to Martha Whiteway, Swift's cousin, and uses gross flattery in promising to publish the *Verses:* "I will then put the little MS. to the press, and oblige the whole *English* nation."[29] For the next twenty-one months we have no reference to King's plans until the following cryptic letter from King to Orrery on 8 July 1738: "Roch [meaning "Rochefoucauld," i.e., the

Verses] is in the press, and shall certainly be published in September or the beginning of the next Term. I believe I mentioned to you the accidents which had retarded the publication of this work so long, when I had the honour of seeing you last."[30] Though the explanation for the delay is missing, the word "accidents" does not suggest any action on Swift's part, and all of the evidence taken together strongly suggests that Swift sought print publication at least two-and-a-half years before its initial publication in London by Charles Bathurst.[31] In general, the publishing history shows that Swift initially sought a local and private audience for his work, aroused the interest of the public, and finally satisfied that interest with print publication.

The problems of publishing the *Verses* did not end in January 1739, for without Swift's permission, King, with the help of Pope and probably others, radically altered the poem, excising 165 lines and all of his notes, and inserting 62 lines from the *Life*. This decision stemmed from a combination of political and aesthetic objections, the former to avoid political controversy and the latter to forestall accusations of vanity on Swift's part. Swift, obviously dissatisfied, arranged to have Faulkner publish a correct version in Dublin, something Swift could have easily done years before. Faulkner also did not publish the poem in its entirety, as it contained gaps to be filled in later by hand.[32]

Thus despite all of Swift's elaborate schemes—the oral circulation of the *Verses,* the hoax of the *Life,* and the use of a London agent—the first printed edition of his poem was an unauthorized distortion. The complexity and variety of Swift's actions point to his awareness of the problems posed by print publication, but in this instance, the complications derived from neither piratical publishers nor Grub Street hacks, but from trusted friends. The entire publishing history of the poem more particularly reveals Swift's combined desire for textual control and publicity. These two authorial impulses end in conflict, for the larger print audience is reached by either a distorted or incomplete text that in turn distorts the publicity Swift hoped to control. As we have seen, this conflict parallels the poem itself. Unable to resolve the problems inherent in print publication, Swift constructs a posthumous fame outside the book trade though still dependent on the printed word. In the end, print is both the cause and the medium of Swift's authorial strategies.

NOTES

I thank the following individuals for their encouragement and helpful criticism: Cora Fox, Sue Uselman, Andrew Hansen, James Woolley, Phillip Harth, Eric Rothstein, Howard D. Weinbrot, and Maya C. Gibson.

1. I refer to the following studies, to which I am indebted: Herbert Davis, "Verses on the Death of Dr. Swift," *The Book Collector's Quarterly* 2 (March-May 1931): 57–73, and Arthur H. Scouten and Robert D. Hume, "Pope and Swift: Text and Interpretation of Swift's Verses on His Death," *Philological Quarterly* 52 (1973): 205–31.

2. See Adrian Johns, *The Nature of the Book: Print and Knowledge in the Making* (Chicago: University of Chicago Press, 1998), 1–48.

3. All citations of Swift's poetry are from *The Poems of Jonathan Swift*, ed. Harold Williams, 2nd ed., 3 vols. (Oxford: Clarendon Press, 1958), hereafter abbreviated *Poems.* Quotations are cited using line numbers in parentheses. For the text of the *Verses*, see *Poems*, 2: 551–72. The tripartite reading often unites those who otherwise disagree about the poem. See, for example, the following studies: Barry Slepian, "The Ironic Intention of Swift's Verses on His Own Death," *Review of English Studies*, n.s., 14 (1963): 249–56; Marshall Waingrow, "*Verses on the Death of Dr. Swift*," *Studies in English Literature* 5 (1965): 513–18; and David M. Vieth, "The Mystery of Personal Identity: Swift's Verses on His Own Death," in *The Author in His Work: Essays on a Problem in Criticism*, eds. Louis L. Martz and Aubrey Williams (New Haven: Yale University Press, 1978), 245–62.

4. For specific discussion of the contrast between friends and enemies, see James Woolley, "Friends and Enemies in *Verses on the Death of Dr. Swift*," in *Studies in Eighteenth-Century Culture*, ed. Roseann Runte, vol. 8 (Madison: University of Wisconsin Press, 1979), 205–32. The Rose speaker has generated the most extensive critical debate surrounding Swift's poem, which has primarily revolved around the relationship between the Rose speech and Swift's attitudes toward himself. For a convincing discussion of this issue, see James Woolley, "Autobiography in Swift's Verses on His Death," in *Contemporary Studies of Swift's Poetry*, eds. John Irwin Fischer, Donald C. Mell, Jr., and David M. Vieth (Newark: University of Delaware Press, 1981), 112–22.

5. For further discussion of the self-mythologizing aspects of the *Verses*, see Brian A. Connery, "Self-Representation and Memorials in the Late Poetry of Swift," in *Aging and Gender in Literature: Studies in Creativity*, eds. Anne M. Wyatt-Brown and Janice Rossen (Charlottesville: University Press of Virginia, 1993), 150, 158–59.

6. See, for example, *Remains of Mr. John Oldham in verse and prose* (1684 and often reprinted) and *The Remains of Mr. Tho. Brown, serious and comical, in prose and verse* (1720). Not surprisingly, Curll published in this genre: *The Remains of John Locke Esq.* (1714) and Richardson Pack, *Major Pack's Poetical Remains* (1738).

7. This use recalls a similar passage in *A Tale of a Tub*, in which Prince Posterity destroys many Grub Street works; see *The Prose Works of Jonathan Swift*, eds. Herbert Davis et al., 14 vols. (Oxford: Basil Blackwell, 1939–68), 1: 20, hereafter abbreviated *PW.*

8. Peter J. Schakel, "The Politics of Opposition in 'Verses on the Death of Dr. Swift,'" *Modern Language Quarterly* 35 (1974): 247. Schakel's context is possible but not necessarily appropriate, and his reading is also open to challenge because most of his examples occur before 1700. For neutral references to the Rose, see Donald F. Bond, ed., *The Spectator*, 5 vols. (Oxford: Clarendon Press, 1965), 1: 10 and Swift, *PW*, 1: 49. For other contemporary references to the Rose (ranging from negative to neutral), see Bryant Lillywhite, *London Coffee Houses: A Reference Book of Coffee Houses of the Seventeenth Eighteenth and Nineteenth Centuries* (London: George Allen and Unwin, 1963), 487–89.

9. See Bryant Lillywhite, *London Signs: A Reference Book of London Signs from Earliest Times to about the Mid-Nineteenth Century* (London: George Allen and Unwin, 1972), 453–57. He also notes that "the rose figures in ancient symbolism as a token of completion, and perfection" (454). Thus Swift may have wanted to link this symbolic association to the culminating episode of his poem. I am grateful to James Woolley and Eric Rothstein for suggesting Swift's generic use of the Rose.

10. James Woolley, "Friends and Enemies," 223.

11. The title pages contain the phrase "Written by Himself, November 1731," a date corroborated by two contemporaneous letters, one from Swift to John Gay and the Duke and Duchess of Queensbury on 1 December 1731 and the other from Gay and Pope to Swift on the same day; see *The Correspondence of Jonathan Swift,* ed. Harold Williams and rev. David Woolley, 5 vols. (Oxford: Clarendon Press, 1963–72), 3: 506, 510, hereafter abbreviated *Corr.* One note can be dated by manuscript additions to line 379 ("When up a dangerous Faction starts") that contain the following phrase: "and so affairs continue till this present 3rd. day of May 1732." Swift may have considered publication at this time, as shown by an advertisement in George Faulkner's *Dublin Journal* of 2 May 1732; the advertisement is reprinted in Irvin Ehrenpreis, *Dean Swift,* vol. 3 of *Swift: The Man, His Works, and the Age* (London: Methuen, 1983), 709.

12. *Corr.,* 4: 152 (1 May 1733), 161 (31 May 1733), 149 (23 April 1733).

13. See *Memoirs of Laetitia Pilkington,* ed. A. C. Elias, Jr., 2 vols. (Athens: University of Georgia Press, 1997), 1: 54–55, hereafter abbreviated *Memoirs.*

14. For the variants, see *Memoirs,* 1: 39, 50, 92, 280, and the corresponding notes in Elias's second volume. For the special case, see 1: 39 and 2: 416–17. Having examined multiple annotated copies of the *Verses,* I can add to the useful information presented by Elias. The manuscript additions in the Forster copy, which is not in an eighteenth-century hand, almost certainly derive from the copy at the Armstrong Browning Library, Baylor University. Edward Dowden's transcription almost certainly derives from the "second" Faulkner edition at the Harry Ransom Humanities Research Center, University of Texas.

15. I am indebted to the following discussions of the *Life,* all of which recognize its burlesque aspects: *The Correspondence of Jonathan Swift,* ed. F. Elrington Ball, 6 vols. (London: G. Bell and Sons, 1910–14), 4: 428–29, n. 3; Ball, *Swift's Verse: An Essay* (London: John Murray, 1929), 268–69; Davis, "Verses on the Death of Dr. Swift," 62–65; *Poems,* 2: 541–43; Ehrenpreis, *Dean Swift,* 708–13, 756–58; and *Memoirs,* 2:433–34.

Both Herbert Davis and Harold Williams unfortunately contribute to the confusion surrounding these two poems. In Davis's 1931 article, he cogently argues for the *Life* as in part a burlesque of the *Verses,* but he later refers to the *Life* as a draft of the *Verses,* though without further comment or evidence; see "The Poetry of Jonathan Swift," *College English* 2 (1940): 114 and "Swift's Character," in *Jonathan Swift 1667–1967: A Dublin Tercentenary Tribute,* eds. Roger McHugh and Philip Edwards (Dublin: Dolmen Press, 1967), 7. In Williams's edition of Swift's poems, he approvingly cites Ball's conclusions and Davis's 1931 article and refers to "the earlier and shorter forms of the poem" (*Poems,* 2: 543). At 202 lines, the *Life* is far shorter than the 484–line *Verses;* therefore Williams believes that the *Verses* is the earlier poem. However, Williams prints the *Life* before the *Verses* and places the year 1731 in the running head for the *Life,* despite the lack of evidence for the poem's composition prior to 1733. Throughout Williams's edition, he arranges the poems by date of composition, not publication, and so his ordering here suggests that Swift wrote the *Life* first, contrary to Williams's explicit statements.

Others have since argued that the *Life* preceded the *Verses,* though without marshaling new evidence or addressing the contrary evidence; see *Collected Poems of Jonathan Swift,* ed. Joseph Horrell, 2 vols. (London: Routledge and Kegan Paul, 1958), 1: xxxiii, 2: 795–96; Ronald Paulson, "Swift, Stella, and Permanence," *ELH* 27 (1960): 299; Paulson, *The Fictions of Satire* (Baltimore: Johns Hopkins Press, 1967), 190; and Scouten and Hume, "Pope and Swift," 207, 208, 213, 215. Pat Rogers is agnostic about which came first, the *Life* or the *Verses,* and prints the *Life* first only out of editorial custom established by Faulkner. At the same time, he states that "there is no real evidence that they [the *Verses*] are a revised text in any way"; see *Jonathan Swift: The Complete Poems* (New Haven: Yale University Press, 1983), 845.

16. For Matthew Pilkington's involvement, see *Memoirs,* 1: 55, 2: 435–36. For the

quotation, see *Corr.,* 4: 371 (31 July 1735). The case for Faulkner's reprint is based on ornament evidence; see D. F. Foxon, *English Verse, 1701–1750: A Catalogue of Separately Printed Poems with Notes on Contemporary Collected Editions,* 2 vols. (London: Cambridge University Press, 1975), 1: 770–71. In *Poems,* 2: 541–42, Williams states that Motte did not publish the *Life,* though one wonders how else Motte could have seen corrected proof sheets. Ball recognizes Motte's involvement in *Swift's Verse,* 269. Part of the mystery surrounding this publication stems from the imprint, which states that the *Life* was "printed for J. ROBERTS in *Warwick-Lane,* and Sold at the Pamphlet Shops &c." James Roberts was the most prolific "trade publisher" of his day, and so his name appeared on books and pamphlets though their copyrights belonged to others in the trade; for more on the complicated subject of "trade publishers," see Michael Treadwell, "London Trade Publishers 1675–1750," *The Library,* 6th ser., 4 (1982): 99–134. Thus Motte employed Roberts as a middleman, though we cannot be certain why he did so. Perhaps Pilkington's intermediary instructed him to or perhaps Motte doubted the poem's authenticity.

Some have suggested that Alexander Pope was involved with the *Life*'s publication. Foxon even suggests that Pope may have written the poem, though he does not present a strong case for this theory; see his *English Verse,* 1: 770. Thomas J. Wise raises the possibility that Pope helped arrange publication of the *Life.* Wise notes that two printer's ornaments appear in the first editions of both the *Life* and Pope's second epistle of his *Essay on Man,* also published in 1733; see *The Ashley Library: A Catalogue of Printed Books, Manuscripts and Autograph Letters. Collected by Thomas J. Wise,* 11 vols. (London: n.p., 1922–36), 6: 35. Williams cites this possibility in *Poems,* 2: 542n. Foxon uses further ornament evidence to show that Edward Say printed this edition of Pope's second epistle; see *Pope and the Early Eighteenth-Century Book Trade,* rev. and ed. James McLaverty (Oxford: Clarendon Press, 1991), 122. Foxon does not mention Say again, and so Pope may have used Say only once, probably to disguise his authorship of the *Essay.* Say, however, had close connections to Motte, having been apprenticed to his father; see D. F. McKenzie, *Stationers' Company Apprentices 1701–1800* (Oxford: Oxford Bibliographical Society, 1978), 242. In addition, J. C. Ross and Michael Treadwell independently show that Say printed portions of the first two editions of *Gulliver's Travels;* see Ross, "The Framing and Printing of the Motte Editions of *Gulliver's Travels*," *Bibliographical Society of Australia and New Zealand Bulletin* 20, 1 (1996): 10–19, and Treadwell, "Observations on the Printing of Motte's Octavo Editions of *Gulliver's Travels,*" in *Reading Swift: Papers from the Third Münster Symposium on Jonathan Swift,* eds. Hermann J. Real and Helgard Stöver-Leidig (München: Wilhelm Fink, 1998), 157–77. After examining printer's ornaments in the *Life,* I find three to be identical to others found in the following work that Ross identifies as Say's: *A Compendious Way of Teaching Antient and Modern Languages* (1728). In short, I can match five of the six ornaments in the *Life* to other work by Say, which strongly argues for Say's printing of the *Life.* Because Say had close connections to Swift's works via Motte and seems to have been involved with printing Pope's works only once, I believe that Say's printing of both the *Life* and the second epistle of the *Essay on Man* is a coincidence that in no way implies Pope's involvement with the *Life*'s publication. I am grateful to James McLaverty for directing my attention to Edward Say as the likely printer of the *Life.*

17. The quoted phrase appears in a letter from Swift to Carteret on 23 April 1733; see *Corr.,* 4: 149.

18. Of course, some readers might therefore conclude that it is Swift's April Fool's joke, but lacking further knowledge they would probably have difficulty distinguishing all the levels of this complex hoax.

19. For the text of *On Poetry: A Rapsody,* see *Poems,* 2: 639–59. For the first quotation about triplets, see Swift's letter to Thomas Beach on 12 April 1735 in *Corr.,* 4: 321. See also

Swift's letter to Pope on 28 June 1715, in which he presents a mixed review of Pope's recent translation of the *Iliad:* "If it pleases others as well as me, you have got your end in profit and reputation: Yet I am angry at some bad Rhymes and Triplets" (*Corr.,* 2: 176). For the Faulkner quotation, see *The Works of Jonathan Swift,* ed. Faulkner, 8 vols., octavo (1746), 8: 138.

20. *Corr.,* 4: 149 (23 April 1733). For other denials, see *Corr.,* 4: 151, 161.

21. *Corr.,* 4: 163 (31 May 1733) and John Boyle, Fifth Earl of Cork and Orrery, *Remarks on the Life and Writings of Dr. Jonathan Swift,* ed. João Fróes (Newark: University of Delaware Press; London: Associated University Presses, 2000), 289. Faulkner also states that readers "were deceived" by the *Life;* see *Works* (1746), 8: 138.

22. *Corr.,* 4: 194, 253. Davis, Williams, and Ehrenpreis suggest that these statements reveal Pope's awareness of Swift's authorship; see Davis, "Verses on the Death of Dr. Swift," 63; *Poems,* 2: 542; and Ehrenpreis, *Dean Swift,* 756–57.

23. Ball refers to the poem as a travesty; see *Swift's Verse,* 268–69.

24. Elias makes a similar contrast; see *Memoirs,* 2: 434. For the text of the *Life,* see *Poems,* 2: 541–50.

25. In addition, all but 11 of these 62 lines are spoken by the "anti-Swift" speaker. These lines were probably chosen to mitigate the vanity and supposed falsehoods that Pope mentions in his letter to Orrery of 25 September 1738; see *The Correspondence of Alexander Pope,* ed. George Sherburn, 5 vols. (Oxford: Clarendon Press, 1956), 4: 130.

26. For further discussion, see *Poems,* 2: 629; Ehrenpreis, *Dean Swift,* 776–78; John Irwin Fischer, "The Government's Response to Swift's *An Epistle to a Lady,*" *Philological Quarterly* 65 (1986): 39–59; and *Memoirs,* 1: 68–69, 2: 449–50.

27. For further details, see David Greenwood, *William King: Tory and Jacobite* (Oxford: Clarendon Press, 1969), 80–86, and *Corr.,* 4: 394.

28. See *Corr.,* 4: 521, 529, 541–42, 550.

29. *Corr.,* 4: 542 (9 November 1736). Ball's and Williams's editions of Swift's correspondence gloss the "little MS" as the *History,* not the *Verses,* though both note that King did not receive the *History* until nine months later. King's statement clearly implies that he already possesses the manuscript. The context of King's letter also questions this gloss. King's following sentence begins with the transitional phrase "As to the history." Also, the *History,* unlike the *Verses,* was not "little." Herman Teerink reads "the little MS" as the *Verses,* though he does so to support his own hypothesis that the *Verses* was first published in 1736; see *A Bibliography of the Writings in Prose and Verse of Jonathan Swift, D.D.* (The Hague: Martinus Nijhoff, 1937), 303–304 and "Swift's *Verses on the Death of Doctor Swift,*" *Studies in Bibliography* 4 (1951): 186–87. Arthur H. Scouten demolishes this hypothesis in "The Earliest London Printings of 'Verses on the Death of Doctor Swift,'" *Studies in Bibliography* 15 (1962): 243–47, but does not comment on Teerink's interpretation of "the little MS." Clive Probyn seems to be neutral on whether "the little MS" refers to the *Verses* or not, but clearly believes that it does *not* refer to the *History;* see "Swift's *Verses on the Death of Dr. Swift:* the Notes," *Studies in Bibliography* 39 (1986): 55 n.

30. Cited in Greenwood, *William King,* 86–87.

31. The death of Motte in April 1738 may have also delayed the publication of the *Verses.* Bathurst was Motte's partner and successor. A further delay may have been owing to the seasonal aspects of London publishing, which peaked during the months in which parliament was in session and the "town" was full. Swift himself often published his works during this period, usually from late autumn through spring.

32. For more on this subject, see Probyn, "Swift's *Verses on the Death of Dr. Swift*" and Stephen Karian, "Reading the Material Text of Swift's *Verses on the Death,*" *Studies in English Literature* 41 (2001): 515–44.

"He Hates Much Trouble": Johnson's *Life of Swift* and the Contours of Biographical Inheritance in Late Eighteenth-Century England

J. T. Scanlan

I

As THE EXAMPLE OF HAROLD BLOOM MAY SUGGEST, GREAT CRITICS SOME-times seem most stimulating not when they convince us, but when they surprise us. Especially now, when the distinction between primary and secondary writing has become blurred, and when a fragmentation in liter-ary studies has fostered different conceptions of evidence within different subspecialties, we may find ourselves drawn to critics not only when they seem indisputably right, but when they are suggestive, provocative, infu-riating, inspiring, or, to use our hallway stamp of approval, when they are "doing interesting work." Harold Bloom's hero, Samuel Johnson, is cer-tainly one such critic, as any number of his surprising, captivating, and thought-provoking utterances indicate. Johnsonians who have spent years trying to "travel over" Johnson's mind, to use his own words, are well acquainted with this attractive feature of his writing and conversation. But Swiftians, too, I should think, would have no trouble making a long list of Johnson's jolting—and arguable—statements. Such a list might include Johnson's preference for Richardson over Fielding, or more accurately, his dislike of Fielding. As Boswell reports, "Fielding being mentioned, Johnson exclaimed, 'he was a blockhead,'" after which Johnson reacts to Boswell's astonishment by asserting, pugnaciously, "What I mean by his being a blockhead is that he was a barren rascal. . . . Sir, there is more knowledge of the heart in one letter of Richardson's than in all of *Tom Jones*."[1] Johnson's denigration of metaphysical poetry in the *Life of Cowley* has become legendary: "The metaphysical poets were men of learning, and to shew their learning was their whole endeavour; but un-luckily resolving to shew it in rhyme, instead of writing poetry they only wrote verses, and very often such verses as stood the trial of the finger better than of the ear."[2] And those of us who remember our college days

99

honestly must admit to a modicum of pleasure upon discovering that Samuel Johnson, of all people, declared of *Paradise Lost* that "None ever wished it longer than it is" (*Lives* 1: 183). Indeed, for many readers, these assertive, argumentative, and plucky statements—coming from a man whom Boswell perceptively viewed as "actuated by the spirit of contradiction" (*Boswell's Life* 4: 429)—go a long way toward defining, for better or worse, the concept "Johnsonian."

But probably none of his commentary on authors and their works is more notorious than what he wrote—and what he said—about Swift. In Johnson's own time, Boswell was taken aback at what he viewed as Johnson's true prejudice against Swift, and doubtless to Swiftians, the following judgment, as Boswell presents it, is particularly boneheaded:

> Johnson was in high spirits this evening at the club, and talked with great animation and success. He attacked Swift, as he used to do upon all occasions. . . . I wondered to hear him say of "Gulliver's Travels," "When once you have thought of big men and little men, it is very easy to do the rest." I endeavoured to make a stand for Swift, and tried to rouse those who were much more able to defend him; but in vain. (*Boswell's Life* 2:318–19)

Perhaps we may mitigate the sting of Johnson's conversational blasts on Swift by remembering that they were conditioned by a variety of contexts, making them questionable as literal guides to what he actually thought about Swift. A similar disclaimer, however, cannot be attached to his *Life of Swift,* written in late 1780 and published in the second six-volume installment of the ten-volume *Lives of the Most Eminent English Poets* (1781): it is undoubtedly his most sustained and mature attempt to comprehend Swift and his works. And for the vast majority of readers—especially Swiftians, surely—the *Life of Swift* is one of Johnson's most unsatisfying works. Boswell himself confidently singled out this work as a locus of Johnson's irrational sentiments: "In the Life of Swift, it appears to me that Johnson had a certain degree of prejudice against that extraordinary man" (*Boswell's Life* 4: 61). In fact, the entire subject of Johnson on Swift, since Boswell's time, has become a curiosity of literary history. More than thirty years ago, as Frederick Hilles reminded us, Michael Foot, a Labour M.P. and editor of Swift, rendered an accurate assessment of Johnson's legacy to the Royal Society of Literature: "I am sorry to have to say it, but the man more responsible for these perennial slanders against Swift was Dr. Johnson."[3] Indeed, Johnson's influence in shaping succeeding literary histories can hardly be underestimated, given his own prominent place as perhaps *the* literary legislator of the late eighteenth century. At least since the late 1960s, Johnson's thoughts on Swift have remained at best perplexing. In the mid 1970s, W. J. Bate perhaps spoke for Johnsonians, Swiftians, as well as general readers of his own time when he wrote that the *Life of Swift* "justly strikes the modern reader" as "hopelessly biased."[4] S. P. T. Keilen more recently has concurred, opening his prize honors essay at Cambridge University by noting succinctly, "The history of the reception of Samuel Johnson's *Life of Swift* (1781) is one of readerly embarrassment and scholarly vexation."[5] When we inquire into Swift's reputation in the late eighteenth century, then, at least we can say that Johnson's own authority as critic and as man of letters inevitably directs the conversation.

This leads to a curious habit of thought in modern literary study. Unless one is inclined simply to write off Johnson as "wrong"—which is always a hazardous enterprise, given the range and depth of Johnson's reading— one is more likely to see Johnson on Swift as something of a problem, something to be figured out, something to be explained. "The usual tendency of the critic," writes Paul J. Korshin on scholars who have trouble with Johnson's views, "has been to assume that Johnson was wrong and to dismiss his mistake with disparagement, or, through rationalization, to explain his fault."[6] Indeed, perhaps the *Life of Swift* remains intriguing because we can hardly believe Johnson could be so downright thick-headed. Johnson on Swift, as a topic, is especially alluring to Johnsonians, I think. Perhaps more than historians would, literary interpreters lean toward asking questions that diminish the bad reputation Johnson's views on Swift have more or less earned. A primary fundamental question emerges: How could a critic as great as Johnson, one who wrote so comprehensively and so enduringly on English literature and on language itself, be so horribly wrong? The secondary question seems inevitable: What are we missing?

In keeping with this twentieth-century disposition to "explain" Johnson on Swift, a fair range of scholars have struggled with Johnson's seeming prejudice against Swift, against his satire, against his singularity, and against his supposedly unbecoming performances as a clergyman. Among the relatively few scholars who have addressed Johnson's *Life of Swift* in light of his entire body of writing, Korshin cuts to the heart of the matter. In "Johnson and Swift: A Study in the Genesis of Literary Opinion," Korshin examines the evolution of Johnson's thought on Swift and penetrates through much of the limited secondary writing, sensibly concluding that "it can be plausibly argued that Johnson was both attracted and repelled by Swift—attracted by the man's brilliance, learning and fearlessness to oppose accepted ideas, repelled by his adherence to repugnant conceptions of humanity. Johnson's attitude toward Swift . . . shows something of his unwillingness to open his mind to Swift's obvious merits . . . and reaches its culmination in the *Life of Swift* with an unfair treatment which Johnson could neither help nor avoid" (Korshin, "Johnson and Swift," 478). It seems hard to argue against the basic soundness of Korshin's informed judgment and its customary attendant scholia.

I do think, however, we may supplement this compelling explanation by inquiring yet again into the specifics of Johnson's biographical research and by comparing his activities to those of other eighteenth-century biographers. But this time, let's shift the critical emphasis away from highlighting Johnson's strengths and, instead, focus for once on Johnson's real weaknesses as a writer—a subject that, given Johnson's unquestionable greatness, tends not to receive the attention it deserves. In other words, let's follow the lead of Maurice Charney, who wonders in his book *"Bad" Shakespeare,* "Can any of Shakespeare be bad? 'Bad' in what sense? . . . [Shakespeare's canonical status] makes it difficult to approach the plays and poems with any sense of the comparative values or the relation of Shakespeare to his fellow dramatists."[7] Much the same, I think, may be said of Johnson in relation to those fellow biographers of the mid- and late eighteenth century—writers whom Johnson usually towered above. In other words, in trying to recover what Johnson actually did on at least one occasion when he writes poorly, I propose in this essay to identify a few of the elements of "bad" Johnson. Furthermore, as the details of Johnson's relations to his predecessors in Swiftian biography will suggest, the essay also underscores the persistence of Swift's canny ability to affect his own literary reputation, long after he died in 1745.

When we look afresh at Johnson's place among his fellow eighteenth-century biographers of Swift, two large issues emerge as worthy of further consideration—and they enable us to challenge or extend earlier explanations of Johnson's understanding of Swift. First, in comparing Johnson's *Life of Swift* to the three principal earlier biographies of Swift—by John Boyle, the fifth Earl of Orrery; by Patrick Delany; and by John Hawkesworth—we find Johnson plainly exhibiting the corners he cut in writing his biography. For once, we see Johnson constrained: he erases, or at least minimizes, those elements of his best biographical writing, amply on display in other biographies. Second, in looking at the widely noticed "buried autobiography" of Johnson's *Life of Swift* and in comparing it to similar autobiographical passages, we find that Johnson's habit of generalizing himself into a prototype of the author—or to use Paul Fussell's phrase, "the writer as representative man"[8]—yields little of biographical value, at least in illuminating the life and writing of the ever-vexing Jonathan Swift.

To be sure, Johnson's biographical thinking on Swift is disappointing, as readers have long sensed; but as we shall see, it is wanting principally because of a tendency of mind that Edmond Malone, whom Boswell once called *Johnsonianissimus,*[9] identified as few else have. Edmond Malone was one of Johnson's friends, as well as a fellow biographer, a fellow

Shakespearean, and a fellow clubman, though Malone was much more well-heeled than Johnson; Malone also thought highly of Johnson's talents as a writer, particularly as a critic of Shakespeare. But Malone was also an uncompromising reader, especially on matters relating to evidence. When the first installment of the *Lives* appeared in 1779, Malone wrote to his friend Lord Charlemont, "The only lives of any value that now appear are those of Cowley, Waller, Milton, and Dryden. The critical parts of this are very amusing and instructive—but in the biographical part, he has, I think, been less amusing than he might have been, from want of industry. He hates much trouble."[10] When the *Life of Swift* finally appeared in 1781 as part of the second and final installment of the collection, Johnson displays this unfortunate "want of industry." That, more than any other single element of the biography, explains both its bad reputation among some readers and its fascination for others.

II

When Johnson began writing his *Life of Swift,* he faced a real problem: much solid work on Swift's life had already been done. More ominously, by the standards of early- and mid-eighteenth-century literary London, the biographical writing on Swift was far superior in both its factual content and its literary execution to the biographical writing then surrounding, say, Addison, Congreve, Prior, Steele, Gay, and maybe even Pope. If "we ask ourselves which authors of that time found biographers of standing before Dr. Johnson embarked on his *Lives of the Poets,*" writes Swift's great editor of a generation ago, Harold Williams, "it will be discovered that Swift has an easy lead over other Augustan writers."[11] The three most important biographies of Swift of the 1750s, and the three principal works on which Johnson relied in writing his *Life of Swift,* are Lord Orrery's *Remarks on the Life and Writings of Dr. Jonathan Swift* (1752),[12] Patrick Delany's argumentative response, *Observations Upon Lord Orrery's Remarks on the Life and Writings of Dr. Jonathan Swift* (1754),[13] and John Hawkesworth's "An Account of the Life of the Reverend Jonathan Swift, D.D., Dean of St. Patrick's Dublin," which appeared as introductory matter to his edition of Swift's *Works* (1755):[14] and, taken together, they cast a rather imposing shadow on a Johnson who in his early seventies was rushing to complete his *Life of Swift* so he could get on to his *Life of Pope,* his last, his longest, and certainly one of his most ambitious biographies. (Johnson was also well aware of the appreciative biographical writing of Swift's cousin, Deane Swift, author of *An Essay upon the Life, Writings, and Character, of Dr. Jonathan Swift* . . . (1755), but as Paul Korshin perceptively notes, Johnson evidently relied on Hawkesworth's biography as his real source for Deane Swift's writing. Johnson even spurned Deane Swift's offer to examine primary documentary evidence.[15]) Perhaps, overall, Johnson recognized that, as Jeffrey Myers has noted, "the *Life of Swift* is almost a minor literary genre in the eighteenth century."[16] A frighteningly simple and specific question now faced Johnson in the twilight of his long, productive, and distinguished career, when he was in his early seventies: What did he think he could add to what had come before? The problem may have been especially acute in that two of the earlier principal biographers—Orrery and Delany—knew Swift personally, and thus their evidentiary contributions had to be weighed and considered seriously. Clearly, Orrery, Delany, and Hawkesworth (who depended heavily on both his predecessors) were much more reliable and authoritative than the knot of fawning Miltonists Johnson believed he encountered when he conceived his vastly more successful *Life of Milton*.[17] This time, Johnson could not write to refute others, as he did so often throughout his career.

In my view, Johnson never provided an adequate solution to this classic problem that besets well-known writers more than is generally assumed. Instead of rethinking his entire conception of the biography, Johnson, writing under deadline pressure, simply deployed a pattern of research and composition that he must have realized had served him well in the past. He decided to consolidate the works of others. But this time, not finding much of an argumentative edge, the results worked against his best talents as a writer. A first cause of Johnson's relative weakness as a biographer of Swift, then—a first element of "bad" Johnson—is his decision to distill, condense, compress, and diffuse the writing of others in his own writing. To be sure, one of Johnson's great talents as a writer—and as a reader, as Robert DeMaria, Jr., has recently shown[18]—is his ability to seize the essence of vast stores of knowledge and translate it into something like wisdom. The *Dictionary* (1755), the *Rambler* (1750–52), and even some of the book reviewing he did for the ill-fated *Literary Magazine: or, Universal Review* (1756–57) are only three of his many acts of literary comprehension, compression, and dissemination. As David Venturo suggests in his recent learned study, *Johnson the Poet,* Johnson's tendency for compression emerged early on: it is discernible in his schoolboy exercises at the Lichfield Grammar School and the Stourbridge Grammar School. And as his moving elegy on Dr. Levet suggests, it persisted to the very end of his life.[19] But what works for some projects is not necessarily transferable to others. And in employing this consolidating habit of mind in order to comprehend Swift, Johnson chooses precisely the wrong method. What he ultimately delivers lacks the punch, the pluckiness, and the incisiveness of many of his other *Lives.* A brief look at how he specifically uses each of his predecessors in Swiftian biography should be enough to indicate the ill consequences of Johnson's well-nigh instinctive consolidating habit of mind.

Lord Orrery's *Remarks* was an instant hit among readers, selling thousands of copies not long after its publication (Williams 116). It went through multiple editions, but as its fame increased, the book earned notoriety for its unsympathetic and relatively unfair portrait of an irascible Swift as an old man. Notably, Johnson rather liked the book—at least some parts of it. While touring the Hebrides, Boswell records that Johnson was once asked "if it was wrong in Orrery to expose the defects of a man with whom he lived in intimacy." Johnson responds, "Why no, sir, after the man is dead, and it is done historically."[20] Johnson also knew personally the author, who not only came from a distinguished family, but whose father, Charles Boyle, the fourth Earl of Orrery, was a major combatant in the so-called Battle of the Books of the late 1690s, having edited the Epistles of Phalaris (*Phalaridis Agrigentinorum Tyranni Epistolae,* 1695) and written against the famed Dr. Bentley.[21] Orrery and his lineage would have been intriguing for anyone writing about Swift's life, given both Swift's work as secretary for Sir William Temple and Swift's own high-spirited satire of the entire mess, *A Full and True Account of the Battel, Fought last Friday, Between the Antient and the Modern Books in St. James's Library* (1710). Given his interests in libraries and debates about books, Johnson may well have had a special feel for Orrery's contribution. Johnson at least had reasons to look favorably on Orrery's biography, in other words. Furthermore, back in 1752, Johnson in fact wrote to Lord Orrery on his *Remarks* and commented to Orrery on the aggressive attention the book was then receiving among pamphleteers. Johnson reassuringly writes that he has "lived long enough among Scriblers" to understand the real reasons for invective in reviews, and he adds, "It would be a very severe censure of those who have attacked the *Memoirs of Swift* to say, they hated the Author without knowing him, and more severe still to say that they could know him and hate him."[22] Additionally, in 1753, when promoting the work of his friend and fellow enthusiast for Shakespeare, Charlotte Lennox, Johnson ghostwrote for Lennox's *Shakespear Illustrated* a thoughtful Dedication to Lord Orrery. In all probability, then, when Johnson came in 1780 actually to use Orrery's *Remarks,* written more than a quarter of a century earlier, he could entertain more than a few justifications to look rather favorably—and debilitatingly—on what Orrery had achieved.

The *Life of Swift* exhibits this unfortunate deference to Orrery—a dependence that helps keep Johnson from achieving the true independence of thought typical of his best criticism. More precisely, since much of Johnson's memorable literary criticism is written in sturdy reaction against another critic or a critical trend, he in this case has a predecessor who does not stimulate him to his best contentious advantage. In short, the critical circumstances this time were fundamentally different from those which nurtured his *Life of Milton,* his *Preface* to Shakespeare (1765), with its challenge to critics like Thomas Rymer who cant about the "unities," his review of Soame Jenyns's *A Free Inquiry into the Nature and Origin of Evil* (1757), or any number of Johnson's lasting adversarial performances. Alas, Johnson seems to have been swayed by much of Orrery's work. As an instance of Johnson's unattractive deference, take, for example, Johnson's rather matter-of-fact description of Swift's education at Trinity College, Dublin. "In his academical studies," Johnson states, Swift

> was either not diligent or not happy. It must disappoint every reader's expectation that, when at the usual time he claimed the Bachelorship of Arts, he was found by the examiners too conspicuously deficient for regular admission, and obtained his degree at last by *special favour,* a term used in that university to denote want of merit. (*Lives* 3: 2)

Orrery handles Swift's residency at Trinity College much better: he includes more detailed knowledge and he writes with more biographical sensitivity. "He lived there in perfect regularity," writes Orrery,

> and under an entire obedience to the statutes: but the moroseness of his temper often rendered him very unacceptable to his companions; so that he was little regarded, and less beloved. Nor were the academical exercises agreeable to his genius. He held logic and metaphysics in the utmost contempt; and he scarce considered mathematics and natural philosophy, unless to turn them into ridicule. The studies which he followed were history and poetry. In these he made a great progress; but to all other branches of science he had given so very little application, that when he appeared as a candidate for the degree of Batchelor of Arts, he was set aside on account of insufficiency

In Orrery's writing, unlike in Johnson's, the reader sees cause and effect, or the unfolding of character in incident and habit. One must keep in mind, too, that in the 1750s, the ostensible recipient of Orrery's biographical treatment, according to its genre as a series of letters from one gentleman to another, was Orrery's own son, Hamilton, who was then himself being educated. "You will not be surprised at such an incident in his life," continues Orrery in direct address to young Hamilton,

> but the fact was undoubtedly true; and even at last he obtained his admission *speciali gratia:* a phrase which in that University carries with it the utmost marks of reproach. It is a kind of dishonourable degree, and the record of it, notwithstanding Dr. SWIFT's present established character throughout the learned world, must for ever remain against him in the academical register at *Dublin.* (*Remarks* 10–11)

In succeeding pages, Orrery adds an unflattering fact: Swift only reluctantly told the whole truth about his degree from Oxford University. In short, when reacting to Orrery's account, Johnson condenses and reshapes things a bit, but to little or no advantageous effect. Johnson offers no criticism of Orrery. And the important incidental facts illustrating in embryonic form Swift's habit of manipulating himself and his reputation in public go entirely unnoticed in Johnson's *Life of Swift*.

On the nature of the evidence of Swift's possible marriage to Esther Johnson, Johnson is also deferent. Johnson adds hardly anything at all to this important biographical matter. While he does claim that a "Dr. Madden" told him that Swift was married "in his forty-ninth year," Johnson turns over the final words in his brief treatment of this significant issue to Orrery. "The marriage made no change in their mode of life; . . . 'It would be difficult,' says Lord Orrery, 'to prove that they were ever afterwards together without a third person' " (*Lives* 3: 31). Johnson seems almost to be looking for a way to dispense with the matter entirely. "In tone and attitude," writes Wayne Warncke in an essay meant to explain away Johnson's unseasonable prejudice against Swift, "Johnson's *Life* most closely resembles Orrery."[23] But that's the problem. Secondary characters in literary biography—the friends and lovers of writers—are pregnant with meaning to the incisive biographer, as any number of first-rate literary biographies indicate. And as we know from many other sources, Johnson's interest in such secondary characters could be profound. But when writing about Swift's curious personal attachments, Johnson's reliance on Orrery obscures his own voice. The *Life of Swift* offers little of the "Johnsonian aether."

Johnson also depended heavily on the writing of Patrick Delany. Delany, who knew Swift much better than Lord Orrery and for a much longer time, responded to the *Remarks* with an aggressive counterattack published under the pseudonym, "J. R." Delany's *Observations Upon Lord Orrery's Remarks on the Life and Writings of Dr. Jonathan Swift* challenges point by point some of the factual grounds for Orrery's conclusions. In at least one way, Delany's response was forward-looking: although Delany casts his response in the same form as Orrery's work—a series of letters from one gentleman to another—the *Observations* is just the kind of argumentative, detailed, and quasilegal examination of evidentiary issues that characterizes the groundbreaking scholarly work of Edmond Malone and other antiquarians of the late eighteenth century.

Johnson knew Delany's book well, but again to his great disadvantage as a writer, Johnson thought well of it. Boswell—always attentive to Johnson's views on Swift, and always ready to return to subjects on which Johnson held surprising views—writes that in April of 1778, Johnson "praised Delaney's [*sic*] 'Observations on Swift' and said that his book and Lord Orrery's might both be true, though one viewed Swift more, and the other less favourably; and that, between both, we might have a complete notion of Swift" (*Boswell's Life* 3: 249). This statement is especially telling for two reasons. First, Johnson presents these views at a time when he was doubtless considering the shape and overall execution of the *Lives,* and particularly Swift's place in that vast work. Second, Johnson not only surprises the young Boswell by refusing to take sides on the Orrery vs. Delany debate, but also proposes his embryonic inclinations for his own *Life of Swift.* In short, Johnson hints here that a solid Life of Swift has in fact *already* been done, but by two writers who need to be understood in a nonadversarial relation to one another.

And what Johnson said in 1778 to Boswell is consistent in large part with what he wrote in 1780. In fact, Delany's own place, as a character, in the *Life of Swift* is almost as prominent as other characters in Swift's life. Again, Johnson's tendency to summarize, reduce, or even to quote at length tends to prevent or frustrate him from developing a comprehensive analysis of Swift's life and works. Johnson clearly has trouble moving beyond Delany's credible, if strongly opinionated, points. Johnson also simply defers to him by quoting him, as he did with Orrery, though this time he quotes at considerable length.

Two points of comparison provide a sense of Johnson's use of Delany. On Swift's known reluctance to wear spectacles, Delany offers a plausible explanation, and one that is in keeping with what he viewed as Orrery's ill-formed judgments on Swift's private life. Swift had taken, Delany argues,

> an obstinate resolution . . . never to wear spectacles. A resolution, which the natural make of his eyes, (large and prominent) very ill qualified him to support. This made reading very difficult to him: and the difficulty naturally discouraged him from it: and gradually drew him, in a great measure, to decline it. And as he was now at a loss how to fill up that time which he was before wont to employ in reading, this drew him on to exercise, more than he ought. . . . His physicians and friends . . . frequently admonished him of doing so: but he paid no sort of regard to their admonitions. . . . The truth is, his spirit was formed with a strong reluctance to submission of any kind. And he battled almost as much with the infirmities of old age, as he did with the corruptions of the times. (*Observations* 146)

This is plausible biography of Swift, at least for the 1750s, as it seeks to explain the relation between Swift's satiric works and the small incidents of his life. Johnson, writing much later, offers a slightly different view. In old age, Swift, writes Johnson, having "desisted from study, had neither business nor amusement; for having, by some ridiculous resolution or mad vow, determined never to wear spectacles, he could make little use of books in his later years." So far, Johnson seems largely to be following the received story. But once Swift is without books, Johnson imagines what that would be like—as best a reader and bibliopole like Johnson could!— and pens the following: "his ideas, therefore, being neither renovated by discourse, nor increased by reading, wore gradually away, and left his mind vacant to the vexations of the hour, till at last his anger was heightened into madness" (*Lives* 3: 47). For Swiftians especially, this must be one of the most unsatisfying passages in the *Life of Swift*. It has none of the anecdotal particularity about private life that Johnson himself desired in biography. And the notion that Swift began to go literally insane in part because he did not have recourse to his books is hardly convincing. At best, Johnson is making up Swift's reality here, largely from the evidence of Delany's book. Perhaps Johnson sensed the weakness of this passage: in the very next paragraph, he shifts to praising Swift's *Polite Conversation* and *Directions to Servants* for their close attention to particulars. Yet the overall effect of this section of the biography is not of sustained narrative, but of implausible explanation, unwarranted generalization, and strained transition.

In other places in the *Life of Swift,* Johnson defers to Delany openly and shamelessly—presenting Delany's views in his own words. Although Johnson often includes Delany's points about Swift throughout the biography, his decision virtually to close the *Life of Swift* with the extended five-paragraph ending of Delany's own *Observations* remains nevertheless startling. The ending of a biography—for any biographer —remains one of its most important sections, as many great literary biographies indicate and as Johnson himself exhibits in other biographies. But in this case, Johnson appears simply to have turned over the close of the "character" section to Delany. Even a brief excerpt delivers a sense of the degree to which Johnson defers to Delany:

> I have here given the character of Swift as he exhibits himself to my perception; but now let another be heard who knew him better. Dr. Delany, after long acquaintance, describes him to Lord Orrery in these terms:
> "My Lord, when you consider Swift's singular, peculiar, and most variegated vein of wit, always rightly intended (although not always so rightly directed), delightful in many instances, and salutary, even where it is most offensive; when you consider his strict truth, his fortitude in resisting oppression and arbitrary power; his fidelity in friendship, his sincere love and zeal for religion, his uprightness in making right resolutions, and his steadiness in adhering to them; his care of his church, its choir, its oeconomy, and its income; . . .
> "All this considered, the character of his life will appear like that of his writings; they will both bear to be re-considered and re-examined with the utmost attention, . . .
> "He lives a blessing, he died a benefactor, and his name will ever live an honour to Ireland." (*Lives* 3: 64–65)

This constitutes roughly half of what Johnson allots to Delany; the entire passage is significantly longer than the three brief paragraphs of criticism of Swift's poetry with which the *Life of Swift* ends. Finally, Johnson's decision to include Delany at such length, and in such an important place in the biography, tends to erase, rather than expose, the Johnsonian imprimatur.

The third biographical treatment of Swift which Johnson knew well and used in writing the *Life of Swift* was the opening biographical volume of John Hawkesworth's edition of Swift, "An Account of the Life of the Reverend Jonathan Swift, D.D., Dean of St. Patrick's Dublin" (1755). Hawkesworth was himself something of a synthesizer, as he unabashedly explains in the opening of the *Account*:

> To gratify that curiosity which great eminence always excites, many accounts have been published of the life of Dr. *Jonathan Swift*. These have mutually reflected light upon each other, ascertained controverted facts, and rectified mistakes. . . . Lord *Orrery's Letters* contained many of the principal events, . . . but sometimes founded on false information: Some of these mistakes were detected by a Volume of Letters signed *J.R.* in which were also some new materials. . . . From a compilation of all these with each other this account is compiled. (*Account* 1)

Thus Hawkesworth declares his function in introducing Swift's works is to adjudicate or authenticate evidence. Further complicating Johnson's relation to this work was Johnson's personal relation to Hawkesworth. As is well known, Johnson knew Hawkesworth not only from the Ivy Lane Club, but from their work on the *Adventurer* in the 1750s. Johnson is typically honest about his relation to Hawkesworth: as Johnson announces in the very first sentence of his *Life of Swift*, he gave Hawkesworth the "scheme" for Hawkesworth's biography—"which I laid before him in the intimacy of our friendship" (*Lives* 3: 1). Needless to say, contemporary scholarship has focused much attention on Johnson's relation to this work, and as Paul Korshin has argued, Johnson followed more or less the overall structure of Hawkesworth's biography when composing his own.[24] Or is that to say that Johnson followed what was originally *his own* "scheme"? Regardless, Korshin has put together a list of parallels of the sort I've presented with the Orrery and Delany, and about them he reasonably concludes, "Although Johnson does not use [Hawkesworth's biography] as his sole source, it is definitely his paradigm, for the order of his own narrative is closely patterned upon Hawkesworth's" (Korshin, "Johnson and Swift" 469). In general, then, in actually composing the *Life of Swift* in relation to the three significant predecessors in Swiftian biographical writing, Johnson not only uses Orrery's *Remarks* and Delany's *Observations* heavily, but uses an analysis and an extension of these two works (and a few others)—Hawkesworth's *Account*. In fact, in the passage earlier quoted—where Johnson diverges from Delany on what happened to Swift once he had to give up reading—Johnson appears to be trying to integrate the broader outlines of Hawkesworth's rendition of Swift's mental decline into his own text.[25]

These patterns of dependence on Hawkesworth are well known among Johnsonians, and have drawn forth even further explanations of Johnson's supposedly prejudicial estimation of Swift. Martin Maner, for example, suspects that in using Hawkesworth, "Johnson experienced a sort of double anxiety of influence—doubt about how to treat both his subject and his chief source. . . . Generally speaking, Johnson's assertive personality leads him to rework Hawkesworth's text by resisting it, as though he were involved in a competitive dialogue with his departed friend."[26] While this point may stimulate us to reconsider Johnson's relation to his literary predecessors in general, it has the tendency of minimizing, or even explaining away, the startling weaknesses of Johnson's writing on Swift. Maner's point is more typical of how a literary critic, rather than a historian, might look at the evidence.

At least as telling, I think, is a consideration of how the evidence illuminates what Johnson actually did when he wrote his *Life of Swift.* And the evidence suggests that he simply tried to evade doing more research— research of the detailed kind that was then becoming more typical in the late eighteenth century as scholarly specialization increased. Stated another way, Johnson exhibits what Malone well understood about his friend—a real disinclination to perform the required scholarly investigations. Furthermore, when Johnson defers to such a degree to Orrery, to Delany, and to Hawkesworth, he allows those who had intimate or professional relations with Swift or his writing to dominate and direct the biography. In "hating much trouble" in executing his *Life of Swift,* Johnson thus frames his biography according to the self-presentations that Swift himself, to a great degree, offered to the world. In short, the *Life of Swift* is a strong indication of the persistence of what we may mean by Swift's "authority."

III

Johnson also weakens his *Life of Swift* by cultivating his penchant to write oblique autobiography. This habit of writing, like his habitual consolidating ability, would also fail him this time around. To be sure, Johnson's autobiographical urge is in part responsible for some of his best writing— particularly in the *Lives of the Poets*—as both specialized and general readers long have noticed.[27] This trait, dependent in part on Johnson's fame as an author, gives his writing real resonance, especially when he expounds on how writers managed the hopes and fears of their literary lives. When Johnson presents an oblique form of himself when writing about another author, readers incline to Johnson's perspective, believing that his writing comes out of real, lived experience. One could turn to many passages in the *Lives* to show how this dimension of his writing intensifies his strong and arresting judgments. Surely one of the most well-known examples appears in Johnson's treatment of Milton's work as schoolmaster in his *Life of Milton* (1779). "It is told," writes Johnson,

> that in the art of education he performed wonders, and a formidable list is given of the authors, Greek and Latin, that were read in Aldersgate-street by youth between ten and fifteen or sixteen years of age. Those who tell or receive these stories should consider that nobody can be taught faster than he can learn. The speed of the horseman must be limited by the power of his horse. Every man that has ever undertaken to instruct others can tell what slow advances he has been able to make, and how much patience it requires to recall vagrant inattention, to stimulate sluggish indifference, and to rectify absurd misapprehension. (*Lives* 1: 99)

Johnson, of course, was himself a schoolmaster—albeit a failed one (perhaps because of his well-known physical oddities)—and readers who know this about Johnson see in Johnson's statement a special conviction. In fact, in generalizing his own experience as a schoolmaster into the broader act simply of instructing others, Johnson asks readers to compare their own real experience in instructing others to the legendary stories (that is, false stories) of what Milton supposedly achieved in the classroom. Johnson's final statement, which at first glance seems harshly blunt, becomes convincing upon reflection:

> Of institutions we may judge by their effects. From this wonder-working academy I do not know that there ever proceeded any man very eminent for knowledge; its only genuine product, I believe, is a small *History of Poetry,* written in Latin by his nephew Philips, of which perhaps none of my readers has ever heard. (*Lives* 1: 101)

In this passage, Johnson includes a specific reference to only one person, and even that fact he somewhat qualifies with the phrase "I believe." The strength of this section in his *Life of Milton* derives from what Johnson learned about teaching through hard experience.

Johnson's *Life of Swift* includes no such resonant passages, and yet in places Johnson clearly depends on buried autobiography to flesh out what he knows about Swift and his works. Jeffrey Myers has paid special attention to the particulars of the possible autobiographical dimension of Johnson's *Life of Swift,* and in his view, "one of Johnson's most common techniques . . . is to state a fact about Swift's life, and then to make a generalization about it which often highlights something about his own life" (Myers 38). This is true enough, and yet Myers's argument does not address why the autobiographical passages in the *Life of Swift* are so inferior to those elsewhere. A brief look at a few autobiographical passages in the *Life of Swift* suggests at least some possible reasons for their failure.

In writing about Swift's presence in Dublin, Johnson writes that "much against his will, he commenced Irishman for life, and was to contrive how he might be best accommodated in a country where he considered himself as in a state of exile." Johnson has little new factual material to add, and he writes, "The thoughts of death rushed upon him at this time with such incessant importunity, that they took possession of his mind when he first waked for many years together" (*Lives* 28–29). Certainly one of Johnson's principal topics, in both conversation and writing, was the fear of death—as any number of sources indicate. But does Johnson's partially auto-biographical deposition particularly illuminate Swift's life? Does it give us as richer understanding of Swift's mind? Does it readjust what has come before, as does Johnson's autobiographical deposition in his *Life of Milton*? Alas, Johnson's dependence on autobiography operates in none of these ways. In that the *Life of Swift* offers no driving Johnsonian argument, Johnson's intensification of the subject of death by means of autobiographical deposition adds very little of quality to the *Life of Swift*. Perhaps one could argue that Johnson included such a passage to substantiate his presentation of Swift wasting away "in exile" in Ireland. But certainly such an effect is weak, lacking the typical force one finds in Johnson's other autobiographical depositions. The autobiographical musing on death does not fundamentally reinforce a typically arresting and memorable "Johnsonian" critical judgment. In this way, the *Life of Swift* differs fundamentally from the *Life of Milton*.

Johnson also delivers autobiographical reflections in a passage intensely critical of Swift's views on linguistic change. As a lexicographer and philologist, Johnson attacks Swift's *Proposal for Correcting, Improving, and Ascertaining the English Tongue* (1712), stating matter-of-factly that Swift wrote the work

> without much knowledge of the general nature of language, and without any accurate enquiry into the history of other tongues. The certainty and stability which, contrary to all experience, he thinks attainable, he proposes to secure by instituting an academy; the decrees of which every man would have been willing, and many would have been proud to disobey, and which, being re-newed by successive elections, would in short time have differed from itself. (*Lives* 3: 16)

This is unsatisfying biography for a number of reasons. First, Johnson clearly uses his own life not to illuminate Swift's intriguing interests in the nature of linguistic change—signs of which are evident throughout Swift's large corpus—but to upbraid Swift for not having the relatively spe-cialized philological knowledge that he himself possessed. Second, as in the passage on death, Johnson does not connect Swift's purported igno-rance of "the history of tongues" to a larger dimension of his intellectual development. Because Orrery, Delany, and Hawkesworth direct Johnson's

Life of Swift, Johnson's incursions into quasi-autobiographical reflection and analysis seem digressions. Johnson's view on Swift and language thus remains largely inert. It remains at best an aside—almost a footnote—penned by a specialist on his specialty. This passage may further be viewed as something of a lost chance, for as Robert DeMaria has noticed, Johnson actually spent a good deal of his energy attempting to conserve and restore the English language. His general views on language and linguistic change were in fundamental ways similar to Swift's. While Swift is perhaps hopeful that he can arrest trendy linguistic change, and while Johnson obviously understands linguistic change more realistically, Swift in fact "speaks for a good part of [the *Dictionary*'s] effort," according to DeMaria.[28] Perhaps Johnson should have included more on Swift's voluminous prose works, where he would have easily found more on Swift's views on language. Regardless, the lasting impression of this passage is one of ill-considered opinion and haste. More broadly, when Johnson depends on his own life to fill out his biographical writing, the very technique or inclination that seems a strength in his *Life of Milton* becomes a weakness in his *Life of Swift*.

IV

As Paul Korshin writes, the *Life of Swift* appears, finally, "hastily truncated" (Korshin, "Johnson and Swift," 468). Writing at the very end of his literary career, Johnson himself knew how much he needed to accomplish quickly. In 1780, he evaluates himself on his birthday, as was his habit. "I am now beginning the seventy second year of my life, with more strength of body and greater vigour of mind than, I think, is common at that age." But he notes, tellingly, "I have not at all studied; nor written diligently. I have Swift and Pope yet to write, Swift is just begun."[29] With his long-planned *Life of Pope* demanding his sustained attention, he probably hoped to proceed as soon as possible to that engrossing enterprise. If this is true, Johnson at least had a good motive to execute quickly his work on Swift. Furthermore, Johnson was behind schedule: as is well known, the publishers had hoped to receive the manuscript two years earlier. Deep personal losses may also have kept him from completing his writing to his own satisfaction between the summer of 1779 and March 1781, when he finished his *Lives*. At just the time he was pressing toward the end, his old and dear friend Henry Thrale suffered a series of strokes and declined rapidly. He died only weeks after Johnson finished the *Lives*. In March of the previous year, his young friend Topham Beauclerk surprisingly died at age forty.[30] Perhaps understandably, then, Johnson relied on two habits of composition that had guided him successfully in the past, but that when applied to his *Life of Swift*, would have deleterious effects.

In the end, Johnson's *Life of Swift* registers a common, and moderately humbling, truth about what causes a widely published writer to write poorly. Almost like contemporary writers working under the pressures of deadlines, contracts, and sometimes age, Johnson unwisely went with what he had used before. But the subject demanded another approach.

Ultimately, perhaps Swift baffled Johnson more than we tend to think. As another of Swift's biographers, David Nokes, confesses in the final pages of his own relatively recent biography of Swift, "the most enduring monster that [Swift] created to provoke and vex us was not Celia or Strephon, or a Struldbrug or a Yahoo, but himself."[31] In short, even had Johnson performed more "primary" research—just the sort of work that younger scholars like Malone trumpeted as necessary—Swift's own paradoxical presence, *his* lasting authority, may still have won the day.[32]

Notes

1. James Boswell, *Boswell's Life of Johnson,* ed. G. B. Hill, rev. L. F. Powell, 2nd ed., 6 vols. (Oxford: Clarendon Press, 1934–64), 2: 173–74. Subsequent references to this work will appear parenthetically in the text and be abbreviated *Boswell's Life.*

2. Samuel Johnson, *Lives of the English Poets,* 3 vols., ed. G. B. Hill (Oxford: Clarendon Press, 1905), 1: 19. Subsequent references to this work will appear parenthetically in the text and be abbreviated *Lives.*

3. Frederick W. Hilles, "Dr. Johnson on Swift's Last Years: Some Misconceptions and Distortions," *Philological Quarterly* 54 (1975): 370.

4. W. J. Bate, *Samuel Johnson* (New York and London: Harcourt Brace Jovanovich, 1975), 537.

5. S. P. T. Keilen, "Johnsonian Biography and the Swiftian Self," *Cambridge Quarterly* 23 (1994): 324.

6. Paul J. Korshin, "Johnson and Swift: A Study in the Genesis of Literary Opinion," *Philological Quarterly* 48 (1969): 464.

7. Maurice Charney, "Introduction," *"Bad" Shakespeare: Revaluations of the Shakespeare Canon* (Rutherford, N.J.: Fairleigh Dickinson University Press, 1988), 9.

8. Paul Fussell, *Samuel Johnson and the Life of Writing* (New York: Harcourt Brace Jovanovich, 1971), 278.

9. James Boswell to William Johnson Temple, *The Correspondence and Other Papers of James Boswell Relating to the Making of the Life of Johnson,* ed. Marshall Waingrow (New York: McGraw-Hill, 1969), 291.

10. Edmond Malone to Lord Charlemont, 5 April 1779, Osborn MS Folder for 1779. James M. and Marie-Louise Osborn Collection, Beinecke Rare Book and Manuscript Library, Yale University.

11. Harold Williams, "Swift's Early Biographers," in *Pope and His Contemporaries: Essays Presented to George Sherburn,* eds. James L. Clifford and Louis A. Landa (New York: Oxford University Press, 1949), 115.

12. John Boyle, Fifth Earl of Orrery, *Remarks on the Life and Writings of Dr. Jonathan Swift, Dean of St. Patrick's, Dublin* (London, 1752). Subsequent references to this work will appear parenthetically in the text and be abbreviated *Remarks.*

13. J. R. [Patrick Delany], *Observations Upon Lord Orrery's Remarks on the Life and Writings of Dr. Jonathan Swift* (London, 1754). Subsequent references to this work will appear parenthetically in the text and be abbreviated *Observations.*

14. John Hawkesworth, "An Account of the Life of the Reverend Jonathan Swift, D.D., Dean of St. Patrick's Dublin," *The Works of Jonathan Swift,* ed. John Hawkesworth, 12 vols. (London, 1755). Subsequent references to this work will appear parenthetically in the text and be abbreviated *Account.*

15. Korshin, "Johnson and Swift," 469–70.

16. Jeffrey Myers, "Autobiographical Reflections in Johnson's 'Life of Swift.'" *Discourse: A Review of the Liberal Arts* 8 (1965): 39.

17. For an overview of Johnson's aspirations in his *Life of Milton,* see Stephen Fix, "The Contexts and Motives of Johnson's Life of Milton," *Domestick Privacies: Samuel Johnson and the Art of Biography,* ed. David Wheeler (Lexington: University Press of Kentucky, 1987) 107–32.

18. Robert DeMaria, Jr., *Samuel Johnson and the Life of Reading* (Baltimore: Johns Hopkins University Press, 1997).

19. David F. Venturo, *Johnson the Poet: The Poetic Career of Samuel Johnson* (Newark: University of Delaware Press, 1999) 36, 162–63.

20. James Boswell, *Boswell's Journal of a Tour to the Hebrides,* eds. F. A. Pottle and C. H. Bennett (New York: McGraw-Hill, 1962), 202.

21. For a comprehensive treatment of the Battle, and for more on Charles Boyle's role in it, see Joseph M. Levine, *The Battle of the Books: History and Literature in the Augustan Age* (Ithaca and London: Cornell University Press, 1991), esp. 59–65.

22. Samuel Johnson, *The Letters of Samuel Johnson,* ed. Bruce Redford, 5 vols. (Princeton: Princeton University Press, 1992), 1: 62–63. For more on the relation between Johnson and Lord Orrery, see Paul J. Korshin, "Johnson and the Earl of Orrery," *Eighteenth-Century Studies in Honor of Donald F. Hyde,* ed. W. H. Bond. (New York: The Grolier Club, 1970), 29–43.

23. Wayne Warncke, "Samuel Johnson on Swift: the *Life of Swift* and Johnson's Predecessors in Swiftian Biography," *Journal of British Studies* 7 (May 1968): 58.

24. See Korshin, "Johnson and Swift."

25. See Hilles, "Dr. Johnson on Swift's Last Years," 370–379 for Johnson's handling of Swift's last years, esp. 376–77.

26. Martin Maner, "Johnson's Redaction of Hawkesworth's *Swift,*" *The Age of Johnson: A Scholarly Annual,* ed. Paul J. Korshin, 2 (1989): 313–14.

27. See Fussell, *Samuel Johnson,* 274–78.

28. Robert DeMaria, *Johnson's Dictionary and the Language of Learning* (Chapel Hill and London: University of North Carolina Press, 1986), 170.

29. Samuel Johnson, *Diaries, Prayers, and Annals,* ed. E. L. McAdam, *The Yale Edition of the Works of Samuel Johnson* (New Haven: Yale University Press, 1958), 1: 301.

30. For a biography of Johnson emphasizing the importance of Johnson's friendships in old age, see W. J. Bate, *Samuel Johnson,* esp. 547–600.

31. David Nokes, *Jonathan Swift, A Hypocrite Reversed: A Critical Biography* (Oxford: Oxford University Press, 1985), 413.

32. I wish to thank the staff of the Houghton Library at Harvard University for their learned and cheerful help. In a lively and penetrating response to a shorter version of this essay, Claude Rawson provided much help as well. In addition, I owe a great deal of my conception of Johnson as a "consolidator" to Richard Murphy, who in recent years especially has provided unlimited opportunities for endless conversation about Johnson.

The Rupert Barber Portraits of Jonathan Swift

Robert Folkenflik

IN A RECENT BIOGRAPHY OF JONATHAN SWIFT, VICTORIA GLENDINNING says of the engraving by Christian Friedrich Fritzch, of which she publishes a degraded copy, "A version of this curious line-engraving of Swift bareheaded was chosen by his friend Lord Orrery as the frontispiece for his *Remarks on the Life and Writings of Dr Jonathan Swift,* so he presumably considered it a fair likeness."[1] What Orrery actually published, the Benjamin Wilson engraving of 1751 (Plate 1), was unattractive enough to lead Sir Frederick Falkiner to claim early in this century that "if we knew no more of it one might surmise that it was spitefully selected by its spiteful author for his disparaging essay."[2] The Wilson is the source of a series of problematic engravings of Swift by S. F. Ravenet, Etienne Fiquet, Alexander Bannerman, Fritzch and others that disseminated Swift's image throughout Europe and America.[3] They may well also have helped to spread the conception of Swift as mad in a century when J. C. Lavater's *Physiognomy* diagnosed character on the basis of engravings when the subject was not at hand.[4] The little-known pastel original of Wilson's engravings and its pastel and miniature progeny are, however, another matter. Those portraits are the highly significant and very different representations of Swift by Rupert Barber upon which I will focus.

While I will discuss Barber's Swift portraits in detail at a later point, it may be best to introduce them here. The first in the series of profile portraits of Swift has a fairly clear provenance. It can be traced back to Alicia Sheridan and her husband, Joseph LeFanu, in the late eighteenth century and may have belonged to Dr. Richard Mead at the time of Wilson's engraving. The line of ownership is unbroken from the eighteenth century. This version, the model for Barber's profile portraits, remains in the family of the late William LeFanu and will be called here the LeFanu version (Plate 2). None of the others is known with certainty before this century. The one I regard as next to be executed is now at Bryn Mawr College, hence the Bryn Mawr version (Plate 3). The possibility that this one, rather than the LeFanu, was owned by Mead and used for Wilson's engraving will be discussed below. My wife and I have owned the next of the pastels in the series since 1977 (frontispiece). I will refer to this one as

Plate 1: Frontispiece engraving to Orrery's *Remarks,* by Benjamin Wilson. Reproduced by kind permission of Robert and Vivian Folkenflik.

Plate 2: "LeFanu" pastel portrait by Rupert Barber. Reproduced by kind permission of the LeFanu family.

the Commemorative version, though that is clearly an act of interpretation. While I think it the only posthumous pastel representation by Barber currently known, I justify the name by the sole undeniable sign of posthumous production in the series, the appearance of "Verses on the Death of Dr. Swift" in the lower right-hand corner. There is also a minia-ture version of this format (Plate 4), though its whereabouts is not known. Two other portraits of Swift by Barber, a full-face bust watercolor after

Plate 3: "Bryn Mawr" pastel portrait. Reproduced by kind permission of Bryn Mawr College's Collection.

Francis Bindon, who painted a variety of portraits of Swift, now at the National Gallery of Ireland (Plate 5), and a miniature version of this one, possibly at Bowhill in the duke of Buccleuch's collection, have a role to play in the story.

Relatively little is known about Barber and his life, and what does appear (with the usual parenthetical fl. 1736–72) in the brief biographical

Plate 4: Miniature portrait by Rupert Barber. Reproduced by kind permission of the National Gallery.

notices in Strickland, Long, Foskett, and other scholarship (including that of so good a Swift editor as Harold Williams and so good a Swift biographer as Irvin Ehrenpreis) is inaccurate. Collectively, they give Barber a father named Jonathan, marry him off to his mother Mary, concoct an uncle Rupert, turn his brother Lucius into a Swede, kill off his father in the 1730s, set Rupert to studying and working at Bath in 1736 and return him to Ireland in 1737, then pack him off again to Bath in 1752, none of which is the case.[5] Thanks to some recent work by A. C. Elias, Jr., on Mary

Plate 5: Watercolor after Francis Bindon. Reproduced by kind permission of the National Gallery of Ireland.

Barber and Louise Lippincott on Arthur Pond, as well as my own findings, a good deal can be corrected and ascertained.

A brief new biography will provide a context for his portraits. Barber was baptized in Dublin on 20 September 1719, the son of Rupert Barber, a woolen-draper and Mary Barber, whose poetry would be published in the

1730s.[6] The junior Rupert was one of four children who lived to adulthood of Mary Barber's nine or ten. The child who appears most often in her poetry, Con—her "fav'rite Son" Constantine—born in 1714, became a distinguished doctor and President of the Dublin College of Physicians.[7] The family lived in Dublin on St. Werburgh's Street in the old business district near St. Patrick's Cathedral from 1705 to 1724 or longer (Elias, *Pilkington* 2: 391 n.). Rupert's younger brother Lucius (baptized 1720), probably taught by Rupert, also became a painter, and Mary Delany sat to him for a miniature (Delany 3: 385, 16 December 1755).[8] He is the "Barbor," whom Horace Walpole lists as dying in London in 1767.[9] Of their sister, born in 1717, Mary Delany comments in 1753 on "Poor Mira . . . a melancholy drooping young woman, and I wish a prospect of her being well settled; but I hear of none" (2: 316). The Barber family lived from 1730 or earlier, at the bottom of Patrick Delany's garden at Delville; that is, before Mary Delany, then the widow Mary Pendarves, married the Dean-to-be, at least that is the import of a passage in Swift's *An Epistle upon an Epistle,* Swift's lampoon on Delany, one of the many poetic satires that sprung up at this time targeting him:

> Here a convenient box you found,
> Which you demolished to the ground:
> Then built, then took up with your Arbour,
> And set the House to R[u]p[er]t B[a]r[be]r.
> (*Poems* 2: 477, ll. 67–70)

Swift clearly meant the father, not the eleven-year-old painter-to-be. "An Answer to the Christmas Box," a mock defense of Delany, gives Rupert Barber, again surely Barber Sr., as the author.[10]

St. Werburgh's Street is very close to the cathedral. Although we do not know when Rupert Sr. met Swift, it is not unlikely that Swift had conversed with him among other drapers in the neighborhood prior to writing in the guise of a draper in 1724–25. We have no evidence that he did so, but Swift enjoyed conversing with the poor and middling in his neighborhood. Ehrenpreis suggests that he may have met Mary in 1728 (Ehrenpreis 3: 635). Swift mentions never having seen her in a letter of 28 March to John Gay expressing the hope that Gay has seen her poem praising Gay's *Fables,* and he later claims in a letter to the Countess of Suffolk that she "was recommended to me by Dr Delany" (26 October 1731) and that he had never visited her (*Correspondence* 3: 278, 501), but it seems unlikely that she would have sent him both son and poem ("*On sending my Son, as a Present, to Dr. Swift, Dean of St. Patrick's on his Birth-Day*") on 30 November 1726 had none of the family met before that.[11] It is worth noting also that she addresses him in the poem as "the DRAPIER" (*Poems* 72), the persona he had first employed during the two previous years, as she does elsewhere in her poetry.

The correspondence of Swift and his friends details their relationships to the senior Barbers. In December 1730 Lady Betty Germaine responded to Swift's request for patronage for Mary. In February 1731 Swift wrote to Mary about her subscription for her poems and to Pope in April regretting her pestering the poet. In September 1731 Lady Betty praised Mary in a letter to Swift but found Mary's husband avariciously taking advantage of patronage that she had brought him, a commission to produce liveries for the Duke of Dorset (*Correspondence* 3: 430, 439–40, 457, 497). In a characteristic undated list by Swift of those grateful and ungrateful to him, Mary rates a "g" and Rupert Sr. a "u" (*Correspondence* 5: 270–71, Appendix xxx). Yet in December 1732 Swift unsuccessfully solicited a place from John Barber, lord Mayor of London and no relation, for Rupert Barber Sr.: "He is of English birth; a very upright honest man, and his wife hath abundance of merit in all respects; they design to settle among you, having turned what fortune they had here, into money (*Correspondence* 4: 92–93). She had gone to England in May or June 1730 and returned on a visit during 1732–33. On 6 September Mary Delany reports, "Mrs. Barber is come to Ireland they say in order to transplant her family in England" (1: 383). It is likely that her children went with her, not her husband, who at some point, possibly in the 1740s, became mentally incompetent. As late as 1755 Mary Delany notes that "Old Mr. Barber is *alive,* drinks his claret, smokes his pipe, and *cares not a pin for any of his family*" (3: 327). Swift remained friendly with Mary Barber throughout his life. He gave her his *Directions to Servants* to publish for her own profit in 1736, and she was one of the few nonclergy given a memorial present in his will dated May 1740.

Mary Barber claims in her Preface that she wrote her poems "*chiefly to form the Minds of my Children,*" and "*A True* TALE" details her educational methods "in modelling her Childrens Minds" (Barber, *Poems* xviii, 7). She certainly worked hard to help her children achieve their ends, cultivating Dr. Richard Mead and Dr. Richard Helsham for Con, John Barber for Lucius, and Arthur Pond for Rupert. A Mary Barber poem of 29 September 1733, addressed to John Barber, "*on committing one of my Sons to his Care,*" imagines young Lucius (or possibly Rupert) as a wild child captured in Ireland who has "not too much *Conscience,* nor too little *Art*" but has the qualities to become a businessman, or perhaps Lord Mayor (*Poems* 232, 233). She puns here on her son's artistic talent.

Young Rupert Barber can be connected to the painter-collector-dealer Arthur Pond from mid-December of 1734 when he (or his mother) advertised that he would take subscriptions for his mother's *Poems,* published in 1735.[12] From 1735–39 he was Pond's only apprentice, though off the books of the Inland Revenue Office. His mother paid Pond the very small fee of £15 a year with no premium or capital sum. Pond painted Mary

Barber in a lost portrait before this time.[13] Rupert's work would have included "scraping smooth the sheets of paper for portraits, grinding and mixing colors, affixing the finished works to straining frames, and other peripheral tasks" (Lippincott 78). Lippincott mentions both that Pond was relatively unknown at this time and that Mary Barber was a friend of Pond's from 1730, but one might also notice that the network of patrons of Pond included Orrery, Mead, and Mary Pendarves (who would in 1743 become Mrs. Delany), all of whom helped Mary Barber at one point or another. Mary Pendarves, who became an amateur landscape artist, studied with Pond among others.

Given the length of Barber's apprenticeship, those inferring that Rupert Barber studied at Bath (every scholar who has published thus far on the matter) have misread Mary Barber's letter to Swift from Bath on 3 November 1736 about Rupert and Constantine: "my son who is learning to paint goes on well and if he be in the least approv'd of in all probability he may do very well at Bath for I never yet saw a painter that came hither, fail of getting more business than he cou'd do." She is not referring to his being there (he was undoubtedly still serving his apprenticeship in London) but to what her teenager would do in the future. The letter claims that she is in Bath both because the waters are the only help for her gout (from which she suffered for years) and "besides this the interest of my children is a great inducement to me for here I have the best prospect of keeping up an acquaintance for them." After speaking of Rupert's prospects, she adds "and I have hopes that Con may settle here." In other words, neither son was on the scene. Indeed, in speaking of renting a house, she intends to take one bigger than she needs, for "if I live till my son the painter goes into business he might be with me" (Swift, *Correspondence* 4: 539). Interestingly, she mentions that Dr. Mead may help Con.

Given Barber's apprenticeship to Pond, the dating of the first of Barber's pastel portraits as 1737, suggested by William LeFanu, the late owner, who believed that Barber returned to Dublin at that time, is unlikely.[14] There is no evidence to show that the apprentice was permitted to leave London during this period. Theoretically at least, all of an apprentice's time belonged to his master. Arthur Pond's *Journal of Receipts and Expenses, 1734–1750*, lists Mary Barber's payment of half the £15 per year every six months or so for Rupert's apprenticeship; however, since Rupert may have been already at Pond's house in December 1734, the apprenticeship may have begun earlier than 1735.[15]

Arthur Pond was a significant choice as master, though he was not an impressive artist. Ellis Waterhouse quotes a Mary Pendarves letter of June 1734: "I hope Mr. Pond will help me too, for his colouring in crayons, I think *the best* I have seen of any English painter" (Delany 3: 485), and adds tartly, "Pond's quality in crayons, to judge from a signed example of 1737

. . . , is little higher than his quality in oils, but his work found favour and imitators as well."[16] In fact, along with his friends George Knapton and William Hoare, Pond participated in a vogue for pastels (or crayons) that was short-lived for him but lasted generally until the end of the century and set the stage for one part of Barber's characteristic output, represented among the Swift portraits by the LeFanu, the Bryn Mawr, and the Commemorative. Lippincott points out that "Joshua Reynolds, the apprentice of [Thomas] Hudson, began in the same manner as Rupert Barber and James George [one of Pond's two later apprentices] and built his career on the models of Richardson, Hudson and Pond" (Lippincott 97), a sobering thought for anyone contemplating the career of Barber. It is also worth noting that Nathaniel Hone, who succeeded Christian Friedrich Zincke as the best enamel miniaturist in England, and Rupert Barber were contemporaries from Ireland in England at roughly the same time.

We do not know from whom Barber learned the technique of miniature enamels, though Dublin was a center of miniature painting.[17] Patrick Noon has compared his "blotchy stippling method" with Hone's miniature style in the 1760s.[18] Barber's enamels have affinities with such mid-century miniaturists as Gervase Spencer and André Roquet. One of Anne Donnellan is at the Ulster Museum, Belfast. The Victoria and Albert has an initialed Barber miniature, and another (unsigned) was displayed at Rothe House in 1999.[19] Besides these and the Barber works discussed in this essay, he is known to have represented Mrs. Delany, Lord Masserene, and Dr. Edward Smyth, this last known only from a Valentine Greene engraving of 1779. An exceptionally good example of his work in miniature will be discussed later. The format of the LeFanu version of Swift is a simple oval, an indication that Barber probably intended it as a model for a miniature, though the degree of finish points to the possibility of pastel production as well. Like pastels, British miniatures flourished around mid-century. An indigenous school of Irish pastelists formed around Robert West and the Dublin Society; Barber's manner was very different from that of West and his followers.[20] Pastels were advantageous to the painter because they were a cheaper and quicker medium than oils, so they cost the sitter less and increased the output. Since they tended in the early eighteenth century to be small bust portraits, they also made fewer technical demands upon the artist in terms of anatomy or composition.

As we have already seen, Mary Barber's whereabouts are not necessarily an indication of Rupert's. Since he married Patrick Delany's niece Bridget Wilson in March 1742, he was back in Dublin between the end of 1739 and the time of his marriage. In the *Dublin Journal* (1743) he is praised in the poetic panegyric "To Mr. Rupert Barber, on his Painting in Ennamel [*sic*]":

> Bless'd Youth whom happy Talents Grace,
> Time shall no more thy Art deface:
> Thy Genius now will be display'd
> In Colours that can never fade.[21]

In the last line the standard trope of praise is wittily more accurate for the enamelist, though the colors of the pastels that are my subject have held up very well. Seven years later another poem in the *Dublin Journal,* "To Mr. Rupert Barber, Enamel Painter, on seeing some Portraits of his Painting in Oil Colours" (1750), recognized his versatility:

> Some Painters in a single Branch,
> The Pencil's Force have shown;
> But to excel, in various Ways,
> Is given to thee alone.
>
> (10–13 February, p. [1])

Faulkner also praised him in a note to Mary Barber's letter to Swift from Bath as "Mr. Rupert Barber, a most eminent painter in crayons and minia-ture."[22] While I am not aware of any oils by Rupert Barber, Anthony Pasquin speaks of a Barber who painted oil portraits in Dublin and the north of Ireland around 1750.[23] This is likely to be Rupert.

From the mid-1740s, the best source of information about Rupert Barber is Mary Delany's letters. While she had been friendly with Mary Barber in England prior to her trip to Ireland in September 1731, she clearly became fond of the whole family to whom her second husband was related by marriage and whose patronage supported them.[24] A number of her letters give a patron's-eye view of domestic details of the life of Rupy and Biddie, as Mrs. Delany styles them, as well as of their three children (a girl and two boys), Dr. Barber, Mary Barber, and Rupert's sister Mira. They display family vignettes and chart his growing success with her help. In 1746 Rupert copied a picture of Lady Stanley and later painted an enamel of Mary Delany. Her friend Mr. Bristowe called it "better done than any he ever saw of Zincke's" and tried to obtain Lord and Lady Chesterfield as sitters for Rupert. Mary herself compared Rupert's portrait of Mrs. Don-nellan to Zincke in 1752. She thinks that such aristocratic sitters as Lord Masserene and the Chesterfields "will bring him into fashion; he is very industrious, and deserves to be encouraged; his wife is a very pretty pru-dent young woman: they have a comical little girl of three years old . . . and he proposes to make her a mistress of his art, as soon as she is capable of learning" (2: 429). One brief anecdote may give some flavor of the relationship. One day the Delanys and their guests went to Rupert Barber's "house at the end of the garden" to eat dinner in the Barbers' absence "in his dining room which looks into Carlingford garden": "Mr. Barber came home when we had half dined, in a great hurry, to burn some of his enamels, little thinking to find his house full of company." (6 June 1747; 2: 461–62). More typically, in early 1753 Mary Delany writes that they "send for our neighbour Barbers in the evening; Rupy reads to us, and our niece helps" (2: 316). In 1753 she judges "Rupy" summarily as "really a very sensible young man" (3: 206).

Barber had another source of income as well as his own art: he bought prints in quantity from his former master, Pond, in order to sell them far from London (Lippincott 35). He was in London in June of 1748 when Mary Delany's friend and correspondent Lady Dysart admired his work and attempted to help him obtain sitters (2: 487). Four years later Mary Delany sees Barber as successful: calling his enamel of Mrs. Donnellan "by much the handsomest likeness," she adds "he is very much improved and has as much business as he can do" (10 April 1752; 3: 116). Her own collections may have been of help to him. Among other works she possessed a pastel self-portrait by Jean–Étienne Liotard, one of the foremost European artists in this medium.

At a late point we come as close as we can to Rupert's own voice when on 9 June 1772 he writes a letter to Mary Delany, now a widow in England following the death of Dean Delany, the only letter by him of which I am aware: "Madam, as your last letter to me was an order to distribute your bounty to your poor pensioners, I saw no necessity to trouble you with an answer; I obeyed your commands *exactly,* and the Kilfoyles, *with the rest,* are *made perfectly happy.* As this letter relates chiefly to my own affairs I must entreat your pardon for troubling you on that head!" (Delany 4: 432). The editor of Delany's letters mentions an engagement with "a very artful person, in a distillery," which Rupert claims has burdened him with his partner's debt. He won a £20 premium for making phials and green glass from the Dublin Society in 1753, and perhaps this venture was related. Barber's letter, mostly devoted to obtaining a loan, is probably the basis for the standard terminus in the collective biographies. It proves he was alive in June 1772, but he was probably still living in 1778 when Mary Delany named him in her will.

I will focus primarily on the Lefanu portrait—the oval profile in pastel that served as the model for the other Barber portraits of Swift (except the full-face portraits)—and the two elaborate pastel portraits derived from it, the Bryn Mawr and the Commemorative. I believe, as do all the others who have touched upon the Barber portraits to this point, that the LeFanu version was taken from the life, and I will later give reasons for thinking so. In the absence of other evidence, I would have suggested that the LeFanu original of Barber versions of Swift was done no earlier than 1740 after the putative completion of Barber's apprenticeship. However, a catalogue reference to a Barber miniature of Swift signed and dated 1739 would seem to make this date more likely.[25] In March of this year a major Bindon portrait was painted and installed in the Deanery. Though Mary Barber paid for Rupert's apprenticeship through the end of the year, and he was in Pond's account book on 7 December for "shooting" and something indecipherable, he was evidently allowed to go back to Dublin, perhaps following this entry. It may be, given his possible presence at Pond's in December 1734, that his apprenticeship ended sometime in December 1739.

In the LeFanu I believe that he was following the example of his master Arthur Pond, whose stark representation of Dr. Richard Mead, the collector and friend of Mary Barber, in an etched portrait after the manner (as it was understood) of Rembrandt was behind Barber's rendition of Swift in a colorful pastel, a medium that Pond helped bring into fashion. Barber might even have had Mead in mind as the proper recipient of one of his Swift portraits, which Mead came to own and which served as the original of the Wilson engraving. It would make a companion to one of Mead's portraits of Pope, in profile without a wig, by Jonathan Richardson, the elder, which was in his collection by 1738 (Wimsatt 205–7).

Rembrandt was in highest regard as a portraitist. Charles Rogers remarked in 1778, "Rembrandt's greatest strength was in Portraits; they had a striking Likeness, and he seized the character of every countenance"[26] Christopher White notes that "In practice it was the bust-length portrait against a plain ground or the half-length portrait . . . , which was most imitated by Rembrandt's admirers" (White, Alexander, and D'Oench 22). Both the *Mead* and the *Swift* were of the former type, and Dr. Mead came to own both. It is also to the point that Benjamin Wilson, the engraver of *Swift* for Orrery, was part of the "Rembrandt Group" that included Pond, Thomas Worlidge, and Wilson's master Thomas Hudson. A poem celebrating Wilson in the *London Magazine* claims: "Rembrandt's wreath to you we must allow/ Since what once Rembrandt was is Wilson now" (quoted by White 41). Pond's portrait obtained a certain notoriety: George Vertue claimed that it made Mead look like "an old mumper as Rhimebrandts [*sic*] heads usually do."[27] What both portraits show is the profile of a man unadorned and "wearing his own hair," as those of the period would have said. Wilson's engraving with its unadmired cross-hatching should also be perceived as an attempt to capture Rembrandt's manner displayed in his engraved portraits. Both Barber's portrait of Swift and Wilson's engraving participate in the Rembrandt vogue (Plate 6).

Barber's image also bears a relation to coin and medal portraiture (where profiles are standard) and to one typical convention of the iconography of writers. In 1745 Jonathan Richardson engraved Swift's friend

Plate 6: Etched self-portrait by Rembrandt. Reproduced by kind permission of Robert and Vivian Folkenflik.

Pope in a similar way (Plate 7), and even earlier Kneller had represented Pope in profile, without wig, laureled (or more accurately, ivied) and wearing a toga (1721). Another like this one but actually laureled, with a shirt under the toga, is at the National Portrait Gallery of England and attributed to Richardson, though David Piper, who notes the rarity of profile portraits in painting—"normal in medals"—thinks it too good for him.[28] In his writings on art Richardson argued that "Painters should take a Face and make an Antique Medal, or Bas-Relief of it, by divesting it of its Modern Disguises."[29] Richardson was a mentor to Barber's master Arthur Pond (Lippincott 20). Dr. Richard Mead, a friend and neighbor of Richardson,

Plate 7: Engraved portrait of Alexander Pope by Jonathan Richardson. Reproduced by kind permission of Robert and Vivian Folkenflik.

owned two of his profile oil portraits of Pope and would come to own Barber's portrait of Swift. Mead opened his collections to students of painting and sculpture, and Barber, who was living close by with Pond, was undoubtedly among them. Like many others, Mead collected what were known as "Heads of Illustrious Persons." Arthur Pond made the connection of such portraits of Pope to coin portraiture even clearer in his engraving of 1745 for William Warburton's edition of the *Essay on Man* (see Wimsatt 190, fig. 43.3).[30] John Flaxman's Wedgwood medallion of Samuel Johnson (1784) provides another example of the "Roman" representation of writers.[31] The drapery in the LeFanu *Swift* is simpler than Pond's robe over a shirt, which, like the Commemorative version, has a vaguely Renaissance suggestion to it. David Piper points out that medallion celebrations of poets were typical of the Renaissance rather than Greek and Rome (Piper 93).[32] The Barber is also a softer image than either the Pond *Mead* or typical Swifts, for reasons I will discuss later.

The drapery of the Commemorative version becomes more complicated, however. The Wilson engravings follow the LeFanu or the Bryn Mawr in the treatment of the hair, but the white collar jutting out beneath the robe is more like the Commemorative. It is possible that Wilson was adding his own accessories, as engravers often do, or that he was bringing it more into line with the Pond *Mead* or another version of the Barber, perhaps the Commemorative or the similar miniature. Since Wilson, an English engraver, was known to have visited Ireland in 1746 and in 1748–50, he may have seen other Barber versions besides Mead's (Crookshank and the Knight of Glin 135). The alternative hypothesis, that Wilson changed the drapery to give Swift a shirt and that Barber then changed his own representation of Swift to follow that of his engraver, strikes me as less likely, as does Barber's waiting until 1751 to execute a commemorative version of his portrait of Swift.

What I say about the Barber portraits is predicated on the versions known to me. I think the basic story will remain accurate, even if currently unknown copies come to light. A version of the Bryn Mawr is said to be in private hands in Ireland, though I have discovered no details as to its whereabouts. The earliest mention I find connecting Barber to a Swift portrait is George Faulkner's advertisement for Orrery's biography (1751) in his *Dublin Journal,* which mentions the "original picture painted by Mr. Barber" and engraved by Wilson.[33] Although the provenance of the Barber Swifts is not entirely clear, the LeFanu can be traced back to the eighteenth century. The LeFanu family descends from the Sheridans, who included Swift's good friend Thomas Sheridan the elder and his grandson, the dramatist, Richard Brinsley Sheridan.[34] However, since the elder Thomas Sheridan died 10 October 1738, I do not believe he could have owned it at any time. Moreover, if the younger Thomas Sheridan owned it at the time of his own biography of Swift (1784), he could have published a better engraving of the Barber *Swift* rather than the poor, unidentified engraving he used. While it is tempting to identify Mead's *Swift* as the Bryn Mawr, which would mean the LeFanu never left Ireland, the logical inference from the Wilson profile engraving is that he was copying from a portrait without any surrounding setting, the LeFanu. In 1754 Dr. Mead's version, claimed in the Sale Catalogue of Mead's collection as the portrait of Swift engraved for Orrery's biography, was sold for £4/14/6 to a Mr. Berners, presumably of the family of Lord Berners.[35] Mead's friendship with Orrery would explain its appearance in his *Remarks on Swift.* Orrery was in London during much of 1751 before the book's publication. Wilson's

Orrery frontispiece limits itself to the oval portrait, although the Bryn Mawr is typical of frontispiece portraits, and therefore would have been highly appropriate in format as a whole, had Mead owned it. These facts and the engraving of Orrery's frontispiece by a London artist in 1751 suggest that Mead had the LeFanu version at the time of his death. However, the case is not beyond dispute. Certain stylistic features (the degree of baldness, for example) seem closer in the Bryn Mawr to Wilson's engraving. Also, it is likely that Barber kept the LeFanu throughout his lifetime as a model to which he could recur for Swift portraits.

The Countess of Orrery disliked Wilson's engraving, but the reception of Orrery's book itself was highly negative among Swift's friends. Following the publication of the *Remarks on Swift,* Orrery was told by Dr. Edward Barry that Mary Barber wrote verses as part of a "*Junto*" against the book, and Con "often used to repeat them, or rather, stammer them." Orrery replied "As to Mother Barber, the Verses and the Son, they move me not," and suggested Thomas Sheridan, the younger, was behind the attacks (*Orrery Papers* 103, 107). Mary Delany also spoke severely about the *Remarks,* and in January 1752 she copied an "epigram" against Orrery that might be the offending lines and at least are typical of the attacks (3: 64–65, 73). Hereafter Orrery would be an unlikely purchaser or recipient of a Barber portrait.

The provenance of the other pastels is only known during the twentieth century. The Bryn Mawr pastel was donated to the College in 1960 by Mary K. Woodworth, who traced the ownership of that version back to Mrs. T. G. Winter in 1936 but no farther.[36] Mrs. Winter sold it to the London dealer Colnaghi, who owned it in 1941 and sold it to a Mrs. Mendelsohn-Bartoldy. Its transmission then is unknown until it was obtained by Pickering and Chatto. Charles Sessler, Inc., of Philadelphia bought it from that dealer, and Mary K. Woodworth bought it from Sessler in 1958.

The Commemorative version is known only from about the same period as the Bryn Mawr. Catalogued by C. A. Stonehill, booksellers of New Haven, Connecticut, in 1939 for $250, it was then sold in April 1948 at Parke Bernet for only $100 (the "ornate gilt frame" is listed as having "some pieces chipped off"), a hint as to why it was reframed (Plate 8). In 1977 the Commemorative version was bought at Swann's Auction House by Dr. Jacob Perlstein, my father-in-law, who gave it to my wife and me at that time. Both Stonehill and Parke Bernet after, however, regarded it as the work of John Russell, R.A. (1745–1806). Although Russell did pastel portraits, I think this is just a familiar case of attributing a work to a better-known artist. The Commemorative is not in Russell's manner and no evidence has been offered for the identification. While the Commemorative differs from both the LeFanu and the Bryn Mawr, which are close in the

ORIGINAL PASTEL DRAWING OF DEAN SWIFT.

330. RUSSELL (John, 1745-1806). Original pastel portrait of Swift, drawn in his memory some years after his death: a profile view in oval, against a brown velvet drape. In the foreground are several volumes of Swift's best known works, and in the lower right-hand corner an open book with verses "On the Death of Dean Swift." Swift's robe and the leaves which are strewn casually over the volumes are in a soft shade of blue, the stained edges of the books being in a muted orange.

Approximate size of drawing, about 19″ by 23″, framed in a very ornate gilt frame, about five inches in width. $250.00

Russell, who was a friend of Sir Joshua Reynolds, was one of the most fascinating portrait painters of the latter part of the 18th century. He worked almost entirely in pastels, and his portraits have a charm and an individuality which place them on almost the same level as those of the great trio, Reynolds, Gainsborough and Romney. Redgrave called him "the prince of portrait painters." He was a constant exhibitor at the Royal Academy, having studied under Francis Cotes, one of the founders of that institution. He painted numerous portraits of the Royal Family, having been made King's Painter in 1789. Other famous personages whose portraits he painted were John Wesley; Philip Stanhope, son of Lord Chesterfield; Bartolozzi, the engraver; William Cowper; Admiral Bligh of the "Bounty"; Mrs. Siddons; R. B. Sheridan, etc.

Plate 8: "Commemorative" framed portrait by Rupert Barber. Reproduced by kind permission of Robert and Vivian Folkenflik.

treatment of the hair, it is like an extant miniature in private hands in both the laurels circling "Verses on the Death of Dr. Swift" and the treatment of the hair. The existence of the miniature also argues for ours as a Barber, since Barber was a miniaturist, and Russell almost never worked in this medium.[37]

The formats also help to show that the pastel portraits of Swift are by the same artist. A general comparison of the Bryn Mawr version with the Commemorative shows many differences, but I think that the first thing to stress is the similarities. William LeFanu's notes give his *Swift* as approximately 16 by 13 inches, pastel on paper. The Commemorative portrait oval is almost the same, with the width a bit over 13 inches; the Bryn Mawr is 15¼ by 13, a little smaller. The portraits are nearly identical in stretcher size, medium, and general format. Both are pastels, employing at times a wet brush or pencil, on paper laid on canvas. Bryn Mawr's stretcher measures 24¼ by 19¾"; ours, 24 by 19⅞".

LeFanu speaks of "replicas" and Sir Frederick R. Falkiner of "repetitions on the sly," but this distorts Barber's artistic practice (LeFanu, *Catalogue* opposite title page; Falkiner 4). Certainly the LeFanu pastel, sometimes called the "sketch" despite its high degree of finish, was meant to serve as the model for Barber's standard artistic efforts, pastel and miniature portraits, and there is no reason to think that one version or even one version in each medium was the necessary expectation.[38] A good example of Barber's practice is the sketch in Dublin at the National Gallery of Ireland of the beggar William Thompson (Plate 9). Barber's signed 1744 recjtangular enamel miniature, now at the New Orleans Museum of Art, identifies Thompson as "Mendicans Dublini" and gives his age as 114 (Plate 10). Speaking of this miniature, unusual in subject and rectangular format among Barber's known works, Basil Long, who regards it as "very good," adds "It is ptd. with considerably more freedom than might have been expected in an enamel of the period" (14). This subject may also be indebted to Pond's interest as collector and artist in Rembrandt. Many of the French and English followers of Rembrandt were attracted to his portraits of old men. Barber's *Thompson* is literally, to use the disdainful phrase Vertue used of Pond's *Mead,* an "old mumper," a beggar.

The full-face portraits of Swift by Barber deserve attention in their own right and provide some evidence about the profile portraits. The putative Barber full-face pastel after Bindon at the National Gallery of Ireland (Plate 5) is probably based on a Deanery Bindon that was not in place until March 1739. This portrait was listed by Sir Walter Scott as owned by Dr. Edward Hill, and in 1913 his great granddaughter sold it to the National Gallery of Ireland (Falkiner 39–40). Walter G. Strickland mentions "a miniature which resembles [this] portrait" as in the hands of J. G. Swift MacNeill in 1913 (Strickland 23). This painting is probably the miniature

Plate 9: Portrait of William Thompson by Rupert Barber. Reproduced by kind permission of the National Gallery of Ireland.

Plate 10: Miniature portrait of William Thompson by Rupert Barber. Reproduced by kind permission of the New Orleans Museum of Art.

of Swift after Bindon (dated 1739) in the collection of the Duke of Buccleuch at Bowhill.[39] Even without this corroborating evidence, I would find convincing Sir Frederick Falkiner's 1908 attribution of the pastel to Barber. Bindon was not a pastelist, and Falkiner claims that he never worked "with the artistic finish, delicacy, and precision which this portrait displays in the sparkle of the eyes, in the deep black eyebrows, in the contours of the double chin and careful curling of the periwig, all of which point to its execution by a skilful [sic] miniature painter" (Falkiner 39–40). The eyes in these Swift portraits are unlike those of earlier representations. While Bindon is known to have painted miniatures, I would add that it lacks the gravitas of the Bindon portraits. Unlike them, however, it shakes free of the suggestion that the artist trained under Mme Tussaud.

The facts I have found suggest that the LeFanu portrait of Swift may have been the last taken from the life, though Bindon's last Swift portrait, painted for Robert Nugent in 1740, also has possible claims (Falkiner 31–36).[40] A letter from Nugent to Martha Whiteway, Swift's cousin who cared for Swift and acted as a kind of manager to him in his last years, reminds her of a portrait ("a head upon a three-quarter cloth") he wishes painted by Bindon (2 April 1740, Swift *Correspondence* 5: 182). This one was certainly painted, though it has been thought lost. A painting possibly of Swift late in life with long white hair under a skull cap is in the collection of the National Gallery of Ireland (Plate 11). Falkiner shrewdly notes that this painting, then in the possession of the Earl of Drogheda at Moore Abbey, corresponds in size and format to the description of the lost Nugent Bindon (Falkiner 35–36).[41] It was attributed at that time (1908) to Stephen Slaughter, but Falkiner calls attention to an identical portrait owned by Godwin Swift, a descendant of Swift's uncle, that the family had always attributed to Bindon (Falkiner 35). Mary Delany comments on Swift near the end: "he was reduced to such a miserable state of idiotism that he was a shocking object; though in his person a very venerable figure, with long silver hair and a comely countenance, for being grown fat the hard lines, which gave him a harsh look before, were filled up." She wrote on 16 November 1745; Swift had died on 19 October (2: 397–98). Her description is in some ways consistent with the various Barber profile portraits, which have hair behind curling below the ear, though there is no reason from them alone to conclude that Swift had reached a period of extreme mental incapacity.

As the son of Swift's friend Mary Barber, the dependent of the Delanys, and someone known to Orrery and Mead, Barber had excellent credentials for entering the Deanery even in the dark days beginning around 1740, as Bindon evidently did. Although we do not know the date of Barber's return, the farther we move from 1739, the less likely Swift was to be a sitter. Even more than the copy after Bindon, the Barber Swifts lack the characteristic severity of most Swift portraits (the Charles Jervas excepted), either because of Swift's mental state or because of the softening effect of pastel as a medium, though I do not think it is simply a matter of Barber's limitations as an artist. It is true that Rupert Barber was likely at an early age to have seen Swift, either at St. Patrick's or when Swift visited Dr. Delany, but on such occasions he would have been unlikely to see him

Plate 11: Portrait of Swift, attributed to Francis Bindon. Reproduced by kind permission of the National Gallery of Ireland.

wigless, and the shift from the balding head of the LeFanu and Bryn Mawr to the more idealized treatment of the hair in the Commemorative suggests that he was moving away from the realistic depiction for which he had no basis in the known representations of Swift. Of course, he may have portrayed Swift later than the winter of 1739–40. Ehrenpreis concludes his biography of Swift by denying the story, best known through Samuel Johnson, that Swift's servants had shown him for money during his years of incompetency (3: 919–20). His denial is based on the assertion of John Lyon, the clergyman responsible for Swift. But Lyon, who would certainly have been eager to deny the story, would have required a strict regime of surveillance to know the facts, and Barber might well have seen Swift bareheaded.

One unconsidered possibility is that Rupert Barber was not working from the life, and that his first portrait of Swift may have been done at any time during his apprenticeship either from a memory of Swift or by way of someone else's portrait, as he had followed Bindon in his National Gallery of Ireland pastel. This hypothesis immediately encounters several problems. Swift did not look this way until relatively late. Also, with the exception of a possible pencil drawing of Swift by Isaac Whood (1730), there is no known model for a profile portrait, and one might ask why Barber would substitute Whood's profile portrait of Swift in the oval for that of Bindon if he were only following another artist (Le Harivel no. 2614, p. 722).[42] I do not think that, even if he knew it and believed it to be Swift, Barber took the turban off the profile by Whood to arrive at his own. Moreover, Orrery would have been unlikely to use a portrait not done from the life. Despite the suspicion of his motives in publishing the Wilson, he thought highly of Wilson, whom he employed to paint portraits of his own sons, which he praised as "very like" (Orrery 2: 115), and Wilson was a better artist than his engraving of Barber's portrait would suggest. The possibility also exists that the three portraits were closer together in time. It is suggestive that the notice of Swift's death in *Dublin Journal* appeared in the same issue as notice of republication of "Verses on the Death of Dr. Swift" and of Andrew Miller's mezzotint of the Bindon portrait of Swift Barber used for his profiles (19–22 October 1745). A posthumous portrait series would make Barber's profiles dependent on a viewing of the body in state following Swift's death or one of Swift's death masks.[43] The history of portraiture contains many posthumous portraits, for commemoration of the dead is a major motive. Hogarth's posthumous profile portrait engraving of Fielding (1762) is said to be based on a lifetime silhouette. I think, however, that Barber's substitution of an unknown profile portrait for the full-face of the Miller-Bindon suggests that he was substituting a lifetime likeness, and a body in an open coffin is an unlikely candidate for a profile portrait. Additionally, the source of Barber's elaborate Swift portraits needs consideration (Plate 12).

The format both of the Bryn Mawr and the Commemorative pastels follows the pattern of Andrew Miller's mezzotint half-length portrait presumably after a lost Bindon of 1744, and could not, therefore, have been executed earlier. A comparison of Barber's own pastel portrait after Bindon with Miller's engraved oval portrait will show how close Barber's work is to a typical Bindon. But Miller's drapery surround, a wreath of oak leaves to the left, books on a mantel, bays to the right circling an open book, are all consistent with the Bryn Mawr and the Commemorative. While the plate reproduced is a proof copy before lettering, the three books

Plate 12: Mezzotint portrait by Andrew Miller, after Francis Bindon. Reproduced by kind permission of the National Gallery of Ireland.

in Miller's engraving are Horace and Plautus with a reversed book in the middle, a standard way of showing the canon on which a writer rests (in this case almost literally). The book is opened to blank pages. The Latin epigraph—*"Istum aget pennâ metuente solvi Fama superstes"*—comes from Horace, *Odes,* 2.2.7: and may be translated "Everlasting fame with untiring wing shall guide him." Beneath the engraving is a coat of arms with the motto *"cum magnis vixissi"* (also from Horace: *Satires* 2.1.76— "I have lived with the great"). But this front-facing portrait of 1744 with its pile of books as straight and stiff as the portrait itself and its literally empty symbolism (the wreath of oak leaves surrounds nothing; the manuscript book is open to empty pages even in the lettered version) is weaker in conception than the Barbers that draw upon it. One sign of the influence of Miller: the velvety drapery of the Barbers is characteristic of mezzotint texture generally and argues against Barber's working from the lost painting itself. I would speculate that Barber first copied Bindon in his full-face pastel now at the National Gallery of Ireland and then produced the miniature version of this Bindon (dated 1739) in the collection of the Duke of Buccleuch at Bowhill. Such work is typical of miniaturists, whose standard productions include portraits by other artists copied on a small scale. Having done that, Barber realized that he could depict Swift from the life in a pose unlike those generally known and that Pond's *Mead* provided a model and participated in an appropriate iconography for honoring a writer. It is typical of an artist newly emancipated from his apprenticeship to show what he can do in the master's way, here in format (the profile portrait befitting a writer, drawn from coin and medal models) and medium (pastel). I think Barber decided in the Bryn Mawr portrait to replace Miller's full-face portrait after Bindon of 1744 with his own profile (or more accurately, near-profile—both eyes are visible) portrait of Swift.

The Bryn Mawr version, in its eighteenth-century frame, displays an oval portrait surrounded by a golden brown to yellow drapery with the head following closely the LeFanu, as does the clothing, which is simply a blue toga-like garment. Oak leaves on the left and laurels (bays) on the right partially circle the closed books, still piled neatly, and the one open to the manuscript poem. The three books are not clearly named, though with the *Drapier's Letters* highly visible on the Commemorative, the source of the "D" on one of the Bryn Mawr books becomes apparent. The poem is "The Petition of Frances Harris," probably chosen as Swift's most popular poem, unless Barber intended the Bryn Mawr portrait for one of the Lords Justices of Ireland, whom the poem comically addresses (*Poems*, 1: 68– 73).[44] It might also have some connection to Lady Elizabeth Germaine, whose father, the Chief Justice, was Frances Harris's employer and whose patronage for the Barbers is discussed above.

While I can find no direct model for the format of the lost Bindon which Miller engraved and Barber followed in the Bryn Mawr and Commemorative portraits, the elements were available. The general pattern of the portrait would evoke no surprise. In 1745 William Hogarth painted a self-portrait in a draped oval resting on three books (as does the Miller engraving of Swift) with attributes below on either side—a palette on the left, his pug on the right. And there were closer parallels for other aspects of the image: in the eighteenth century a number of author portraits, including Hogarth's engraving of Henry Fielding, contain books open and closed on a mantel beneath a portrait oval or *l'oeil-de-boeuf*. An undated engraving of Charles Churchill after the Irish artist J. H. O'Neal depicts the poet in an oval with open books to right and a closed book on the left. Earlier, an engraved oval portrait of Sir Francis Wortley (1652) has two books below on each side, closed on the left and the topmost open on the right, a format closer to the Barber portraits than the Miller.

Barber's symbolic garlands are worth more inquiry. Andrew Marvell's "The Garden" (1681) describes men's quests to "win the palm, the oak, or bays;/ And their uncessant labours see/ Crowned from some single herb or tree." Although in Barber's portraits books, not the poet, are encircled with oak and laurel, the tradition is both clear and by the eighteenth century familiar. The English laureateship as a poet's public office dates securely only to the time of Dryden, though it harkens back through William Davenant to Ben Jonson, who received a butt of sack from the king, and even to Skelton. In the Renaissance Sir Philip Sidney pondered the link between the poet and the laurel: "I think (and think I think rightly) the laurel crown appointed for triumphing captains doth worthily (of all other learnings) honour the poet's triumph." But it was hardly of recent vintage. Petrarch had crowned himself with laurel at the Capitol in Rome in 1341. Virgil established the tradition (*Eclogues* viii, 11–13), though the laurel is linked to poetry as early as Hesiod. Portraits of authors, especially poets, appeared with laurels over their heads like halos or supported by putti, surrounding their oval portraits or extended to them by Apollo. More commonly, like William Davenant, represented in the 1673 folio of his works as "Poet Laureate to two Great Kings," or Michael Drayton, with no claim to office (1613), they were crowned with laurels. The portraits mentioned above of Pope by Kneller and Richardson, who also portrayed both Milton and himself laureated, attest to the familiarity of the symbol in eighteenth-century portraiture. Pope himself in praising Addison's *Dialogues Upon the Usefulness of Medals* (1721) imagines a Temple of Fame for British worthies displaying "in fair series laurell'd Bards."[45] A double crown, however, would have been silly. Perhaps Bindon was influenced in his choice of program and Rupert Barber in following his intermediary Miller by Mary Barber's praise of Swift in "Written for my Son, and spoken by him, at a public Examination for Victors": "A Patriot Race shall sing the Drapier's Praise /And civic Crowns shall mingle with His Bays" (*Poems* 190).

The laurel encircling a book was infrequent, though it can be found in the nonportrait frontispiece to Richard Burton's *Choice Emblems, Divine and Moral* (London, 1680). I am not aware of a balanced representation of symbolic circlets of leaves around books in any portrait. The combined celebration of patriotic and artistic glory is unusual, though a closer model might turn up in an engraved frontispiece portrait of a writer of the seventeenth or eighteenth century.

The Commemorative (frontispiece), unlike the Bryn Mawr, is clearly a posthumous representation, hence my speculative date of 1745, following the death of Swift. Here, though the format is quite similar, the effect is very different. The coloring of the drapery is darker, probably in recognition of the occasion. The oval profile portrait is more idealized with Swift given hair that the other two versions show him not to have had, much as Johnson was given the abundant hair of an Irish model in Joseph Nollekens's bust. The books to the left bear two clear titles. Swift's warning against English financial depredations, the *Drapier's Letters,* surrounded by the oak leaves, now discloses more clearly than in the Bryn Mawr the association with Irish patriotism. Since Barber's father was a draper, and his mother addressed Swift several times as the "Drapier" in her poems, this book had autobiographical meaning for Barber as well. The other title is Swift's most popular book, *Gulliver's Travels.* The book whose spine we cannot see may be taken as volume two of that two-volume work. A wreath of laurels surrounds the best known passage in "Verses on the Death of Dr Swift," one of Swift's only poems that despite its excellence could not be used in a portrait of the living poet:

> Fair Liberty was all his Cry;
> [For] her he stood prepared to die
> For her he boldly stood alone
> For her he oft expos'd his own.
> Two Kingdoms just as faction led,
> Had set a Price upon his Head
> But not a Traytor could be fou[nd,]
> To sell him for Six Hund[red Pound.]
> (cf. *Poems,* 2: 566–67, ll. 347–54)

The lines continue (355–66), though progressively fewer words appear or appear legibly beneath the leaves. This writing, which contains variants from those noted by Williams, is clearly not a copy of an actual manuscript. Swift provides his own panegyrical elegy. Barber's use of it attests to the posthumous production of the Commemorative portrait. The use of this format for commemorative purposes is highly appropriate: medallion profile portraits were frequent on eighteenth-century funerary sculpture, such as Louis François Roubiliac's monuments to George Lynn, John, 2nd duke of Montagu, and Field Marshall George Wade. In this version and the Bryn Mawr, Swift is Irish laureate as well as Irish patriot.

If I am right about the dates of the known versions, Barber may have made one pastel (the LeFanu) and one miniature in 1739 or later but by 1744, another in pastel following Miller's 1744 mezzotint of Bindon but before Swift's death, then a different version in each medium after Swift's death in 1745 but before the Wilson engraving and probably close to the death. The LeFanu may well be the last portrait of Swift taken from the life, and Orrery probably for good reasons thought it a "fair likeness," in Victoria Glendinning's phrase. But the engravings of Wilson and his followers, which continued to influence readers from the mid-eighteenth century, were not. The Barber Swifts—stark, like the LeFanu, or idealized, like the Commemorative—convey a melancholy dignity different from the severe churchman of the Bindons or the witty satirist of the Jervases and deserve to be better known than the representations of Swift best known in the eighteenth century, the engravings derived from Rupert Barber's original portrait.

NOTES

I am indebted to many scholars, curators, and others, especially the late Jack Perlstein, to whose memory this essay is dedicated. Mary K. Woodworth of Bryn Mawr did the primary work on provenance and was assiduous in attempting to discover facts about the Barber portraits of Swift. A. C. Elias, Jr., is a fount of Swift and Mary Barber information. Hermann Real sent me a packet of copies of his Swift engravings. Jane MacAvock, Curator of Prints and Drawings at the National Gallery of Ireland, and her courteous colleagues were helpful in Dublin, as were Muriel McCarthy of Marsh's Library, and Desmond Fitzgerald, the Knight of Glin. I am also grateful to Brian Allen, director of the Mellon Center; Paul Caffrey; Louise Lippincott; Carol Campbell, at Bryn Mawr; Joan H. Sussler and Anna Malicka at the Lewis Walpole Library, and Kathleen M. Kemmerer. None of those mentioned above is responsible for my interpretations or any errors.

1. Victoria Glendinning, *Jonathan Swift* (London: Hutchinson, 1998), opposite 149.

2. Though dated 1752, Orrery's *Remarks* appeared in November 1751. Sir Frederick R. Falkiner, "The Portraits of Swift," *The Prose Works of Jonathan Swift,* ed. Temple Scott, 12 (London: George Bell and Sons, 1908), 52. A replacement for this account of Swift iconography is long overdue. It is outdated, faulty, and illustrated only with two modern re-engravings. That said, it was a great improvement on what came before and still worth reading. Both Pope and Johnson have been better served than Swift. Swift sometimes claimed he did not like to be painted: "I have been fool enough to sit for my Picture at full length by M[r] Bindon for my L[d] Howth" (*The Correspondence of Jonathan Swift,* ed. Harold Williams 5 vols. [Oxford: Clarendon Press, 1963], 4: 352 [16 June 1735]). For Pope, see William Kurtz Wimsatt, *The Portraits of Alexander Pope* (New Haven and London: Yale University Press, 1965). For Johnson, Herman W. Liebert, "Portraits of the Author: Lifetime Likenesses of Samuel Johnson," *English Portraits of the Seventeenth and Eighteenth Centuries* (Los Angeles: William Andrews Clark Memorial Library, 1974), 47–88, and Morris R. Brownell, *Samuel Johnson's Attitude to the Arts* (Oxford: Clarendon Press, 1989), esp. chap. 7. The recent edition of Orrery's *Remarks,* ed. João Fróes (Newark: University of Delaware Press, 2000), gives Wilson's engraving as appearing in the Millar (London) first and fourth editions and all the Faulkner (Dublin) editions except the third

(31) , which was engraved by Samuel Wheatley. The rectangular format of the Wilson in the Dublin editions suggests that it comes later than the London. The quotation below the engraving is from Pliny, whose letters Orrery also published in 1751: *"Cives aliquos virtutivus pares & habemus & habebimus, gloria neminem"* (We have had other citizens of equal virtues, but we shall have no one with such glory). In "Jackal and Lion: A Note on Orrery's 'Remarks on Swift,'" Seumas O'Sullivan gives brief consideration to the illustrations and their reception. See *The Rose and Bottle and Other Essays* (Dublin: Talbot Press, 1946).

3. Lady Orrery commented to her husband that "Millar's second Edition of *Rem. &c.* I this day received, . . . the head piece of Swift [is] very soft; who graved it? I like it better than Falkners" [*sic*]. See *The Orrery Papers,* ed. The Countess of Cork and Orrery. (London: Duckworth, 1903), 2: 275, 30 November 1751. She was unknowingly praising Ravenet over Wilson. Ravenet's looks left, the rest look right—an indication that he was following Wilson, not engraving the original portrait and that the later engravings followed Ravenet. He also engraved the third and fifth London editions.

4. See John Caspar Lavater, *Essays on Physiognomy,* trans. Henry Hudson (London, 1789–98), 1: 194 for Samuel Johnson interpreted on the basis of engravings of portraits, including the highly idealized Knole portrait by Sir Joshua Reynolds. I discuss and illustrate these engravings in "Samuel Johnson and Art," *Samuel Johnson: Pictures and Words* (Los Angeles: William Andrews Clark Memorial Library, 1984), 100–102 and figure 11.

5. Walter G. Strickland, *A Dictionary of Irish Artists* (Dublin and London: Maunsel and Company, 1913), 1: 20–23; Basil S. Long, *British Miniaturists* (London: Geoffrey Bles, 1920), 14; Daphne Foskett, *Dictionary of Miniature Painters* (London: Faber and Faber, 1972), 1: 148; *The Poems of Jonathan Swift,* ed. Harold Williams, 2nd ed. (Oxford: Clarendon Press, 1958), 2: 477 n., 486–87 n. While Williams recognizes that Rupert Barber was married to Mary Barber, the index identifies him as the painter, the probable source of this error. Irvin Ehrenpreis, recognizing that there must be a Rupert in the painter's father's generation hypothesizes an uncle by that name. See *Swift: The Man, His Works, and the Age* (London: Methuen, 1983), 3: 636. Strickland sends Rupert Barber on a second nonexistent trip to Bath by misreading one of Mary Delany's letters to a friend at Bath. See Mary Delany, *The Autobiography and Correspondence of Mary Granville, Mrs. Delany,* ed. Lady Llanover. (London: Richard Bentley, 1861), 3: 116. J. J. Foster, *A Dictionary of Painters of Miniatures,* ed. Ethel M. Foster (London: Philip Allen, 1926), gives Lucius Barber as a Swede (11), as does the National Gallery of Ireland's *Illustrated Summary Catalogue of Drawings, Watercolours and Miniatures,* comp. Adrian Le Harivel (Dublin: National Gallery of Ireland, 1983), 6.

6. A. C. Elias, Jr., "Editing Minor Writers: The Case of Laetitia Pilkington and Mary Barber," *1650–1850: Ideas Aesthetics, and Inquiries in the Early Modern Era* 3 (1997): 145 n. See also his edition of *Memoirs of Laetitia Pilkington* (Athens and London: University of Georgia Press, 1997). Although Mary Barber's birth is always given as 1690, Elias, pointing to the first recorded child in October 1705, casts some doubt on the date. She died 14 July 1755. My information on the children's dates of birth and the family's early whereabouts also comes from Elias. For Mary Barber's poems, the only readily available modern edition is *The Poetry of Mary Barber 1690–1757,* ed. Bernard Tucker (Lewiston, N.Y.: Edwin Mellen Press, 1992), though it cannot always be counted upon for accuracy, as with the death date in the title. I quote her *Poems on Several Occasions* (London, 1735).

7. The phrase comes from *"A True TALE"* (Barber *Poems*). Con is the only child named in Mary Barber's poetry. The file on Constantine in the College of Physicians contains some useful information about him, but not about his parents or siblings.

8. This is probably the signed miniature enamel of "Mary Granville" illustrated by Basil Long (fig. 62) and owned by Lord Treoven.

9. See *The Works of Horatio Walpole, Earl of Orford* (London: 1798), 3: 496. Actually, the newspaper item on which Walpole relies (at the Lewis Walpole Library in his "Book of Materials") spells the name correctly, gives the date as 31 October 1767, and calls him only a miniaturist.

10. Harold Williams thinks it may be the work of Thomas Sheridan (Swift, *Poems,* 2: 487). Turning Delany's dependent into the author is one of the actual author's jokes.

11. For Mary Barber's poem, see *Poems,* 71.

12. An advertisement in the (London) *Daily Courant* dated 19 December 1734 states that Rupert Barber will deliver copies to subscribers at Pond's Covent Garden house as of 1 March. The notice appeared in the issue for 17 January 1735. See George P. Mayhew, *Rage or Raillery: The Swift Manuscripts at the Huntington Library* (San Marino, Ca: The Huntington Library, 1967), 110 n.

13. See Louise Lippincott, *Selling Art in Georgian London: The Rise of Arthur Pond* (New Haven: Yale University Press, 1983), 45, 95. The portrait of Mary Barber may well be that in Dr. Richard Mead's collection, sold in 1754. See n. 35 below for the *Catalogue.*

14. *A Catalogue of Books Belonging to Dr. Jonathan Swift* (Cambridge: Cambridge University Library, 1988), opposite title page.

15. "Arthur Pond's Journal of Receipts and Expenses, 1734–1740," ed. Louise Lippincott, *The Walpole Society* 54 (1988): 220–333. Pond lists prints bought by Mary Barber (17 July 1735; £1/1). Rupert Barber buys a set of prints for £1/1 on 14 December 1735, borrows £2/2 on 9 September 1736, another £2 on 2 December 1736, £1/1 on 20 December 1738, which he repays on 26 February 1739. Barber incurs a charge of £1 for "shooting" and something illegible on 7 December 1739. But he was probably in Ireland on 31 May 1745 when Pond marks his receipt of £2/17 which he "had dispurst" for "Mr Rupert Barber," along with £4/8 for prints (Pond, 269).

16. Ellis Waterhouse, *Painting in Britain 1530–1790* (Harmondsworth: Penguin Books, 1978), 334.

17. Daphne Foskett, *British Portrait Miniatures* (London: Spring Books, 1968), 95.

18. Patrick J. Noon, "Miniatures on the Market," in John Murdoch et al., *The English Miniature* (New Haven and London: Yale University Press, 1981), 170.

19. See Paul Caffrey's Catalogue *John Comerford and the Portrait Miniature in Ireland, c. 1620–1850* (Dublin: Kilkenny Archaeological Society, 1999), 20 and color plate 10.

20. Anne Crookshank and the Knight of Glin, *The Painters of Ireland c. 1660–1920* (London: Barrie & Jenkins, 1979), 71.

21. *Dublin Journal,* 8–12 November 1743, p. [2].

22. Note to Mary Barber's letter to Swift from Bath, *Works of Jonathan Swift* (Dublin, 1767), 16: 135 n.

23. Anthony Pasquin [pseudonym of John Williams], *An Authentick History of the Professors of Painting, Sculpture & Architecture Who Have Practised in Ireland* (London, [1797]), 23.

24. See her letter of 25 November 1731: "Mrs. Barber is still in England, she has not yet published her works; I wish she may not spend more money in pursuing this affair than the subscription will answer" (Delany, 1: 319). Mary Barber had been in England from 1730. Both she and Mary Pendarves subscribed to Matthew Pilkington's *Poems on Several Occasions* (1730). See Ehrenpreis, 3: 686.

25. Sotheby's *Sale Catalogue: Portrait Miniatures,* 28 October 1974, #15. This cannot be, as we will see later, the copy of the miniature I illustrate.

26. Quoted by Christopher White in Christopher White, David Alexander and Ellen D'Oench, *Rembrandt in Eighteenth Century England* (New Haven: Yale Center for British Art, 1983), 22

27. Quoted by Lippincott, 90 from George Vertue, Ms. Notebooks, *Walpole Society* 22

(1934), 3: 125–26. Mead disliked Pond's etched portrait of him, though Orrery bought a painted version in 1744, and Mead himself capitulated and bought one likewise in 1746.

28. See David Piper, *The Image of the Poet: British Poets and their Portraits* (Clarendon Press: Oxford, 1982), 63, 75 and plate 80. Cf. Wimsatt, 217–19 (fig. 54), attributed to Richardson. See also Section VII, "Coins and Medals," in Desmond Shawe-Taylor's catalogue *Genial Company: The Theme of Genius in Eighteenth-Century Portraiture* (Nottingham: Nottingham University Art Gallery, 1987), 53–65.

29. Jonathan Richardson, *An Essay on the Theory of Painting* (London, 1725), 209.

30. An engraved profile portrait by William Hoare of Warburton, wigless and wearing a robe-like garment, appears as the frontispiece to the fifth volume of Warburton's edition of Pope (1769).

31. See Chauncey Brewster Tinker, *The Wedgwood Medallion of Samuel Johnson* (Cambridge: Harvard University Press, 1926), frontispiece.

32. The Renaissance also displayed an interest in profile portraits of authors more generally, as for example Marco Zoppa's laureated *Head of a Poet,* reworked very early in the sixteenth-century by Peter Paul Rubens (c. 1432–c. 1478; now at the National Gallery of Victoria, Melbourne).

33. *Dublin Journal,* 19–23 November 1751, quoted in *Prince of Dublin Printers: The Letters of George Faulkner,* ed. Robert E. Ward (Lexington: University Press of Kentucky, 1972), 40 n. Wilson's name is misspelled in the advertisement.

34. William LeFanu traced it back to his ancestor Alicia Sheridan who married Joseph LeFanu in 1781, and he believed she had it from her father, Thomas Sheridan the younger, Swift's biographer and godson. LeFanu thought that Sheridan in turn had it from his father or by way of Dr. Mead. A copy of his "Notes" was sent me by the family of William LeFanu.

35. *A Catalogue of Pictures . . . of the Late Richard Mead, M. D.* (London, 1754), vi.

36. Details of the Bryn Mawr provenance come from the Woodworth mss. and correspondence, Mariam Coffin Canaday Library, Bryn Mawr College. When the brass plaque was placed on the elaborate original frame is not known. It was typical of Barber's master Arthur Pond to use the best gold frames for his pastels, taking a loss on their cost but undoubtedly contributing to their sale as well as their appearance (Lippincott, 81). Such original frames on both the Bryn Mawr and the Commemorative versions suggest that Barber understood the necessity.

37. Both the Knight of Glin and Jacob Simon of the National Portrait Gallery (London) have informed me that they also find the attribution to Russell unconvincing.

38. Two miniatures of Swift by Barber were known to exist in the 1970s; the one discussed earlier of which I am aware, but cannot locate (Plate 7), is like the Commemorative. Frustratingly, it appears to be signed. The "p^t" for pinxit is fairly clear and what may be part of the B in Barber. The other (or another) miniature, listed as in the Charlemont inventory, dated 1739. See Sotheby's, #15. James Caulfeild, 1st Earl of Charlemont (b. 1728), was a likely early owner of Barber's work. Though he was too young to know Swift, Mary Delany mentions him as a patient of Dr. Constantine Barber in 1756 (3: 455). See n. 39, below.

39. For the miniature, see H. A. Kennedy, *Early English Portrait Miniatures in the Collection of the Duke of Buccleuch,* ed. Charles Holme (London, Paris, New York: "The Studio," 1917), 42. For details, including the inscription and date on the reverse "F. Bindon, 1739," and the size (¾-inch oval), as well as a description of the subject as "almost full face, wearing ecclesiastical dress," I am indebted to the Duke of Buccleuch and his staff. This enamel portrait, listed by Kennedy as "Perhaps by Rupert Barber," is "Catalogued as by F. Bindon, but more probably after a painting by him." The possibility exists that the inscription of the date refers only to the date of Bindon's original. This miniature may be

that listed as Charlemont's in n. 38, above At the wide-ranging Exhibition "Fair Liberty! Was All His Cry: Jonathan Swift and His Contemporaries" mounted by Bruce Arnold at the National Library of Ireland (July 1999), an oil painting of Swift in a private collection was identified as by Barber, but the modern inscription on the rear draws on the passage in Falkiner, and the painting has no resemblance to Barber's work.

40. For a poetic commentary on this portrait, see William Dunkin, "An Epistle to R——b——t N——g——t, Esq. with a Picture of Doctor Swift" in *Select Poetical Works of the Late William Dunkin, D.D.* (Dublin, 1769), 2: 169–74. It includes a description of Swift as but "a shadow of the Dean."

41. See *Illustrated Summary Catalogue of Paintings,* comp. Adrian Le Harivel and Michael Wynne (Dublin: National Gallery of Ireland, 1981), no. 4069, p. 251.

42. See Glendinning's illustration, opposite 149. The attribution is uncertain. Arthur S. Marks suggests in a forthcoming essay on Barber in *Swift Studies* that this drawing relates to a painting of John Rudge. I am grateful to Professor Marks sending me for a rough draft of his essay after the Dublin Congress.

43. T. G. Wilson, "A Hitherto Undescribed Death-Mask of Dean Swift," *Journal of the Royal Society of Antiquaries of Ireland* 81 (1951): 107–14 and "Swift's Death-Masks," *Review of English Literature* 3 (1962): 39–58.

44. "To Their Excellencies the Lords Justices of Ireland. The Humble Petition of Frances Harris, Who Must Starve, and Die a Maid If It Miscarries" (1701). Ehrenpreis says, "Perhaps no poem by him has been more often reprinted" (2: 32).

45. Marvell, "The Garden," in *The Complete Poems,* ed. Elizabeth Story Donno (Middlesex: Penguin Books, 1996), 100, lines 2–4. Sidney, *An Apology for Poetry,* ed. Geoffrey Shepherd (Manchester: Manchester University Press, 1973), 120. Pope, "To Mr. Addison, Occasioned by his Dialogue on Medals," *Minor Poems,* ed. Norman Ault and John Butt, *The Twickenham Edition of the Poems of Alexander Pope* (London: Methuen, 1964), 6: 204, line 61. For the laurel, see J. B. Trapp, "The Owl's Ivy and the Poet's Bays, an Inquiry into Poetic Garlands," *Journal of the Warburg and Courtauld Institutes,* 21 (1958): 227–55, and Robert J. Clements, *Picta Poesis: Literary and Humanistic Theory in Renaissance Emblem Books* (Roma: Edizione di Storia e Letteratura, 1960), especially 34–36, 42–45.

Swift's Mythopoeic Authority

Ann Cline Kelly

JONATHAN SWIFT, EVEN BEFORE HIS DEATH, WAS A LEGENDARY OR mythic figure, and through the nineteenth and twentieth centuries, his was a name to conjure with. Swift's larger-than-life presence gives him a massive authority, which is enlisted to support a variety of arguments. Paradoxically, Swift's authority as a myth grew out of his lack of authority as a writer. Typically Swiftian works present uncertain ironies that make their points of view ambiguous or suspect and contain elements completely antithetical to one another, so that the point is in doubt. The print-constructed "Swift" (signaled with quotation marks) implied by such works is amphibious, inconsistent, and freakishly unpredictable. Both Swift himself and others create "Swifts" with these qualities. Because of Swift's fragmentary and contradictory statements, as well as his penchant for never explaining himself, fundamental questions about the man are still unanswered. Were his allegiances to England or Ireland? Was he ever married? Was he frigid or libidinous? What was the nature of his religious belief? Was he a Jacobite? How far did his sympathy with the underclass extend? The diversity of answers to each of these questions reinforces the confusion surrounding Swift. Because neither Swift's writings nor historical records illuminate clearly who Swift was and what he stood for, the myth of Swift develops without the constraint of authoritative evidence—indeed, it develops *because* of the lack of authoritative evidence.[1]

Swift's lack of authority is epitomized in the fact that all but a handful of his works are published anonymously or pseudonymously. Swift is not responsible for his utterances—nobody is or somebody else is. The relation between Swift and his mouthpieces is impossible to determine. To what degree does Swift share the sentiments of the *Tale*-teller, Bickerstaff, Gulliver, Cadenus, the Church-of-England man? Because Swift's works seldom bear his name, and many other writers borrow it, the Swiftian canon is notoriously uncertain. While there is documentation (mostly from his letters) to establish Swift's authorship of many pieces attributed to him, many others are in dispute. And Swift cannot be counted on to tell the truth. For example, although Swift took out advertisements to inform the world that "The Life and Genuine Character of Doctor Swift" was spurious, a large number of scholars do not believe him.[2]

Swift's Whig enemies, enraged over the derailment of their agenda caused by the *Conduct of the Allies* and other Tory tracts, belittled Swift as a hack, buffoon, and machiavel, in other words, as someone whose claims to authority should not be accepted. Instead of countering those images, Swift wrote a number of poems containing a namesake character, "Swift," who embodies the vices the Whigs ascribe to him. In 1713, for example, after the Whigs lambasted him for his appointment to the Deanery of St. Patrick's, seemingly in reward for his service to Harley as unofficial minister of propaganda, Swift published an epistle to Harley that reinforces their suspicions. In the poem, an imitation of an Horatian epistle, Swift characterizes "Swift" as a Grubstreet writer, who receives a surprise invitation to dinner from Harley. In response to the invitation, Swift's "Swift" stupidly stammers, unable to complete a sentence. After their friendship evolves, Harley names Swift as Dean. The poem offers no justification for this action. Once installed as Dean, Swift loses control over his financial situation and blames others for his failures:

> (The wicked laity's contriving,
> To hinder clergymen from thriving),
> Now all the Doctor's money's spent,
> His tenants wrong him in his rent;
> The farmers, spitefully combined,
> Force him to take his tithes in kind. . . .
>
> ("Horace, Epistle 7.1, Imitated and
> Addressed to the Earl of Oxford" 105–10)

Abandoning his responsibilities in Dublin, Swift's "Swift" shows up at Harley's gate, asking to be relieved of the deanship unless Harley gives him money to cover his expenses. The epistle to Harley confirms what Swift's Whig enemies had been saying all along: he was not worthy of preferment, and the only reason he got it was because of his friendship with Harley. Worse still, the poem makes Swift look like an extortionist. Journalist Abel Boyer snorts, "Who else should be so *hardy* as to offer such balderdash to a *prime minister?*"[3] Instead of using the epistle to Harley to establish his probity and his dignity, Swift does the opposite, annexing new scandals to his name.

In 1722, Swift presents an extended portrait of himself in "Journal of a Part of a Summer," in which he describes his visit to his friends the Rochforts in Gaulstown. How this poem got into print is a mystery, but Swift's enemies believed (I think correctly) that he himself was responsible. In the poem, the "Swift" character passes his days reading, playing backgammon, drinking, and fishing. The most eventful episode in the long visit is his falling out of a boat. Throughout, Swift depicts himself as passive and foolish, in need of Mrs. Rochfort to organize his life. That such a man could be considered an authority on anything is patently ridiculous. Similar depictions occur in the Market Hill poems. In "The Grand Question Debated," primarily narrated by Lady Acheson's maid, Swift characterizes himself as a scruffy cleric who cuts no figure at all—"For the Dean was so shabby and looked like a ninny,/That the Captain supposed he was curate to Jenny." The Dean is silenced by the Captain: "he durst not so much as once open his lips,/ And, the Doctor was plaguily down in the hyps" (153–54, 177–78). In "A Panegyric on the Dean," also narrated by Lady Acheson, Swift creates a "Swift" with the skills of a butler, farmhand, or cookmaid. He shows himself a whiz at making butter, but his real triumph is his construction of "his and her" outhouses. In a mock heroic address, Lady Acheson commends him—"you have raised your generous mind/To works of [an] exalted kind" (297–98). These publications raised questions about Swift's character—not only did he represent himself without the dignity that a man in his station should assume, he also seemed to be humiliating his friends by holding them up to public ridicule.

"The Life and Genuine Character of Dr. Swift" shows the mixed opinions about Swift's eminence as a writer in a debate between two friends, one pro-Swift, one anti-Swift. The pro-Swift argument is brief and abstract, while the anti-Swift argument is long and detailed. Few claims are made for Swift's authority as a writer or a moralist, and those are contested. "Tis owned he was a man of wit" is answered by "Yet many a foolish thing he writ"; "He was an honest man, I'll swear" is answered by "Why sir, I differ from you there" (73–74, 80–81). In his final self-portrayal, "Verses on the Death of Dr. Swift," Swift also suggests that most people think of him as marginal and ephemeral. In the much debated conclusion of the poem, Swift may or may not be justifying himself and seeking to command respect through the narration of an "impartial" speaker, who links him with elevated principles like liberty, truth, and justice. The image of Swift as a champion of high principles, though, is undermined by other elements in the poem itself as well as by Swift's celebrity as the author of a *Tale of a Tub,* the Bickerstaff papers, "Mrs. Harris' Petition." That celebrity sank his bids for positions of authority—director of an English Academy, Historiographer Royal, or an Anglican Bishop—which were met with hoots of derision.

The mystery of who Swift really was created a market for libels masquerading as true confessions. In a Whig-authored pseudo diary, "Swift" says, "When I studied Astrology . . . and was Isaac Bickerstaff (for I must own that I have gone through as many Changes as my Splendid Shilling, and hope that I have many more to go through yet), I calculated my own

Nativity [astrological prediction of life]. . . . I must be a whore, if a Woman; a P[arso]n, if a Man; but was irreversibly determin'd to be . . . the Reverend Dr. S——t; a Boy, a Collegian, a P—n, a Poet, a Politician, and a Lover." In another diary, the Whig "Swift" puppet lists his professions as "Rector, Vicar, Dean, Author, Translator, and Scribler, and many other things" and elsewhere in similar texts confides that "[Though my] three Characters of Clergyman, Critick, and Examiner, may seem inconsistent . . . I can easily reconcile them."[4] *An Answer to the Proposal for the Universal Use of Irish Manufactures* (1720) illustrates the confusion of Swift's multiple print-constructed identities. It is a strange production in which a right-thinking English "Swift" denounces a subversive Irish-leaning "Swift." The English "Swift" accuses the Irish "Swift" of being a satanic master of shifts and disguises, an "evil Genius," the "Serpent"— "sometimes he is a Priest, sometimes a Philosopher, and at other times a Tradesman; but for the most part, a Ballad-Maker, a Punster, and a Merry-Andrew."[5] During Swift's lifetime, this latter identity prevails, making the name "Swift" synonymous with contradiction, subversive irony, and underclass values—not magisterial authority.

Can we point to some works where Swift seriously presents himself or his persona as an authority? The *Battle of the Books,* though ostensibly a support of Sir William Temple's view that the Ancients were in all ways superior to the Moderns, undercuts its own thesis and ends in midair. The *Project for the Advancement of Religion* outlines policies to encourage devout behavior, but unsettling statements intrude to make readers wonder whether Swift is really advocating hypocrisy.[6] A magisterial tone dominates the *Proposal for Correcting, Improving and Ascertaining the English Tongue,* but as critics both in Swift's time and our own have pointed out, Swift fails to abide by the linguistic strictures he lays down and booby traps the proposal with political subtexts.[7] As Mr. Examiner, Swift argues seriously against the Whig agenda, and as a Church of England man, argues seriously for the maintenance of the Test Act. The authority of these arguments, however, is deconstructed by Swift's reputation as the author of *A Tale of a Tub,* which is dedicated to a prominent Whig (Lord Somers) and seems to mock the Established Church, perhaps even Christianity itself. In the 1720s and 1730s, Swift—sailing under the flags of both the Dean and the Drapier—assumed the pose of an expert in economics, who insists that the English exploitation of Ireland is not only inhumane but unprofitable. But these pro-Irish positions are called into question by Swift's extremely negative references to Ireland and to the Irish. While some read these references as ironic, others take them literally. Swift is the master of mixed assertions and double voicing. As Mikhail Bakhtin emphasizes, the voice of authority is monologic, not heteroglossic like Swift's.[8]

During Swift's life, "Swift" seemed to stand for little besides inconsistency, scandal, and mystery—a combination of elements that made him a very popular topic and stimulated a constant stream of publications. The print-projected "Swift" took on a life of its own—or more accurately *lives* of its own. Mythopoesis begins in earnest after Swift's death in 1745 and develops in various generic patterns that each create a different "Swift." There is a romance "Swift" entangled with several women simultaneously; a tragic "Swift," whose lack of Christian faith and overweening ambition make him mad and morbid; a comic "Swift," whose antics recall the trickster characters of the fabliaux; and finally, an epic "Swift," who embodies a variety of noble abstractions. Multiplicity is a hallmark of mythologized figures and adds to their preternatural aura. They are not knowable in ordinary terms and defy existing categories. In *Joan of Arc: The Image of Female Heroism,* for instance, Marina Warner itemizes Joan's various manifestations in chapter headings: Prophet, Harlot of Armagnacs, Heretic, Ideal Androgyne, Knight, Amazon, Personification of Virtue, Child of Nature, Saint, Patriot.[9] As Roland Barthes notes in *Mythologies,* "the knowledge contained in a mythical concept is confused, made of yielding, shapeless associations. One must firmly stress this open character of the concept; it is not at all an abstract, purified essence; it is a formless, unstable, nebulous condensation." Barthes adds that the bizarre contradictions of the mythologized figure and its persistence in cultural discourse put it on another plane, above and beyond the quotidian, and in doing so, translate it into a generalized signifer of transcendence, available for appropriation.[10] Paradoxically, then, a lack of authority gives rise to the mythic character, which then functions as the epitome of authority because of its monumental cultural presence.

Such is the case with Swift. During his lifetime, Swift was ridiculed as a buffoon, an atheist, a timeserver, a barbarian, an opportunist—identities that made his name buzz in people's ears and created a market for gossip about him. After his death, the continued fascination with Swift stimulated mythopoesis that kept his name in circulation. Swift became famous for being famous. His fame eclipses the particular scandals that had brought him to prominence in the first place and endows him with mythic authority. As Barthes explains, in myth, "meaning leaves its contingency behind; it empties itself, it becomes impoverished, history evaporates, only the letter remains" (117). The provocative ambiguities of Swift encourage the assignment of different significations to the "letter" representing him. His works are interpreted in a variety of ways; his life is embellished with fictions premised on divergent views of his nature. When Swift is represented as an authority, he is usually separated from the lurid lore of his personal history and appears as a disembodied icon of Virtue, Truth, or Wisdom. His words are often wrenched out of context or new words are put in his mouth that better suit the purpose. As Barthes notes, "Myth is a *value,* truth is no guarantee for it" (123). Fictionalizing is another term for mythopoesis.

In that light, perhaps it is possible to understand how Swift, mythologized on the one hand as the cruel lover of multiple women or a husband who refuses openly to claim his wife, on the other hand, can be cited as an authority on courtship and marriage. In the mid-eighteenth century, Samuel Richardson's Pamela denounces Swift's *Letter to a Very Young Woman on her Marriage* as a text that "must disgust, instead of instructing." Richardson's Clarissa believes that Swift was not for those with a "pure eye" or a "pure ear."[11] By the late century, though, Swift's *Letter* began to be reprinted in collections of essays designed for young ladies. *The Lady's Pocket Library* (Philadelphia, 1792) lists Swift's letter in the following company: "Miss [Hannah] More's Essays, Dr. Gregory's Legacy to his Daughters, Lady Pennington's Unfortunate Mother's Advice, Marchioness of Lambert's Advice of a mother to her daughter, Mrs. Chapone's Letter on the Government of the Temper."[12] Placing Swift among these writers of courtesy literature addressed to women effaces his identity as a misogynist.

In another surprising turnabout, despite the doubts of the Archbishop of York and many others that Swift was a Christian, he subsequently is mythologized as religious authority and exemplar. In a pamphlet published by the Religious Tract Society, for example, Swift is characterized in an heroic way as a Christian soldier: "When Dr. Swift was arguing one day with great coolness, with a gentleman who had become exceedingly warm in the dispute, one of the company asked him how he could keep his temper so well. 'The reason is,' replied the dean, 'I have truth on my side.'"[13] Here words are put in "Swift's" mouth to epitomize his moral leadership. In a similar way, ventriloquism is used in a fake autobiography published shortly after Swift's death to show his religious devotion. In it he apologizes for his offensive writings, saying "GOD alone knows my heart . . . to HIM I appeal for all my thoughts."[14] In 1775, one of Swift's sermons is included in a collection called *The Family Chaplain,* and in 1814, he is one of the featured authors in *The Churchman Armed Against the Errors of the Time* published by the Society for the Distribution of Tracts in Defence of the United Church of England and Ireland.[15] Miraculously, too, a lost manuscript containing an "Evening Prayer" is found in the nineteenth century. (It appears both in the editions of the collected works published by Sir Walter Scott and Thomas Roscoe.) This bogus prayer is unlike anything Swift ever wrote. Cited by some biographers as evidence of Swift's hidden faith, the prayer invokes Christ's mercy and the hope of resurrection. Swift—known for his godlessness during his lifetime—is rehabilitated, mostly by fellow Anglicans, as a true believer.

In another posthumous twist of fate, Swift's writings become the gold standard of English prose, a contrast to a general view during his lifetime that he specialized as an author in sensationalism and vulgarity. When Swift put his name forth as the possible director of an English academy, for instance, John Oldmixon quotes blasphemous swearing from *A Tale of a Tub* and homey dialect from "Mrs. Harris's Petition" to show how preposterous it is that Swift act as a "Refiner of our Tongue."[16] After Swift's death, though, critics and scholars reevaluate Swift as a writer. Ignoring works containing billingsgate, scatology, or colloquialisms (meaning most of Swift's output), they mythologize Swift as a master stylist. In a *Short Introduction to English Grammar* (1762), Robert Lowth pronounces Swift to be "one of the most correct, and perhaps our very best prose writer." In *Lectures on Rhetoric and Belles Lettres* (1783), Hugh Blair makes Swift the "standard of the strictest Purity and Propriety" in English prose and uses excerpts from Swift's writings throughout his text as examples of perfection.[17]

Swift's larger-than-life legends and his indeterminate political principles have encouraged a variety of ideologues to construct him as a founding father or prominent proponent of their causes. He has been hailed by both conservatives and liberals, capitalists and Marxists. Ireland, in particular, has been fertile but contentious ground for Swiftian mythopoesis. During the Time of Troubles in Ireland and its aftermath, Swift was defined in radically different ways, depending on which camp did the defining. Faced with the prospect of exclusion by a Catholic majority who had won their political rights, some Protestants, particularly W. B. Yeats, install Swift as one of the governing gods of a "national mythology" that embraces and equally empowers both colonial Protestant and native Catholic.[18] Other Protestant writers of the time acknowledge Swift's negative remarks about Catholics and Presbyterians, but emphasize his authority as a founding father of Irish nationalism by citing his hatred of the Ascendancy absentee landlords and his desire to uplift all Irish, including the Catholic majority, who, they said, looked upon him as a savior. P. S. O'Hegarty, for instance, argues that although Swift was a Church-of-Ireland man, his desire for Irish independence inspired both Catholic and Protestant leaders, "not only Flood and Grattan but every Irish leader after them down to Arthur Griffith. That public opinion that he so magnificently called into being . . . was the same public opinion which O'Connell recreated."[19] These writers often point to the Jack and the Dane [Dean Swift] stories in Irish to argue that Swift was part of native folk culture.

Militant Catholic nationalists would have none of this line of reasoning and reject Swift's authority to speak for the Irish nation. Daniel Corkery, in "Ourselves and Dean Swift," declares that the idea that Swift could have sympathy for the Catholics of Ireland "is just about as wrong as an idea can be," for he hated and despised them. Of Swift's presence in the "Jack and the Dane" tradition, Corkery sarcastically notes that "It is true we come on stories about the Dean in the Gaeltacht, comic and scurrilous stories only . . . they still bear the marks of having been translated from the English." At the same time, Corkery decries how the Anglo-Irish have spread the myth that native Irish "wish [Swift] a God of their Gaelic Olympus and even imagine that he was secretly of their faith. So are 'correct' ideas of Irish history spread abroad in the world."[20] In the *Catholic Bulletin,* Dermot Curtin, argues that the glorification of "Swift"—whom he calls "the enemy" throughout the essay—is another Ascendancy tactic to enslave the natives. Curtin urges real Irishmen to turn their backs on Swift and his Anglo-Irish boosters for "these men detest the whole heart of our national and spiritual being: they seek to impose themselves on it as its overlords and judges."[21] The intense polemics of the early century have subsided into moderation, but "Swift" is still being called upon to drive political points home.[22]

Swift's political authority is also in demand outside of Ireland. Last year I was called up by an administrative assistant for a conservative Republican senator, who was sure that Swift had said something about the moral bankruptcy of social programs for the poor. Could I find the reference, so that the senator could use it to add gravitas to a budget-cutting speech to Congress? I was horrified that the "Swift" I imagined as a friend of the poor and downtrodden might be enlisted as an advocate of ideas opposed to their interests, but the incident reminded me that we each mythologize Swift in different ways. Swift's capacity to carry wildly varying valences has given him life everlasting as a protean abstraction, which translates, paradoxically, into concrete cultural authority.

NOTES

1. This paper summarizes part of an argument I make in my book, *Jonathan Swift and Popular Culture: Myth, Media, and the Man* (New York: Palgrave, 2002).

2. See *Jonathan Swift: The Complete Poems,* ed. Pat Rogers (New Haven and London: Oxford University Press, 1983), 844–45. In his endnote annotations to the poem, Rogers summarizes the welter of conflicting theories about this poem's authorship. For new perspective on the poem, see Stephen Karian's essay elsewhere in this volume. My citations of Swift's poems are from Rogers's edition, with line numbers indicated parenthetically in the text.

3. Abel Boyer, *The Political State of Great Britain* (London, 1713), qtd. Ehrenpreis, 2: 677.

4. *A Hue and Cry After Dean S——t; Occasion'd by a True and Exact Copy of Part of his own Diary* (London, 1714), 14; *Dr. S——'s Real Diary; Being a True and Faithful Account of Himself* (London, 1715), A3r.; [Thomas Burnet], *Essays Divine, Moral and Political . . . Collected from the Works of J. S——t, D— of St. P——k, and author of the Tale of a Tubb* (London, 1715), iv.

5. *A Defence of English Commodities. Being an Answer to the Proposal for the Universal Use of Irish Manufactures . . . Written by Dean Swift* (London, 1720), in *The Prose Works of Jonathan Swift,* ed. Herbert Davis, 14 vols. (Oxford: Blackwell, 1939–62) (Appendix A), 9:268.

6. A debate on this issue in recent times was instigated by Leland Peterson's "Swift's *Project:* A Religious and Political Satire," *PMLA,* 82 (1967), 54–63. Entering the fray were Donald Greene, Phllip Harth, and Jan R. Van Meter.

7. In *Swift and the English Language* (Philadelphia: University of Pennsylvania Press, 1988), I treat arguments about the seriousness of Swift's proposal in Chapter 6, "How Possible to Improve Discourse: The Proposal for an Academy," 89–119.

8. See *The Dialogic Imagination: Four Essays,* ed. Michael Holquist, trans. Caryl Emerson and Michael Holquist (Austin: University of Texas Press, 1981; rpt. 1987).

9. Marina Warner, *Joan of Arc: The Image of Female Heroism* (New York: Knopf, 1981).

10. Roland Barthes, *Mythologies,* trans. Annette Lavers (New York: Hill and Wang, 1972; rpt. 1995), 119ff. Further page references to Barthes will be included parenthetically in the text.

11. "Samuel Richardson on Swift," in *Swift: The Critical Heritage,* ed. Kathleen Williams (London: Routledge and Kegan Paul, 1970), 103–4.

12. This is item #1619 in the *Bibliography of the Writings of Jonathan Swift,* ed. Herman Teerink; revised and corrected by Arthur H. Scouten (Philadelphia: University of Pennsylvania Press, 1963). The bibliography lists eight reprints of Swift's "Letter to a Young Lady," all of them in the late eighteenth century, 380–82.

13. "Moral and Christian Duties," in *Anecdotes. Miscellaneous* (London: The Religious Tract Society, 1840).

14. *A Funeral Elegy on the Father of His Country, the Rev. Dr. Jonathan Swift* (broadside) (Dublin, 1745).

15. *The Family Chaplain: Being a Complete Course of Sermons Upon the Festivals and Fasts . . . as Prescribed by the Book of Common Prayer* (London, 1775); *The Churchman Armed Against the Errors of the Time* (London: 1814).

16. John Oldmixon, *Reflections on Dr. Swift's Letter to Harley* (1712) in *Poetry and Language,* ed. Louis Landa, Series 6; number 1 (Ann Arbor, Mich.: Augustan Reprint Society, 1948), A3r–A3v.

17. Robert Lowth, "Preface," *A Short Introduction to English Grammar* (London, 1762; rpt. Menston, England: Scolar Press, 1967), ii; Hugh Blair, *Lectures on Rhetoric and Belles Lettres,* 2 vols. (London, 1783); rpt. Harold Harding, ed. (Carbondale and Edwardsville: Southern Illinois Press, 1965), 188.

18. William Butler Yeats, "Introduction to *Words on the Window-Pane* (1934) in *Fair Liberty was all his Cry: A Tercentenary Tribute to Jonathan Swift,* ed. A. Norman Jeffares (New York: St. Martin's Press, 1967), 186–87.

19. P. S. O'Hegarty, "Jonathan Swift: Irishman," *The Bell* 10 (September 1945): 487.

20. Daniel Corkery, "Ourselves and Dean Swift: *Lives* by Stephen Gwynn" [review] *Studies* 18 (1934): 215, 215n.

21. Dermot Curtin, "Our Gaelic Democracy: Teaching the Lessons of Its History (with special reference to Swift)," *Catholic Bulletin* 23 (July 1933): 592.

22. For a history of the appropriation of Swift as an authority by various Irish factions, see Robert Mahony, *Jonathan Swift: The Irish Identity* (New Haven: Yale University Press, 1995).

Hints Toward Authoritative Conversation: Swift's Dialogical Strategies in the Letters and the Life

Brian A. Connery

> Speech is commonly judged the truest character of the mind, the surest test of inward worth, as that which discloseth the *hidden man of the heart,* which unlocketh the closets of the breast, which draws the soul out of her dark recesses, into the open light and view, which rendereth our thoughts visible, and our intentions palpable. Hence, *loquere, ut te videam,* Speak, that I may see you, or know what kind of man you are, is a saying which all men, at first meeting, do in their heart direct to one another.
>
> —Isaac Barrow

SWIFT HAD NO BOSWELL. CONSEQUENTLY, THOUGH CONVERSATION'S importance to him is abundantly clear, the bulk of Swift's conversation, unlike Johnson's, is lost to us. Conversation was regarded in the early eighteenth century as the medium par excellence for combining reason and sociability and so improving one's understanding. Swift's project, off and on for some thirty-odd years, of compiling material for *A Compleat Collection of Genteel and Ingenious Conversation,* as well as his composition of *Hints towards an Essay on Conversation,* bespeaks a valuing of conversation extraordinary even within his talk-loving culture.[1] His remarks on the proprieties and improprieties of conversation suggest the thoroughness with which he had considered the subject, indicate a high degree of self-consciousness in conversation, and might be taken to imply that he considered himself a fine conversationalist. In his correspondence from Ireland to his friends in England in the 1720s, Swift frequently laments their inaccessibility specifically for conversation, and, in their replies, Swift's conversation not infrequently serves synecdochally as a substitution for Swift himself, the object of his friends' longing. John Arbuthnot, for instance, writes in 1714, "I am sure I never can forgett yow, till I meett with, (what is impossible) another whose conversation I can so much delight in as Dr. Swifts & yet that is the smallest thing I ought to value you

159

for."[2] Yet though we have Swift's "remarks" aplenty, we have no records specifically of his conversation.

This essay surveys Swift's early biographers, several of his own published works, and his correspondence in order to develop a sense of his conversational principles and habits.[3] As will become clear, the extant material is filled with gaps, suppressions, holes, and absences, such that we can only exclaim, with the Tale-teller's editor, "*Hic multa desideruntur.*" These gaps and absences, however, like those in his published works, may be regarded as purposeful and strategic; that is, his own remarks on conversation and his practice, as reported by himself and others, suggest both social and rhetorical principles that, if followed, would result in those gaps and absences. Like those in his writing, these gaps may be read as distinctively Swiftian.

Swift recommends, in his writing about conversation, the suppression of various manifestations of the self in the interest of the collective construction of conversation. Self-seeking, self-assertion, self-promotion—and the various kinds of conversational performance that overtly enact these—are represented as counter to conversation's ends of mutual edification, entertainment, and sociability. "Politeness" becomes purposeful not in its favorable reflection upon the polite speaker (as numerous contemporary guides to conversation suggested) but in its support and furthering of conversation's goals. Indeed, both Swift's practice and his writings suggest that politeness in conversation is frequently constituted by *not* speaking.

Rather than a negative nonaction, not speaking is potentially a positive contribution to conversation as well as to the authority of the (non)speaker. It is also, as Swift's practice and writings suggest, an effective rhetoric. Silence simultaneously signals the potential end of conversation and offers the opportunity for assent; it provides the opportunity for the auditor to make a judgment of both speaker and speech.

There are two significant types of silence in conversation: the relatively involuntary silence of the excluded and of those silenced by other conversants, and the self-imposed silences of those within the conversation who either defer to others or strategically do not say what they might say or what they might be expected to say. Both types of silence figure in Swift's understanding of conversation.

THE AUTHORITY OF INCLUSION AND EXCLUSION, *OR* SWIFT, THE WITS, THE WEAVERS, AND THE WOMEN

> He never thought an honour done him
> Because a duke was proud to own him:
> Would rather slip aside, and choose
> To walk with wits in dirty shoes:

Despised the fools with Stars and Garters,
So often seen caressing Chartres.
He never counted men in station,
Nor persons had in admiration;
Of no man's greatness was afraid,
Because he sought for no man's aid.
—*Verses on the Death of Dr. Swift,* 319–28

Using speech as a model for discourse, we can identify the lower and upper limits of discursive authority as, respectively, *permission to speak* and *the capacity to end the conversation.*[4] As in his writings, in what we can glean from his correspondence and early biographers, Swift seems attentive to both the threshold of conversational authority (that is, access to the attention and attendance of others), and to authority's upper extreme (that is, the claim to having the last word). While Swift is attentive to the a priori authority customarily granted speakers because of *who they are,* he seems frequently to want to suspend the operation of such authority *within* conversation. That is, such authority may (or may not) be instrumental in the speaker's inclusion in the conversation, but once admitted to conversation all speakers are to be granted a provisional equality of authority, and everyone deserves to be treated, for better or worse, with openness and frankness.

In his writings, of course, he frequently chooses and constructs pseudonymous personae on the basis of their presumed a priori authority—a Member of the House of Commons in Ireland, or a Church of England Man; but he just as frequently chooses a speaker whose a priori authority places him in a subject position at or outside the boundaries of the conversation (for example, the Drapier), whose authority to speak is questionable and whose permission to speak is earned (or, in some cases, like those of the Tale-teller or the Modest Proposer, forfeited) on the basis of the speech rather than on the basis of the speaker's identity.

Swift's own circulation in a number of different social circles subjected him to the challenges of maintaining his identity in a variety of subject positions that varied in the degree of authority they entailed. When we think of Swift in conversation, we most likely think of one or more of the following groups: the wits and politicians in London in the reign of Queen Anne, Swift's Anglo-Irish circle in Dublin (including Patrick Delany, Thomas Sheridan, Charles Ford, Esther Johnson, Rebecca Dingley, Laetitia Pilkington), the weavers and tradespeople of the liberties of St. Patrick's, or perhaps the coterie of Lord and Lady Acheson at Market Hill. Among both the higher orders and the lower orders, Swift was often out of his class.

His delight in disrupting the expectations raised by signifiers of class and consequent authority is manifest throughout his work and correspondence, and he frequently implies that distinctions of class interfere with sociable relations and conversation. He enjoys seeing his "betters" confronted with the assumption of equality by himself or his peers, and he enjoys the confusion which results, exactly the sort of confusion which politeness is supposed to remedy. He reports in the *Journal to Stella* on a trip to the Cockpit with the Duke of Ormonde: "My friend Penn came there, Will Pen the quaker, at the head of his brethren, to thank the duke for his kindness to their people in Ireland. To see a dozen scoundrels with their hats on, and the duke complimenting them with his off, was a good sight enough" (*Journal* 2.464–65; 15 January, 1711–12). In an earlier report from London in 1711, giddy with his own increasing sociability, Swift had bluntly told Stella, "I love to be the worst of the company" (*Journal* 1.272).

When he is excluded, however, he tends toward fury: "I found 4 of them at whist [at Lady Clarges], Lady Godolphin was one. I sat by her, & talked of her Cards &c, but she would not give one Look, nor say a word to me. She refused some time ago to be acquainted with me. You know, she is Lady Marlbroughs eldest Daughter. She is a fool for her Pains, & I'll pull her down" (*Journal* 2.631; 2 March 1712–13).

One senses that the greatest reward offered to Swift by the Harley ministry was his admission to their conversation. Much later in life, Swift observed to the Countess of Suffolk that "One who asks nothing, may talk with freedom" (*Corr.* 3.484; 27 July 1731), and he seems to have experimented with this principle in the company of Harley and Bolingbroke and to have been admitted to their conversation on his own terms. His lack of ulterior motive, his disregard for the potential profitability of his relationships, allowed him to ignore rank and to speak freely. Deane Swift observes, "Neither would he have stooped to converse with the greatest monarch in *Europe,* upon any terms lower than equality" (360).

For similar reasons, it was extremely important to him that he had initially been summoned by Harley rather than having had to make an appointment, that is, that he had been authorized by Harley rather than having had to attempt to authorize himself: "I would endeavor that my betters should seek me by the merit of something distinguishable, instead of my seeking them" (Deane Swift 360).

On the other hand, his London journal records Swift's own increasing delight in reporting to callers that he is not at home, excluding them from his conversation. These exclusions indicate Swift's disdain for place-seekers and self-promoters, who would propel themselves into his conversational sphere while contaminating conversation with their personal ambition. Swift's comments about conversation indicate that participants must be free of motives other than mutual edification and entertainment: a participant who seeks favor spoils conversation, either through self-promotional performance or humiliating self-abasement. Nonetheless, at least in London during a period of increasing celebrity and authority, Swift's pleasure in being sought, like his pleasure in being identified as the author of a good pamphlet or poem, may sometimes have led him to excesses: "Mr. Gay (saith he) will tell you that a nameless person sent me eleven messages before I would yield to a visit" (Deane Swift 360).

Swift's accounts to Stella of his familiarity with Harley and Bolingbroke suggest a fairly consistent view (however irregularly practiced) of how rank should and should not come into play in conversation. Swift expects that familiarity will be accompanied by sincerity and frankness:

> I called at Mr. secretary's . . . and one thing I warned him of, Never to appear cold to me, for I would not be treated like a school boy; that I had felt too much of that in my life already; that I expected every great minister, who honoured me with his acquaintance, if he heard or saw any thing to my disadvantage, would let me know it in plain words, and not put me in pain to guess by the change or coldness of his countenance or behavior; for it was what I would hardly bear from a crowned head. (*Journal* 1.230; 3 April, 1711)

Significantly, Swift sees frankness as extending to forthright criticism "if he heard or saw any thing to my disadvantage." Moreover, the relation is reciprocal: Swift's willingness to submit to frank advice and criticism authorizes him, in turn, to advise and criticize.

Toward the end of his London career, Swift writes to Stella:

> I dined with Ld. Treasurer & shall again to morrow, which is his day when all the Ministers dine with him. He calls it whipping day; it is always on Saturday; and we do indeed usually railly him about his Faults on that day. I was of the Originall Clubb when onely poor Lord Rivers, Lord Keeper, & Lord Boling-broke came, but now Ormonde, Anglesea, Lord Steward, Dartmouth, & other Rabble intrude, and I scold at it, but now they pretend as good a Title as I, & indeed many Saturdays I am not there: the Company being too many I don't love it. (*Journal* 2.599; 9 January, 1712–13)

Swift's playfulness with the metaphor of rank in this passage indicates that a ranking continues into the discursive realm, but that the ranking among conversational familiars does not necessarily correspond to that of society at large. That is, within the coterie of Harley, Swift has a legitimate "Title," while Lords such as Ormonde and the nouveaus constitute "Rabble." Swift also clearly indicates that the Saturday "whipping day" was a semi-institutionalized gathering, most probably initiated by himself, during which Harley complacently received the well-meant, frank, and playful criticisms of his social inferiors, an occasion that must have been dear to Swift.[5] Subsequently, in correspondence from Ireland, Swift makes his principle clear, reminding Harley that "When I was with you, I have said more than once, that I would never allow Quality or Station to make any reall Difference between Men" (*Corr.* 2.44; 3 July, 1714).

After his London career, Swift no doubt had to make some adjustment to his new companions in conversation. As early as 1711, he had written to Ford that he had so little respect for "the Quality" in Dublin, that if he returned to Ireland, "I will talk Politicks to the Farmers, and publish my Works at Trim" (*Corr.* 1.257; 8 September, 1711). And to an extent, this is what he did. After the *Drapier Letters,* Swift regarded himself and was regarded by his contemporaries as well as by his early biographers as "absolute Monarch in the *Liberties,* and King of the Mob" (Pilkington 1.35). He seems to have been more willing to admit his inferiors into his company than had been the case in London, and some biographers suggest that he seems to have entered into a more monologic mode of discourse, moving away from the free and easy conversation he had relished with his London companions.

A number of reasons can be assigned for this alteration. First is the very obvious pleasure of being listened to and considered seriously. While he had found his entrée into polite London conversation enchanting, Swift ultimately always wanted more than the bare minimum authority of permission to speak and advise. In later life, he not infrequently complains of being "weary of being among Ministers whom I cannot govern" (to Thomas Tickell, *Corr.* 3.138; 7 July, 1726). It must have been gratifying to find people who not only listened to him but took his advice. Writing to Gay, he is very clear: "I would have society if I could get what I like, people of middle understanding, middle rank, very complying, and consequently such as I can govern" (*Corr.*4.17; 4 May, 1732).[6]

There is also his continuing and worsening physical debility. Both the *Journal* and his correspondence frequently remark on the bouts of "giddiness," that is, the vertigo and the crashing in his ear, the symptoms of Ménière's syndrome that increasingly tormented him; he always retreated from society when afflicted, being "mortified" to be in company in this condition, no doubt because unfit for conversation. One imagines that even with these symptoms, however, he would be capable of holding forth to people who listened to him and did not demand overmuch that he listen in return. Swift writes to Pope, a fellow sufferer,

> a man subject like us to bodily infirmities, should only occasionally converse with great people, notwithstanding all their good qualities, easinesses, and kindnesses. There is another race which I prefer before them, as Beef and Mutton for constant dyet before Partridges: I mean a middle kind both for understanding and fortune, who are perfectly easy, never impertinent. (*Corr.* 3.285; 10 May, 1728)

I think, however, that Orrery overstates the case in describing a Swift who is seduced by the power he is allotted in keeping company with people not his equals: "It is a matter of astonishment to find the same person, who had enjoyed the highest and the best conversation, equally delighted with the lowest and the worst: and yet it is certain, from Swift's settlement in Dublin . . . his choice of companions, in general, shewed him of a very depraved taste" (Orrery 67–68). Delany takes exception to this characterization of Swift's companions: "The meanest man I ever heard of his conversing with, during this period, was Mr. Worrall, a clergyman, a Master of Arts, a reader, and a vicar of his cathedral" (Delany 90–91). Unlike Orrery, Delany seems to be using the word "conversing" with a precision that excludes Swift's meetings with the weavers. Nonetheless, it is clear that Swift discovered that he could indulge his own desire to speak and to be heard attentively by including within his conversational sphere those who might otherwise and earlier have been excluded.

In principle, then, Swift seems to incline toward inclusiveness rather than exclusiveness, particularly if he himself is in danger of being excluded. He maintains with a high degree of consistency, for instance, that women should not be excluded from conversation and urges that conversation itself will be improved by their inclusion. Much of his advice to and criticism of women is designed, at least superficially, to make them fit conversational companions. In his *Proposal for Correcting, Improving, and Ascertaining the English Tongue* he remarks at some length about women's capacity to refine and improve the language and avers "that since they have been left out of all Meetings, except Parties at Play, or where worse Designs are carried on, our Conversation hath very much degenerated" (*PW* 4.13). In *Hints towards an Essay on Conversation,* he similarly laments the degeneration of conversation because of the exclusion of women, dating the "highest Period of Politeness" to the early part of Charles I's reign, when "Several Ladies, whom we find celebrated by the Poets of that Age, had Assemblies at their Houses, where Persons of the best Understanding, and of both Sexes, met to pass the Evenings in discoursing upon whatever agreeable Subjects were occasionally started" (*PW* 4.94–95).

However, while Swift's liberality to women, as perhaps with weavers, may extend to the lower limits of authority, that is, to the inclusion of women within his conversational sphere, it appears perhaps not to have extended to the suppression of a priori gendered authority within the conversation itself. A curious incident recounted by Laetitia Pilkington seems representative of Swift's humor, his conversational principles, and, perhaps, his behavior with women:

The last time he was in London, he went to dine with the Earl of Burlington, who was then but newly married. My Lord, being willing, I suppose, to have

some Diversion, did not introduce him to his Lady, nor mention his Name: 'Tis
to be observed, his Gown was generally very rusty, and his Person no Way
extraordinary.—After Dinner, said the Dean, "Lady Burlington, I hear you can
sing; sing me a Song." The Lady looked on this unceremonious manner of
asking a Favour with Distaste, and positively refus'd him; he said, she should
sing, or he would make her. 'Why, Madam, I suppose you take me for one of
your poor paultry English Hedge Parsons; sing when I bid you." As the Earl did
nothing but laugh at this Freedom; the Lady was so vext that she burst into
Tears, and retired.

His first Compliment to her when he saw her again, was "Pray, Madam, are
you as proud and as ill natur'd now, as when I saw you last?" to which she
answered with great good Humour,—"No, Mr. Dean, I'll sing for you, if you
please." From which time he conceived great Esteem for her. (Pilkington 1.38)

As the incident unfolds, a variety of the principles discussed above are
enacted. Swift assumes a conversational sphere in which a priori authority
is suspended and in which, consequently, as a member of the party, though
of unknown rank, and perhaps even "the worst of the company" as signified by his "rusty Gown," Swift asserts implicitly the suspension of
ceremony and assumes the willingness of all members of the party to edify
and entertain all others. He recognizes (or Pilkington recognizes) Lady
Burlington's contrary assumption that rank and ceremony are continually
operative, and Swift makes the point clear by pointing to the question of
his identity (and, thus, his a priori authority to request a song) as the
decisive factor for Lady Burlington. Her subsequent greeting, identifying
him as "the Dean," makes clear how the question of identity has been
resolved and has become decisive. But it is her acquiescence to his subsequent scolding of her as being "proud and ill natur'd" in withholding her
talents from a seeming nobody that indicates her submission to his frankness and her acceptance of his rules for conversation—and for their
relation—on which he conceives his esteem for her.

The bullying nature of this exchange seems exhibited by Swift most
frequently though certainly not exclusively with women—particularly Esther Johnson, Esther Vanhomrigh, Lady Acheson, and Laetitia Pilkington.
Nonetheless, one might argue, his expectation of the submission of these
women to his "plain talk" is little different from his expectation of himself
and of Harley, discussed above, to acquiesce to one another's frankness.

The incident is also typical of Swift in both his writing and his conversation in the manner of his withholding information, particularly regarding
his identity, as a means of both subverting his a priori authority and of
ensuring that subsequent authority is the product not of his bare assertions
of authority but of his authorization by others, a practice to which we will
return.

GOOD CONVERSATION NOT QUOTABLE; *OR,* WHY SWIFT HAD NO BOSWELL

While Swift was not without reporters on his remarks—we have Laetitia Pilkington and Deane Swift's accounts, for example—we have little of what might be truly called conversation. There are the famous remarks—the sending of the roast back to the kitchen to be cooked a little less well done, for example (Pilkington 1.27). Samuel Johnson admired one verbal encounter sufficiently to record it in his *Life of Swift,* that is, Swift's riposte to Richard Bettesworth: "'Mr. Bettesworth,' answered he, 'I was in my youth acquainted with great lawyers, who, knowing my disposition to satire, advised me, that, if any scoundrel or blockhead whom I had lampooned should ask, *Are you the author of this paper?* I should tell him that I was not the author; and therefore I tell you, Mr. Bettesworth, that I am not the author of these lines'" (Johnson 3.23).

One can see why Johnson would have admired the response. Yet the example may indicate a crucial difference between the conversational style of Johnson, which we have in abundance, and that of Swift, which we have hardly at all. In Swift's response to Bettesworth, as in so many of Johnson's own famous lines, Swift exercises the upper limit of authority: the riposte is a conversation stopper.

Johnson's conversations as recorded by Boswell frequently offer a classic plot line, an exposition, a rising action through dialogue, a climactic authoritative remark by Johnson, and the falling action and denouement. Johnson seems ever seeking to assert his utmost authority, and the consequence is the *termination* of conversation, the necessary effect of highly authoritative pronouncement.[7] As a result, he utters exactly the sorts of magisterial remarks that get recorded. Boswell, of course, discursively nudges Johnson in this direction, feeding him topics on which to pronounce authoritatively; moreover, since Boswell is always taking a sort of mental dictation, it is unsurprising that Johnson's remarks have a dictatorial or authoritarian quality to them—both the discursive context and the amanuensis tended, no doubt, to deform even nonauthoritative comments into authoritative ones. In any case, it may be that less of Swift's conversation is recorded than Johnson's, not only because of the lack of a Boswell, but because of its greater casualness and relatively less assertiveness and consequent authoritativeness.

All of Swift's early biographers agree that Swift's practice in conversation reflected a strong belief in the usefulness of dialogue for refining ideas and dispelling illusions. When conversants subordinate personal performance to collective disinterested engagement with ideas, as Ann Cline Kelly remarks, "the flexible give-and-take of everyday talk is most effective in winnowing out error and reinforcing the natural bonds between men" (207–208). In *Hints towards an Essay on Conversation,* Swift suggests that conversation can be perfected merely by the attempt "to avoid a Multitude of Errors, which, although a Matter of some Difficulty, may be in every Man's Power" (*PW* 4.87). The sense of this observation, I believe, is that beyond the easy "give-and-take of everyday talk," which is within the capacity of all people, the primary requirement of conversation is the *suppression* of those pronouncements, motives, and influences that might lead to conversation's deterioration, deformation, or extinction. Among these, we might include ambitions to authority.

Wit, sometimes considered the sine qua non of conversation in the late seventeenth and early eighteenth centuries, is praised by Simon Wagstaff, and, thus, ironically denigrated by Swift, in the "Introduction" to *Ingenious Conversation,* exactly for its conversation-stopping qualities:

> When this happy Art of polite conversing, shall be thoroughly improved; good Company will be no longer pestered with dull dry tedious Story-tellers, or brangling Disputers. For, a right Scholar of either Sex, in our Science, will perpetually interrupt them with some sudden surprizing Piece of Wit, that shall engage all the Company in a loud Laugh; and, if after a Pause, the grave Companion resumes his Thread, in the following Manner; well; but, to go on with my Story; new Interruptions come from the Left and Right, until he be forced to give over. (*PW* 4.117)

As the collected "wit" of *Ingenious Conversation* demonstrates, most often the problem with "wit" is its utter banality. But the inability of any of the conversants in *Conversation* to maintain a thread for more than two or three lines reflects also the ways in which the self-centered pursuit of wit disrupts the flow of conversation. Swift urges that most conversants should avoid attempts at wit: "Few are qualified to *shine* in Company; but it is in most Mens Power to be *agreeable.* The Reason, therefore, why Conversation runs so low at present, is not the Defect of Understanding; but Pride, Vanity, ill Nature, Affectation, Singularity, Positiveness; or some other Vice, the Effect of a wrong Education" (*Thoughts on Various Subjects; PW* 4.244). Similarly, in his *Hints,* Swift insists that conversation "requireth few Talents to which most Men are not born, or at least may not acquire without any great Genius or Study" (*Hints, PW* 4.87). Conversation does *not* require wit; in fact, wit disturbs conversation.

Raillery, on the other hand, often mistaken as abuse or witty insult by would-be wits ("what is generally called Repartee, or being smart . . . It now passeth for Raillery to run a Man down in Discourse" [*Hints; PW* 4.91]), as described by Swift, actually subordinates self-assertiveness in a socializing gesture of deference: "Raillery was to say something that at first appeared a Reproach or Reflection; but, by some Turn of Wit unexpected and surprising, ended always in a Compliment, and to the Advantage of the Person it was addressed to" (*Hints; PW* 4.91).[8] Raillery, then, is distinguished by its *generosity* of spirit, as signified by its always climaxing with a compliment. Unlike other forms of wit and unlike ridicule, Swift's version of raillery, as described, necessarily includes—indeed, is defined by its inclusion of—a supportive, sociable gesture, which complements the display of wit with attention to the companion's virtue.

Significantly, rather than noting his wit, Swift's early biographers most consistently remark on his habitual punctuation of conversation with silences, though they differ in their accounts thereof. Delany says Swift tried to speak briefly and then wait for others to take up the thread of conversation; if they did not (and Irvin Ehrenpreis suggests that they might very well learn to hesitate), Swift felt entitled to speak once again (Delany 203; Ehrenpreis 3.90).

Deane Swift is the most effusive commentator on Swift's conversation. He points to Swift's eagerness to listen to others, his habitual assumption of the role of moderator in disputatious conversation, and his systematic deference to the judgment of others:

> If any point, whether religious, moral, or political, happened when he was present to be controverted in a circle of his acquaintance, he was fond to listen with great attention to the merits of the argument: And, if any doubt remained, after a fair discussion of the point, he would recapitulate the sum of what had been said; then state the matter in the clearest light, and appeal unto the unbiased judgment of the youngest person in company. (Deane Swift 368)

Of his silences in conversation, Deane Swift explains:

> Swift talked a great deal in all companies, without engrossing the conversation to himself. His rule of politeness in this case was, that every man had a right to speak for a minute; and when that minute was out, if nobody else took up the discourse after a short pause of two or three moments, the same person had an equal right with any of the rest of the company, to speak again, and again, and again, and so on the whole evening. His chief delight, however, was to entertain and be entertained in small circles. (Deane Swift 366)

It should be noted that these systematic silences are silences of inclusion—invitations to others to speak—rather than the sort of cold silence of exclusion against which Swift had warned Harley, as recounted above, or which he experienced from Lady Godolphin.

Orrery concurs with Deane Swift's account of Swift as raconteur, reporting that "He told a story in an admirable manner" (Orrery 226), but as Deane Swift emphasizes, the entertainment was reciprocal: "He was by no means in the class of those who pour down their eloquence like a torrent, driving all before it. Far from any desires of that sort, he equally loved to speak and loved to hearken" (Deane Swift 367).

Dr. Johnson, as one might expect, took note in his *Life,* of the earlier biographers' comments on Swift's conversation and, particularly, of his silences: "He did not, however, claim the right of talking alone; for it was his rule, when he had spoken a minute, to give room by a pause for any other speaker." Johnson immediately adds that, "Of time, on all occasions, he was an exact computer" (3.31). Johnson's inference and implication, of course, is that Swift's allowance of silences and his deference to other speakers (and his reciprocal expectation of deference from them) was a principle that he imposed upon himself—in order to control his own inclination to dominate conversation. That Johnson should assume such a tension may be attributed either to his sense of Swift's true character or to his own character and habits—or to both.

Swift warns strenuously in *Hints* of the way in which straightforward attempts to dominate conversation are liable to redound upon the speaker, leading to deauthorization rather than to the desired heightened authority: "Nothing is more generally exploded than the Folly of Talking too much, yet I rarely remember to have seen five People together, where some one among them hath not been predominant in that Kind, to the great Constraint and Disgust of all the rest" (*Hints; PW* 4.88). Wits—or would-be wits—do not engage in conversation as Swift would define it: "The two chief Ends of Conversation are to entertain and improve those we are among, or to receive those Benefits ourselves. . . . When any Man speaketh in Company, it is to be supposed he doth it for his Hearer's Sake, and not his own" (*Hints; PW* 4.92). Nonetheless, there are those whose seeming intention to "entertain" others is merely a screen for their own self-aggrandizement: "I know a Man of Wit, who is never easy but where he can be allowed to dictate and preside; he neither expecteth to be informed or entertained, but to display his own Talents . . . he chuseth to frequent those who are content to listen, and profess themselves his Admirers" (*Hints; PW* 4.90).[9] Modesty is the necessary precondition for conversation, as suggested pointedly by Swift's remark in *Hints:* "Of such mighty Importance every Man is to himself, and ready to think he is so to others; without once making this easy and obvious Reflection, that his Affairs can have no more Weight with other Men, than theirs have with him; and how little that is, he is sensible enough" (*Hints; PW* 4.89).

Self-promotion by way of self-abnegation is the route to authority prescribed—and I think practiced—by Swift. A good conversationalist, then, tends—or at least represents herself as tending—to selflessness: "Another general Fault in Conversation is, That of those who affect to talk of themselves" (*Hints; PW* 4.88). Even avoiding oneself as the subject, excessive self-imposition upon the conversation is nothing but pedantry, "the too frequent or unseasonable obtruding our own Knowledge in common Discourse, and placing too great a Value upon it" (*Hints; PW* 4.90). Indeed, one of the healthful effects of conversation is the exercise of self-control; conversation is moderating. Thus, Swift famously defines madness as the absence of self-control in speech:

> He said, that the difference betwixt a mad-man and one in his wits, in what related to speech, consisted in this: That the former spoke out whatever came into his mind, and just in the confused manner as his imagination presented the ideas. The latter only expressed such thoughts, as his judgement directed him to chuse, leaving the rest to die away in his memory. (*Discourse of Free Thinking; PW* 4.49).

In short, Swift was acutely conscious of the less-is-more principle applied both to conversation and to writing. Self-abnegation renders self-interest invisible, while self-promotion is always grounds for incredulity and deauthorization. As he advised Knightley Chetwode, himself prone to self-aggrandizement,

> The world will never allow any man the character which he gives to himself, by openly confessing it to those with whom he converses. Wit, learning, valour, great acquaintance, the esteem of good men will be known, although we should endeavor to conceal them, however they may pass unrewarded, but I doubt, our own bare assertions, upon any of those points, will very little avail, except in tempting hearers to judge directly the contrary to what we advance. (*Corr.* 4.476; 28 April, 1731)

These comments, late in Swift's conversational and authorial career, in addition to indicating his principles regarding self-(re)presentation in conversation, seem strikingly applicable to his habit of publishing anonymously, that is, "endeavoring to conceal" his character. So many of the speakers in his satires "tempt" the readers "to judge" their own characters "directly the contrary to what [they] advance."

SWIFT'S CONVERSATIONAL ABSENCES, OR THE PLEASURES OF ANONYMITY

As he frequently reports and demonstrates in the *Journal to Stella,* Swift thoroughly enjoyed conversations with unwitting others about his anonymous or pseudonymous publications. Deane Swift records in some detail a conversation between Swift and Bishop Sheridan, in which Swift cannot resist the coup de grace of claiming authorship of *The Contests and Dissensions:*

> Having met with old bishop Sheridan at his uncle William Swift's in Dublin, the bishop after some little conversation with him about the affairs of England, asked him if he had read *The Description of the Contests and Dissensions between the Nobles and Commons in Athens and Rome* and what reputation it carried in London. The Doctor told him with a good deal of modesty, that he had read it, and that as far as he had observed, it was very well liked at London. Well, surely bishop Burnet is one of the best writers in the whole world! Bishop Burnet, my lord, said the Doctor? Why, my lord, Bishop Burnet was not the author of that discourse. Not the author of it, said the bishop? Why sir, there is never a man in England except the bishop capable of writing it. I can assure your lordship, replied the Doctor, bishop Burnet was not the author of it. Not the author of it, said the bishop? Pray sir, give me your reason, your reason, Mr. Swift, for thinking so. Because, my lord, that discourse is not written in the bishop's style. Not in the bishop's style, replied old Sheridan, with some degree of contempt? No, my lord, that pamphlet is I think wholly different from the style of the bishop. Oh, Mr. Swift, replied Sheridan, I have had long acquaintances with your uncles, and an old friendship for all your family, and really I have great regard for you in particular. But let me advise you, let me advise you Mr. Swift, for you are still a very young man. I know you have a good share of abilities, and are a good scholar; however, let me assure you notwithstanding, that you are still a great deal too young to pronounce your judgements on the style of authors. I am greatly obliged to your lordship, replied Swift, for the good opinion you are pleased to entertain of me, but still I am to assure your lordship that Bishop Burnet was not the author of that discourse. Well, sir, if Bishop Burnet was not the author of it, pray sir let me know who it was that did write it? Why, really, my Lord, I writ it myself. And this was the first time that he ever acknowledged himself to be the author of that famous tract. (Deane Swift 121–23)

While the self-identification as author was clearly irresistible and is the perfect climactic line for the exchange and the anecdote, it fails Swift's rule about bare assertions about oneself. On subsequent occasions, Swift remained silent, leaving to others the discovery of his authorship As in Pilkington's account of Swift's first encounter with Lady Burlington, the achieved effect, contrary to that of the exchange with Bishop Sheridan, is that the final word in the conversation is deferred until after the conversation's end. Swift's silence, his *non*claim of authorship (and authority), leaves the decisive discovery to his auditors who fill the postconversational silence by assigning him authorship and thus authorizing him. *They* get the final word, while he gets the authority.

The experience of hearing others talk about his work while he maintained his secret was nonetheless pleasurable, a pleasure that he shared with Stella in his letters. For instance, he reports on a gathering including Robert Harley, Matthew Prior, and Lord Peterborow at Harley's:

> They began to talk of a paper of verses called Sid Hamet. Mr. Harley repeated the part, and then pulled them out, and gave them to a gentleman at the table to read, though they had all read them often: lord Peterborow would let nobody read them but himself: so he did; and Mr. Harley bobbed me at every line to take notice of the beauties. Prior rallied lord Peterborow for author of them; and Lord Peterborow said, he knew them to be his; and Prior then turned it upon me, and I on him. I am not guessed at all in town to be the author; yet so it is: but that is a secret only to you. (*Journal* 1.60)

Similarly, upon publication of *The October Club,* Swift reports to Stella:

> I was tonight at lord Masham's; lord Dupplin took out my new little pamphlet, and the secretary read a great deal of it to lord treasurer; they all commended it to the skies, and so did I, and they began a health to the author. But I doubt lord treasurer suspected: for he said, This is Dr. Davenant's style; which is his cant when he suspects me. But I carried the matter very well. (*Journal* 2.470)

"Carrying the matter very well" is important in Swift's representation of his character by means of *not* representing his character. It is important that *others* discover his authorship without his assistance, that they assign him the role of author on the basis of their own recognition, that they, in effect, authorize him, rather than that he authorize himself.

Swift can, of course, be frustrated when his silence or secrecy prevents him from being discovered, as he writes to Stella regarding his attempts to reconcile the feuding Harley and Bolingbroke in 1711: "Do you know . . . if there be no breach, I ought to have the merit of it? 'Tis a plaguy ticklish piece of work, and a man hazards losing both sides. 'Tis a pity the world does not know my virtue (*Journal to Stella* 1.333–34).[10] Swift is clearly much happier when the news circulates, as it did about his authorship of *The Conduct of the Allies:*

> The printer called early this morning, told me the second edition went off yesterday in five hours, and he must have a third ready to-morrow, for they might have sold half another . . . [the secretary] tells me, the Dutch envoy designs to complain of that pamphlet. The noise it makes is extraordinary. It is fit it should answer the pains I have been at about it. . . . Some lay it to Prior, others to Mr. secretary St. John, but I am always the first they lay everything to. (*Journal* 2.427–28)

The pleasure of such incidents, in which Swift circulates among his readers unknown and then is credited, lies not in the discrepancy between Swift's knowledge and his companions' ignorance, nor simply in the challenge, the game of carrying off a jest successfully. In another letter to Stella, Swift reports on a gathering in which he was the central player in a group joke: "I dined to-day in the city with Dr. Freind at a third body's house, where I was to pass for some body else, and there was a plaguy silly jest carried on, that made me sick of it" (*Journal* 1.207). As this incident suggests, the pleasure is neither in convincing someone that he is someone else nor in letting someone discover that he is *not* someone else; it is in having someone recognize who he *is* and then authorizing him. In the incident reported above, on the other hand, that pleasure is lacking, and the ruse is but a "plaguy jest."

Swift's principles regarding conversation, as I've reconstructed them here, suggest a modern man who tends, whiggishly, toward inclusivity in his conversational sphere, who recognizes the postconstitutional paradoxes that authority circulates and is socially constructed and that therefore self-suppression is an effective mode of self-authorization, and who rhetorically manipulates these inclinations and recognitions into a mode of speaking that was highly successful in achieving authority without claiming it. The degree to which Swift actually practiced his principles is unknowable: his conversations are lost. In some instances, his principles seem at odds: he was clearly fond of conversation with women, but one senses that he often used his authority as both a public figure and a male within these conversations. The degree to which his irony, that is, his self-consciousness in this behavior, mitigated his sometimes alarming aggressiveness, seems to me minimal.[11] Similarly, Orrery reports Swift "dictating" to the weavers, and Swift himself with an indeterminate degree of irony reports late in life seeking company that he can "govern." Nonetheless, as this paper suggests, Swift was well aware and well-practiced in governing and dictating, that is, in exercising the upper limits of authority, through silence and self-negation.

His practice of observing silences in conversation and of moderating conversations, as reported by Deane Swift, seems similarly potentially strategic: he assumes a "moderate" stance—much like that of the Church of England Man, or the Examiner—and this "moderation" accrues authority to him, which he then musters as he sees fit. Modesty is the ruse of the proud, as Swift explains:

> To be vain, is rather a Mark of Humility than of Pride. Vain Men delight in telling what Honours have been done them, what great Company they have kept, and the like; by which they plainly confess, that these Honours were more

than their Due; and such as their Friends would not believe if they had not been told: Whereas a Man truly proud, thinks the greatest Honours below his Merit, and consequently scorns to boast. I therefore deliver it as a Maxim; that whoever desires the Character of a proud Man, ought to conceal his Vanity. (*Thoughts on Various Subjects; PW* 4.245)

Or, whoever desires the character of an authority ought to conceal his authoritativeness.

NOTES

1. There exists already ample commentary on Swift's formal *writing* about conversation. In particular, I have benefited from Ann Cline Kelly's "Swift's *Polite Conversation: An Eschatological Vision*," *Studies in Philology* 73 (1976): 204–24, and Herbert Davis's "The Augustan Art of Conversation," in *Jonathan Swift: Essays on His Satire and Other Studies,* (New York: Oxford University Press, 1964): 260–76. A fine overview of eighteenth-century conversational rhetoric is offered in Leland Warren's "Turning Reality Round Together: Guides to Conversation in Eighteenth-Century England," *Eighteenth-Century Life* 8, 3 (1983): 65–87. As might be expected, and as I've suggested, there is a longer and broader tradition of writing about the conversation of Samuel Johnson. Of particular value are John C. Ward's "Johnson's Conversation," in *SEL: Studies in English Literature, 1500–1900* 12, 3 (1972): 519–33; Glen J. Broadhead's "Samuel Johnson and the Rhetoric of Conversation," *SEL: Studies in English Literature 1500–1900* 20, 3 (1980): 461–74; and Catherine N. Parke's "Johnson and the Arts of Conversation," in *The Cambridge Companion to Samuel Johnson,* ed. Greg Clingham (Cambridge: Cambridge Univesrity Press, 1997): 18–33. The bulk of commentary on Swift, as one might expect, focuses upon *polite* conversation, the relation between conversation, manners, and civility. Kelly explains, in an overview of her article, that "Because 'manners' are a necessary passport to the circles of wealth and position, 'how to' books on the subject of gentility have always been popular. Swift, we will see, considered the audience for these books crypto-barbarians, fundamentally lacking in human sociability and reason, yet shrewdly aware that they needed to seem civilized" (210). Davis, similarly, hooks his comments onto Swift's presumed social conservatism: "I believe that Swift . . . had formed his ideal of conversation not after the fashion of courts or clubs or coffeehouses or taverns, but after the older fashion of the great country houses" (e.g., at Sir William Temple's Moor Park) (262). Irvin Ehrenpreis discusses conversation's importance to Swift almost entirely in terms of its signification of polite character: "Conversation was Swift's real measure of manners" (*Swift: The Man, His Works, and the Age,* vol. 3, *Dean Swift* [Cambridge: Harvard University Press, 1983], 91).

2. Jonathan Swift, *The Correspondence of Jonathan Swift,* ed. Harold Williams (Oxford: Clarendon Press, 1963): 2.122 (12 August 1714). Subsequent references to Swift's correspondence, hereafter abbreviated as *Corr.,* will appear parenthetically in the text. References to *The Journal to Stella,* hereafter appearing parenthetically in the text and abbreviated as *Journal,* are to Swift's *Journal to Stella,* ed. Harold Williams, 2 vols. (Oxford, Clarendon Press, 1948).

3. Swift's works and biographies are cited parenthetically in the text. Citations refer to the following editions: John Boyle, Earl of Orrery, *Remarks on the Life and Writings of Dr. Jonathan Swift* (London, 1752) [Orrery]; Patrick Delany, *Observations upon Lord Orrery's Remarks on the Life and Writings of Dr. Jonathan Swift* (1754) [Delany]; Irvin Ehrenpreis,

Swift: The Man, His Works, and the Age, 3 vols. (Cambridge: Harvard University Press, 1962–1983) [Ehrenpreis]; Samuel Johnson, "Swift," *The Lives of the Most Eminent English Poets,* vol. 3 (London: Methuen, 1896) [Johnson]; Laetitia Pilkington, *Memoirs of Laetitia Pilkington,* ed. A. C. Elias, Jr., 2 vols. (Athens and London: University of Georgia Press, 1997) [Pilkington]; Deane Swift, *An Essay upon the Life of Jonathan Swift* (London, 1755) [Deane Swift]; Jonathan Swift, *Jonathan Swift: The Complete Poems,* ed. Pat Rogers (New Haven and London: Yale University Press, 1983) [*Poems*]; and Jonathan Swift, *The Prose Works of Jonathan Swift,* ed. Herbert Davis et al., 14 vols. (Oxford: Basil Blackwell, 1939–1968) [*PW*].

4. In the course of a larger project, I have surveyed the vast and disparate literature of authority—political, ontological, and rhetorical—both in the long eighteenth century and in the twentieth. The model of discursive authority that I apply here—and that I find apt for discussion of Swift generally—is derived from Bruce Lincoln's *Authority: Construction and Corrosion* (Chicago and London: University of Chicago Press, 1994).

5. It's interesting to note that what Harley seems to have allowed is a ritualized or institutionalized time at which Swift had permission to satirize, or railly, or criticize him. And Swift relishes this opportunity. The letter from Arbuthnot quoted above, lamenting the unavailability of Swift's conversation, similarly notes Swift's capacity to deliver personal criticism in conversation: "I shall want often, a faithfull monitor, one that would vindicate me behind my back & tell me my faults to my face" (*Corr.* 2.122). For all that has been said about Swift's savage indignation, these seem stunning and telling examples of how his criticism could be defused by a friendly reception. One wonders if the source of Swift's apparent anger is less the stupidity of politicians and hacks than their unwillingness to acknowledge his criticism, that is, their resistance to giving him permission to speak.

6. In his *Verses on the Death,* Swift similarly characterizes his familiars in Ireland: "His friendship there to few confined,/Were always of the middling kind" (439–40).

7. Johnson remarks in the *Adventurer* about the ways in which striving for conversational triumph may compromise thoroughness or produce deviations from truth: "But while the various opportunities of conversation invite us to try every mode of argument, and every art of recommending our sentiments, we are frequently betrayed to the use of such as are not in themselves strictly defensible: a man heated in talk, and eager of victory, takes advantage of the mistakes or ignorance of his adversary, lays hold of concessions to which he knows he has no right, and urges proofs likely to prevail on his opponent, though he knows himself that they have no force: thus the severity of reason is relaxed, many topicks are accumulated, but without just arrangement or distinction; we learn to satisfy ourselves with such ratiocination as silences others; and seldom recall to a close examination, that discourse which has gratified our vanity with victory and applause." See *Adventurer* No. 85 in *The Yale Edition of the Works of Samuel Johnson,* vol. 2 (New Haven: Yale University Press, 1963), 41.

8. Swift's conception of raillery seems to me to be exemplified in his poems to Stella. In light of Swift's definitions of raillery and wit, I think that Irvin Ehrenpreis has mischaracterized Swift's conversation in one of his accounts: "Though both Temple and Swift esteemed conversation as the most deeply satisfying kind of recreation, Temple detested the raillery and witticisms in which Swift rejoiced. 'Those squeez'd or forc'd strains of wit', Temple called them, 'that are in some places so much in request, tho' I think commonly men that affect them are themselves much fonder of them than any of the company.' 'Raillery is the finest part of conversation', said Swift; wit and ridicule are 'the meaner parts' of conversation, said Temple" (*Swift: The Man, His Works, and the Age,* vol. 1, *Mr. Swift and His Contemporaries* (Cambridge: Harvard University Press, 1962), 110. Swift's definition of raillery, excised in Ehrenpreis's quotation, includes a generosity of spirit which distinguishes it from the wit and ridicule to which Temple was antipathetic. My

argument in this paper suggests that Swift was much more in alignment with Temple than Ehrenpreis indicates. Laetitia Pilkington remarks that raillery, as defined in *Hints* (quoted above) was Swift's invariable habit: "as I found the Dean always prefac'd a Compliment with an Affront, I never afterwards was startled at the latter (as too many have been, not entering into his peculiarly ironical Strain), but was modestly contented with the former which the Surprize rendered doubly pleasing" (Pilkington 1.29).

9. Pilkington reports on the occasion on which she first met Charles Ford in terms similar to those which Swift includes regarding his "man of Wit": "There now came in, to sup with the Dean, one of the oddest little Mortals I have ever met with: He formerly wrote the *Gazetteer;* and upon the Strength of being an Author, and of having travelled; took upon him not only to dictate to the Company, but to contradict whatever any other Person advanced Right or Wrong, till he had entirely silenced them all: And then having the whole Talk to himself (for, to my great Surprize, the Dean neither interrupted nor shewed any Dislike of him), he told us a whole String of Improbabilities" (Pilkington 1. 31).

10. It may well be that Swift expected Stella to spread the word about his inter-ministerial diplomacy. In a similar vein, immediately following his remarks on the ministers, Swift switches to complaining about the lack of Irish thanks for his work in obtaining the First Fruits: "I thought the clergy in convocation in Ireland would have given me thanks for being their solicitor, but I hear of no such thing. Pray talk occasionally on that subject, and let me know what you hear" (*Journal to Stella* 1.334).

11. Of this behavior, Dr. Johnson remarks with some acuity: "This authoritative and magisterial language he expected to be received as his peculiar mode of jocularity; but he apparently flattered his own arrogance by an assumed imperiousness, in which he was ironical only to the resentful, and to the submissive sufficiently serious" (3.31).

Part III
Gender, Class, Swift

Swift, Women, and Women Readers:
A Feminist Perspective on Swift's Life

Louise Barnett

JAMES BOSWELL DESCRIBES HOW A SCOTTISH LADY ONCE ASKED DR. Johnson if he believed that no man was naturally good. Johnson replied, "No, madam, no more than a wolf." Boswell then asked, "Nor no woman, sir?" and received the predictable response. "No, sir." At this, Boswell recounts, "Lady MacLeod started, saying low, 'This is worse than Swift.'"[1] Her comment, made in 1773, reflects a view of Swift on women that has waxed and waned in popular and critical opinion without ever going entirely out of fashion. As Donald Berwick writes in his study of Swift's reputation, "More and more . . . hatred of the Dean was to center on his treatment of women."[2]

Recent criticism, however, has been dominated by efforts to understand Swift's attitude toward women in more complex and less judgmental terms. Where, for example, the scatological poems have been treated as eruptions of Swiftian misogyny, they are now more commonly read as examples of Swift working in an established genre.[3] And however satiric Swift might be about women in general, the birthday poems to Stella and the tribute to Vanessa, "Cadenus and Vanessa," demonstrate appreciation of individual women. Swift, we are further reminded, was also an enlightened exponent of education for women and of a gender-neutral humanity.[4]

In questioning at least some of these assertions I will be working on a feminist reading of Swift's life in relation to women, one that examines what earlier women readers have written about Swift. While I would not argue, as Nora Crow does, that "women bring to the interpretation of Swift certain gender-specific advantages over men," I do believe that there can be a gender difference in the evaluation of some data (Crow 233). For example, those women whose lives seem most exemplary to men are not necessarily instructive in the same manner to women.

Down through history male critics have gallantly lauded Esther Johnson—who I will refer to as "Stella" in recognition of the fact that our only interest in this woman is because of her association with Swift. These critics have often condemned Swift for his role in their relationship and concomitantly found Stella to be a repository of many virtues. Even men who have been her partisans have found the anecdotes Swift adduced to illustrate her wit less than impressive: Dr. Johnson accurately remarked that "the smart sayings which Swift himself has collected afford no splendid specimen."[5] Swift praised Stella generously, but an evaluation of this praise might be tempered by Johnson's further comment that "if Swift's ideas of women were such as he generally exhibits, a very little sense in a lady would enrapture, and a very little virtue astonish him" (Johnson 42).

Biographers and critics have in fact primarily valued Stella for her long years of devotion to a famous man on his terms, terms that gave her very little latitude and him a great deal. Swift seems to have cared deeply for Stella, but he reserved the right to express his feeling in the most limited and circumscribed manner and in no public sense to admit his preference. He was also involved with another woman for fourteen of the twenty-seven years Stella spent in Ireland. She might have presided over his table when he entertained, but she had no official position there.

When Stella was dying, Swift's preoccupation with his own approaching loss seemed to eclipse concern for her feelings. In what must be one of the most egocentric utterances in literature, he upbraided the dying woman in his final birthday poem for her: "Me, surely me, you ought to spare."[6] Perhaps his buying a watch for Stella when her time was clearly running out simply indicates a denial of her approaching death so strong that he was unable to think of her feelings, or perhaps the watch was something she had always wanted rather than a token of tactlessness—but what must Stella have thought as Swift prayed over her "to raise up some other in her place, with equal disposition and better abilities."[7]

Swift insisted that Stella be moved out of his deanery lest by dying there she should implicate him in scandal. Surely whatever had been said about Swift and Stella was by now stale news, more than a quarter century old. Stella and her companion Rebecca Dingley had lived in the deanery—routinely and openly—while Swift was away. And yet, in 1728, when he was sixty years old and had no realistic hope of further advancement, the risk of scandal was apparently enough to justify treating this companion of so many years unceremoniously.

Male writers have noted these facts with some sympathy for Stella without pursuing the case into an explicitly feminist analysis. Those who have condemned Swift's treatment of Stella have done so because he inflicted an irregular position on her. As Mark Twain wrote in the margin of Thackeray's book on Swift, "That it was her fate to suffer 21 years of a love so trifling as Swift's ought to entitle her to the world's compassion for all time."[8]

Margaret Oliphant, writing in 1894, is the first writer to suggest that some of this sympathy may be both misguided and gender based. "Appearances of blighted life or unhappiness there are none in anything we know of [Stella]," she wrote. She then asked, at some length, "Is it perhaps a certain mixture of masculine vanity and compassion for the gentle feminine creature who never succeeded in getting the man she loved to marry her, and thus failed to attain the highest end of woman, which has moved every biographer of Swift, each man more compassionate than his predecessor, thus to exhaust himself in pity for Stella?"[9]

Writing in 1913, Margaret Woods echoed Mrs. Oliphant's view, although for a more traditional reason. Stella should not be pitied or considered "badly used," Woods asserted, because "she was the respected, the admired, the tenderly loved companion of a man who was not only a great genius but a great personality." Woods believed that as Swift's "acknowledged wife" Stella "would have found [his tiresome ways] still more tiresome, and complained as much as good wives do, which is often a good deal."[10]

Oliphant and Woods both illustrate a decidedly gender-based perspective, but neither is a feminist, or much of a researcher for that matter. Their views of the Swift-Stella relationship are creatures of sentimental idealization rather than historical recuperation. Except for unreliable stories, we have no evidence of dissatisfaction in Stella, but since we have no firm evidence of any other sort, certainty about Stella's state of mind is unwarranted.

To a feminist biographer, the very lack of any evidence of Stella that has not been channeled through Swift should be one of the most salient facts of her history. Marginalized in life, after her death, insofar as it was within Swift's power, she was deliberately erased as an independent voice. How much more of a sense of Stella's personality we would have today if even a few of the forty-one letters she wrote to Swift between 21 September, 1710 and 6 June, 1713 had survived.[11]

From a feminist perspective Stella is particularly memorable for this erasure—the absence of enough information about her to form an opinion or reach a conclusion, and, above all, the silence of her own voice. Swift commended Stella to a prospective suitor by stating that he had never seen "that person whose conversation [he] entirely valued but hers," without specifying what made her conversation so valuable (*Correspondence* 1: 146). In the essay he wrote after her death he does specify: "She never had the least absence of mind in conversation, nor [was] given to interruption, or appeared eager to put in her word by waiting impatiently till another had done." She never, he continued, "spoke much at a time" (*Prose Works* 5: 230).

If we compare these remarks with Swift's severe condemnation of so-called "learned ladies" who have a reputation for "impertinent talkativeness," we arrive at a picture that contemporary sociolinguistics has often substantiated: the male holding forth to the attentive and generally silent female.[12] As Mary Pendarves, the future Mrs. Delany, described Swift in a letter to her sister (1733), "He talks a great deal and does not require many answers."[13]

Even strong partisans of Stella have generally failed to mention that her will set aside twenty pounds for a memorial tablet that was not raised during the seventeen years that Swift outlived her.[14] Yet the memorializing of the dead appears to have been a preoccupation of his, in keeping with his observation that most people wish to be remembered after their deaths. "We observe, even among the Vulgar," he wrote, "how fond they are to have an Inscription over their Grave" (*Prose Works* 4: 244). As Dean of St. Patrick's, Swift wrote to members of several prominent families to tell them that their family's funerary monuments in the cathedral were in need of repair. He was indignant if they failed to respond.[15] He also occupied himself with erecting a monument to Lady Betty Germain's sister Penelope, who had died in Ireland some thirty years before at the age of twelve, a task no member of her family had undertaken or thought of undertaking until Swift broached it to Lady Betty. When taxed on the subject by the Dean, Lady Betty could remember only imperfectly when her sister had been born and when she had died (*Correspondence* 4: 5).

Much earlier in his life, Swift had proclaimed his intention of erecting a marble monument to Anne Long, Esther Van Homrigh's beautiful cousin whom Swift had known briefly and admired. Shortly after her death, he wrote to the Rev. Thomas Pyle, Anne Long's pastor, avowing his intention to place a monument over her grave "if no other of her friends will think fit to do it." He continued: "I had the honour of an intimate acquaintance with her, and was never so sensibly touched with any one's death as with hers. Neither did I ever know a person of either sex with more virtues, or fewer infirmities." (*Correspondence* 1: 280).

Swift also placed a tablet in St. Patrick's in memory of his servant, Alexander McGee. It reads in part: "His grateful master caused this monument to be erected in memory of his discretion, fidelity and diligence in that humble station" (*Correspondence* 2: 422–23). According to Patrick Delany, Swift had intended to style himself more warmly as "friend and master," but was persuaded otherwise (*Correspondence* 2: 423 n.). If McGee's discretion, fidelity, and diligence deserved such acknowledgment, Stella surely merited at least the simple memorial she had requested, a tablet indicating that she had lived and died.

Swift was no exception to his own observation that people wish to have a memorial: Brian Connery suggests that "the urge to memorialize himself

. . . and be memorialized is, perhaps, the largest theme of Swift's work."[16]
In addition to the memorializing of self apparent throughout his poetry,
Swift composed his own epitaph and gave extremely precise instructions
for the monument on which it would appear: "A Black Marble of   Feet
square, and seven Feet from the Ground, fixed to the Wall, may be erected,
with the following Inscription in large Letters, deeply cut, and strongly
gilded" (*Prose Works* 13:149).

Swift's failure to implement Stella's last instructions for such a re-
membrance is consonant with other omissions and withholdings. Stella is
rarely called by name in his writings. The *Journal to Stella* refers to her as
MD, thought to be an abbreviation for "My Dears," a term that presumably
includes Rebecca Dingley.[17] And the poems call her Stella, which she has
also become for posterity. Above all, in Swift's correspondence and elsewhere in his writings, her designation is some permutation of *friend*—"our
friend in Grafton Street," "my most valuable friend," etc.—that appella-
tion with which Swift thought to disarm public censure, private reproach,
and his own psyche. When she was dead, he did refer to her by her actual
name. He wrote at that time what Herbert Davis has described as a conventional tribute, full of praise but not personality (Davis 96). This may be
why commentators so often seize upon a detail from this description of
Stella, that she was "a little too fat" (*Prose Works* 5: 227); at least it
suggests a real person rather than the congeries of perfections created by
the tribute's other adjectives: *beautiful, graceful, agreeable.*

Swift protested too much that his feeling for Stella was simply friendship because this rubric freed him from the implications of a sexual relationship, which is, after all, a common distinction between friendship and
love. The putative secret marriage between Swift and Stella begged to be
invented to explain what otherwise seems to the ordinary world to be
inexplicable behavior: that is, a significant yet nonsexual friendship lasting
many years between two people who appear to have no impediment to
marriage.

Evelyn Hardy has observed that biographers accept or reject the marriage according to caprice;[18] it is, in point of fact, difficult to do otherwise
since whatever disproves this maddening biographical datum may just as
easily prove it. Irvin Ehrenpreis, among others, rejects the idea because
Stella signed her will "Esther Johnson, spinster."[19] But if the marriage was
secret, she was bound to have done or not done whatever was appropriate
to the existence of an unmarried woman.

Male critics have sometimes failed to understand why Stella might want
a secret marriage. For Ricardo Quintana, if such a ceremony took place,
"the explanation must be sought not in the realm of reason but of non-
sense."[20] For Ehrenpreis, Stella "had nothing to gain from an unacknowledged, invalid marriage that left both of them living as celibate friends (3:

405 n.). Thomas Sheridan, on the other hand, explains the marriage by saying that Stella pined because of the "indelible stain fixed on her character, and the loss of her own good name, which was dearer to her than life."[21] But a secret marriage would not have remedied this problem since "good name" is a public rather than a private matter. If the issue were instead Swift's relationship to Vanessa, as has also been conjectured, marriage—however invalid or publicly unacknowledged—"would have given Stella some private satisfaction in a world in which women had no recognized vocation but marriage."[22]

A secret marriage seems unlikely for one brutal, if equally unprovable reason: namely, that Swift had exactly the relationship he wanted with Stella without marriage, and she did not have the leverage to override his wishes. This was clear in 1704 when a man who did want to marry Stella appeared.[23] Since Swift did not marry Stella himself when faced with a suitor for her hand, it must have been clear to her at that time that he never would.

Swift's snobbery further militates against the idea of marriage to Stella. While Swift did not preserve the letters of the woman whose conversation pleased him above that of all others, he did save any number of trifling letters from aristocratic women. In 1735 he wrote to Lady Elizabeth Germain that when he left England he had burnt the letters he had received from ministers, "but," he continued, "as to the letters I receive from your Ladyship, I neither ever did or ever will burn any of them. . . . For I never burnt a letter that is entertaining, and consequently will give me new pleasure when it is forgotten" (*Correspondence* 4: 344).

Many of those who similarly reject the secret marriage have proffered explanations ranging from impotence to consanguinity in seeking to account for Swift's failure to marry Stella.[24] Less dramatically, Richard Krafft-Ebing's idea of "sexual anesthesia," which "does not exclude nonsexual tenderness" or "require impotency," seems tailor-made for Swift, as does his example of a man who wanted to marry "but only on rational grounds."[25] Perhaps it is even more suited to Swift apologists: in providing a scientific sounding rubric for Swift's condition, it strips his behavior of oddity and disarms disapproval.

Given the initial puzzle of the Swift-Stella relationship, other details without sufficient context have teased biographers into bizarre speculations. Swift wrote to Esther Van Homrigh, "Vanessa," that a woman who did business for him had told him that she had heard that he visited Vanessa accompanied by "little master."[26] Ehrenpreis, always eager to dampen any potentially lurid flames, assumes that this was a charity child from Stella's household. He has a curious footnote that this child must have been "like the girl mentioned in [Stella's] will," an inexplicable remark since the only child mentioned in Stella's will is Bryan M'Loghlin.[27] Moreover, if Swift was as insistent on discretion as all his behavior suggests, he would hardly have taken a child from Stella's sphere into Vanessa's; this explanation is patently absurd. At the same time, it is hard to imagine who might have accompanied Swift on such a clandestine visit.

Sybil LeBrocquy conjectured that this was an illegitimate child of Vanessa's fathered by Swift who, after Vanessa's death, was taken in by Stella as an object of her charity.[28] This would be the Bryan M'Loghlin that Stella specifies in her will with what seems to be unusual generosity. LeBrocquy has been assiduous in researching this matter and constructing a possible scenario, but it all hinges upon the identity of "little master." Were this to be merely a private way of referring to some common acquaintance, like "Glass Heel" for Charles Ford, the hypothesis of the child fathered by Swift falls.[29] Having no children of her own, Stella might well have become so attached to Bryan M'Loghlin that she provided for him in her will somewhat more generously than might have been expected.[30]

As for the more tempestuous and secret relationship Swift carried on with Vanessa, his efforts to marginalize and erase *her* are more understandable. That they were less successful was due as much to the difference in economic circumstance between Stella and Vanessa as to any difference in temperament: Vanessa's fortune gave her a power of assertion and self-indulgence that Stella lacked.

Vanessa preserved not only Swift's letters to her, but copies of her own letters to him. His influence was such, however, that her instructions to her executors to publish this correspondence were not carried out during Swift's lifetime: Sheridan's son tells us that soon after Vanessa's death the letters were on the verge of being published when his father, "getting intelligence of it . . . applied so effectually to the executors, that the printed copy was cancelled" (Freeman 39). Nor do we know how censored the correspondence that survives may have been. Because of Vanessa's system of numbering, we can be fairly certain that many letters are missing, and it is improbable that Vanessa herself destroyed them.

What letters there are are sufficiently remarkable, especially in light of the view that Vanessa ceaselessly pursued a reluctant Swift.[31] In this standard interpretation, while Swift attempted to disengage himself for fourteen years, Vanessa preyed upon his compassion by parading her griefs before him.

In 1767 Dr. George Berkeley, one of Vanessa's executors, several times assured Dr. Delany that the correspondence contained "nothing which would dishonor the character or bring the least reflection upon Cadenus." LeBrocquy comments: "One can only conclude that Dr. Berkeley saw nothing unfitting in an elderly Dean assuring a young woman of his adoration, so long as he did so in a foreign language" (LeBrocquy, *Cadenus* 42). A more recent critic has made much the same argument without LeBrocquy's irony. Wanting to deflate some of Swift's compliments in French to Vanessa, David Nokes suggests that writing in French was "like a promise with fingers crossed. Somehow it doesn't quite count. Otherwise," Nokes concludes, "what he says here is frankly dishonest." This is clearly an unacceptable interpretation for Nokes, who wants to invalidate these compliments in keeping with his own view that Swift's "esteem and honour for Stella were always greater than for Vanessa" (Nokes 261). He seems to find it inconceivable that a man might simultaneously tell two different women that each was paramount in his affections.

A similar reading can be found in Ehrenpreis, with some admission that Swift was partially responsible for encouraging Vanessa, or at least for allowing "compassion" to overcome his desire to stay away. In short, the thesis advanced by Bishop Berkeley has remained intact in the hands of Swift's most prominent twentieth-century biographers. Of the dashes that Swift suggested to Vanessa as a way of conveying tender epithets in their letters without writing the actual words, Nokes says that Vanessa "seized on his idea . . . with great enthusiasm, and strewed her letters with these cryptic symbols of affection" (257). Swift's announcement that he was coming to see her at Celbridge "called forth a whole battery of strokes" (258). When Swift responded with his own set of dashes, Nokes remarks that this "hail of strokes [is] too profuse to be intense" (259).

Ehrenpreis says that he will "pass over the many piquant or touching sentences from Swift's letters to Vanessa because they would misrepresent the general effect of a man straining to transform a romantic obsession into a placid, playful intimacy" (3: 395). Such passages should not be overlooked, however, for they are unique in Swift's writing. They are, in fact, so arresting that Ehrenpreis could legitimately fear their effect on his idea of Swift's striving for a "placid, playful intimacy." At the same time, his admission that there are "many" such sentences is surely an argument for engaging rather than ignoring them.

In contrast to such attempts to minimize Swift's feelings in the correspondence, Margaret Woods described the letters to Vanessa as "far indeed from bearing out the view, improbable in itself, that for some twelve years Vanessa besieged Swift with a love which he consistently discouraged" (Woods 1239–40).

Reviewing the Swift-Vanessa correspondence in 1933, Alyse Gregory commented on Swift: "He who understood society as a thief understands his jemmy, with the same grim stealth, or as a hangman knows his knots, did not comprehend so much about the heart of a girl."[32] Passing over Gregory's rather sinister comparisons, it is possible to agree with her conclusion, for if Swift wanted merely Ehrenpreis's "placid, playful intimacy" with Vanessa, he was, at the age of fifty-four, extraordinarily naive in writing to her on 5 July, 1721: "Cad— assures me he continues to esteem and love and value you above all things, and so will do to the end of his life, but at the same time entreats that you would not make yourself or him unhappy by imaginations" (Freeman 132). He may have expected the second clause to cancel the first, but since the first is an emphatic and absolute declaration, and the second a vague and weakly couched plea, there is little likelihood that the sentence moderated the passionate feelings that Vanessa expressed to him so often.

Some critics have assumed that Swift's third-person references were a means of dissociating himself from the sentiments attributed to Cad—although he uses the same device by calling himself Presto in the *Journal to Stella*. But in this respect, too, he must have known that for Vanessa the use of this special name simply reinforced a tender intimacy.

The letter does contain some of the instructive precepts that Swift was apt to inflict on everyone he cared for, and it provides in addition a quite ordinary account of his own activities, which was also meant to be exemplary. But these passages are outweighed by those that Ehrenpreis would pass over as "piquant" or "touching." The peremptory "settle your affairs, and quit this scoundrel island" might have disheartened Vanessa, had it not been followed by the seductive phrase, "and things will be as you desire." What Swift might have meant by this has understandably eluded those commentators who do not want to accuse him of bad faith, but we can be more certain of what Vanessa would have thought upon reading it. She was, after all, the woman who had written to Swift that he was the one "unexpressible passion" of her life (Freeman 129).

The letter continues with Swift reiterating his sentiments in French: "Rest assured that you are the only person on earth who has ever been loved, honored, esteemed, adored by your friend."[33] Perhaps Swift was merely crossing his fingers as he wrote, figuratively speaking, as he penned this sweeping declaration, but Vanessa would not have known this. More important to a biographical investigation of Swift, he surely understood how she would take these words. To Vanessa, French must have seemed to be a token of their special relationship, the language associated with love.

Swift concluded in English, "I drank no coffee since I left you, nor intend till I see you again. There is none worth drinking but yours, if myself be the judge" (Freeman 133). "Drinking coffee," repeated so often in Swift's letters to Vanessa, is unlikely to mean the sex act, but it is redolent of eroticism nevertheless. Whatever it meant to Swift and Vanessa, these many references to drinking coffee are hardly plausible as mere literal utterances. They articulate and underscore intimacy.

Certainly there were times when Swift wrote lightheartedly to Vanessa, and times when he wrote of mundane matters without those piquant or touching passages that Ehrenpreis refuses to cite. But the nonplayful sort of intimacy is rarely absent. Commenting on the dissatisfactions each had expressed with company, Swift tells Vanessa: "The worst thing in you and me is that we are too hard to please, and whether we have not made ourselves so, is the question. At least I believe we have the same reason" (Freeman 138). To say that Swift might have written thus to someone else—a good friend, a relative—is beside the point. He was writing to a woman who had declared her love for him, and to whom he had used the word "love" in his letters. However Swift meant it, love would have been the unspoken subtext in Vanessa's reading of this declaration of affinity.

Swift's general condemnations of women provide a context for his praise of Stella and Vanessa. In fact, he praises the two favored women only by constructing them as different from all other women, who are, for him, *bestes en juppes,* monkeys, disgusting female yahoos, a tribe of bold, swaggering, rattling Ladies, unclean belles, or decaying prostitutes. Even Swift's praise of Stella is mixed with unflattering physical details— supposedly evidence of his sensible determination to see women as human beings rather than goddesses. My reading is otherwise. Although references in the birthday poems to Stella's gray locks, wrinkles, and obesity are only faint reflections of the criticism leveled against the female body elsewhere in Swift's writings, they seem to erupt into the poetic context from Swift's very loathing of female physicality, as if he cannot keep himself from taking notice of bodily decay, even within a context celebrating nonphysical attributes. (He similarly erupts inappropriately in the "Letter to a Young Lady on her Marriage.") It is surely a compliment for affection to transcend physical decay, but it is hardly complimentary to draw attention to the process.

Reading her birthday poems, Stella might have felt as we may imagine Swift's early fiancée Jane Waring felt upon hearing from her prospective bridegroom that beauty of person meant nothing to him, cleanliness everything.[34] Many years later, Laetitia Pilkington was to observe Swift singling out a dirty old woman in a crowd of beggars and saying, as he gave alms to everybody but her, "that though she was a Beggar, Water was not so scarce but she might have washed her Hands."[35] The female body was always problematic for Swift, always a suspect site of uncleanliness.

Those women Swift liked and admired had bodies, too, but Swift preferred to look away from this fact and foreground those character traits that qualified them for his friendship. References to the physical beauty of Stella and Vanessa are abstract and hurriedly presented. Swift intends to draw a sharp line when he tells Vanessa that compared to her, other women are animals in skirts, but of course Vanessa, too, is an animal in skirts, that is, a physical being—even if Swift is determined to ignore it. *Why* he wanted to ignore it seems clear enough: bodies suggest the kind of relation-ship Swift did not want to have with women.

What has captivated recent feminist critics of Swift is what they regard as his enlightened departure from essentialism. In a "Letter to a Young Lady on her Marriage" he stated uncategorically, "I am ignorant of any one Quality that is amiable in a Man, which is not equally so in a Woman . . . nor do I know one Vice or Folly, which is not equally detestable in both" (*Prose Works* 9: 92–93). This has led some feminists to believe that Swift espoused a gender-free ideal of character and behavior. But those who read the above statement as a passe-partout to gender equality should keep in mind the equality of another sort that Swift advances in this same text. Those women who do not display the proper deference to males need not be supposed to be women, Swift wrote. They should instead be treated like "insolent Rascals disguised in Female Habits, who ought to be stripped, and kicked down Stairs" (*Prose Works* 9: 93).

Swift's ideal woman is actually stripped of any quality identifiably female except the docility to take instruction. She is then endowed with the desirable qualities of men. Instead of making the argument for equality for women, Swift makes the conservative argument of merit, the merit of male qualities or merit as determined by himself. Stella and Vanessa were assid-uously formed by Swift, and he hoped that Deborah Staunton Rochefort, to whom the "Letter" was written, would follow in their footsteps. Pilkington relates that Rochefort did not take Swift's advice as a "Compliment, either to her or the Sex" (Pilkington 1: 63–64). Nor should we today. The reader who applauds Swift's assertion of genderless qualities of character must be equally prepared to condemn his sustained diatribe against women, the generality of whom he pronounces unworthy of respect and of limited educability: their best efforts to improve their minds will fall short of the "Perfection of a School-Boy" (*Prose Works* 9: 92–93).

Perhaps Swift genuinely believed in one set of qualities for both sexes, but we will look in vain in his writings for the consequences that such a belief might be expected to produce. To put Swift's view in perspective, Evelyn Hardy compared it to that of his contemporary, Daniel Defoe (Hardy 191). In the *Essay upon Projects,* written in 1697, Defoe stated: "I cannot think that God Almighty made [women] . . . with souls capable of the same accomplishments as men, and all to be only stewards of our houses, cooks, and slaves."[36] Defoe moves from a transformation of atti-tude about women to a suggestion of their empowerment, a step Swift never took. The scrap he throws to women is inclusion in after-dinner conversation, which merely means more opportunity to approve male discourse with the Stella-like behavior Swift commended in his descrip-tion of her life: "Wise men . . . could easily observe that she understood them very well, by the judgment shewn in her observations, as well as in her questions" (*Prose Works* 5: 236). Only in sexist terms was Stella the perfect *conversationalist;* what she was in reality was the perfect audience. Swift could imagine nothing higher for women.

NOTES

1. James Boswell, *Boswell's Journal of a Tour to the Hebrides with Samuel Johnson,* ed. Frederick A. Pottle (New York: McGraw-Hill, 1961), 170.

2. Donald Berwick, *The Reputation of Jonathan Swift 1781–1882* (New York: Haskell House, 1965), 53.

3. Ellen Pollak, "Swift Among the Feminists," *Critical Approaches to Teaching Swift,* ed. Peter Schakel (New York: AMS Press, 1992), 66, sums up feminist criticism from the 1970s on as identifying "the misogyny [sic] of Swift's writing as a cultural, rather than a merely personal phenomenon." See Nora Crow, "Swift and the Woman Scholar," in *Pope, Swift, and Women Writers,* ed. Donald C. Mell (Newark: University of Delaware Press, 1996), 222–38, for a more detailed treatment of recent feminist critics of Swift.

4. Margaret Ann Doody, "Swift Among the Women," *Critical Essays on Jonathan Swift,* ed. Frank Palmeri (New York: G. K. Hall, 1993), 20–21; Crow, "Swift and the Woman Scholar," 225–26.

5. Samuel Johnson, *Lives of the English Poets,* ed. George Birkbeck Hill, 3 vols., 2nd ed. (Oxford: Clarendon Press, 1958), 3: 42.

6. Jonathan Swift, *The Poems of Jonathan Swift,* ed. Harold Williams, 3 vols. 2nd ed. (Oxford: Clarendon Press, 1958), 2: 766.

7. Jonathan Swift, *The Prose Works of Jonathan Swift,* ed. Herbert Davis, 14 vols. (Oxford: Shakespeare Head Press, 1939–68), 9: 254, hereinafter *Prose Works.* In a letter to John Worrall, 15 July, 1726, Swift writes: "I have bought her a repeating gold Watch for her Ease in winter Nights." *The Correspondence of Jonathan Swift,* ed. Harold Williams, 5 vols. (Oxford: Clarendon Press, 1963–65), 3: 141, hereinafter *Correspondence.*

8. Coley B. Taylor, *Mark Twain's Margins on Thackeray's Swift* (New York: Gotham House: 1935), 45.

9. Mrs. M. O. W. Oliphant, *Historical Characters of the Reign of Queen Anne* (New York: Century Company, 1894), 99–100.

10. Margaret Woods, "Swift, Stella, and Vanessa," *The Nineteenth Century and After* 74 (December 1913): 1246.

11. Herbert Davis, *Stella: A Gentlewoman of the Eighteenth Century* (New York: Macmillan, 1942), 51.

12. Sociolinguistic studies indicate that male speakers conversing with women take longer speech turns, interrupt more frequently, and are generally more assertive speakers. See Don H. Zimmerman and Candace West, "Sex Roles, Interruptions and Silences in Conversation," in *Language and Sex: Difference and Dominance,* eds. Barrie Thorn and Nancy Henley (Rowley, Mass.: Newbury House, 1975), 105–25; John J. Gumperz, *Discourse Strategies* (Cambridge: Cambridge University Press, 1982), 154–55; and David Graddol and Joan Swann, *Gender Voices* (Oxford: Basil Blackwell, 1989), 170–72.

13. *The Correspondence of Jonathan Swift, D.D.* ed. F. Elrington Ball, 4 vols. (London: G. Bell and Sons, 1910–14) 4: 436 n.

14. Stella's will contained the following provision: "I desire that a decent monument of plain white marble may be fixed on the wall, over the place of my burial, not exceeding the value of twenty pounds sterling." Cited in William R. Wilde, *The Closing Years of Dean*

Swift's Life, 2nd ed. rev. (Dublin: Hodges & Smith, 1849), 97. Apparently the memorial tablet was erected not long before the year 1780 (Ball 4: 462 n). Wilde observes, 121 n.: "Both her own name and that of Steevens are misspelled in it. The precise date of its erection has not been ascertained; but it does not appear to have been set up during the Dean's lifetime."

15. When the heirs of the Duke of Schomberg ignored Swift's repeated overtures to set up a monument to the deceased Duke, Swift had a memorial tablet pointedly inscribed: "His reputation for virtue prevailed more among strangers than the kindredness of his blood prevailed among his own folk" (*"Plus potuit fama virtutis apud alienos/Quam sanguinis proximitas apud suos"*). See *Correspondence* 3: 468 and 468 n. The intensity of his feeling on the subject may be gauged by a letter to Lord Carteret in April of 1730 in which Swift vows that if the family tries to obtain the body to avoid paying for a monument, "I will take up the bones, and make of it a skeleton, and put it in my registry-office, to be a memorial of their baseness to all posterity" *(Correspondence* 3: 390).

16. Brian A. Connery, "Self-Representation and Memorials in the Late Poetry of Swift," in *Aging and Gender in Literature,* eds. Anne M. Wyatt-Brown and Janice Rossen (Charlottesville: University of Virginia Press, 1993), 157.

17. *Journal to Stella,* ed. Harold Williams (Oxford: Clarendon Press, 1948), passim. Crow, cited above, notes that throughout the *Journal* Swift refers to MD as "sirrahs," "lads," and "boys."

18. Evelyn Hardy, *The Conjured Spirit: A Study in the Relationship of Swift, Stella, and Vanessa* (London: Hogarth Press, 1949), 173.

19. Irvin Ehrenpreis, *Swift: The Man, His Works, and the Age,* 3 vols. (Cambridge: Harvard University Press, 1983), 3: 405 n.

20. Ricardo Quintana, *The Mind and Art of Jonathan Swift* (Oxford: Oxford University Press, 1936), 233.

21. Thomas Sheridan, *The Life of the Rev. Dr. Jonathan Swift,* 2nd ed. (London: J. F. & C. Rivington, 1787), 322.

22. Modern commentators have generally accepted Williams's cautious attribution of the poem "On Jealousy" to Stella—*Poems* 2: 736. Her jealousy of Vanessa is discussed by John Middleton Murry, in *Jonathan Swift: A Critical Biography* (London: Jonathan Cape, 1954), 279–80, and David Nokes, *Jonathan Swift, A Hypocrite Reversed* (Oxford: Oxford University Press, 1985), 217, both of whom accept the secret marriage.

23. Swift's letter to the Rev. William Tisdall concerning his intentions toward Stella reveals Swift's own desire to maintain her in a virginal state: "Time takes off from the lustre of virgins in all other eyes but mine." *Correspondence* 1: 45–46.

24. Lady Mary Wortley Montagu was an early proponent of the impotence theory. See *The Complete Letters of Lady Mary Wortley Montagu,* ed. Robert Halsband, 3 vols. (Oxford: Clarendon Press, 1967), 1: 273–76 and 3: 56, 56 n.; see also Leslie Stephen, *Swift* (New York: 1898), 140. The consanguinity hypothesis rests upon the idea that both Swift and Stella were natural children of Sir William Temple, and it, too, has had a long history. Sybil Le Brocquy, *Swift's Most Valuable Friend* (Dublin: Dufour Editions, 1968), 12–20, reproduces in its entirety an anonymous article asserting the relationship that appeared in *The Gentleman's and London Magazine* of November 1757.

25. Richard Krafft-Ebing, *Psychopathia Sexualis,* cited in Maxwell Gold, *Swift's Marriage to Stella* (New York: Russell and Russell, 1967), 130.

26. *Vanessa and Her Correspondence with Jonathan Swift,* ed. A. Martin Freeman (Boston: Houghton Mifflin, 1921), 104.

27. Ehrenpreis, 3: 94 n. Stella's will contained the following bequest: "I bequeath to Bryan McLoghlin (A child who now lives with me, and whom I keep on charity), twenty-five pounds to bind him out apprentice as my executors or the survivors of them shall think

fit." Cited in Wilde, *The Closing Years,* 100. Wilde is the best source for Stella's will, which is no longer extant.

28. Sybil LeBrocquy, *Cadenus* (Dublin: Dolmen Press, 1963), 52.

29. Ball annotates Swift's reference to "Glass Heel" in a letter to Vanessa: "Like Achilles Ford was believed to be invulnerable save in an unimportant place" (3: 59 n). Victoria Glendinning, *Jonathan Swift: A Portrait* (New York: Henry Holt, 1998), believes that "Little Master" was a dog (195).

30. LeBrocquy notes that the bequest to M'Loghlin was a considerable sum of money: "In that year the fee paid to apprentice a boy was 3 pounds and a suit of clothes" (*Cadenus* 115).

31. This is the view of the most recent male biographers of Swift, Ehrenpreis (3: 380–83) and Nokes (259–62). Ehrenpreis refers to Vanessa's "emotional blackmail" (3: 94), while Nokes depicts a Swift attempting to cheer up a woman given to "morbid self-pity" (259).

32. Alyse Gregory, "Stella, Vanessa, and Swift," *Nineteenth-Century and After* 113 (June 1933): 759.

33. The original reads: *"soyez assuree que jamais personne du monde a ete aimee, honoree, estimee, adoree par votre ami que vous"* (Freeman 133).

34. Swift to Miss Jane Waring, 4 May 1700: "These are the questions I have always resolved to propose to her with whom I meant to pass my life; and whenever you can heartily answer them in the affirmative, I shall be blessed to have you in my arms, without regarding whether your person be beautiful, or your fortune large. Cleanliness in the first, and competency in the other, is all I look for" (*Correspondence* 1.36).

35. Laetitia Pilkington, *The Memoirs of Mrs. Laetitia Pilkington,* 3 vols. (New York: Garland, 1975; facsimile of Dublin edition, 1748–54), 1.153. In this instance Swift might have been unreasonable: Lewis Mumford has documented a scarcity of water among the poor in large urban centers at the beginning of the Industrial Revolution. See *The City in History: Its Origins, Its Transformations, and Its Prospects* (New York: Harcourt-Brace-Jovanovich, 1961), 463 and passim.

36. Cited in F. Bastian, *Defoe's Early Life* (Totowa, N.J.: Barnes and Noble, 1981), 198.

Swift, Reynolds, and the Lower Orders

Sean Shesgreen

THE NAMELESS EDITOR OF THE FIFTH EDITION OF *A BIOGRAPHICAL HIS-tory of England* (1824), looking back on his enlargement of James Grang-er's (1723–76) book from two volumes to six hefty tomes, feared he had done wrong to devote so much space to those people who appear in the last of its twelve classes of subjects: "Persons of both Sexes, chiefly of the lowest Order of the People, remarkable from only one circumstance in their Lives, namely such as lived to a great Age, deformed Persons, Convicts, &c."[1] "I have, perhaps, in the foregoing strictures, extended the sphere of it [biography] too far," he frets. "I began with monarchs, and have ended with ballad-singers, chimney-sweepers, and beggars" (Granger 6: 179) His misgivings, prompted by the increasingly vexed atmosphere surrounding England's class stratification in the nineteenth-century, contrast with his very next sentiment, connecting the center of social life with its margins in a demotic and antihierarchic way that has become a central tenet among Bakhtinian theorists of literature and cul-ture: "But they that fill the highest and the lowest classes of human life, seem, in many respects, to be more nearly allied than even themselves imagine. A skillful anatomist would find little or no difference, in dissect-ing the body of a king and that of the meanest of his subjects; and a judicious philosopher would discover a surprising conformity, in discuss-ing the nature and qualities of the minds" (Granger 6: 179). The paradox about the "many respects" in which the highest and lowest are united is the focus of this essay investigating Jonathan Swift's (1667–1745) and Joshua Reynolds's (1723–92) lives and works for the contrasting and bizarre illustrations they offer about what seems, at first glance, to be little more than a vague cliché mixing medieval Christian ideas of equality with modern Enlightenment notions of uniformity.

I

Swift was keenly interested in the lower orders. Ireland's and England's dregs, from city and country, fill up his writings, as they filled up his life.

Paupers, beggars, street hawkers, prostitutes, criminals, outcasts, lunatics, charlatans, and marginal people are the subjects of poems, pamphlets, and proposals that flowed continuously (and incongruously, some thought) from the pen of the Dean of St. Patrick's Cathedral. In his poetry, they populate "A Description of the Morning" (1709), "A City Shower" (1710), "The Progress of Beauty" (1720), "The Description of an Irish Feast" (1720), "Clever Tom Clinch Going to Be Hanged" (1727), "Mary the Cook-Maid's Letter to Dr. Sheridan" (1732), "A Beautiful Young Nymph Going to Bed" (1734), and a host of other verses.[2] In his prose, they surface in "A Short View of the State of Ireland" (1728), "A Modest Proposal" (1729), "The Humble Petition of the Footmen in and about the City of Dublin" (1733), and "Directions to Servants" (1745), where the lower orders are treated in a spectrum of captious tones ranging from light irony to humorless savagery. Two representative pieces, the first in verse and the second in prose, exemplify the censorious tones Swift adopts to describe the marginal and outcast, especially street vendors and beggars.

"Verses made for Women who cry Apples, &c," a suite of six undated satiric rhymes first published by George Faulkner in 1746, was allegedly composed to help street hawkers sell their wares; to that end, these jingles were written in the voice of the poet speaking as a set of female street-mongers.[3] How do the lower orders fare in these jocular, self-incriminating verses? Not well. In their professional dealings, these costermongers are a false, deceptive lot whose apparent trade is food or medicine but whose real commerce is sex or dirt. For example, they promote "ripe" asparagus by claiming it has diuretic powers:

> Ripe 'Sparagrass,
> Fit for Lad or Lass,
> To make their Water Pass.

Or they sell oysters for the intestinal therapy, entirely imaginary:

> Charming Oysters I cry,
> My Masters come buy,
> — — — — — —
> Your Stomach they settle.

They hawk the same oysters as an aphrodisiac:

> [Your Stomach they settle,]
> And rouse up your Mettle,
> They'll make you a Dad
> Of a Lass or a Lad.

They also boost oysters as an infallible cure for infertility in married women, whom they crude-mindedly divide into sluts and scolds, a taxonomy that likely mirrors their own social world:

> And, Madam your Wife
> They'll please to the Life;
> Be she Slut, or be she Scold,
> Eat my Oysters, and lye near her,
> She'll be fruitful, never fear her.

Finally and predictably, they fib about their prices, exaggerating the cheapness of the fruits they vend:

> Come buy my fine Wares,
> Plums, Apples, and Pears,
> A hundred a Penny,
> In Conscience too many,
> Come, will you have any.

Their personal lives are of a piece with their professional customs, for they are generally no better than they should be. So they practice sanitary habits and sexual behaviors said to be common to the Irish Catholic underclasses. They reek of the stinking things they vend: "Come, follow me by the Smell,/Here's delicate Onyons to sell." And of course they procreate bountifully: "My Children are seven." But as parents, they are indifferent, even malevolent, toward their offspring: "I wish them in Heaven." They consort with men who are drunks and laggards, whose values they no doubt share:

> My Husband's a Sot,
> With his Pipe and his Pot,
> Not a Farthing will gain 'em,
> And I must maintain 'em.[4]

II

In certain prose works of Swift's (but not in all), the "meaner people" have the same faults they possess in his verse, but the Dean's jocularity and half-cynical indulgence turn first disciplinary and then punitive. His "Proposal for Giving Badges to the Beggars in all the Parishes of Dublin" (1737) advocates that the poor be treated in severe and humiliating ways; yet he signed it "Dean of St. Patrick's," "J. Swift," and "M. B. Drapier" in order to avow its contents using the full weight of his public reputation in its most imposing aspects.[5] In it, he views the greatest part of Dublin's beggars as a set of strollers who "ought to be whipped as a most insufferable Nuisance, being nothing else but a profligate Clan of Thieves, Drunkards, Heathens, and Whoremongers, fitter to be rooted out off the Face of the Earth, than suffered to levy a vast annual Tax upon the City."[6] To prevent their mischief-making, he argues in a public voice for badging them with tags "well sown upon one of their Shoulders, always visible, on Pain of being whipt and turned out of Town; or whatever legal Punishment may be thought proper and effectual" (*Prose Works* 13: 132–33). Adopting a private and confessional tone, he claims an authority on his subject that is individual: "I am personally acquainted with a great Number of Street Beggars," Swift writes, adding that for several years past, "I have not disposed of one single Farthing to a Street Beggar, nor intend to do so until I see a better Regulation; and I have endeavored to persuade all my Brother-walkers to follow my Example, which most of them assure me they do" (*Prose Works* 13: 134, 135).

In words that distantly echo the King of Brobdingnag's description of the English as the "most pernicious race of little odious vermin that nature ever suffered to crawl upon the surface of the earth," the essay caricatures all mendicants, declaring that without exception there is "not a more undeserving vicious Race of human Kind than the Bulk of those who are reduced to Beggary, even in this beggarly Country." Their viciousness takes forms predicted in Swift's verse: they have too many children, making Ireland "the only Christian Country where People contrary to the old Maxim, are the Poverty and not the Riches of the Nation; so, the Blessing of Increase and Multiply is by us converted into a Curse" (*Prose Works* 13: 135). Conflating beggars with criminals and violent brigands, he claims they steal, rob, and menace: "He and his Female are Thieves, and teach the Trade of stealing to their Brood at Four years old; and if his Infirmities be not counterfeit, it is dangerous for a single Person unarmed to meet him on the Road" (*Prose Works* 13: 134). Their indolence, for which they have only themselves to blame, compounds their other faults: "Among the meaner People, nineteen in twenty of those who are reduced to a starving Condition, did not become so by what Lawyers call the Work of God, either upon their Bodies or Goods; but meerly from their own Idleness, attended with all Manner of Vices, particularly Drunkenness, Thievery, and Cheating" (*Prose Works* 13: 135).

What is to be done with them? The answer depends on their status and conduct. Dublin's native beggars clogging shopkeepers' doors ought to be met by "a 'Prentice with a Horse-Whip" whose task should be "to lash every Beggar from the Shop, who is not of the Parish, and doth not wear the Badge of that Parish on his Shoulder" (*Prose Works* 13: 138). Those mendicants who have left England to settle in Ireland—by a bizarre reversal in the direction of colonial immigration, Dublin had become a mecca for British beggars—should be put "into Bridewell, and after a Month's Residence, having been well whipt twice a Day, fed with Bran and Water, and put to hard Labour, they should be returned honestly back with Thanks as cheap as they came" (*Prose Works* 13: 136–37). What about so-called "foreign" beggars, that is, mendicants from rural Ireland who are "foreign" to Dublin? "Must they be left to starve?" Swift asks, in a question that is not entirely rhetorical. "No," he answers, "but they must be driven or whipt out of Town; and let the next Country Parish do as they please, or rather after the Practice in *England,* send them from one Parish to another, until they reach their own Homes." A beggar native to a parish is known to the squire, priest, minister, or relative, the Dean declares. "If he be not quite maimed, he and his Trull, and Litter of Brats (if he hath any) may get half their Support by doing some Kind of Work in their Power, and thereby be less burthensome to the People" (*Prose Works* 13: 133). Such passages, with their low cant terms like "Trull" and animal imagery like "Female," "Litter," and "Brood," are so derogatory, and their exhortation to whipping is so brutal and misanthropic, that the reader might wonder if Ireland's master ironist is here masquerading as the projector of the "Modest Proposal."

III

In his everyday life, by contrast with his writings, Swift treated the lower orders quite leniently, as his indulgence of Dublin's street hawkers and benevolence toward his own household servants demonstrate. A convoluted, but revealing episode in Swift's life (brought to light by Ehrenpreis) shows that he treated Dublin's outcast street vendors with tolerance, generosity, and even fondness.[7] Lord Orrery, in *Remarks on the Life and Writings of Dr. Jonathan Swift* (1752), alleges that the Dean's "command" over a circle of Dublin ladies was such that "you would have smiled to have found his house, a constant seraglio of very virtuous women, who attended him from morning till night, with an obedience, an awe, and an assiduity, that are seldom paid to the richest, or the most powerful lovers; no, not even to the Grand Signor himself."[8] This passage, written after Swift's death, gave Patrick Delany "great concern" because he rightly sensed its sexual innuendo, proclaimed by the tendentious words "Lovers" and "seraglio." Delany, in *Observations upon Lord Orrery's Remarks on the Life and Writings of Dr. Jonathan Swift* (1754), defended his friend, admitting that Swift did indeed maintain a following of women in Dublin: "Swift kept a greater, and much more extended Seraglio than the Grand Seignor," Delany declares, confessing that he himself "had the honour, to be admitted, (more than once) to bear him company in his visits to them."9 These visits "were always by day-light: and for the most part, in the most open and public parts of the city. But yet truth obliges me to own, that he also visited some of them, even in by-alleys, and under arches; (places of long suspected fame)" (Delany 131).

Delany reveals the identities of this "seraglio's" members: "One of these mistresses sold plums, another, hob nails; a third tapes; a fourth, ginger bread; a fifth knitted, a sixth darned socks and a seventh cobbled shoes, and so on." Next he describes the appearances of these women and their conditions: "One of these mistresses wanted an eye: another, a nose: a third, an arm: a fourth, a foot: a fifth, had all the attractions of Agna's *Pollipus;* and a sixth, more than all those of Aesop's hump, and all of them as old at least as some of Louis the XIVth's mistresses, and many of them, (for I must own he had many) much older" (Delany 131–32). In a letter to Sheridan, Swift gave these women nicknames, a few based on their call-ings but most upon their diseases or missing limbs: Flora, Stumpantha, Cancerina, Pullagowna, Friterilla, Stumpy (one of his favorite, so called "from the fame of her wooden leg"), and another with the same common condition bearing the sobriquet Stumpa-Nympha (Delany 134, 133).

Finally Delany describes how the Dean treated these women, who surely seemed to their patron nothing less than allegories of the Irish nation itself. The account of his bounty to them ought to be read against the backgrounds of his legendary miserliness and the practice of most alms-givers, then and now, which is to give charity to indigents without speaking to them.

> He saluted them with becoming kindness: asked them how they did, how they throve: What stock they had? &c. And as mistresses, all the world owns, are expensive things, it is certain he never saw them but to his cost. If any of their ware were such, as he could possibly make use of, or pretend to make use of, he always bought some: and paid for every half-penny-worth, at least sixpence: and for every penny-worth, a shilling. If their saleables were of another nature, he added something to their stock: with strict charges of industry and honesty. (Delany 132–33)

Delany observes that the number of Swift's patrons was "beyond my counting" and concludes: "And I must once more own, (for truth exacts it of me) that these mistresses were very numerous: insomuch, that there was scarce one street or alley or lane in Dublin, its suburbs, and its environs that had not, at least one or more of them" (Delany 133). When they died he buried them with church honors but without church fees or onerous church regulations: "Cancerina is dead," he lamented to Sheridan on 27 March 1733, "and I left her go to her Grave without a Coffin and without Fees."10

As well as coddling the women beggars of Dublin, Swift also indulged his servants, even when they were troublesome and faithless. For three years, he tolerated the shenanigans of his Irish valet Patrick, who was feckless, irresponsible, and drunken; and when he finally fired him, he gave him £3–10 in severance pay (Ehrenpreis 2: 552–53). He considered Alexander McGee "the best servant in the world"; when McGee died, the Dean complained that he had known "few greater losses in life" (Ehrenpreis 2: 422–23). He buried McGee in St. Patrick's Cathedral, where he erected a small monument (still standing) in his memory. Most signally, he elevated his common household servants into arbiters of his literary style. The Dublin publisher, George Faulkner, records that when he came to issue the Dean's collected works, their author, who was obsessed with matters of style and especially clarity, laid down, as a condition, "that the editor should attend him early every morning, or when most convenient, to read to him, that the sounds might strike the ear, as well as the sense the understanding" (Ehrenpreis 3: 783–84). In actual fact, the volumes were prepared a little differently. For purposes of clarifying his style, Swift read his works in the presence of two men servants from his household, and "when he had any Doubt, he would ask them the Meaning of what they heard; which, if they did not comprehend, he would alter and amend until they understood it perfectly well, and then would say, *This will do; for I write to the Vulgar, more than to the Learned*" (*Prose Works* 13: 202–203). As well as providing him with occasional subjects about which to write reformatory tracts and light verses, the lower orders in Swift's household helped mold the style and shape the technique of his collected prose and poetry.

IV

Beggars and street characters played an even more important but somewhat different role in the art and life of Sir Joshua Reynolds. While Swift satirized the lower orders, Reynolds took the opposite tack: he idealized them in his paintings to such an extent that they are unrecognizable. Only when we know the parts they played in the rituals of his studio can we identify them in his art or understand how extensively he used them and how radically he transformed them.

Throughout his career, Reynolds paid street people of all kinds to model for him in his atelier.[11] In *Iphigenia,* he sketched the Greek heroine after a "battered courtesan," while in *Venus Chiding Cupid for Learning to Cast Accounts* (1771) he apparently drew "Venus" from "some girl in low life of thirteen or fourteen years of age," probably a teenage prostitute (Postle, *Angels* 23, 65). His most famous model was George White, whom William

Hazlitt described as "a common mendicant at the corner of a street, waiting patiently for some charitable donation."[12] In Reynolds's atelier, White, "an Irishman, once a paviour, then a beggar," took on successively the roles of a nobleman, a bandit, a Renaissance pope, assorted saints, and various wise men: his most celebrated role was as the protagonist of *Count Hugolino and His Children in the Dungeon as Described by Dante* (1773).[13]

Though the artist employed a spectrum of adults from the marginal and outcast classes, he also used children as models: "Sir Joshua was incessantly practicing from hired models, and from children—beggar children," according to James Northcote (1746–1831), an apprentice who studied with him, lived in his house for some years, and kept a detailed and hagiographic account of his master's studio practices.[14] Indeed the portraitist preferred indigent children before all other models, valuing them for their cheapness, compliance, and disposability. More than that, he believed their "looks and attitudes, being less under the controul of art, and local manners, are more characteristical of the species than those of men and women," according to Northcote.[15] They first appeared in his appointment book in 1759, when a terse entry for 5 April reads, "Boy 6," that is, a sitting for a poor boy who would model at 6 P.M.[16] His appointment book for 6 March 1770 carries an entry for a "Beggar child" typical of at least 150 such entries for sittings with indigent child models who, between 1770 and 1773, came to his studio in droves. "Good G-d! how he used to fill his studio with such malkins," Northcote exclaimed in a conversation with James Ward; "you would have been afraid to come near them, and yet from these people he produced the most celebrated pictures" (Fletcher 121).

Though these children were nameless to Reynolds, one of them is known to us. The youth portrayed in *The Boy with Cabbage Nets* (1775) was among the artist's most habitual models in the 1770s (Postle, *Angels* 75). The boy posed for *The Infant Samuel* (1776), *A Fortune Teller* (1777), and several studies of children reading; the figure in *The Schoolboy* (c. 1776–77), according to a contemporary, is "almost his absolute portrait."[17] Though he appears in Reynolds's sitter book under the anonymous sobriquet "Net Boy," he was identified by a man who met him in the painter's atelier as William Mason, "an orphan of the poorest parents, and left with three or four brothers and sisters, whom he taught, as they were able, to make cabbage-nets, and with these he went about with them offering them for sale, by which he provided both for their maintenance and his own. What became of him afterwards, I know not. Sir Joshua has told me, when talking of his beggars, that when he wanted them again they were very frequently never to be found" (Cotton 57).

Mason posed for several studies in which he read or carried books, as he does in *The Schoolboy*. Exhibited at the Royal Academy in 1777 and praised by Horace Walpole as "very fine, in the style of Titian," this portrait of Mason was bought for fifty guineas by the second Earl of Warwick who hung it alone in the library at Warwick Castle, where, as one modern scholar remarks without irony, it stood as "an image of learning within an appropriate setting."[18] Thus did Reynolds, celebrating the link between books and children, construct the adored young scholar of the Enlightenment upon the destitute and illiterate street waifs of London.

In the 1760s, appointments with urchins like Mason followed within a day or two after engagements with named children having their portraits painted, indicating that street youths served as lay sitters for Peter Toms, George Roth, Northcote, and the other students who served as Reynolds's drapery men and kept his assembly line moving. In painting likenesses such as *Master Hare* (1788) or *Master Crewe as Henry VIII* (1775–76), his wittiest portrait of a child from an elite family, the artist took the faces of his aristocratic subjects, dismissed them, and substituted beggars in their place. When he had done the face, he had an assistant finish the portrait, calling upon members of his own household or street urchins to model the subject's hands, arms, and legs (Postle, *Reynolds* 61–62).

In the 1770s and '80s, however, Reynolds turned to allegories and fancy pictures, painting very young children and babies, even to the neglect of portraiture (Postle, *Angels* 59). For these genres, he employed beggar children not as lay sitters but as living models who appear in his oils as saints, prophets, angels, fortune tellers, imps, shepherds, and (rarely) streetwise urchins (Postle, *Angels* 7). Beginning early in the 1770s, he devoted weeks, even months, solely to painting street boys and girls, sketching just their heads. Often he had a student add bodies at a later stage, but occasionally he sold these likenesses simply as face paintings (Postle, *Angels* 74). All his young models, referred to in his sitter-book only as "boy" or "child," were painted in a high style: "Fuscous colours characterise the paintings of neglected, mendicant children, who seem to appear like weeds outside of conservatories and gardens," Patricia Crown observes aptly.[19]

Reynolds painted indigent children so often and so successfully that he established a new subgenre of fancy pictures devoted to the very young, illustrated by *A Child's Portrait in Different Views: Angels' Heads* (c. 1787) showing the countenances of boys and girls from different angles to resemble a cluster of cherubim. Until his death, such fancy pictures making urchins into angels and angels into urchins, formed an increasingly important and lucrative part of his artistic production. Snatched up by members of fashionable society, these paintings fetched higher prices than his portraits of comparable size; in 1772, when Reynolds was charging thirty-five guineas for portraits, he charged Lord Irwin fifty guineas for *The Shepherd Boy* (1770–71) of the same size (Postle, *Angels* 7, 59).

Though fifty guineas was his standard fee for fancy pictures of beggars, it was not his top figure: he charged Alderman Boydell a hundred guineas for *Puck* (1789–90), celebrated for the impish magic of its Shakespearean subject, which Sir Joshua said he painted from a little child he found sitting on his doorstep at Leicester Fields one day.[20]

His best-known fancy pictures are all likenesses of beggar children from this period. *Infant Jupiter* (1774), *A Sleeping Girl, The Children in the Wood,* and *The Piping Shepherd* exemplify his transformation of orphans into emblems of ideal pathos and refined sensibility. He kept *The Piping Shepherd* (1771–73) in his possession until his death, when he bequeathed it to his niece Mary Palmer (Postle, *Angels* 58–59). After her death in 1821, it passed to George Phillips; he bought it for the astronomical sum of £430.10s, an amount surpassed only by the prices paid for Reynolds's large subject pictures and his designs for the *Nativity* at New College, Oxford (Postle, *Reynolds* 59). (A rough sense of the present-day worth of £430.10s is offered by the fact an agricultural worker earned 9/4d a week in 1824 but a hand-loom weaver, whose trade was depressed, earned a penny an hour or 6/- a week for seventy-two hours labor in the 1830s.)[21] Benjamin Robert Haydon, present at the auction when *The Piping Shepherd* fetched this price, captured the painting's place within the aesthetic of late eighteenth-century sensibility, describing it as

> one of his finest emanations of his sentiment. The look of his [the shepherd's] eyes, the tone of his complexion, the grace of his motion, the pressure of the upper lip on the flageolet, the actions of the fingers, the tone of the background fill the mind with those associations of solitude and sound which are so affecting in Nature when the melancholy strain of the flageolet comes to my ear across a meadow or dell. The colour of this exquisite harmony with the idea of a yellow leaf in Autumn opposed by a dark sky, fills the mind with associations of melancholy and music. I think it the most complete hit in expression and colour that he ever made.[22]

In addition to serving as lay sitters for portraits and live models for fancy pictures, beggar children played a number of other, more consequential roles in Reynolds's painting. For example, beyond providing mechanical assistance, infant beggars worked catalytic effects on Reynolds, prompting him to discover materials—poses as well as subjects—that did not come to mind spontaneously. The observant Northcote illustrates the children's unique agency when he describes how one particular indigent actually dictated to Reynolds, instead of the other way around. On a certain day, when Reynolds was working in his studio

> the Beggar Infant, who was sitting to him for some other picture, during the sitting, fell asleep; Reynolds was so pleased with the innocence of the object,

that he would not disturb its repose to go on with the picture on which he was engaged, but took up a fresh canvas, and quickly painted the child's head as it lay before it moved; and as the infant altered its position, still in sleep, he sketched another view of its head on the same canvas (Northcote 1: 284–85).

Commenting on this event, the admiring Northcote remarks that here Reynolds "may be said also to have produced [a work of art] by an accident" (Northcote 1:285). Naturally, he is blind to the crucial role played by what he calls "the object," that is, the infant, who begins as a mechanical model but turns into a powerful inspiration for *Children in the Woods,* one of Reynolds's most successful fancy pictures, exhibited at the Royal Academy in 1770.

In *Children in the Woods,* Reynolds's debt to beggar children, however striking, is limited to a single case of inspiration, though perhaps such cases were repeated from time to time. But Reynolds, like Swift, was also indebted to the lower orders for a more fundamental acquisition than the occasional pose or subject of a fancy picture. According to Northcote, "Sir Joshua was incessantly practicing from hired models, and from children— beggar children . . . his incessant practice from the models enabled him to acquire that mechanical dexterity which made him so famous." Just as Swift was indebted to his household servants for what is most characteristic about his style—its lucidity—so Reynolds was indebted to street children for what is most distinctive and fundamental about his technique, his dexterity and painterly eloquence.

V

However essential children were to Reynolds, both formally and materially, they were not cosseted in his studio, as privileged children were. "When the children of the nobility were brought to him," Northcote relates, "he was able to paint them quite rapidly. Oh! What grand rackets there used to be at Sir Joshua's when these children were with him! He used to romp and play with them and talk to them in their own way; and, whilst all this was going on, he actually snatched those exquisite touches of expression which make his portraits of children so captivating" (Fletcher 78). By contrast, he treated beggar children brusquely. They were furniture, as appears in Northcote's revelation that "When any of the great people came, Sir Joshua used to flounce them [child beggars] into the next room until he wanted them again" (Fletcher 121). Naturally he only hired distressed children who, "being dependant people, were quiet and gave no trouble," Northcote writes, in a remarkable tale in which he parallels his attitude to horses with Sir Joshua's to beggars:

The Prince of Wales one day sent to offer me any of his horses to paint from, but I didn't avail myself of his kindness, for I found I could obtain what I wanted so much more comfortably at a livery stables. Now Sir Joshua felt this same thing strongly, and was for ever painting from beggars, over whom he had complete command and leaving his mind perfectly at liberty for the purposes of study! (Fletcher 121).

The detachment that Northcote here attributes to Reynolds is confirmed by an accident that happened in the artist's studio, though the importance of the event lies in the rubric under which the apprentice, speaking in his master's voice, thinks it worth telling at all. One day, Northcote reveals, a very young beggar infant whom Reynolds was painting plunged from the lap of its mother "who carelessly let the child fall over her arm on the floor, which, as she sat at the time in a chair raised some height above it, made the fall very considerable; but, by great good fortune, the child received no material injury from the accident" (Northcote 1: 285). The tragedy that had been averted, Northcote's narrative makes clear, was double, involving the wretched child and the great artist. The child received no "material" injury, though the extent of its hurts is not disclosed. But in a far more important register, the careless mother, Northcote reveals, "had nearly given a finale to Sir Joshua's studies from this subject" (Northcote 1: 285).

VI

In romantic studies of beggar infants and children, Reynolds generally took care not to hint at the actual conditions of poor London children, as Hogarth and Gainsborough did in their art. In this regard, as Martin Postle points out, the portraitist's *Beggar Boy and His Sister* (1775) is "unusual among his fancy pictures in that it depicts the child in a role which approximated his status in life, an impoverished urchin eking out a living by selling cabbage nets on the streets of London" (Postle, *Angels* 84). By contrast, Hogarth—in the genre that he invented, the progress—regularly depicted city urchins in every shade of misery and vice, from the little boy molested by his tyrannical sister in "Noon" to the gang of gamesters in the "First Stage of Cruelty" who threaten, with their sadistic iniquities, the very future of the nation. The more sympathetic Gainsborough focused on the plight of rural children. In *Margaret Gainsborough as a Gleaner* (1750s), he illuminated the grim realities faced by rural children who were forced to labor hard in order to save the harvest. In *Girl with a Penny* (1780), he evokes the extreme poverty of rural children while alluding to the indigence of the very beggar boys and girls, rural and urban, who modeled for him. By this allusion, he also hints at the vexed commercial bargain that bound laboring children to artists (Postle, *Angels* 90). The Nacton House of Industry, a workhouse for boys and girls established in 1758, congratulated itself on providing useful employment for children "who otherwise would have figured nowhere but in a landscape of Gainsborough's, the spawn of gypsies, lying upon a sunny bank half naked, with their bundles of stolen wood by their sides."[23] But the realities of modeling for Gainsborough and other artists contradicts this idealized and self-serving fable; after all, holding intricate, torturous poses for indefinite periods of time (a sitting with Reynolds could run to five hours) at the demands of peevish artists was exacting and irksome for squirming children who may well have seen artists' ateliers as elegant sweatshops. Northcote, who worked in the next room to Reynolds when he had no other sitters but beggars, "would often hear the voice of a child, 'Sir,—Sir, I'm tired.' There would be a little movement, another half-hour would pass, and then the plaintive repetition, 'Sir!—I'm tired" (Leslie and Taylor 1: 358).

In his personal life, Reynolds was certainly aware of the plight of the poor children of London who sat to him. His private response to their difficulties appears in an "annoying" incident that occurred in the 1790s. One day, according to a report in the *Morning Herald,* a mob gathered outside the artist's grand house at No. 47 Leicester Fields.[24] A little girl of eighteen months had been abandoned at his doorstep, following the custom of the time by which the poor left infants at the houses of the rich in the expectation that the latter would admit, adopt, or sponsor them in some way. As the crowd swelled, its members battered on Sir Joshua's door, demanding that he take in the foundling. Reynolds refused.[25] So the throng appealed to the benevolence of a nameless gentleman walking by, who ordered the infant to be carried to his home.[26]

In distancing himself from the lower orders, Reynolds stood apart not just from the gentleman passerby and Jonathan Swift, but also from his fellow artists Gainsborough and Hogarth. All his life, Hogarth was personally involved in the Foundling Hospital: he gave the hospital big sums of money, supervised its wet nurses, and designed uniforms for its orphans. Late in life, he and Jane took a number of foundlings into their home in Chiswick; when the hospital called for the children's return after William Hogarth's death, Jane protested, demanding to keep them until the end of the year so that "they would enjoy the benefit of a run in the Country for the Summer Season, which in all probability would quite establish their Healths."[27]

Gainsborough's daughter Margaret wanted to adopt one of her father's favorite models, Jack Hill from Richmond, who is pictured in the *Cottage Children or the Wood Gatherers.*[28] Her impulse may have originated with the artist, as this tale suggests:

Gainsborough, who often found the models for his pictures of children by chance in the streets or fields, was walking near his house one day at the close of this year when he was accosted by a beggar woman, who was accompanied by a little boy of singular beauty. The painter, noticing the child, gave the woman some money and asked her to call upon him in Pall Mall on the following day and bring her charge with her. She came, and Gainsborough had the child washed and dressed and was so impressed by his appearance that he offered to take entire charge of him from that time forth. The woman, who proved to be the boy's mother, asked for a few days to consider the matter. At the end of that time she returned and told Gainsborough that she could not part with her child; not it appears, on account of parental affection, but because during the preceding twelve months he had earned by begging about seven shillings a day (Whitley 232).

VII

No doubt there are as many different ways of accounting for these reverse symmetries between Swift and Reynolds as there are current critical approaches. Scholars with biographical and historical biases, in order to explain the gulf between Swift's literary severity and personal indulgence, might point to his hatred of humanity, which he himself contrasted with his love of individuals:

> I have ever hated all Nations professions and Communityes, and all my love is towards individualls for instance I hate the tribe of Lawyers, but I love Councellor such a one, Judge such a one for so with Physicians (I will not Speak of my own Trade) Soldiers, English, Scotch, French; and the rest but principally I hate and detest that animal called man, although I hartily love John, Peter, Thomas, and so forth. (*Correspondence* 3: 103)

This well-known antithesis in Swift's attitude seems especially helpful in accounting for the satiric tone of "Verses made for Women who cry Apples &c," which aim at the type rather than the individual, but also take as their targets, not just the human, but the literary. As so much of Swift's poetry does, "Verses" targets poetic idealization, more specifically, the romanticized street characters of sentimental rhymes churned out by Swift's friend John Gay. Gay, in his *Trivia: or, The Art of Walking the Streets of London* (1716), viewed city hawkers through rose-colored lenses:

> Successive Crys the Season's Change declare,
> And mark the Monthly Progress of the Year.
> Hark, how the Streets with treble Voices ring,
> To sell the bounteous Product of the Spring!
> Sweet smelling Flow'rs, and Elder's early Bud,

> With Nettle's tender Shoots, to cleanse the Blood:
> And when *June's* Thunder cools the sultry Skies,
> Ev'n *Sundays* are prophan'd by Mackrell Cries.
> Wallnuts the *Fruit'rer's* Hand, in Autumn, stain,
> Blue Plumbs, and juicy Pears augment his Gain;
> Next Oranges the longing Boys entice,
> To trust their Copper-Fortunes to the Dice.
> When Rosemary and Bays, the Poet's Crown,
> Are bawl'd, in frequent Cries, through all the Town,
> Then judge the festival of *Christmas* near,
> *Christmas,* the joyous Period of the Year.[29]

Gay's lyrical poem, an urban pastoral, harmonizes the rhythms of the seasons with the cycles of the liturgical calendar with the shouts of London's hawkers, whom he represents as picturesque and benevolent agents and avatars of prelapsarian bounty. Swift's astringent "Verses," opposing low, mundane reality to high, poetic mythmaking, took aim at this kind of idealization, which also proliferated in the Cries of London, a popular genre of word and image in which saccharine likenesses of hawkers are accompanied by honeyed texts that exaggerate the virtues of the foodstuffs and wares sold on the streets of the capital: "Fair Lemons & Oranges," "Ripe Speargas," "Fat Chickens," "Fine Writing Inke."[30] Behind the Dean's critical attitude lies a sensibility illustrated in a comic episode from Swift's *Journal to Stella,* where, writing about the vicissitudes of daily life in London, he complains of one street vendor in particular, "a restless dog crying Cabbages and Savoys plagues me every morning about this time, he is now at it. I wish his largest Cabbage was sticking in his Throat."[31] In turning to Reynolds, traditional-minded scholars might contrast Swift's economy of feelings about the individual (as opposed to the type) with the painter's fondness for the general and indifference to the particular, articulated in his *Discourses,* practiced in his portraits, and expressed existentially in his conduct.

Psychologically minded critics, on the other hand, might view Swift, a Protestant living in a Catholic country, an "English grandee" settled in Ireland, and a rich gentleman dwelling in a nation of women beggars, as a marginal person in a marginal world, whose wretched inhabitants he ultimately came to identify with, an identification he openly acknowledged in verse:

> He's all the day saunt'ring,
> With labourers bant'ring,
> Among his colleagues,
> A parcel of Teagues,
> (Whom he brings in among us

And bribes with mundungus.)
Hail fellow, well met,
All dirty and wet:
Find out if you can,
Who's master, who's man.[32]

For Swift, there was no escape from Dublin and its "dirty and wet" Tea-gues, whose poverty, disease, and misery were "indescribable," but whose cause he embraced.[33] But that embrace may have come at the price of a measure of self-hatred, hinted at in the self-deprecating verses just quoted. That Swift felt some ambivalence toward himself and that he inclined to self-loathing as well as self-pity are suggested by the fact that, in reflecting on his exile to Ireland, he identifies himself with vermin, writing to Boling-broke of dying "here in a rage, like a poisoned rat in a hole" (*Correspondence* 3: 383).

With regard to Reynolds, psychologically inclined critics might note his professional interest in and idealization of prepubescent children untainted by erotic experiences; a preference for such youths looks like a denial of those aspects of human existence lost when the individual is "corrupted" by sexual experiences. In his personal life, Reynolds labored to deny his own sexuality; according to Northcote, he worked incessantly "and suffered nothing to turn his attention from it [painting]; no pleasure, no feelings of any kind were allowed to stand in the way" (Fletcher 77). He neither wedded nor patronized prostitutes, as his friend Samuel Johnson did, when he was young. And he never contemplated marriage, as Swift did twice. From another angle, this extreme repression of adult sexuality, with an attendant aversion to the body and its "lower" functions, may have rein-forced economic motives, traditional artistic practices, and professional training in shaping his studio practice. Reynolds's mentor was Thomas Hudson, whose genius failed him without exception after he had painted a sitter's head, so that "he was obliged to apply to one Vanhaaken to put it [the head] on the shoulders and to finish the drapery, both of which he was himself totally incapable" (Northcote 17). Reynolds, from his earliest days, devoted himself to painting only faces; he assigned the "inferior" parts of the body (as well as the clothes that disguise those parts)[34] to underlings: students, assistants, and drapery men like Giuseppi Marchi, whom he brought to England with him from Rome for that purpose in 1752, at the start of his career (Northcote 32). Certainly the prevailing psychodynamic behind his art is the denial of the body and the severe repression of adult eroticism, enacted socially in the hierarchical arrangement of his studio practice and mirrored aesthetically in his idealized face painting.

At the other end of the spectrum, contemporary theorists influenced by Bakhtin might see both men as bourgeois spectators drawn to and repelled by their own antithesis in the lower orders, whom they compulsively needed to portray, survey, classify, exploit, and reform.[35] Like some new theoretical insights, however, this reading making symbolically central those who are economically and culturally marginal is strikingly similar to Granger's remarks about the affinities between the highest and lowest social classes.

These analyses, rooted in individual and collective perspectives, might be complemented by an understanding based upon social practice. Between the seventeenth and eighteenth centuries, elites in England from both the aristocracy and upper-middle class staged a withdrawal from the lower orders in public and private life, Lawrence Stone has shown.[36] In public life, for example, they ceased to ride at the head of great cavalcades, removing instead to shuttered coaches and curtained sedan chairs. In private realms, they stopped eating in great halls staffed by servants; instead they withdrew to particular dining rooms where, in order to enjoy complete privacy, they even served themselves from "dumb waiters." Swift, who died in 1745, and Reynolds, who died in 1792, lived on different sides of what has been called "the great withdrawal." Their behaviors toward the lower orders offer exemplary illustrations of the practices of elites on both sides of that divide, practices accentuated by the fact that Reynolds lived in cosmopolitan London, while Swift resided in Dublin, little more than a big market town with a population of 58,045 in 1682, according to the estimate of Sir William Petty.[37]

NOTES

1. James Granger, *A Biographical History of England,* 5th ed., 6 vols. (London, 1824): 1: x.

2. I am indebted to Carole Fabricant for suggesting some of these titles; in writing this essay, I have been guided by her book, *Swift's Landscape: A Revised Version* (Notre Dame: University of Notre Dame Press, 1995), the most comprehensive and incisive account of Swift's thinking available.

3. These verses are accepted as Swift's by every editor of his poetry.

4. Jonathan Swift, *Swift's Poems,* ed. Harold Williams, 3 vols. (Oxford: Clarendon Press, 1937) 3: 951–53. All quotations from "Verses" are drawn from Williams's edition of Swift's poems.

5. "M. B. Drapier" appears in a medallion portrait of Swift as Dean on the title page.

6. Jonathan Swift, *Prose Works of Jonathan Swift,* ed. Herbert Davis (Oxford: Blackwell, 1959), 13: 139; hereafter cited parenthetically in the text as *Prose Works.*

7. Irving Ehrenpreis, *Swift: The Man, His Works, and the Age,* 3 vols. (London: Methuen, 1962–83), 3: 813–20.

8. John Orrery, *Remarks on the Life and Writings of Dr. Jonathan Swift* (London, 1752), 128.

9. Patrick Delany, *Observations upon Lord Orrery's Remarks on the Life and Writings of Dr. Jonathan Swift* (London, 1754), 131.

10. Jonathan Swift, *The Correspondence of Jonathan Swift,* ed. Harold Williams, 5 vols. (Oxford: Clarendon Press, 1963–65) 4: 130. Hereafter cited parenthetically in the text as *Correspondence.*

11. The Victorian painter William Powell Frith believed he had found the model for Reynolds's *Infant Baptist,* then an old man. In his late sixties, the man identified Reynolds as a "deaf gent" with an ear trumpet. Agreeing to work as Frith's model, the man supposed that Frith too would ask him to remove his shirt "as the deaf gent did." Told by Frith that this was not necessary, the man asked, "Then why did the old gent make me take off all but my trousers and give me a crook to hold? There was a lamb in the picture as the old gent done" (Martin Postle, *Angels and Urchins: The Fancy Picture in 18th-Century British Art* [Nottingham: Djanolgy Gallery, 1998], 63).

12. Brian Allen, *Toward a Modern Art World: Studies in British Art I* (New Haven and London: Yale University Press, 1995), 135.

13. Charles Robert Leslie and Tom Taylor, *The Life and Times of Sir Joshua Reynolds,* 2 vols. (London, 1865), 1: 385; Postle, *Angels and Urchins,* 7.

14. Ernest Fletcher, *Conversations with James Northcote* (London: Methuen, 1901), 77.

15. James Northcote, *The Life of Sir Joshua Reynolds,* 2nd edition, 2 vols. (London, 1819), 1:298.

16. Martin Postle, *Sir Joshua Reynolds: The Subject Pictures* (Cambridge: Cambridge University Press, 1965), 61.

17. William Cotton, *Sir Joshua Reynolds's Notes and Observations on Pictures* (London, 1859), 57.

18. Walpole is quoted in James C. Steward, *The New Child: British Art and the Origins of Modern Childhood 1730–1830* (Berkeley: University Art Museum, 1995), 145; the quote about the "image of learning" is also Steward's, *New Child,* 145.

19. Patricia Crown, "Portraits and Fancy Pictures by Gainsborough and Reynolds: Contrasting Images of Childhood," *British Journal for Eighteenth-Century Studies* (1984) 7: 161.

20. Nicholas Penny, ed., *Reynolds* (New York: Abrams, 1986), 322.

21. John Burnett, *A History of the Cost of Living* (Harmondsworth: Penguin, 1969), 249–50.

22. Benjamin Haydon, *The Diary of Benjamin Robert Haydon,* ed. William B. Pope, 5 vols. (Cambridge: Harvard University Press, 1960–64), 2: 337.

23. Sidney Webb, *English Poor Law History* (London: Longman's, 1929), Part I, 127–29.

24. For a description of this residence (as well as a masterful account of the painter's career), see Richard Wendorf's *Sir Joshua Reynolds: The Painter in Society* (Cambridge: Harvard University Press, 1996), 112.

25. It well may be Reynolds's servants, knowing their master's will or following his instructions, who refused to open the door.

26. My narrative of these events is based upon William T. Whitley, *Artists and their Friends in England,* 2 vols. (London: Medici, 1928), 2: 127–28.

27. Jenny Ugelow, *Hogarth: A Life and World* (London: Faber and Faber, 1997), 704.

28. William T. Whitley, *Thomas Gainsborough* (London: Smith, 1915), 292–93.

29. John Gay, *Trivia: or, The Art of Walking the Streets of London* (London, 1716), Book II, 40–41.

30. These captions are drawn from Marcellus Laroon's *Cryes of the City of London drawne after the Life,* which, first published in 1687 and regularly republished until 1821, was certainly known to Swift.

31. Jonathan Swift, *Journal to Stella,* 2 vols. (Oxford: Clarendon Press, 1948), 2: 581.

32. Swift, *Poems,* 3: 856.

33. Constantia Maxwell, *Dublin under the Georges, 1714–1830* (London: Faber and Faber, n.d.), 138.

34. Northcote records that Reynolds "either could not or would not take the trouble to give a sufficient look of reality to them [draperies]. He would throw a piece of muslin over the back of a chair, in order to see the character of it, but seldom troubled himself to do more" (Fletcher 211).

35. Peter Stallybras and Alon White, *The Politics and Poetics of Transgression* (Ithaca: Cornell University Press, 1986), 128, 193.

36. Lawrence Stone, *The Family, Sex, and Marriage in England, 1500–1800* (New York: Harper and Row, 1977), 253–58.

37. Maxwell, *Dublin Under the Georges,* 138. Maxwell gives the population of London in 1700 as 674,350; she also notes that James Whitelaw took a census of Dublin that put the count at 172,091 in the years 1798–1805. Whitelaw's figure suggesting that Petty's may be too low, but it confirms the view that Dublin was regarded as a big town rather than a city as this time.

Part IV
Swift and Ireland

Swift, Postcolonialism, and Irish Studies: The Valence of Ambivalence

Robert Mahony

TRUISM AS IT IS THAT LITERARY THEORY OUGHT ALWAYS TO BE SUPported by evidence, the evidentiary import of an item of information already known in literary or historical studies, if considered from a theoretical perspective, may increase markedly. To give a personal case in point, an article of mine on Jonathan Swift published a few years ago cited one such item which seems to me now to have more significance as evidence than I noticed then:

> He was no revisionist in terms of a sectarian colonial history. He accepted, for instance, the inflated numbers for the Protestant victims of 1641 hallowed by generations of propaganda: commenting in his own copy of Clarendon's *History of the Rebellion* upon the author's estimate of "Forty or Fifty Thousand of English Protestants murther'd," Swift wrote in the margin "at least."[1]

Swift's marginal note was hardly my discovery. His copy of Clarendon has long been preserved in Archbishop Marsh's Library in Dublin, and the comment here, along with the rest of such material then available, was published in Herbert Davis's edition of Swift's *Prose Works*.[2] I cited the comment as part of an argument about Swift's efforts to adjust Irish Protestant colonial perceptions of their situation in the 1720s. Because this population had been subjected to eight decades of propaganda about Protestant victimization in the early stages of an Irish Catholic rising that began in 1641, when (it was held, inaccurately) many thousands were massacred,[3] a fear of Catholics was deeply cultivated among them, and consequently a psychology of dependence upon England, by whose military efforts under Cromwell the rising had eventually been crushed. Swift's marginal note on Clarendon indicates that he accepted this colonial fear of Catholics as having an historical basis in the events of 1641.

When he started in earnest to intervene in Irish affairs in the 1720s, however, Swift was clearly, if implicitly, confuting the applicability of the "lesson" by then traditionally derived from those events, that Catholics were to be feared and that dependence upon England (or, following its union with Scotland, Britain) was necessary to hold their bloodthirsty natures in check. For the combination of such fear and dependence in the Irish Protestant understanding of their situation had led them not to resist, however they might resent, British measures that by the 1720s had severely restricted both the political liberties of this settler population and the opportunities available for their economic advancement. Swift attempted to displace this sense of helpless dependence upon England (and implicitly, though only implicitly, the fear of Catholics that underlay it) by fostering economic self-reliance. Since the Westminster Parliament had forbidden the export of Irish wool, for instance, he pressed in his *Proposal for the Universal Use of Irish Manufacture* of 1720 for Irish people of all ranks to wear home-produced woollen goods and to cease importing cloth from Britain or abroad. This would strengthen the Irish economy directly by supporting domestic industry and stemming the outflow of Irish capital to British and foreign suppliers. As an avenue to prosperity, moreover, as he pointed out in later writings, this was far superior in the long term to the common practice of rackrenting tenants, which indeed enhanced the income of the Irish gentry in the short term but precluded longer-term economic development by exacerbating the poverty already widespread in the countryside.[4] Rackrenting was also, of course, a form of oppression to which Swift as a moralist (and, not incidentally, as a Christian minister) strenuously objected.

The weight of evidence, I believe, supports that argument, but Swift's marginal note on Clarendon is puzzling nonetheless, for it implies a counterweight, and in Swift's own mind. It is still generally the case that Swift is regarded as a cosmopolitan exiled to the provinces, a case he repeatedly makes himself; that the provincialism with which he was confronted was that of his native land renders his case bitterly piquant. He didn't think of himself, or at least preferred not to think of himself, as Irish except in geographical terms; but his note implies that he shared with those of his Irish Protestant, colonial stock a sense of heritage that he could reveal in an unguarded moment as he read Clarendon's *History,* pen in hand. In one sense, this impression amounts to his being no more than human, a point latent in my argument but perhaps too easily taken as rhetorically dismissable in the service of a weightier interpretive goal. My object here, then, is to refine that argument, a task facilitated by reference to aspects of postcolonial theory as this has become applied to Ireland in recent years, especially as it offers loci of ambivalence; and thereby to assess the value of postcolonialism in approaching Swift. In that refinement Swift's marginal note on Clarendon plays a telling part.

But to begin with the larger issue, postcolonialism has found a place in the study of Irish history and literature generally, and of Swift specifically, only since about the mid-1980s. Most commentators upon Swift beyond

Ireland itself had previously shown a reluctance to acknowledge his Irish concerns as any more than peripheral to their subject; there was as well the general critical belatedness that Edward W. Said observed in 1983: "what we might call advanced contemporary criticism has not come round to Swift."[5] The delay between the emergence of academic postcolonial theory and its application to Ireland might at first glance seem peculiar, given the apparent amenability of such a discourse to the country's political and cultural history. First, Ireland was dominated for centuries by England, its larger and richer neighbor. Second, this had the effect, at a deeper level, of advantaging cultural developments initiated by the colonial power at the expense of the language, religious life, and social habits native to the Irish population, ultimately transforming Ireland from a country its colonizers found very strange indeed (if we are to accept the complaints of sixteenth- and seventeenth-century Englishmen like Fynes Moryson, Edmund Spenser, and Sir John Davies) into a cultural province of England. That was no accidental transformation, and the policies underlying it were informed not only by concerns for English security—since Ireland could become a base for aggression from England's enemies—but also by a sense of superiority analogous to the overt racism of later European colonizations beyond Europe's frontiers. Finally, and at a deeper level still, that transformation occurred in good part because the notion of England's superiority was over the centuries sufficiently internalized in the mentalities of native Irish people that many willingly collaborated in the task of anglicizing their own land. In all these respects, Ireland would appear a very appropriate site for postcolonial explorations.

There are, of course, factors that would contest the country's suitability in this respect, and probably accounted for the relative lateness of academic postcolonialists' attention to it. Since postcolonial theory developed at its outset upon the model of European interactions with subjugated non-European peoples, applying it within an entirely European context can seem problematic. That non-European paradigm is premised upon differences most palpably of race, with issues of culture, religion, and language flowing from that initial and obvious difference, and it may be questioned whether this is really a suitable paradigm for examining the relationships of European peoples among whom culture, religion, and language, in varying order, are the primary elements of difference, with race a metaphor at best for such differences, as really a synonym for "nation." It is true, of course, that differences of culture among European peoples were often articulated in terms remarkably similar to racism, and to consider the issue with due comprehensiveness it is worth noting that the long history of Ireland's struggle for freedom (whether for autonomy or independence) from its European neighbor was a struggle as well, at least by the eighteenth century, with an internationally imperial power, which poses a distinction between that conflict and a number of intra-European struggles involving more restrictedly powerful countries and their weaker neighbors—Prussians or Austrians with Slavs, for instance.

Postcolonial discourse might also seem of contestable relevance to the Irish situation in that, while its initial academic proponents tended to study colonial enterprises that were mainly undertaken in modern or early modern times, Ireland was partially colonized from the later twelfth century by Anglo-Norman adventurers intervening by invitation in an Irish royal dispute. As was true of many later extra-European colonizations, of course, this one developed a strong strategic imperative as well. A second and more comprehensive colonization of Ireland got underway in the sixteenth and seventeenth centuries, impelled by a mixture of strategic and religious motives. Because neither the native Irish nor the descendants of the Anglo-Norman colonists embraced the new religious polity of the English Reformation, English and Scottish Protestants were settled in Ireland, displacing the earlier, Catholic colonists (by then called the "Old English") from positions of local governance and, more effectively than they, subjugating the Catholic native Irish; the resentments of both Catholic groups broke out in 1641. This renders the colonial history of Ireland certainly longer and arguably more complicated than those of most of the colonial ventures beyond Europe that initially provided subjects for academic postcolonial literary and historical theorizing. On the other hand, it is appropriate to notice that the Irish achievement, or near achievement, of independence in 1922 took place only slightly more than a generation before most non-Europeans colonized by European powers gained their own political liberty; that near confluence of effort among these subjected peoples to break away from the imperial grip, and the fact that it was conducted, in Ireland and by many of those subjected peoples, in the English language, would certainly invite comparing these anti-imperial struggles. A final difference from the early subjects of postcolonial study again has to do with Ireland's European geography, on account of which the Republic of Ireland has become a relatively wealthy country since its independence in 1922. Its prosperity was indeed impeded in the first half-century of independence by continuing economic dependence upon Britain, but accelerated in the last decade of the twentieth century, owing in no small part to its membership in the European Union. Other former European colonies have become wealthy as well, of course, but nearly all of these were so thoroughly populated by European immigrants that the indigenous populations were marginalized or nearly exterminated; in Ireland the settler population never amounted to more than a quarter of the whole.

Such divergences from the postcolonial norm probably account for Ireland's absence from synoptic essay collections meant to facilitate graduate instruction in postcolonial theory, like *The Empire Writes Back,* which appeared in 1989.[6] By that point, however, a number of prominent Irish commentators had already been drawn to consider their country in post-colonial terms precisely because of its very long colonial history, marked by the often violent subordination of its political and economic interests and of its native people, and by the generalized, manifestly dominating, and often resented influence of the colonizing power. Irish subordination and resentment had in the nineteenth century, indeed, prompted both a nationalist political movement and a grand historiographical narrative of resistance, which after the achievement of independence for most of the country in 1922 developed a teleological bent all but sanctifying the attainment of nationhood. Though from the later 1930s this Irish variant upon the Whig interpretation of history began to be countered in Irish academic circles by a "revisionist" historiography, which sought to displace the privilege accorded to resistance and teleology, demotic nationalism was slow to show the effect. As Luke Gibbons puts it, opening his *Transformations in Irish Culture,* "Ireland is a First World country, but with a Third World memory."[7] Academic revisionism was impelled the more urgently, and with broader effect, after the outbreak of the "Troubles" in Northern Ireland in 1968, when the violent reaction from Protestant fringe elements to largely Catholic civil rights demonstrations, not effectively resisted and occasionally abetted by the local police, revitalized old-fashioned popular nationalism, with its hard-and-fast polarities and its paramilitary tradition, embodied in the Irish Republican Army. By the late 1970s, revisionism dominated both history writing and reportage upon the Northern "Troubles" in the Irish Republic. Almost inevitably, a reaction set in, exemplified by the Field Day Theatre Company, founded in 1980, which combined theatrical productions, academic pamphleteering, and the eventual publication in 1990 of the *Field Day Anthology of Irish Writing.* Field Day was intended to critique the revisionary enterprise by analyzing the roots of conflict in Ireland instead in terms that emphasized their colonial nature.[8] Colin Graham, taking strenuous issue with the parallel between Irish nationalism and the current Irish application of postcolonial theory, has noted that those allied with Field Day and others did not articulate from the first their attraction to the emergent discourse [9] (which may have some bearing upon their neglect by the editors of *The Empire Writes Back*), but by the end of the 1980s postcolonialism was clearly established as the alternative to revisionism, an interpretive key for the academic study of Irish history, literature, and culture.

The conventional extra-European postcolonial model was nonetheless incongruent for Ireland, even if geography and all that it entails could be elided, since Irish history presents a good many examples of the colonizing class, people of British heritage, habits, and religion, offering resistance to the continuance of British domination. Traditional Irish nationalism, especially as it developed from the middle of the nineteenth century, held this group of "patriots" in particular esteem, not least because they were Protestants who, in succeeding generations, stood apart from the main body of their own coreligionists by advancing the cause of Irish freedom. A major thrust of British colonialism following the Reformation was sectarian, encouraging Protestant settlers to think of themselves as "British" (even though denied the full economic and political rights of Britons); Irish nationalism could demonstrate through its patriotic Protestant genealogy its morally superior nonsectarianism, its determination to submerge confessional differences in a common Irishness. From the initial perspective of academic postcolonialism this genealogy certainly runs counter to the strict polarity of colonizer and colonized set forth in the writings of Frantz Fanon, for instance. To take such prominent patriots as Henry Grattan, Thomas Davis, John Mitchel, and Charles Stewart Parnell positively into postcolonialist theoretical account expands the category of "Irish" to include the patriotic nonnative (ethnically speaking, to be sure, since they all considered themselves unimpeachably Irish in national terms). But, as Colin Graham indicates:

> post-colonial criticism evolves as an ethical criticism. It is diagnostic of a political and historical situation, in that it identifies who is the coloniser and who the colonised—but it also morally evaluates this colonial relationship as one in which a wrong is done to the colonised, whose integrity, space and identity is taken over and controlled against his/her will.[10]

Graham deplores the amenability of this postcolonialist ethical privilege to "a narrative which celebrates the entity of the nation as the logical and correct outcome of the process of anti-colonial struggle" (30) and which is thus conducive to an exclusivist and sentimental bent in Irish nationalism; but such an ethical thrust obviously enables those who are morally committed to the cause of the oppressed, even if ethnically different from them, to join the "colonised." Indeed, as early as Albert Memmi's influential *The Colonizer and the Colonized* (1957), available in English since 1965, a full chapter was devoted to "The colonizer who refuses,"[11] and though Memmi was thinking explicitly of the sort of European who champions the freedom of non-European natives, the concept is easily adaptable to the Irish colonial situation.

From a later and different perspective, the Subaltern Studies Group considering Indian circumstances has developed a line of commentary and criticism from the implications of the fact that indigenous peoples, in their progress toward independent statehood, frequently adopt the language and culture of the colonizing power.[12] This fact certainly has relevance to

Ireland's nonnative "subalterns," already equipped with the colonizer's language and culture, who not only embraced the native cause and articulated it in terms the colonizer could understand, but by doing so provided a model for the masses. Their paradigmatic significance is the greater, indeed, because they laid and refined the rhetorical foundations in English for Irish aspirations to freedom—whether autonomy or outright separation—for the most part during a period (roughly, from the first third of the eighteenth to the last third of the nineteenth century) in which the language of most people in Ireland gradually shifted from Irish to English. That popular linguistic shift also reflects "subalternist" observations, in that only after its completion did (or could) that part of Ireland dominated by indigenous people realize the freedom to which they aspired. In other words, that freedom came attended by a kind of cultural-linguistic self-colonization; and for all its prosperity and European aspirations, some still would consider the Irish Republic a cultural colony of Britain. Especially from a "subalternist" perspective, such a defect in the Republic's independence is glaring, and one for which the compensation—that in its progress to political freedom Irish nationalism could boast of a *Protestant* patriot genealogy— is at least dubious.

In view of considerations like these, it is hardly surprising that some Irish commentators themselves have strong doubts about the applicability of postcolonial theories to the Irish literary and historical situation.[13] And the greater number, however amenable to postcolonialism, are far from uniform in approach. For its application may partake both of the strictly construed ethical terms of the discourse as initially articulated, which adhere closely to nationalist polarities of colonizer and colonized and valorize the advance of the "nation" from colonial bondage, with some mild adaptations to account for the geography and history of Ireland's colonization, and the more ambiguously valenced "subalternist" terms, which actually interrogate the strictness of those polarities and nationalism itself. Yet, whether viewed as a facilitator of the nationalist struggle for freedom from Britain, or as a dissenting subaltern, Swift can be fitted into this Irish postcolonial model: he was certainly a dissenting subaltern, and a rhetorical founding father of Irish nationalism. His is of course a peculiar fit, for Swift was a creature of manifold contradictions and ambivalences, not the least of them about Ireland and the Irish, whom he defended without loving or even liking very much. Though he contributed to the "grand narrative" of Irish nationalism, he could hardly have foreseen as much, for it was well after his death that rhetorical strategies he initiated to assist those of his own settler, colonizing stock to see their own interests as distinct, even diverging, from those of Britain were taken up to make the case for the rights of the native Irish, again in the face of British imperial domination. And from the perspective of those who study the subaltern, that "grand narrative" of nationalism is suspect as replacing one hierarchy with another, aping the colonizer: native nationalism reacts to imperial nationalism by following its model. Or, as Seamus Deane puts it, Ireland has had "for at least two hundred years British nationalism as a predominant political and cultural influence. In fact, Irish nationalism is, in its foundational moments, a derivative of its British counterpart" (7). Colin Graham applies the Subaltern Studies Group's critique of nationalist ideology more directly to the Irish case, since Irish nationalism developed in a hierarchical and exclusivist form during the nineteenth century (regardless of any rhetorically privileged Protestant genealogy) to lend a false homogeneity to the Irish Republic it shaped (40–42). Hence by his being put posthumously to the service of nationalism, however inadvertent on his part this may have been, Swift becomes implicated in a project students of the subaltern would deplore and subvert, rendering him more a cautionary than a positive subject for postcolonial study.

There is a nice propriety in such an ambivalent position for Swift within the broad school of postcolonialist discourse, his functioning as either a Protestant model to be emulated for his protonationalism, or as a marker of how nationalism itself subverts its ideals by emulating the colonialist enterprise it resists. This contrast echoes his own ambivalences about Ireland, his homeland, which he regarded as a place of exile, and about the Irish themselves, both his own Protestant stock whom he defended even as he castigated their habits of consumption, and the native Catholics whose idleness, deceitfulness, and thievery he denounced as much as he did their being oppressed. Swift is all the more suitable in this respect for postcolonial consideration given the emergence of special attention to varieties of ambivalence within this discourse, an area that its promoters have had to confront and by which they have become in some measure fascinated. As Graham notes, "the discipline is moving into a new phase in which the ethically-loaded dichotomy of coloniser/colonised is becoming less fixating, while the ambiguities and cultural dislodgments of imperialism are becoming more attractive" (33). We might even suggest that the efforts of the Subaltern Studies Group and others, not necessarily in full agreement with them, like Edward Said, have brought to the fore in postcolonial studies the valence of ambivalence. Although ambivalence (allied and sometimes identified with paradox) is a familiar idea in Swift studies and a common usage in Irish Studies generally, as a broad term it may appear too old-fashioned for the areas that postcolonial theorists have preferred to distinguish as, for instance, hybridity or liminality. But it is arguable that these are species of the genus ambivalence, for all share, though perhaps in differing degrees, the features of lacking certainty, of a somewhat makeshift assemblage from competing notions, which fit Ireland itself, writ large, as they do Swift.[14]

Its own grappling with ambivalence renders contemporary postcolonialist theorizing not only useful for approaching Swift's Irish writings, but quite distinct from earlier approaches. For these in varying degrees found it uncomfortable that, unlike Grattan, Davis, Mitchel, or Parnell, Swift did not espouse so much the historic political rights of Irish Catholics, the great bulk of the oppressed classes in Ireland, as he did the political and economic interests of his own class, the colonizers of British descent living in Ireland, who appeared to him an oppressed class of their own. The historical record of interpretations of Swift's Irish writings shows a long-standing rift, dating from Francis Jeffrey's assessment of Walter Scott's edition of Swift's *Works* in the *Edinburgh Review* in 1816, between taking these writings as genuinely patriotic in their opposition to British maltreatment of Ireland, and viewing that opposition instead as hypocritical. In a tone of cool dismissal Jeffrey argued that Swift cared very little in fact about Ireland, as evidenced by his frequent expressions of discomfort or even disgust at his perceived exile in Dublin, and that his advocacy of Irish interests against English should be understood as a means of berating or embarrassing the Whig administration that had dislodged his friends at Queen Anne's death in 1714 and ended whatever hopes Swift still retained of achieving his more exalted and metropolitan ambitions.[15] With varying emphases, Jeffrey's argument was echoed frequently in the nineteenth century, notably by the poet Thomas Moore in 1824, the advanced nationalist John Mitchel in 1869, and the British Conservative politician A. J. Balfour in 1897.[16] The line of approach developing from Moore and Mitchel, furthermore, through such "Irish-Irelanders" as the journalist D. P. Moran at the end of the nineteenth century and, a generation later, the academic Daniel Corkery, held that since Swift was himself entirely, even aggressively complicit in the project of Protestant supremacy in Ireland that was underpinned by British power, his complaints about the misuse of that power to disadvantage Protestants in this or that particular respect are simply petty.[17]

On the other hand, what we may term the nationalist or "patriotic" argument accepts that there was a large element of the personal in Swift's antipathy to the British administration during his time in Ireland, and even that he was clearly uncomfortable in the country, but maintains that these take nothing from his hatred of oppression, nor of course from the fact that Ireland then, as so often in the hundreds of years of its being ruled from Britain, was oppressed. He had, furthermore, inspired patriots like Grattan and Tone at the end of his century, and was seen by mainstream nationalists in the nineteenth as their ideological and certainly their rhetorical ancestor. Fixed in the patriotic pantheon by the Young Ireland movement of the 1840s and evoked reverently and repeatedly in their influential newspaper, *The Nation,* he was important to the long struggle for Irish freedom, however mixed his motives, for what he wrote and for its effects well after his death. This remains the established view of Swift in Ireland, justifying a folk tradition of affection for "the Dean" (often spelled "the Dane," to evoke stage-Irish pronunciation—reflecting in miniature the self-mockery so often part of Irish self-understanding; the ambivalence, indeed, of Irish acceptance of Swift) that has withstood whatever evidence of his disliking Ireland and the Irish themselves scholars may discover. His patriotic reputation may be constructed but has become genuine for all that.

As though attempting to resolve these contradictory approaches, the view began to be formulated about a century ago that Swift was fundamentally an humanitarian, a hater of oppression in all its forms, and that he saw such oppression at first hand in Ireland; he was moved to protest, then, less by patriotism than by morality. This view, embraced particularly by British left-of-center commentators like H. W. Nevinson, R. C. Churchill, and Michael Foot, has become quite generally accepted, especially outside Ireland, and has the advantage, for partisans of Swift, of downplaying the personal features of his animosity toward the Whigs and thus shielding him from accusations of hypocrisy.[18] Its emphasis upon universal over specifically Irish ideology, however, was regarded in Ireland for many years as unsatisfactory, not only disregarding or at least subordinating the palpable influence Swift's writings had had upon generations of nationalists but playing as well into the hands of those, like D. P. Moran and, later, Daniel Corkery, who assailed that influence as illegitimate even as they accepted Swift's general stance against oppression. For such "Irish-Irelanders," opposition to high-handedness as a universal ideal was insufficiently Irish and opened Swift to a renewed charge of hypocrisy as profiting from Protestant supremacy within Ireland even while decrying as oppressive British measures that subordinated Irish Protestant political and economic interests to those of the British homeland.

For much of the twentieth century the lines were drawn thus: within Ireland there was a popular view of Swift that was decidedly favorable to the notion of him as a patriot, a precursor of the movement for independence that was ultimately successful, or mostly successful; there was a small cohort of naysaying idealists, mainly in Ireland, who thought him hypocritical; and the scholarly mainstream internationally regarded him as more a humanitarian than an Irish patriot, but found some delight in the persistence of the attitude general in Ireland, in good part because few enough of our literary subjects retain popular interest anywhere centuries after their deaths. The emergence of postcolonial theory as a guide to literary and historical study in recent years would seem to alter this situation, for as it has brought Ireland and Swift himself under its lens, its application to Swift's Irish writings may be seen as a fin de siècle attempt to rescue Swift from the dilemma long dogging his reputation. It has the attraction of absorbing at once the notion of Swift as universally emancipatory in opposing oppression, and, under the character of ambivalence, both of the features that would seem to undercut the purity of such advocacy: the pleasure he undoubtedly took in vexing the Whigs he hated and his own adherence to a colonial class within Ireland and advocacy of its interests.

At the beginning of a new century, mixed motives hardly garner the blame they did in the early decades of the twentieth, when ideologues walked the earth with o'erweening confidence. Nationalists, communists, fascists, Freudians could look upon themselves, and expect to be perceived by others, as idealists. In our postmodern era, we have discovered that the monument idealism raised to Ideology has feet of clay, and we accept impurities as inevitable: as evidence, in fact, of the human. In postcolonialist terms, we can see that the colonial enterprise corrupted the colonisers even as it oppressed the natives. This is an argument forcefully extended to Swift himself by Wolfgang Zach, in a paper read at the Second Münster Symposium on Jonathan Swift in 1989:

> Swift's Anglo-Irish dilemma of identity and his "schizophrenic" position as an anti-colonial colonialist are central to understanding his personality and his writings. If Swift did suffer from self-hatred even to the point of wishing never to have been born . . . his Anglo-Irishness must be seen as the major cause of this self-destroying urge.[19]

The burden of Zach's argument is that Swift ought not be taken uncritically as an Irish patriot, that the psychological ambivalence he demonstrates so often in his work and correspondence emerges as well in his despising the Irish, whom he yet defended. This can appear a conundrum, but if developments in postcolonial theory can be said to comport with ambivalence, it does not have to be taken as a disabling contradiction. Our recognizing that colonialism damages even those who enforce it, or profit from it, need not occlude our perception of its effects as oppressive upon the native population. Indeed, since the postcolonialist analytical process combines diagnosis and evaluation, as indicated in Colin Graham's succinct overview quoted above, we may notice the impact of colonialism even upon those analyzing it. Diagnosis may seem to precede moral evaluation, but their relationship within the analytical process is concurrent: we must identify colonialism itself, in the first instance, as morally questionable if we are to probe and evaluate its effects. It is morally based questioning that enables the perception of those effects. The exercise of perception can even reveal elements of our own cultural colonialism in our very attempts to identify and analyze aspects of the colonial enterprise. By recognizing that to be human is to incorporate ambivalence, most certainly in Swift's case, postcolonialist attention to him can effect a compromise between the nationalist interpretive camp and that disposed to emphasize his hypocrisy, accepting his (and perhaps indeed our own) complicity in oppressive evil because that is countered by a rhetoric opposing such evil, and because the word lives more broadly than the man could.

A postcolonialist discourse of this sort applied to Swift would explain his apparent contradictions in dealing with Ireland better than the sort of thinking that presses for his essential hypocrisy, his nationalist purity or even his overarching humanitarianism. Such a discourse, furthermore, can find ample justification in Swift's comments upon those of his own stock, the Protestant Irish (or, as he preferred to call them, the "English living in Ireland"). Not that Swift condemned himself as a colonizer, for it is in terms of his advancing the interests of these Protestant colonizers that he saw himself as very much the patriot. But he recognized that colonialism as practiced in Ireland in his day corrupted the Protestant Irish even as (through the very agency of Irish Protestants) it oppressed the Catholic natives, while reserving to Britain the ultimate blame for this corruption and oppression. It is significant that in a letter to Lord Peterborough in 1726, following a very unsatisfactory meeting on Irish affairs with Sir Robert Walpole that Swift had asked Peterborough to arrange, Swift implies a marked distinction between the modern British and the ancient Greek and Roman practice of colonialism. The very first of a considerable list of grievances, in fact, is that the descendants of those who conquered Ireland are "called and treated as *Irishmen,* although their fathers and grandfathers were born in *England,*" whereas "they ought to be on as good a foot as any subjects of *Britain,* according to the practice of all other nations, and particularly of the *Greeks* and *Romans.*"[20] Thucydides provides the major classical articulation of the idea that those who ventured forth from the mother country to found a settlement on other shores continued to enjoy the rights and freedoms of those remaining in the homeland.[21] Nowadays, Swift was complaining (intending that his letter to Peterborough be read by Walpole), such settlers, descended from those British Protestants enjoined to colonize Ireland in the seventeeth century, were considered by those in power at home to be as much "the colonized" as the natives. They should be entitled to the same rights as those who remained in Britain, but their oppression by the British parliament's restrictions on their liberties and trade indicates that they were thought no better than the native Irish by whose rebellion in 1641 and support for Jacobitism in 1689–91 their forebears had suffered.

This is explicitly a colonialist argument, and moreover an exaggerated one, since Irish Protestants had far broader civil rights than the Catholic natives. Rather than support a contention for the postcolonialist suitability of Swift's dissidence, it would seem to renew the case for his oppositional-ism made by those who view him as a hypocrite: since the displacement of his Tory friends in 1714, his side had been losers in the political arena, and he saw that losing side as defending tradition. His defense of Ireland is thus a reflexive defense of old ways, a new reflex, in fact, for it is only after the Declaratory Act passed into law that Swift began publicly to promote Ireland's interests. Indeed, when for Walpole's benefit he holds in 1726 that the present practice in English government of Ireland defies old, long-standing usage in the relations of colonies to mother countries, dating to classical times, he does not explicitly state that such usage was the case in Ireland, which would hardly have been truthful; Walpole's treatment of Ireland was not that different from that of earlier English postrevolution governments, though adverting to this would not have advanced Swift's argument. Rather, his point is at one with his overall political conserva-tism. As Carole Fabricant reminds us, Swift's conservatism incorporates elements that inspire radicals in our own time.[22] Certainly his defense of the old—resonating with his Augustinian-Tory distrust of benevolent progress—opposes a political system that our contemporary left under-stands (and maybe our right as well) as the emerging stages of industrial capitalism and bourgeois government.[23] Swift is, one might say, so far to the right in his day as to lend posthumous support to the left in ours. That is a paradox in keeping with the nature of his writings and with the man himself.

All the same, postcolonialism offers a suitable approach to Swift be-cause he recognizes, in that same letter to Peterborough and thus to Wal-pole, that the government's denial of classical equity to Irish Protestants—which points to Britain's corruption as the colonial power— has had the effect of corrupting the colonists, as demonstrated by their resorting to oppressing the native (Catholic) population in order to maintain their social standing. Here he clarifies for Walpole's sake a theme constant in his Irish writings; indeed, that immoral behavior breeds more of the same hearkens to the tenor of many of his other writings as well. This neo-Augustinian view of human and political relations involves the writer as well as those whose interests he defends, so encompassing Swift's own ambivalences about Ireland. His assertion that the colonial power's ineq-uity had corrupted the Protestants colonizing Ireland problematizes his support for the latter's colonial project: favoring the principle of privileg-ing the colonial class, which allows him to argue for their interests, he yet decries its practical impact upon the native Irish. Treating the settlers thus— in the Irish instance by curbing their opportunities for economic advancement—leaves them little recourse but to prosper by oppressing their tenantry. By rights, they ought to be considered as British as those in Britain; deprived of those rights, they fall into habits like importing luxuries and squeezing the native tenants, both of which damage their own national economic well-being. While Swift lays the responsibility for this upon Britain, he is in fact most scathing about the misdeeds, economic in the first instance but implicitly moral, of the settler population itself.

Here we may turn again to Swift's marginal note in his copy of Clarendon. He accepts the facts of Ireland's history, as he saw them, citing the (supposed) many thousands of dead at the hands of Catholics in 1641; but implicitly, throughout his Irish writings, he rejects the contemporary application of this historical "lesson." Irish Protestant tradition understood the 1641 Rising as revealing the true character of Irish Catholics, both native and Old English, as savage, deceitful, and determined to exterminate Protestantism. This lesson of history was drummed home each year on 23 October, the date the Rising had begun in 1641, a statutory holiday in Ireland observed by compulsory attendance at commemorative services in every parish. So understanding the Catholic threat comported with the anti-Royalist and anti-Catholic fervor of English Parliamentary opinion in the 1640s and had become firmly established in Ireland following the defeat of the Irish Jacobite regime of 1689–91. But in Britain, from the Restoration onward, the Irish Catholic Rising of the mid-century had ceased to have pressing significance: it was normalized as another instance of the constant threat Catholic power posed to Protestants, like that of Queen Mary in England or the St. Bartholomew's Day Massacre in France during the sixteenth century. The Gunpowder Plot was commemorated annually, of course, and anti-Catholic outbursts could be sparked by more modern instances like the Popish Plot, but the elites in English society understood domestic Catholicism as posing little active danger to Britain.[24] Swift was taking a view rather like that in Britain about the Catholic threat, that it was historical and still dangerous internationally but not domestically. In Ireland, moreover, the "penal laws" enacted in the Irish parliament restricting the economic freedom of Catholics, disarming them and curtailing their political liberties, had deprived the Catholic population of the sort of leadership and access to weaponry they had in the 1640s. Hence, to Swift, Catholics were no longer a threat within Ireland either, though his arguments to Irish Protestants were couched in economic rather than antisectarian terms. Indeed, he saw Presbyterians, not Catholics, as the genuine and pressing danger to the condition of Ireland, for by the 1720s they seemed to him equipped, by virtue of their economic power and their alliances with the Whig ministry in England, to disestablish the Church of Ireland.

Swift's internally normalizing the Irish Catholic threat in a "British" rather than an Irish Protestant fashion, then, underlies his economic recommendations to the Irish colonial classes; it also anticipates the subaltern postcolonial observation that a nation colonized begins to regain its freedom by, ironically, aping attitudes of thought identified with the colonial power. For Swift, this was a mental stance to which his prolonged periods in England, first as secretary to Sir William Temple and later as confidant and propagandist for the Tory ministry of Queen Anne's final years, would have habituated him: the critic Francis Jeffrey, writing a century after the fact, noted that when Swift was close to power in England during that later period the condition of Ireland never concerned him at all. He had become "cosmopolitan," a habit of mind that enabled him perhaps to discern Ireland's situation more objectively once he returned in 1713 as Dean of St. Patrick's Cathedral, to live the rest of his life in the country of his birth. His so intimating himself with the British or cosmopolitan perspective upon affairs of state heightened the force of his intervention in Irish political controversy from 1720; it also, however, impeded his success in altering Irish Protestant self-understanding vis à vis Irish Catholics and British politicians. For that self-understanding was in its nature "colonial": Catholics were more abundant and proximate than was common in Britain, which the colonial consciousness could not ignore as Swift seemed to imply it should; the "Britishness" of the colonial was not that of the Englishman. It was, indeed, ambivalent, at once British and Irish (though not "native" Irish), in a sense that Swift saw as crippling.

Swift's refusal to privilege the historical Catholic threat over the facts of the present, which include British arrogance, even (when he turns to the Wood's halfpence scheme with *The Drapier's Letters* in 1724) misgovernment, and contemporary Irish Catholic impotence, was too sophisticated for his own people in Ireland. They could not discard the reflexive anti-Catholicism that blinded them to what he saw as their economic interest and actually kept them manipulable by British politicians, acting thus as a kind of self-colonization that impeded their prosperity as much as British economic restrictions did. Irish Protestants behaved, indeed, as though in concert with the very British colonial policies they resented: their understanding of themselves as a people at risk inhibited the development of the self-confidence and, thereby, the will to resist such policies that Swift promoted. In *A Modest Proposal* he found the metaphor to engage this contradiction. Recommending that Protestants eat Catholic babies inverts the historical victimhood that Irish Protestant tradition inculcated as ever latent and thus mocks the perpetuation of this victim mentality as obtuse. And in its bleak succinctness that work mocks his genuine recommendations for Irish self-sufficiency as well, directly by raising only to discard them, indirectly by advocating cannibalism instead, which presses Irish self-sufficiency to an absurd literalism.

The ironies of the *Modest Proposal* in particular comport with the overarching irony of Swift's Irish career during his life and posthumously. For his message that Irish Protestants ought not to act like colonials, but like

British people themselves, abroad but in possession of the selfsame rights as British subjects, translated in time as an argument for equal rights with those of British subjects, for Irish people as Irish. Swift came to inspire successive generations of not only Irish nationalists who wished to loosen the link with Britain, so that their equal rights with the British might be respected, but also separatists who sought to break the link altogether, to achieve such respect. Yet the British connection, which was for Swift personal as much as political, was the very foundation of his prescribing a more self-assured "Britishness" among the Protestant Irish. The discourse of postcolonialism accommodates this irony of his (inadvertent) service to the "grand narrative" of Irish nationalism, even including the twist that the "British" quality of self-assurance he pressed for adoption by the colonials only became a reality (of sorts) for the "natives" in their achievement of independence. What he prescribes for the colonials, that is, those with a "subalternist" perspective would describe of the colonized, not least (and ironically again) in that Irish independence, gained at the expense of the colonials, came at the cost to the natives themselves of becoming more "British," forsaking their language and much of their culture.

The very susceptibility to irony in Swift's case thus suits the notice that postcolonialist critics have given to what may largely be termed ambivalences. The ironies of Swift's writings and of the career they made for him in Ireland are apparent, of course, quite independently of any postcolonialist perspective. Indeed, those who adopt that perspective should be cautious not to conflate Swift the writer with the Swift more broadly perceived, whose rhetoric proved later so amenable to the cause of Irish nationalism—though his tendency to overstatement in his writings on Ireland was certainly conducive to that amenability, and what occasional propensity to overstatement we may find in the rhetoric of Irish nationalism itself may owe some debt to him. Yet the fact remains that underpinning these writings was Swift's hatred of oppression as he saw it firsthand in Ireland, whether defined as inflicted ultimately by British policy or at closer hand by Irish Protestants. And his moral impulse aligns with the ethical basis of postcolonial discourse, both for its rhetorical value to the later anti-British formulations of Irish nationalism and for his criticism of the oppressed themselves—Irish Protestants for their tendencies to self-colonization and their compensatory squeezing of the Catholic poor, and indeed those poor for so commonly enduring Protestant oppression by embracing personal moral degradation. Combining with its tolerance for ambivalence, that ethical foundation renders postcolonialism a discourse more accommodating to Swift's Irish writings than more exacting earlier critical stances or contemporary theories.

Swift remains, of course, an awkward subject for postcolonialist inquiry, and that is appropriate, for he fits awkwardly any systematic discourse—his work and life manifest abundant ambivalences, contradictions, paradoxes. But Ireland is itself a somewhat awkward fit for postcolonialism; the strains and disjunctions of its own history defy any totalizing inclination in that discourse. More comprehensively than most other critical systems, however, postcolonialism can embrace the paradoxes that Swift and Ireland both present—and not least that paradox they present together, the fact that Irish nationalism, an ideology that took a separatist form Swift would have resisted, would well after his death take his promotion of Protestant Ireland's political equality with Britain, and his moral determination of Britain's inequity in ignoring or rejecting this parity as genealogical and rhetorical underpinning for its own ideological principles. That is certainly an irony befitting Swift, and one that instances the word's enduring well beyond the man.

NOTES

Earlier versions of this paper were prepared for presentation at a roundtable discussion on "The Authority of Swift," chaired by Professor Brian Connery at the Tenth International Congress on the Enlightenment, University College, Dublin, July 1999; and a symposium on "Puzzling Evidence," chaired by Professors David Scott Kastan and David Armitage at the Folger Institute, Folger Shakespeare Library, Washington, D.C., in April 2000. My thanks are due to the participants in both fora for their comments.

1. Robert Mahony, "The Irish Colonial Experience and Swift's Rhetorics of Perception in the 1720s," *Eighteenth-Century Life* 22, n.s. 1 (February 1998): 69. This essay continues the examination of issues raised in that article and in another, "Protestant Dependence and Consumption in Swift's Irish Writings," in *Political Ideas in Eighteenth-Century Ireland,* ed. S. J. Connolly (Dublin: Four Courts Press, 2000); 83–104.

2. Herbert Davis, ed. *Miscellaneous Pieces, Fragments and Marginalia [Prose Works of Jonathan Swift,* vol. 5] (Oxford: Blackwell, 1962), 299. Davis's commentary indicates that Swift read Clarendon's *History of the Rebellion and Civil Wars in England* (Oxford: 1706–07) for the fourth time in 1741; the dates of marginalia are, however, unknown.

3. The number of Protestants massacred in 1641 very quickly became the subject of intense debate which lasted well into the nineteenth century; it has never been resolved, but contemporary historians estimate that in the early months of the Rising there were actually between two and five thousand Protestants killed who were not soldiers. For a brief synopsis of the debate and the modern consensus about the number of victims, see Mahony, "Irish Colonial Experience," 74, n. 14.

4. This argument is elaborated in Mahony, "Protestant Dependence and Consumption."

5. Edward Said, "Swift as Intellectual," *The World, the Text, and the Critic* (Cambridge: Harvard University Press, 1983), 72. By the time this work appeared, however, there had already been published the early deconstructionist study by Terry Castle, "Why the Houyhnhnms Don't Write," *Essays in Literature* 7, 1 (1980): 31–44.

6. Bill Ashcroft, Gareth Griffiths, and Helen Tiffin, *The Empire Writes Back: Theory and Practice in Post-Colonial Literatures* (London: Methuen, 1989). In more recent introductory volumes, the Irish experience has continued to be ignored, as in *Contemporary Postcolonial Theory: A Reader,* ed. Padmini Mongia (London: Arnold, 1996), treated

perfunctorily, with bemusement, or cursorily, as by John McLeod, *Beginning Postcolonialism* (Manchester: Manchester University Press, 2000).

7. Luke Gibbons, *Transformations in Irish Culture* (Cork: Cork University Press, 1996), 3.

8. See Seamus Deane's introduction to a collection of essays by Terry Eagleton, Fredric Jameson, and Edward Said, *Nationalism, Colonialism, and Literature* (Minneapolis: University of Minnesota Press, 1990), esp. 6–18.

9. Colin Graham, "'Liminal Spaces': Post-Colonial Theories and Irish Culture," *The Irish Review* 16 (autumn–winter 1994): 35.

10. Ibid., 30. Later references to this article are cited by page number only.

11. Albert Memmi, *The Colonizer and the Colonized* [*Portrait du Colonisé précédé du Portrait du Colonisateur,* 1957], trans. Howard Greenfeld (New York: Orion, 1965), 20–44.

12. Graham, "Liminal Spaces," 30 ff., quotes from Ranajit Guha, "On Some Aspects of the Historiography of Colonial India," *Subaltern Studies: Writings on South Asian History and Society,* I (Delhi: Oxford University Press, 1982) and demonstrates the applicability to the Irish situation of the Subaltern Studies Group's critical method.

13. The strongest objections have been raised by Liam Kennedy, "Modern Ireland: Post-Colonial Society or Post-Colonial Pretensions," *Irish Review* 13 (winter 1992/93): 107–21. Among the best arguments in a spectrum of doubts nuanced more specifically toward literature are Bruce Stewart, "'The Bitter Glass': Postcolonial Theory and Anglo-Irish Culture—A Case Study," *Irish Review* 25 (winter/spring 1999–2000): 27–50, and Edna Longley, "Postcolonial *versus* European (and Post-Ukanian) Frameworks for Irish Literature," *Irish Review* 25: 75–94.

14. Hybridity is most closely associated with studies by Homi K. Bhabha, especially the exploratory "The Other Question," *Screen* 24, no. 6 (1983): 18–36, and the more assured (if also more opaque) "Signs Taken for Wonders: Questions of Ambivalence and Authority under a Tree Outside Delhi, May 1817," in *'Race,' Writing, and Difference,* ed. Henry Louis Gates, Jr. (Chicago: University of Chicago Press, 1986), 163–184, reprinted in Bhabha's *The Location of Culture* (London: Routledge, 1994). Graham, "Liminal Spaces," 42, n. 16, adapts his title here from Said, *Culture and Imperialism* (London: Chatto and Windus, 1993), 159–96.

15. Francis Jeffrey, "Jonathan Swift," *Edinburgh Review,* 27 (September 1816): 1–58.

16. Thomas Moore, *Memoirs of Captain Rock* (London: Longmans, 1827), 123–27; John Mitchel, *The History of Ireland from the Treaty of Limerick to the Present Time* (Dublin: Duffy, 1869), 2: 76–94; A. J. Balfour, "Biographical Introduction" in *The Works of George Berkeley, D.D.,* ed. George Sampson (London: Bell, 1897), 1: lii–lvi.

17. D. P. Moran, "The Pale and the Gael," *New Ireland Review* 11, no. 4 (June 1899), reprinted in Moran's *The Philosophy of Irish Ireland* (Dublin: Duffy, 1905), 32–51; Daniel Corkery, "Ourselves and Dean Swift," *Studies* 23 (June 1934): 203–18, and "The Nation that was not a Nation," *Studies* 23 (December 1934): 611–22.

18. H. W. Nevinson, "Where Cruel Rage," *Essays in Freedom and Rebellion* (New Haven: Yale University Press, 1921), 67–74; R. C. Churchill, *He Served Human Liberty: An Essay on the Genius of Jonathan Swift* (London: Allen and Unwin, 1946); Michael Foot, "Round the Next Corner: The Pursuit of Jonathan Swift," *Debts of Honour* (London: Picador, 1981), 181– 212.

19. Wolfgang Zach, "Jonathan Swift and Colonialism," in *Reading Swift: Papers from the Second Münster Symposium on Jonathan Swift* (München: Wilhelm Fink, 1993), 99.

20. *Correspondence of Jonathan Swift,* ed. Harold Williams (Oxford: Clarendon Press,1963) III, 132.

21. Thucydides, *Peloponnesian War,* I: 34, describing a dispute between Corinth and its

erstwhile colony Corcyra, records the Corcyrans' remark that "Colonists are not sent abroad to be the slaves of those who remain behind, but to be their equals," trans. Rex Warner (Harmondsworth: Penguin, 1954), 32.

22. Carole Fabricant, "Swift's Political Legacy: Re-membering the Past in Order to Imagine the Future," in *Locating Swift: Essays from Dublin on the 250th Anniversary of the Death of Jonathan Swift, 1667–1745,* eds. Aileen Douglas, Patrick Kelly, and Ian Campbell Ross (Dublin: Four Courts, 1998), 180–200 *passim,* esp.193–94.

23. Edward Said, "Swift's Tory Anarchy," *The World, the Text, and the Critic,* 62.

24. In 1687 Sir William Petty actually proposed, as a solution to the Irish problem, transporting most of the Irish to Britain, where the transplanted Catholics would still amount to a small minority of the expanded British population. His "Treatise of Ireland, 1687," was submitted to King James II, but Petty died shortly thereafter and it was left in MS, to be first published in *The Economic Writings of Sir William Petty,* ed. C. H. Hull (Cambridge: University Press, 1899), 2: 545–621.

Speaking for the Irish Nation:
The Drapier, the Bishop, and the Problems of
Colonial Representation

Carole Fabricant

WHEN SWIFT, AS M. B. DRAPIER, ADDRESSES "THE WHOLE PEOPLE OF Ireland" in his famous Fourth Letter, written to bring about defeat of William Wood's coinage scheme, whom exactly is he speaking to?[1] And, more germane to my concerns here, whom is he speaking *for?* The general consensus has been that "the whole People" refers only to the small circle of the Anglo-Irish elite and the established church to which Swift belonged—a position reflected in R. F. Foster's contention that the "restricted and exclusive views of Swift" typified "Ascendancy attitudes."[2] I read the Drapier's Fourth Letter very differently, as a document that articulates the interests of a broad spectrum of Irish society and that invokes a conception of nationhood considerably more comprehensive than these sectarian constructions would indicate. I will be offering evidence for this reading later in my discussion; however, my primary aim here is not to offer an interpretation of a particular text but rather to examine a number of interrelated theoretical and historical issues that underpin the questions I pose at the outset. In the absence of such examination, it is impossible adequately to address questions of the Drapier's viewpoint, audience, and representative, or nonrepresentative, status. More broadly, I want to explore the contradictions, and in the process weigh the meaning, of Protestant attempts to speak for the Irish nation in the first half of the eighteenth century. To this end I will be focusing primarily on Swift, but also considering texts by George Berkeley and (more briefly) Thomas Sheridan.[3]

I

The example of Swift, one of many instances in which a member of a privileged minority purports to represent an oppressed majority through the figure of "the whole nation," points up the relevance of current theoretical investigations into the question of who can legitimately speak for whom in situations where a clear power differential exists: in the case of Ireland, where the nationalist spokespersons, on the strength of their membership in their country's social and religious elite, can be considered complicit with the colonizers even if treated by them as subordinates. In such circumstances, do Anglo-Irish acts of speaking as the nation silence the colonized Catholic majority (by subsuming the latter's voice into their own) or do they, on the contrary, enable the colonized to be heard by giving them a voice they would otherwise lack? One of the assumptions underlying this essay is that there is no simple, or single, answer to this question—that the answer varies according to a number of specific factors while at the same time limited by the political and historical constraints operating on both speaker and spoken for. One important aim here is to establish some grounds for distinguishing those circumstances in which such representation can function constructively, to minimize hierarchically based exclusions and expand the field of expression, from those circumstances in which this mode of representation shows its "violent" side, functioning to suppress differences and to impose a monolithic structure of order.

The whole problematic of "speaking for" has considerable resonance given recent poststructuralist critiques of both identity and representation, which challenge the very grounds upon which one individual or group can speak for another. Gayatri Chakravorty Spivak's highly influential essay "Can the Subaltern Speak?" has helped to crystallize the theoretical and ideological stakes in this line of questioning, as have various recent formulations of a feminist epistemology.[4] Donna Haraway, for example, rejects "a politics of semiotic representation" for a "politics of articulation" in analyzing the speciousness of certain advocacy claims by Western environmentalists "speaking for" endangered species in distant lands and by antiabortion activists purporting to "speak for" the fetus.[5] Linda Alcoff agrees about the dangers in such acts of representation but nevertheless reminds us that these acts are not in all cases detrimental since there are times when we do need someone "to advocate for our needs."[6] Bringing this whole question closer to home (that is, Ireland), Vincent Cheng considers this problematic both in terms of the endeavors by English and American scholars to represent Irish literature through "a hegemonic reading of a native son like Joyce" and in terms of a newly politicized Joyce made to represent all of postcolonial Irish literature, thereby in effect functioning to marginalize or even silence less canonical Irish writers. Noting several examples in which white "first world" males have written books purporting to recount the true-life stories of first-person female and/ or "third world" narrators (for example, the English vicar Toby Forward's publication, under the name Rahila Khan, of what claimed to be an Indian feminist's true experiences struggling to survive in Margaret Thatcher's

Britain), Cheng observes, "From [such examples] one might conclude that it is better not to speak for others at all, not to intervene so as not to act like Haines (in the 'Telemachus' episode of *Ulysses*). On the other hand, such a retreat from 'representation' and 'speaking for' is frequently politically detrimental or even suicidal."[7]

Joyce himself directly addressed this question in his most explicitly anticolonialist piece of writing, "Ireland, Island of Saints and Sages," which lists a number of Irish "patriots" from the late eighteenth century onward whom he judged to be legitimate spokesmen for the cause of Ireland despite the fact that many were Protestant and unable to claim "even a drop of Celtic blood"; after all, he reminds us, "to deny the name of patriot to all those who are not of Irish stock would be to deny it to almost all the heroes of the modern movement."[8] Joyce was thinking here primarily of nineteenth-century leaders such as his much-revered and repeatedly mourned Parnell. But what about the Irish protonationalists of the first half of the eighteenth century, whose notion of an independent Ireland was of a nation enjoying political and legal parity with England, similarly ruled by an established church and by a religiously-defined class (enjoying a power bolstered by both the Penal Laws against the Catholics and the Test Act against the Dissenters) that seemed to evidence little concern for the rights of the Catholic majority, or even of other Protestant denominations that were not Anglican?[9]

In this situation, acts of representation—specifically, of speaking for the oppressed or the colonized—become particularly fraught (if not indeed, on the face of it, a blatant contradiction in terms), and seem inconceivable without postulating a bad faith or false consciousness of mammoth proportions. Such acts seem to provide powerful justification for Gilles Deleuze's insistence on "the indignity of speaking for others" and his assertion that "only those directly concerned can speak in a practical way on their own behalf."[10] And yet, Spivak too has a point (even though she chooses to overlook the compelling circumstances, namely the *événements* of May 1968, motivating his protest) when she challenges Deleuze on this matter, deriding the idea that we, as intellectuals (or relatively privileged members of society), should simply back off in silence and let the oppressed speak for themselves: an act that conveniently absolves us from the responsibility of intervening in intolerable situations and that assumes the possibility of transparency, of an end to the need for all representation. But as Spivak succinctly reminds us, "representation has not withered away."[11] Certainly it showed little sign of withering away in eighteenth-century Ireland, where, when the oppressed *did* speak for themselves, it was often both literally and figuratively in another language, one that required translation into the idiom of power to have any effect within the governing structures of society.

Once again we can look to Joyce for a pertinent comment on this state of affairs—specifically, in his essay, "Ireland at the Bar," which describes the celebrated trial in Galway of one Myles Joyce, accused of murdering a family in the town. Because he spoke only Irish and "seemed stupefied by all the judicial ceremony," he was forced to depend on the services of an interpreter, who would listen to his lengthy and involved explanations, punctuated by wild gesticulations and imprecations to the heavens, and then succinctly translate to the judge, "He says no, your worship." Not surprisingly, he was found guilty and executed. James Joyce transforms this episode into a comprehensive metaphor of Ireland's plight: "The figure of this dumbfounded old man, a remnant of a civilization not ours, deaf and dumb before his judge, is a symbol of the Irish nation at the bar of public opinion."[12] We might think of this essay as an extended reflection on the problematic of representation within a colonial context. One may well be tempted to interpret the parabolic account as a call for an end to all representational modes of expression so that the native would be able to state his case directly to a jury of his peers, without having to negotiate the system of falsifying mediations inherent to colonialist rule. However, even if Ireland were independent of Britain, an exclusively Irish-speaking denizen from the wilds of Connemara would be likely to encounter formidable difficulties in trying to communicate to his fellow countrymen in a nation divided (even without a colonial presence) along linguistic, cultural, class, and regional lines. (How much more difficult would he find the task of stating Ireland's case to the world at large!) In this sense effective representation may be seen as a necessary (if insufficient) condition for creating a just society. And indeed, one might argue that it is precisely this kind of representation that is embodied in Joyce's essay, which was originally written in Italian while he was staying in Trieste, and which in effect sets its author up to be the successful translator and advocate so conspicuously missing in the courtroom that condemned Myles Joyce.

In making this point, I am very far from wishing to argue that the oppressed can never speak effectively without outside help—that their position always and necessarily forces them into a state of dependency on others, along the lines of Marx's small peasant proprietors, who "cannot represent themselves; they must be represented."[13] On the contrary, this essay proceeds on the assumption that the oppressed in eighteenth-century Ireland—or, to be more accurate, the *most* oppressed by far among the various groups *unevenly* victimized by British colonialism, the Catholics—were not simply silent and passive recipients of help from above but did in fact speak for themselves on a number of occasions and in a variety of ways, in words as well as in deeds: through the versified expressions of violation and loss by Gaelic poets such as Dáibhí Ó Bruadair (David O'Bruadair) and Aodhagán Ó Rathaille (Egan O'Rahilly); through the accounts of native historians such as Hugh Reilly and Sylvester O'Halloran, intent upon correcting misrepresentations of the Irish perpetuated by their British and Anglo-Irish counterparts; through regular Jacobite gatherings at St. Stephen's Green in Dublin to celebrate the Pretender's birthday; and through acts of rebellion and social unrest, such as the Hougher disturbances in 1711–12 in the west of Ireland and the Dublin riots of the 1720s.[14]

But if I decline to treat the Catholics in terms of an undifferentiated mass of docile, mute oppression, I also want to avoid treating the Anglo-Irish as a monolithic class of oppressors, all of whose speech acts (conceived in the broadest terms) must be understood as modes of colonialist repression and/or appropriation, which would lead to the argument that taking seriously the nationalist sentiments expressed by a member of their class is necessarily tantamount to "allow[ing] the colonizer to speak for the colonized" because it "perniciously renders invisible the indigenous Irish themselves."[15] My disagreement with this view is based on several considerations. For one thing, it prevents us from making some important distinctions among the different parties, subclasses, and individuals who constituted its membership: between Whigs and Tories, between the English and the Irish interest, between Hanoverians and Jacobites—as well as between those who walked the meaner streets of Dublin, mingling with the tradesmen and the homeless, and those who confined their movements to the fashionable sections of Georgian Dublin, relying on carriages to prevent contaminating contact with "the rabble"; between those who fostered connections with the native Irish culture (including Swift's friends the antiquarian Anthony Raymond, Rector of Trim, who embarked on an English translation of Geoffrey Keating's classic history of Ireland, *Foras Feasa ar Éirinn,* and the clergyman Patrick Delany, who was patron to the last of the great Irish harpist-bards, Turlough Carolan), and those who rejected all aspects of Irish culture as expressions of a barbarism inimical to the putative height of civilization embodied in their "mother" country, England. Swift's poem, *The Description of an Irish Feast,* based on the Irish verses *Pléaráca na Ruarcach,* attributed to Hugh MacGauran and set to music by Carolan, exemplifies Swift's own interest in Irish popular culture. In each of these cases, the act of speaking for Ireland necessarily conveyed its own distinct set of nuances and implications. The challenge is to acknowledge individual differences in this regard without (as has been the case with many recent histories) losing the forest for the trees—without becoming so fixated on specific examples that the larger outlines of Ireland's colonial subordination to Britain disappear from view, leaving what appears to be a level playing field, unencumbered by the lopsided power relationships that necessarily affected all forms of representation and limited what individual acts of "speaking for" could mean and do.

II

Another problem with viewing the Anglo-Irish as a monolithic class of oppressors is that such a view ignores the contradictions of their hyphenated identity and their complex history, which positioned them as both colonizers and colonized: as members of a group subordinated and exploited by England even as they functioned as the agents of British colonial rule in Ireland. These contradictions may be glimpsed, for example, in the "migrating pronouns" of Swift's Irish tracts, where "we" and "our" slip in and out of contexts in which they refer, sometimes alternately, sometimes simultaneously, to the original English settlers, to the Irish-born Protestants, and to the "whole people" of Ireland, including (at least in theory and potential) the Catholics. The following passage from the Drapier's Fourth Letter points to the porous line that exists between "us Irish" conceived of as a general, national group, and "us Irish" conceived of as a more specific, sectarian group laying claims to a privileged English heritage; it shows how the word "our" can at one and the same time conflate and sharply differentiate the two: "Our *Neighbours, whose Understandings are just upon a Level with Ours* (which perhaps are none of the *Brightest*) have a strong Contempt for most Nations, but especially for *Ireland:* They look upon us as a sort of *Savage Irish,* whom our Ancestors conquered several Hundred Years ago" (*D,* 10: 64). What these words at once reveal and try to deny is that the "us" who are considered "a sort of *Savage Irish*" include *both* the "old Irish" *and* the subsequent waves of English settlers (including members of Swift's own family), who were viewed as being contaminated by their new surroundings and as eventually merging with the Irish "natives." The speaker's immediate recoil from this recognition and rush to identify with "our [not the expected *their*] Ancestors," who "conquered [the *Savage Irish*] several Hundred Years ago," rather than establishing the grounds of his separation from the latter, serves mainly to underscore the ambiguity of his position and his awareness that, from the perspective of the English observers—which is to say, the observers who *matter* in the political scheme of things—he will always be lumped together with these "savages." The shift here from the initial "our" and "ours," which situates Swift as an Irish denizen distinct from his "neighbours," the English, to the final "our," which reconfigures him as an Englishman, no longer merely a "neighbour" but now a blood brother and fellow conqueror, undergoes yet another reversal in the sentence immediately following, which once again establishes a clear distinction between, on the one hand, "I" and "you" (the speaker and his Irish audience) and on the other, "they" (the deluded and supercilious beings across the Channel): "And if I should describe the *Britons* to you, as they were in *Caesar*'s Time, when they *painted their*

Bodies, or Cloathed themselves with the Skins of Beasts, I should act full as
reasonably as they do" (*D,* 10: 64). Here the Englishman's gaze, which
regularly reduces the Anglo-Irish as well as the native Catholics to "savages," is thrown back at him as the Irish are invited to step through the
looking glass and see the English themselves as primitives—a procedure
aided by the use of the same pronoun to refer both to the "savage" Britons
of Caesar's time and to the putatively "civilized" Britons of Swift's own
day. While this invitation is, strictly speaking, being extended specifically
to other members of his own class, the reversal mechanism Swift recommends offered an even more effective strategy for the native Irish Catholics, in whose hands it could be transformed into a far more subversive tool
for relativizing established hierarchies of value and status—for calling the
very construct of "savage" into question.

In this passage two very different solutions to Swift's identity crisis (so
to speak) are presented: either to reject as erroneous the identification with
Ireland's native population and reaffirm ties to the "master race"; or to
accept this identification but use it to turn the tables on those who have
made it a sign of innate inferiority. Swift's inability to make a definitive
choice between these alternatives produced fissured texts whose speakers
at times embrace the collective category of "us"—even on occasion expanding it to include Africans, American Indians, and other "savages"—
while in other instances strenuously affirming a more limited "us," defined
by its "purer" English roots. From this confusion of pronouns and signifiers we can derive no small insight into why the question of whom Swift
is speaking for in his writings is so problematic.

That these confusions had broad historical roots is evident from their
presence in texts produced by other Anglo-Irish writers contemporaneous
with Swift—Berkeley's tract, *A Word to the Wise; or An Exhortation to the
Roman Catholic Clergy of Ireland* being a case in point. Addressing his
Catholic counterparts in his role as Bishop of Cloyne, Berkeley begins and
ends his exhortation with affirmations of solidarity with them. At the
outset he asks rhetorically, "Do we not inhabit the same spot of ground,
breathe the same air, and live under the same government? why, then,
should we not conspire in one and the same design, to promote the common good of our country?"; and he closes by assuring his audience, "I
consider you as my countrymen, as fellow-subjects, as professing belief in
the same Christ."[16] In between these two assertions of a communal and
seemingly all-inclusive "we," however, the first-person pronouns signify
two more restrictively defined groups: the body of church officials (Anglican and Catholic alike, including the pope himself, lauded for his "endeavor[s] to put new life into the trade and manufactures of his country"
[*W,* 247]), who have the responsibility of setting a moral example for the
slothful Irish natives; and the privileged Protestant class, whose domestic

economy depends on the labor of native Catholic servants and who (at least indirectly, through their political and psychological ties to the British) own colonies—and slaves—abroad. In *A Word to the Wise* Berkeley moves ideologically and linguistically between these distinct groups, in the process offering up three very different models for conceptualizing who constitutes "the Irish nation," and what the act of speaking on its behalf means.

One passage in particular sheds revealing light on this ambivalence of identification. Describing a "kitchen-wench" in his household who refused to carry cinders because she felt it was beneath someone "descended from an old Irish stock," Berkeley declares:

> Never was there a more monstrous conjunction than that of pride with beggary; and yet this prodigy is seen every day in almost every part of this kingdom. At the same time these proud people are more destitute than savages, and more abject than negroes. The negroes in our plantations have a saying, If negro was not negro, Irishman would be negro. (*W*, 237)

Having put forward an expansive view of an Ireland where national definition transcends sectarian (if not class) divisions, Berkeley is suddenly pulled back into the vortex of his immediate surroundings: a world of pronounced social and cultural differences governed in no small part by racial classifications. It is as though Berkeley's more liberal tendencies must give way under the pressure exerted by the immense stigma attached to the category of "Irishman"—a category to which he himself both does and doesn't belong. That the equation of "Irishman" and "negro" is being made here, not by the colonial class across the channel but by the black slaves themselves, adds a level of irony, and a further layer of humiliation, to Berkeley's equivocal status. Although the plantation negroes are presumably referring in this comparison to the native Irish—the "poor white trash" of Britain's nearby colony—even the merest threat that through some perceptual or taxonomic slippage the category of "Irishman" (through the eyes or on the lips of slaves no less!) could include those of Berkeley's own class creates a source of extreme tension that threatens to disrupt the detached, magisterial tone of *A Word to the Wise*.

What we see here is a movement common to many Anglo-Irish texts of the period: as they approach the "heart of darkness," the savage or the negro at the center of their most obsessive and terrified apprehensions, they reveal not only the schizophrenia generated by their hyphenated status but also the phobic strategies designed to put these fears to rest.[17] For Berkeley this means falling back on prevailing stereotypes by labeling the native Irish "a lazy, destitute, and degenerate race" who are "wedded to dirt on principle" (*W*, 238, 242). Having already linked the Irishmen's "innate hereditary sloth" to their "Scythian blood" (*W*, 235), he now presents a more fully articulated expression of the race theory that guarantees his separation from the native Catholic population: "In Holland a child five years old is maintained by its own labour; in Ireland many children of twice that age do nothing but steal, or encumber the hearth and dunghill. This shameful neglect of education shews itself through the whole course of their lives, in a matchless sloth bred in the very bone, and not to be accounted for by any outward hardship or discouragement whatever. It is the native colour, if we may so speak, and complexion of the people" (*W*, 244).

For a man so open to enlightened ideas of national and religious unity, Berkeley gets racially ugly very quickly—a circumstance perhaps not all that surprising given his untroubled acceptance of slavery as biblically defensible. Having magnanimously swept aside the sectarian grounds for distinguishing the Anglo-Irish from the "native" Irish by asking, "Why should . . . the different roads we take to heaven prevent our taking the same steps on earth?" (*W*, 235), but loth to jettison the system of hierarchies that ensures his own privileged position in society, Berkeley has little option but to play the race card as a way of affirming radical difference—and, by implication, vindicating his own sense of entitlement. This is a card Swift too can play, though in his case a sense of complicity in the "degenerate race" he excoriates functions to destabilize the clearcut racial hierarchy we discern in Berkeley's texts, which lack the kind of complex satiric and ironic mechanisms capable of revealing speaker and savage as mirror images of one another, as opposite sides of the same coin rather than as simple antitheses. (Think of Gulliver's horrified recognition of his own close resemblance to the Yahoos.)

A Word to the Wise, then, speaks for the most conservative and elitist elements in contemporary Irish society, but at the same time it gives voice to a quite different perspective, which in part helps to explain the highly favorable response it received from the Roman Catholic clergy of the Diocese of Dublin, who, in a letter first appearing in the *Dublin Journal* of 18 November 1749, "return[ed] their sincere and hearty thanks" to "that great and good man," Berkeley, and expressed their determination "to comply with every particular recommended in [the exhortation] to the utmost of their power."[18] Although this response was obviously motivated by a number of highly pragmatic and self-interested concerns and might strike us today as a perfect example of what we now commonly refer to as colonial mimicry, it attests at the same time to a genuinely liberal dimension of Berkeley's tract, which, in spite of the at times insufferably condescending tone adopted toward the Catholic clergy, created a forum in which the latter could carry on a dialogue with a Protestant Bishop, the very symbol of Ascendancy power, about "the nation"—invoking references to "the public good" and "the true patriot" generally reserved for the lips (and pens) of only those within the inner circles of power.[19] Thus in *A Word to the Wise,* Berkeley—without abandoning the ideology, and consequently the prejudices, of his class—does more than speak for the narrow interests of a small elite. In this sense he, like Swift, though in a less subversive and destabilizing way, highlights the contradictions of colonial representation in eighteenth-century Ireland.

III

Swift not only embodied the problematic of colonial representation, he specifically identified it *as* a problem and foregrounded it throughout his writings, spotlighting the entire spectrum of difficulties involved in acts of articulation in a colonial context. On the most basic level, his works highlight the difficulties surrounding the act of speaking per se within the contemporary state of affairs—not surprisingly, given his continuing battles against government censorship, which included surveillance of his mail, confiscation of his papers, and prosecutions (not to mention jailings) of his printers. As he explained in a letter to Pope, "I dare not publish [my sentiments on publick affairs]: For however orthodox they may be while I am now writing, they may become criminal enough to bring me into trouble before midsummer."[20] And suggestively anticipating the (albeit far more severe) problems of Myles Joyce in the colonial courtroom, Swift dramatized his own judicial victimization at the hands of Lord Chief Justice William Whitshed, who was determined to punish Swift to the full extent of the law (and beyond) for his authorship of *A Proposal for the Universal Use of Irish Manufacture,* falsely claiming that "the Author's design was to bring in the Pretender" and angrily sending the jury back nine times to reconsider their verdict after they had found the printer of the pamphlet not guilty (*SP,* 9: 27)—a circumstance that makes Swift question the efficacy of all judicial appeals, since lawyers and judges "will just give themselves time to libel and accuse me, but cannot spare a minute to hear my defence" (*SP,* 9: 33). These personal libels went hand in hand with the slander of the nation at large; hence Swift also protests against the "[false] Rumours industriously spread" about Ireland in English newspapers (*D,* 10: 53) and the fact that "no Minister ever gave himself the Trouble of reading any Papers written in our defence" (*D,* 10: 64). Note the shift in pronouns, from "*my* defence" to "*our* defence," which underscores the close link Swift saw between personal and national persecution at the hands of England.

It is true, of course, that Swift's circumstances were far more favorable than many others among his countrymen; thus, when confronted by a biased and overzealous judge resolved at all costs to punish him (through his surrogate, the printer Edward Waters), he was able to prevail upon higher authorities to issue a *nolle prosequi,* which won Waters his freedom and ended his own legal liability.[21] Hence to view Swift as the quintessential victim of British colonialism in Ireland would be in effect to occlude the vast body of Irishmen who were far more egregiously victimized, not only by Britain's economic policies but also by Irish legislation that defined them as second-class citizens in their own place of birth. There is no question but that Swift's tendency to offer up his own experiences as a symbol of Ireland's colonial afflictions skirts the danger of becoming an appropriative gesture of the kind discussed earlier. At the same time, his formulations, however personal, often provide access to the experiences of less privileged members of Irish society, articulating grievances suffered even (at times especially) by the lower ranks in society and thereby enabling the latter's voices to be heard along with his own. This is certainly true of those instances in his Irish tracts where, referring to "consumptive Bodies like ours" (*D,* 10: 63) and ironically confessing his "degenera[cy]" in "not [being] easy without *Bread* to my Victuals," he characterizes himself as lacking the basic necessities of life, a potential famine victim whose dramatized plight speaks far more directly for the masses of rural native inhabitants than for the Anglo-Irish gentry in Dublin, whose lavishly spread dinner tables and continually catered-to appetites are in fact the subject of satiric or censorious treatment in other of Swift's tracts (most memorably in *A Modest Proposal*).[22]

My point here is simply this: As long as we view Swift's situation in an appropriately critical way, not as exemplary of all the afflictions imposed on Ireland by British colonialism but instead, as emblematic of a whole range of such afflictions as they *variously* and *unevenly* affected different groups within Irish society, we can fruitfully talk about Swift's "representation" of Ireland without falling into the trap of letting his enormous symbolic presence and rhetorical power silence, or render invisible, the rest of his aggrieved countrymen. To use a present-day analogy, we might think of the way that the putative sufferings of the (seemingly ubiquitous) middle class in the United States have been regularly invoked over the past decade or two to protest against various inequities in the system and to support a variety of proposed reforms. The main effect of this invocation has been an almost total displacement, a consignment to near-invisibility, of those groups in society—the working poor, the unemployed, the homeless—who bear the real brunt of the current global economy. Too often the difficulties that professional couples who earn six-figure salaries face in buying a house in a fashionable suburb or in sending their children to private schools come to stand in for the severe deprivations suffered by an underclass without access to the most basic necessities of life. Nevertheless, I would argue that their act of speaking for the economically afflicted can, *under certain circumstances,* function in more enlightened ways as well, enabling a clearer understanding of those developments in the domestic and world economy that have significantly affected not only their lives but also the lives of the less privileged, and providing the grounds for a *meaningful, nonappropriative* sense of identification with the truly deprived, based on recognition of the widening gap between the (obscenely) rich and the rest of society, middle class and poor alike, and the consequent need for a redistribution of society's resources. Whether in terms of eighteenth-century Ireland or late twentieth-, early twenty-first-century United States, representational acts embody the conflicting impulses, and contradictory political potential, inherent in all endeavors to speak simultaneously for oneself and others within a framework defined by pronounced social and political inequalities.

Consider, for example, Swift's protestation against Englishmen being given the chief employments in Ireland that should by rights go to native-born Anglo-Irishmen, where he argues that these (very recent and often temporary) English transplants "had no common ligament to bind them with us; they suffered not with our Sufferings, and if it were possible for us to have any Cause of Rejoycing, they could not rejoyce with us."[23] On one level this protest has a rather narrow focus: the misfortunes of those within Ireland's privileged class who have in effect been cheated out of better jobs by carpetbaggers from across the channel. Even if this situation were to change for the better, no Catholic or Dissenter was likely to benefit directly from the expanded access to these sorts of positions. And yet, on another level, Swift's outcry may be said to articulate the grievances of a much broader spectrum of the population. In class terms, it speaks for the many Protestants who were far from prosperous—those referred to in Thomas Sheridan's acid observation: "This is the Modern way of Planting Colonies. . . When those who are so unfortunate to be born here, are excluded from the meanest Preferments, and deem'd incapable of being entertain'd, even as common Soldiers, whose poor stipend is but Four pence a Day."[24]

Going even beyond this expanded conception, Swift's protest may be said to speak for the Irish nation as a whole in other crucial ways. For one thing, it focuses attention on the presence of suffering as an inescapable consequence of British policies toward Ireland—*suffering,* not mere discomfort or inconvenience. For another, it insists on the validity of a peculiarly Irish body of experiences, wholly alien to an English sensibility and mode of valuation ("[they] had no common ligament to bind them with us"). Finally, it underscores the fundamental inequity of a situation in which people are denied participation in the very institutions and political mechanisms that govern their lives. Texts such as this one bear out Joep Leerssen's conclusion that "Swift seemed to regard the division between

Protestants and Catholics as less important than the one between Irish interest and English interest," a position he considers "Swift's most important contribution to the development of Irish Patriotism."[25] Advocacy of this Irish interest meant that the deprivations endured by thwarted Anglo-Irish place-seekers, in themselves hardly indicative of Ireland's worst hardships, could be transformed into a vantage point from which the nation's severest problems were able to be seen more clearly and understood within the broader context of a system in which the "sufferings" of relatively well-off Protestants were merely (so to speak) the tip of the iceberg—a point, indeed, explicitly acknowledged by the Swiftian persona "A. North" (a "Country Gentleman, and a Member of *Parliament*") upon noting the severity of his own economic problems: "But the Sufferings of me, and those of my Rank, are Trifles in Comparison of what the meaner Sort [Shopkeepers, Farmers, Pedlars, common Labourers] undergo."[26]

IV

The problems of representation in Swift's Ireland cannot be fully comprehended without considering the very basic level of political representation: specifically, the failure of the Irish legislature to speak effectively for the interests of its constituents. Obviously its most blatant shortcoming was its failure to represent the majority of the population; but even within the limited parameters of a colonial Protestant institution it failed to function meaningfully as a representative body, most dramatically because it effectively ceased having any independent existence after 1720, when the so-called Declaratory Act, insisting on the full rigors of Poynings's Law, asserted the right of the Westminster Parliament to pass laws binding on Ireland and to act as the final court of appeal in all Irish cases, the explicit aim being to "better secur[e] the Dependence of the Kingdom of Ireland upon the Crown of Great Britain."[27] The Drapier's scornful rejection of the very term "*depending Kingdom*" on the grounds that it is "a *modern Term of Art;* unknown . . . to all antient *Civilians,* and *Writers upon Government*" (*D,* 10: 62) is an obvious response to this Act, as was Swift's publication (in the same year the Act was passed) of *A Proposal for the Universal Use of Irish Manufacture,* which declares the invalidity of laws that "*bind Men without their Consent.*"[28] The Act's humiliating subjection of Ireland was still fresh in Swift's mind over a decade later, when he came to write *Verses on the Death of Dr Swift* and included a reference to "Fools of Rank, a mungril Breed,/Who fain would pass for Lords indeed"; in a note to Faulkner's edition, Swift glosses these lines with a pointed allusion to the Declaratory Act: "The Peers of *Ireland* lost a great Part of their

Jurisdiction by one single Act, and tamely submitted to this infamous Mark of Slavery without the least Resentment, or Remonstrance."[29]

The Declaratory Act obviously produced a major political crisis in Ireland; but also, and more to the point of my specific concerns here, it produced a major crisis in representation, making it in certain crucial ways impossible for *any* group in Ireland to speak for the Irish, since the official channels and structures of representation had been removed from Irish soil and transferred to London. This circumstance haunts all of Swift's political writings throughout the 1720s, many of which at one and the same time insist on the necessity for acts of representation and dramatize the futility of attempting them. These writings depict the Act's debilitating effects in terms of Ireland's reduction to little more than a puppet, mechanically uttering words put into its mouth by those pulling the strings (either the English themselves or their flunkeys in Ireland); as Swift wryly observed to Pope, "I have often wished . . . that a political Catechism might be published by authority four times a year, in order to instruct us how we are to speak and write, and act during the current quarter" (*SP*, 9: 33). The puppet imagery is made explicit in a poem such as *Mad Mullinix and Timothy,* where the titular Mullinix, a stand-in for a half-crazed beggar known as Molyneux who roamed the streets of Dublin during Swift's time spouting Tory sentiments, engages in alternately abusive and comical dialogue with Timothy: namely, Richard Tighe, a staunch Whig and Walpole supporter who was a member of both the Irish Parliament and the Irish Privy Council.[30] Mullinix describes the state of Irish affairs through an extended analogy to a Punch show, invoking a putatively universal definition—"Thus *Tim,* Philosophers suppose,/*The World consists of Puppetshows*" (*MM,* 123–24)—to delineate Ireland's very specific situation:

> So at this Booth, which we call *Dublin,*
> Tim thou'rt the Punch to stir up trouble in;
> You Wrigle, Fidge, and make a Rout
> Put all your Brother Puppets out,
> Run on in one perpetual Round,
> To Teize, Perplex, Disturb, Confound.
>
> (*MM,* 127–32)

Tighe would have struck Swift as perfect material for a Punchinello given his slavish exertions on behalf of the English interest in Ireland, which included informing on Swift's friend Sheridan to the authorities in Dublin Castle after Sheridan delivered a provocatively titled sermon, "Sufficient unto the Day is the Evil thereof," on the anniversary of King George's accession.[31] Tighe's example conflates the roles of informer and puppet, revealing both as stooges incapable of independent thought or action, who mouth the words and perform the gestures demanded of them by those pulling the strings behind the scene. Thus Timothy, having been convinced that his image needs a complete overhaul, pleads for guidance in learning how to become just like Mullinix. The latter is only too happy to comply, readily seizing the reins of control: "Be studious well to imitate/ My portly Motion, Mien, and Gate./Mark my Address, and learn my Style,/When to look Scornful, when to Smile" (*MM*, 223–26). Timothy's eagerness to join the ranks of Dublin's madmen foreshadows the depiction of Ireland's new Parliament House in *A Character, Panegyric, and Description of the Legion Club* as a lunatic asylum whose members "sit a picking Straws" and "dabble in their Dung" (49; 52), acting like typical Bedlamites while they "Sell the Nation for a Pin" (48).

If we were to think of this situation in rhetorical terms, we might describe the impact of the Declaratory Act as a reduction of Ireland to the status of England's persona: a figure lacking an independent existence, set up to mouth the words decreed by an authorizing power, in much the same way that the fictive speakers in Swift's works utter the words written by their author (though note that in both cases the inability to exert total control from above, combined with bursts of anarchic energy from below, creates political and rhetorical situations of marked subversive potential). Obviously Ireland was a real place peopled by flesh-and-blood inhabitants; but we can think of it as a "creation" of England in the sense suggested by Declan Kiberd when he observes, "If Ireland had never existed, the English would have invented it; and since it never existed in English eyes as anything more than a patchwork-quilt of warring fiefdoms, their leaders occupied the neighbouring island and called it Ireland."[32] Within this conceptual framework it is possible to understand Swift's utilization of personae in his political writings (after 1720 in particular) as a means of turning the tables on England: of wresting back control and voice from the self-proclaimed master ventriloquist and asserting Ireland's right to speak for itself. To be sure, this strategy is based on mechanisms of repression in that the goal of *Catholic* Ireland's independence and *its* right to speak for itself, no longer subordinated to the laws and institutions of both British- *and* Protestant-dominated Ireland, is what can never be expressly articulated in Swift's writings—what must be displaced onto Protestant Ireland's struggle against British rule.

Yet here again, as in earlier-noted instances, the basic paradigm Swift offers, in this case through his persona strategy, is capable of being appropriated for considerably more subversive ends. And indeed, Swift himself, in his posthumously published tract, *Reasons Humbly Offered to the Parliament of Ireland For Repealing the Sacramental Test, in Favour of the Catholicks,* goes a long way toward demonstrating the possibilities of such appropriation by creating a (pro-) Catholic speaker who powerfully refutes the official Protestant interpretation of the Rebellion of 1641, replacing it with a view consistent with that of Catholic historians at the time.[33] That the tract was intended as an ironic piece, part of Swift's polemical works in support of the Test Act, does not negate the fact that many of its positive constructions of Irish Catholics occur also in Swift's nonironic texts.[34] Nor does it negate the subversive force of Swift's use of a persona in this instance to turn the tables on not only the English but also the Irish Protestant "ventriloquists" by presenting a political and historical perspective that belies the official "scripts" of both dominant groups: "It is well known, that the first Conquerors of this Kingdom were *English Catholicks*, subject to *English Catholick* Kings. . . . It is confessed, that the Posterity of those first victorious *Catholicks* were often forced to rise in their own Defence, against new Colonies from *England,* who treated them like mere native *Irish,* with innumerable Oppressions."[35] Here the speaker deftly turns on its head the argument based on conquest that was commonly adduced by *Protestants* to rationalize their domination of Ireland; he underscores the impossibility of locating an originary or foundational moment in Irish history capable of justifying Protestant claims to be the rightful rulers of the country. Moreover, the protest against being treated "like mere native *Irish,*" usually voiced by the Protestants in Ireland (on occasion, by Swift himself) miffed at English *hauteur* toward them, here takes on a rather satirical tone through its being uttered by a Catholic. The shift in voice and perspective exposes both the absurdity of the Anglo-Irish complaint and the injustice of the English stance of superiority toward Ireland.

V

The Drapier's affair provided Swift with a set of circumstances ideally suited to his combined political and rhetorical use of personae. The seeming anomaly of having a (mere) tradesman represent all of Ireland pales in comparison with the infinitely greater anomaly of having William Wood—"a *Single, Rapacious, Obscure, Ignominious* PROJECTOR" (*D*, 10: 35)—and the corrupt, hibernophobic Robert Walpole determine what is best for Ireland. Compared with the "fraudulent representations of Wood" (*D*, 10: 47), the Drapier's acts of representation seem almost unproblematic. The fact that there was so broad a consensus opposed to the coinage scheme meant that the Drapier could plausibly claim to speak for the whole nation without having to deal with pesky questions about how this claim could be reconciled with the obvious social and religious divisions in Irish society.[36]

Although partly inspired by William Molyneux's *The Case of Ireland
. . . Stated,* the Drapier's Fourth Letter shifts the emphasis of the case for
Ireland's legislative independence from the historical precedents and common law argument spotlighted by Molyneux to the assertion of natural
rights: "by the Laws of GOD, of NATURE, of NATIONS, and of your own
Country, you ARE and OUGHT to be as FREE a People as your Brethren
in *England*" (*D,* 10: 63). The subsequent *Letter to Molesworth* extends this
thread of argumentation, citing the influence of "dangerous Authors, who
talk of *Liberty as a Blessing, to which the whole Race of Mankind hath an
Original Title*" (*D,* 10: 86). The Drapier's assertion of natural rights necessarily (whether consciously intended or not) extends their application to all
of Ireland's inhabitants, without exception; it is what Thomas Bartlett
terms "the Achilles' heel of the whole Protestant position," since "natural
rights could not be restricted to Englishmen, nor to Englishmen born in
Ireland, nor to Irish Protestants: they were inherent in all mankind."[37]

There is another telling difference between *The Case of Ireland . . .
Stated* and the Drapier's Fourth Letter. Molyneux makes a point of defining "the people of Ireland" for whom he speaks as the Protestants of
English origin. He claims, for example, that "it was only the *Antient Race*
of the *Irish,* that could suffer by [Henry II's] Subjugation," while "the
English and *Britains* that came over and Conquered with him [along with
their descendants], retain'd all the Freedoms and Immunities of *Free-born*
Subjects," and he offers highly sectarian accounts of particularly polariz-
ing events in Irish history, such as the upheavals of the year 1689, "when
most of the Protestant Nobility, Gentry, and Clergy of *Ireland,* were driven
out of that Kingdom by the Insolencies and Barbarities of the *Irish Papists.*"[38] Swift, on the contrary, exploits the specific occasion to convey a
picture of Irish society that transcends such sectarian conflicts, stressing
instead his citizenship in "a Country, where the People of all Ranks,
Parties, and Denominations, are convinced to a Man, that the undoing of
themselves and their Posterity for ever, will be dated from the Admission
of [Wood's halfpence]" (*D,* 10: 60). Of course, given that the Letter (not to
mention the entire campaign to defeat Wood's patent) depended for its
credibility and effectiveness on refuting the false reports widely circulat-
ing that the anti-Wood opposition was in essence a Catholic plot against
British Protestant interests, the Fourth Letter does affirm the specifically
Protestant character of the opposition, enumerating at the outset the ruling-
class institutions and officials, including "the two Houses of Parliament,
the Privy-Council . . . [and] the Lord-Mayor and Aldermen of Dublin" (*D,*
10: 54), that have declared themselves against the coinage, and later stating, "it is the *True English People of Ireland,* who refuse [Wood's half-
pence]; although we take it for granted, that the *Irish* will do so too,
whenever they are asked" (*D,* 10: 67).[39] This statement reflects something

of the same patronizing tone noted earlier in Berkeley's exhortation to the Catholic clergy. At the same time, it reveals Swift's awareness that, having asserted the natural right of all mankind to liberty and government by consent, it was no longer possible to simply leave the Catholics out of the picture, nor to ignore the importance of their support.

Under the circumstances, the surprise is not that Swift in this Letter distinguishes between the Protestant people of Ireland and the Catholic natives, but that he gives this distinction so little emphasis, subordinating it instead to a vision of solidarity among all groups in Irish society. The internal logic of the Fourth Letter demands that "the Whole People of Ireland" include the Catholic population, even though existing political conditions demanded that the latter be excluded. The Drapier deals with this impasse by in effect acknowledging that the Catholics must be part of the opposition, but specifically on terms consistent with Ascendancy rule. The central contradiction governing *The Drapier's Letters* lies in their need to avoid undermining this rule while at the same time expanding the oppositional base against Wood to include groups in society ordinarily ignored when advocating for the people of Ireland. The Drapier cannot explicitly incorporate the Catholics into this expanded conception of nationhood, but in a sense they are allowed to sneak in the back door through a series of displacements in which religious divisions are replaced by class differences that are at least somewhat more assimilable into a national ideal. Thus in an earlier letter, the Drapier asserts his credentials by telling us, "I am no inconsiderable Shop-keeper in this Town. I have discoursed with several of my own, and other Trades; with many Gentlemen both of City and Country; and also, with great Numbers of Farmers, Cottagers, and Labourers" (*D,* 10: 16). He deliberately presents a list of the humblest groups in Irish society (several of which were composed largely of Catholics), whose opinions about Wood's proposed coinage are accorded as much attention as the views of "the two Houses of Parliament, [and] the Privy-Council" invoked in the subsequent letter. The Drapier's Fourth Letter may be the one that most explicitly asserts his role as speaker for "the Whole People of Ireland," but it is only when we consider all of the Letters together that we can fully appreciate the extent to which Swift manages to accomplish that aim—even as he avoids taking the final step that would pull the rug from under his own feet by negating the grounds of his class's privileged position in Irish society.

VI

Swift's activities as M.B. Drapier proved highly efficacious, of course, culminating in the revocation of Wood's patent in August 1725. I want to conclude this discussion, however, not with an example of Swift's success in representing the Irish nation but with a consideration of (what were far more typical) his frustrated attempts in this regard, exemplified by writings of his that dramatize the profound difficulties, even at times the impossibility, of such representation. A case in point is *A Letter to the Archbishop of Dublin concerning the Weavers,* which not only failed to achieve its ostensible purpose but was never even published in Swift's lifetime, despite his assertion that he was writing to "offer my notions to the publick."[40] Herbert Davis, referring to this and several other tracts written in 1729, comments that "the real problem is to explain why they were not printed," and concludes that the reason must have been "that mood of despondency to which [Swift] often gives expression in these unpublished pieces."[41] I want to consider this "despondency" further, not only as dejection over Ireland's deteriorating economic conditions (which included a serious famine during the course of that year), but also in terms of Swift's deepening sense of the futility of all forms of representation designed to make this situation known to others and thereby bring about relief.

The opening of the *Letter to the Archbishop* immediately foregrounds the act of representation as one of the text's central preoccupations by having Swift describe a meeting with the corporation of weavers in the woollen manufacture, "when he who spoke for the rest and in the name of his absent brethren" delivered what he said was "the opinion of the whole body"—namely, that Swift write something to "persuade the People of the Kingdom to wear their own woollen Manufactures" (*L,* 12: 65). This request ironically underscores the failure of previous Swift interventions (most obviously his *Proposal for the Universal Use of Irish Manufacture* nine years earlier) to achieve their goal, while at the same time highlighting the conditions and hence the limitations of the representational act. Were Swift to accept this advocacy role for the corporation, it would place him at not one, but two removes from those he is supposed to speak for; the absent body first represented by one of their own would now be re-represented by someone completely outside of their group. This problem of the gap created by standing in for what is absent takes on an additional dimension through Swift's subsequent suggestion that the weavers "apply themselves to the Parliament in their next Session" with a view toward "prevail[ing] in the House of Commons to grant one very reasonable request" (*L,* 12: 71)—namely, vote to wear clothing made only of Irish manufacture. Elsewhere in Swift's writings, the distance between the formally constituted representative bodies of society and those seeking representation is satirically magnified through the use of speakers who are at the very bottom of the social hierarchy, as in the poem, *The Petition of Frances Harris,* and *The Humble Petition of the Footmen in and about the City of Dublin,* where lowly members of the Irish servant class farcically present their cases to the most powerful officials in the land.[42] Swift's advice to the weavers to petition Parliament with their grievance, if not similarly satirical, nevertheless conveys a hint of absurdity given the Irish Parliament's record of caving in to English pressures and doing little to oppose its restrictions on Irish trade. The subtext is clear: even if Swift were to devote the rest of his life to representing the weavers in his writings, they would still not be meaningfully represented—no more than Ireland itself could ever be under the prevailing circumstances.

Almost every existing problem with regard to representational acts within the Irish context is touched upon in the *Letter to the Archbishop,* including political reprisals against protest, the frustration of the advocate whose advice has repeatedly been ignored, and the unreliability of those seeking to be represented. But what is perhaps the most interesting feature of the *Letter* with respect to this theme is Swift's suggestion that there is something about the Irish situation so peculiar and aberrant that it falls outside the scope of representation altogether: "For, I will not deny to your Grace, that I cannot reflect on the singular condition of this Country, different from all others upon the face of the Earth, without some Emotion" (*L,* 12: 65). The same point is made even more dramatically in his tract, *Maxims Controlled in Ireland,* where Ireland's radical otherness is conveyed through a series of conditional clauses suggesting monstrosity: "For, if we could conceive a nation where each of the inhabitants had but one eye, one leg, and one hand, it is plain that, before you could institute them into a republic, an allowance must be made for those material defects, wherein they differed from other mortals."[43] Indeed, this entire tract is based on the premise of Ireland's irreducible singularity as the only place in the world where otherwise universal principles do not apply. It is this grotesque and unenviable uniqueness that makes Ireland's problems impervious to the numerous recommendations for "improving the trade of Ireland" by "referring us to the practice and example of England, Holland, France, or other nations" (*M,* 12: 131).

It is possible to argue that Swift speaks most powerfully for the Irish nation, not when he is clearly articulating the interests of his countrymen in works like *The Drapier's Letters,* but when he is indicating Ireland's resistance to normal modes of representation due to the "unspeakable" nature of its conditions. The claims of unrepresentability that pervade Swift's post-1720 political writings function, among other things, as an ironic counterpart to the overabundance and violence of representation that England inflicted on its "dependencies." Looking at a later period in Irish history, Seamus Deane has located "a narrative of strangeness" about a country whose condition "cannot be represented at all or . . . still has to be represented."[44] Swift's distinctive twist on this narrative, and very possibly his strongest claim to being an Irish patriot, was his transformation of the (to him) inherent strangeness of Ireland, as a country with an alien language and culture, into the artificially produced strangeness of a country deformed and rendered unrecognizable by colonialism. We can see a microcosm of this transformation in Swift's letter of 30 June 1732 addressed to Dean Brandreth:

> I think I was once in your county, Tipperary, which is like the rest of the whole kingdom, a bare face of nature, without house or plantations; filthy cabins, miserable, tattered, half-starved creatures, scarce in human shape; . . . a parish church to be found only in a summer-day's journey, in comparison of which, an English farmer's barn is a cathedral; a bog of fifteen miles round; every meadow a slough, and every hill a mixture of rock, heath, and marsh. . . . There is not an acre of land in Ireland turned to half its advantage; yet it is better improved than the people; and all these evils are the effects of English tyranny: so your sons and grandchildren will find it to their sorrow.[45]

This passage begins with a speaker indistinguishable from an Englishman confronting the dreaded heart of darkness on an expedition into deepest Africa, or an Anglo-Irishman railing in disgust against the native savagery of the land to which a malevolent fate has condemned him; it ends with the forceful, angry voice of an Irish nationalist, exposing the almost indescribable wretchedness of Ireland as a manifestation of the barbarism not within but without: the barbarism emanating from, and created in the name of, English "civilization." A half-century ago, George Orwell argued that Swift spoke (if only partially and contradictorily) for the forces of anarchy; several decades later, Norman O. Brown noted the ways in which Swift spoke for the id, not for civilization but for its discontents.[46] In the spirit of these interpretations, I want to suggest that Swift also spoke for those extreme aspects of eighteenth-century Irish society that resisted all forms of rational explanation and verbal closure. The exposure of the mechanisms of sexual sublimation (as in *A Tale of a Tub*'s "Digression on Madness") that prompted Brown to view Swift as a kind of pre-Freudian psychoanalyst also allows us to understand Swift as one who adamantly rejected those mechanisms of political and linguistic repression that enable the supposedly civilizing processes of rationalization and normalization to take place on a historical level, that conceal from view the unassimilable vis-à-vis the established institutions of polite society.

In a different time and place, Aimé Césaire powerfully protested against similar manifestations of so-called civilization, also within a colonial context, by exposing the savagery at the very core of refined European culture, the "unctuous and sanctimonious cannibalism" regularly staged as normal political operations in the French National Assembly. His observations, based chiefly on the twentieth-century experience of Martinique, have their own peculiar applicability to eighteenth-century Ireland: "Colonization: bridgehead in a campaign to civilize barbarism, from which there may emerge at any moment the negation of civilization, pure and simple."[47] To describe this civilizing campaign, even in an eloquent way, is not remarkably difficult given a sufficient level of education and socialization. But how—with what language and mode of address—does one record the "negation" of civilization: those moments that can erupt suddenly, at any time, and tear apart the smooth fabric of social and rhetorical sublimations? For Césaire the answer is an impassioned outcry that sets up, but then quickly subverts, expectations of a sober philosophic "discourse": that consists in sentence fragments, fierce ejaculations, and a generic olio of satire, diatribe, historical reportage, and theatrical dramatizations. For Swift, the answer was a body of writings with built-in satiric mechanisms enabling them to self-destruct at the same time that they give voice to the madman, the cannibal, the excrementalist, and others functioning outside of the sublimation machine; writings that on occasion cast doubts on their own powers of communication and persuasion by remaining fragmentary and/or unpublished despite their intended appeal to the public; writings that insist on the absolute, monstrous singularity of the Irish condition, which no established modes of explanation can adequately describe.

The enormities of twentieth-century history have foregrounded the problem of trying to speak the unspeakable, to represent that which falls outside the boundaries of normal human experience; they have forced us to ask (in George Steiner's words) "whether language itself can justly communicate, express, give rational or metaphoric constructs to the realities of modern torture and extermination."[48] But what about eighteenth-century Ireland? Could its conditions really have been so horrible that they defied the signifying powers of language as well as the conventions of rational discourse? On the face of it this seems to be a gross exaggeration of the facts—as do Swift's impassioned diatribes on the existing situation. Sooner or later most of us are probably moved to ask ourselves, What was this guy's problem anyway? Why the constant negativity and vituperation, the repeated outcries against the circumstances of his existence, given a mode of life more privileged than desperate and a position in society many would have considered enviable? I think that Swift on some level realized the inevitability of such questions, and that this realization made him even more strident in his denunciations as well as more overwhelmed by a sense of the sheer hopelessness of trying to get his point across, given the power of sublimating mechanisms to turn shit into the products of high culture and to replace aberration or pervasive disease with the varied forms of normalcy. In the years since his death we can see the effect of these mechanisms in the way that his most disturbing and obscene works have been, when not dismissed as morally loathsome or ignored altogether, converted into models of ironic prose or satiric dexterity deserving of literary canonization or, alternatively, in the way in which his extreme diagnoses of the Irish condition have been turned on himself, normalizing the depicted situation while pathologizing the author.

These mechanisms have tended to be kinder to Swift's contemporaries. Thus, for example, what we might term the "civilized barbarism" of the genial, philosophically detached Bishop Berkeley—his defense of slavery in the name of religion and his urging that planters baptize "those who belong to them" since "their Slaves would only become better Slaves by becoming Christians" and "it would be of Advantage to their Affairs, to have Slaves who should *obey in all Things their Masters according to the Flesh, . . . in Singleness of Heart as fearing God*"—has been converted by subsequent critical commentary into a stage in the upward march of human progress: "While to a later age it may seem no great service to blacks to argue that they could lawfully be both Christians and slaves at the same time, the case is otherwise. . . . Berkeley took a step, however tentative and tiny, when he argued for greater intensity and responsibility in trying to Christianize blacks."[49] It is tempting to recall here Césaire's discovery of "howling savagery" in the writings of "the Western *humanist,* the 'idealist' philosopher" (the reference here is to Renan), as well as his scathingly sarcastic look at various French so-called "scientific" and philosophic texts that blithely normalize slavery—for example, Lapouge's "*it must not be forgotten that* [slavery] *is no more abnormal than the domestication of the horse or the ox.*"[50]

And leaving behind individual cases altogether, we might think of the ways that rationalizing and normalizing techniques have been appropriated by certain kinds of recent "revisionist" historiography in order to represent aspects of the Irish past in a putatively dispassionate, objective manner.[51] With regard to the Great Famine, this has meant (once again) invoking historical relativism in order to examine the events of 1845–52 in a detached, clinical fashion, devoid of the ideologically engaged tone of earlier nationalist historiography. Thus Mary Daly, for one, having warned her readers against "adopting a late-twentieth-century attitude of moral superiority," turns the catastrophic events of that period into a less than remarkable (because part of a recurring) scenario that called forth government relief measures that, however inadequate, are not subject to second-guessing, much less to condemnation by later historians.[52] The transformation, in Daly's study, of millions of starved and displaced bodies into a largely administrative problem immune to moral judgments is the very opposite of the mercilessly *de*sublimating strategy of Césaire as he reconverts European industrial growth and economic prosperity into "the highest heap of corpses in history."[53] It is equally inimical to Swift's desublimations of what passed for civilization in his day, which also entailed recovering heaps of dead bodies from underneath layers of abstraction and repressed material realities: for example, the Irishmen lured to the American colonies under false pretenses, to be used as colonial foot soldiers, "as a Screen [for the English settlers] against the Assaults of the *Savages*," and afterward to "fill up Trenches with their dead Bodies."[54]

Which brings us to one final casualty of these rationalizing and normalizing procedures, colonialism itself—which has virtually been eliminated from a number of recent historical narratives through their assimilation of eighteenth-century Ireland into contemporary European models of governance. Thus Jacqueline Hill, noting that in Ireland "politics was mainly the preserve of an aristocracy . . . claiming rights that derived, in part at least, from conquest," insists that "there was nothing unusual, by contemporary standards, about that. Aristocratic preeminence was to be observed all over Europe, and it was frequently explained in terms of conquest."[55] In a similar vein, S. J. Connolly, acknowledging Ireland's "many-sided subordination" but seeing it as no different from that of Southern Italy, Norway, or Poland during this period, argues that "*Ancien régime* Europe offers many examples of territories or historic nations under the domination of foreign rulers. . . . Yet none of [these nations] is normally described as a case of colonial rule. Why then should Ireland, alone in Western Europe, be considered for that status?"[56]

Why indeed? Clearly there were many in Swift's own day who asked that very same question (or a variant thereof) and who answered it with unequivocal assurances of Ireland's normalcy in this regard, emphasizing the array of familiar benefits it offered both its own and England's ruling class (the only ones deemed worth considering in this matter). It was these kinds of descriptions that drove Swift to distraction, provoking his most mordantly sarcastic and vehement denunciations. Much of the exceedingly bleak commentary in *A Short View of the State of Ireland* was designed to counter the reassuringly rosy reports made about the country by contemporary pamphleteers, such as John Browne in his *Seasonable Remarks on Trade* (1728), who promoted Ireland's alleged wealth as a source of growing profit for England, portraying the colony as "a milch Cow [which], if we let it run into good Pasture . . . will overflow our Pails."[57] The same perverse and/or deluded attitude is attributed in the *Short View* to those who come to Dublin for brief visits, frequenting the homes of the privileged few and then returning to England to spread the word that Ireland's inhabitants "wallow in Riches and Luxury."[58] Swift tells us that "with regard to the Affairs of this Kingdom, I have been using all Endeavors to subdue my Indignation" (*SV*, 12: 5), but the body of the pamphlet shows that not even his most vaunted satiric and rhetorical skills can transmute this sense of outrage into something more restrained, more socially acceptable, more literary ("But my heart is too Heavy to continue this Irony longer" [*SV,* 12: 10]). As a response to the complacent reports of English visitors to the country (and the Irish "Man-pleaser[s]" eager to curry favor with them [*SV,* 12: 12]), Swift again insists on the appalling singularity of Ireland's situation, which removes it from any possible comparison with other countries—even, one must assume, those of the ancien régime. Having enumerated a series of disastrous circumstances besetting Ireland, he concludes, "And in this, as in most of the Articles already mentioned, we are an Exception to all other States or Monarchies that were ever known in the World" (*SV,* 12: 9).

The language of the *Short View* is extreme and uncompromising; it moves between the starkest of concrete, factual details ("The Families of Farmers, who pay great Rents, living in Filth and Nastiness upon Buttermilk and Potatoes, without a Shoe or Stocking to their Feet" [*SV,* 12: 10]) and tropes whose very banality is used for shock effect ("One Thing I know, that *when the Hen is starved to Death, there will be no more Golden Eggs*" [*SV,* 12: 12]). Should we be inclined to interpret this (and similar tracts) as a distortion of the actual state of affairs through vituperative exaggeration, we must at the same time be prepared to entertain the possibility that the comforting, familiarizing descriptions of all those, whether in the eighteenth century or today, who reject Swift's diagnoses distort reality in another way—and perhaps with far more pernicious results in the sense that, unlike exaggeration, the latter practice does away with reality altogether, removing the problem from view and making disappear those who stand witness to its appalling results. Thomas Sheridan's version of the *Short View,* his own graphic account of a journey he took from Dublin to Dundalk, published in the *Intelligencer* No. 6, which emphatically endorses the picture of wretchedness offered by Swift with its enumeration of the dismal objects he encountered en route (including "Carrs loaden with old musty shrivel'd Hydes," "tattered Families flitting to be shipped off to the *West-Indies,*" and large colonies of beggars "all repairing to people our Metropolis"), explicitly addresses the possible challenges to his (and Swift's) perception of the Irish condition:

> It may be objected, What use it is of to display the Poverty of the Nation in the manner I have done. In answer, I desire to know for what Ends, and by what Persons, This new Opinion of our flourishing State has of late been so Industriously advanced. One thing is certain, that the Advancers have either already found their own Account, or have been heartily promised, or at least have been entertained with hopes, by seeing such an Opinion pleasing to those who have it in their power to reward.[59]

Sheridan's point here is as relevant to our own interpretations of eighteenth-century Irish history as it was to his contemporary detractors. Mere avoidance of the impassioned criticism pervading his own and Swift's accounts of Ireland in favor of serene testimonies to the nation's normal development or flourishing state does not equate to a detached, objective viewpoint. Indeed, it can just as readily be an expression of flagrant partiality and self-interest. Sheridan does not make any claim here for the objective truth of his own position. He does, however, invite us to consider what there is to gain, in the personal and political terms suggested above, from the relentless exposure of Ireland's singularly miserable conditions; and if we conclude that the answer is nothing, to wonder why we should reject the testimony of people like himself and Swift for the complacent reports of a well-functioning society provided by those who stand to profit from reassuring the ruling powers about the status quo in which they have so great an investment.

It is perhaps in the *Intelligencer* No. 6 that Sheridan comes closest to approximating Swift's perspective and mode of expression; yet even this piece falls well short of the emotional and linguistic extremity of the *Short View*. Verbal excess is one of the signs under which Swift (like Césaire) attested to the outrages of his time; and while excess by definition can never be consonant with an exact representation of historical reality, its operations *can* bring to the level of consciousness, and thus help render discernible, those elements in an extreme situation that refuse accommodation to official historical narratives rooted in standardized models of explanation and resolution. Another sign under which Swift offered witness to the times was the very opposite of verbal excess: spareness, starkness, silence—the terse recognition that mere words cannot communicate the enormities that the writer or speaker wishes to, indeed *must*, convey. Faced with the absurdities of Ireland's economic situation as regulated by English interests, Swift is moved to note that "there is something so monstrous . . . something so sottish, that it wants a Name, in our Language, to express it by."[60] This awareness did not of course prevent Swift from producing a very substantial number of words in the course of a long life devoted to commenting on, satirizing, and urging measures to improve the state of affairs in Ireland. Nevertheless, I want to conclude by suggesting that Swift's contribution to Irish history rests not only on what he said but also on what he *didn't* say—or, to be more precise, on what he kept insisting he *couldn't* say: rests in no small measure on his demonstration that the struggle to represent Ireland's situation, and through that struggle to underscore its unrepresentability due to man-made (politically inflicted) deformation, was a task not to be evaded even by an Anglican churchman in relatively cushy circumstances who could, if he chose, have spoken in the confident, magisterial tones of the Ascendancy.

NOTES

1. Swift, *The Drapier's Letters* (1724), in *Prose Works of Jonathan Swift*, ed. Herbert Davis, 14 vols. (Oxford: Basil Blackwell, 1939–68), 10: 53–68. Hereafter abbreviated *D* and cited parenthetically in the text by volume and page number.

2. R. F. Foster, *Modern Ireland, 1600–1972* (London and New York: Penguin, 1988), 175. Technically the term "Protestant Ascendancy" is anachronistic when applied to Swift since it did not come into use until the 1780s. However, it is possible to argue, along with Jacqueline Hill, that the term nevertheless "serves to describe the political reality in Ireland from the mid-seventeenth to the nineteenth century" (*From Patriots to Unionists: Dublin Civic Politics and Irish Protestant Patriotism, 1660–1840* [Oxford: Clarendon Press, 1997], 9). For additional insight into the historical background and meaning of the term, see Kevin Whelan, *The Tree of Liberty: Radicalism, Catholicism and the Construction of Irish Identity,* Critical Conditions: Field Day Essays and Monologues (Notre Dame: University of Notre Dame Press, 1996), 107–10.

3. Although all three of these "speakers for the Irish nation" were Anglican—indeed, officials of the Church of Ireland for at least some period in their lives—a distinction needs to be made between the Anglo-Irish background and tradition of Swift and Berkeley on the one hand, and on the other, the Irish Protestantism of Sheridan, who came from a native Gaelic-speaking family, the O Sioradains (or O'Sheridans) of county Cavan, that converted in the first half of the seventeenth century, forging relationships with high-ranking members of the Protestant Church (such as William Bedell, Bishop of Kilmore) while retaining its ties to Irish culture. For details of this family history, see Fintan O'Toole, *A Traitor's Kiss: The Life of Richard Brinsley Sheridan, 1751–1816* (New York: Farrar, Straus and Giroux, 1998 [1997]), 3–10.

4. See Gayatry Chakravarty Spivak, "Can the Subaltern Speak?" in *Marxism and the Interpretation of Culture,* eds. Cary Nelson and Lawrence Grossberg (Urbana and Chicago: University of Illinois Press, 1988), 271–313.

5. Donna Haraway, "The Promises of Monsters: A Regenerative Politics for Inappropriate/d Others," in *Cultural Studies,* eds. Lawrence Grossberg, Cary Nelson, and Paula A. Treichler (New York and London: Routledge, 1992), 311–12.

6. Linda Alcoff, "The Problem of Speaking for Others," in *Who Can Speak? Authority and Critical Identity,* eds. Judith Roof and Robyn Weigman (Urbana and Chicago: University of Illinois Press, 1995), 116.

7. Vincent Cheng, "Of Canons, Colonies, and Critics: The Ethics and Politics of Postcolonial Joyce Studies," *Cultural Critique* 35 (1996–97): 89. I use the terms "first world" and "third world" as a convenient and familiar shorthand reference, but the quotation marks placed around them indicate my agreement with such critics as Arif Dirlik and Aijaz Ahmad, who argue that "the transnationalization of production calls into question earlier divisions of the world into First, Second, and Third Worlds" (Dirlik, "The Postcolonial Aura: Third World Criticism in the Age of Global Capitalism," *Critical Inquiry* 20 [1994]: 350) and that under present global conditions "we live not in three worlds but in one" (Ahmad, *In Theory: Classes, Nations, Literatures* [London and New York: Verso, 1994 (1992)], 103).

8. "Ireland, Island of Saints and Sages" (1907), in *The Critical Writings of James Joyce,* eds. Ellsworth Mason and Richard Ellmann (Ithaca: Cornell University Press, 1959), 162.

9. The views of Anglo-Irish nationalists in the early part of the eighteenth century are commonly described as "colonial nationalism," implying their strict containment within an imperial framework and their supposed difference from "real" nationalism; see, for example, the Introduction to J. G. Simms, *War and Politics in Ireland, 1649–1730,* eds. D. W.

Hayton and Gerard O'Brien (London and Ronceverte, W. Va.: Hambledon Press, 1986), xiii–xiv. Often the term is used in an overtly pejorative way, as when Foster declares that "many of [Swift's] arguments carry the authentic exclusiveness and brutality of colonial nationalism" (*Modern Ireland,* 181). But see D. George Boyce's cogent counterargument that "it is misleading . . . to refer to Protestants' sentiment as 'colonial nationalism,' as if it were in some way to be distinguished from the mainstream of the Irish nationalist tradition." Boyce, *Nationalism in Ireland,* 3rd ed. (London and New York: Routledge, 1995 [1982]), 107.

10. See "Intellectuals and Power" (1972), in *Language, Counter-Memory, Practice: Selected Essays and Interviews by Michel Foucault,* ed. Donald F. Bouchard (Ithaca: Cornell University Press, 1977), 209.

11. Spivak, "Can the Subaltern Speak?," 308.

12. James Joyce, "Ireland at the Bar" (1907), in *The Critical Writings,* 198.

13. In *The Eighteenth Brumaire of Louis Bonaparte,* Marx attributes this need for outside representation to the small peasants' lack of unity and class consciousness. See *Marx: Later Political Writings,* ed. and trans. Terrell Carver, Cambridge Texts in the History of Political Thought (Cambridge: Cambridge University Press, 1996), 117.

14. On Catholic discontent, see, for example, Archbishop Hugh Boulter's account, in a letter to the Duke of Newcastle (11 June, 1726), of "the popish rabble coming down to fight the whig mob" on the Pretender's birthday in 1726, in the process "assault[ing the Lord Mayor, Sheriffs, and some aldermen, attended with a number of constables] with stones, bricks, and dirt" (Hugh Boulter to the Duke of Newcastle, 11 June, 1726, in *Letters Written by His Excellency Hugh Boulter to Several Ministers of State in England, and Some Others,* vol. 1 [Dublin, 1770], 65–66). For a general overview of Catholic activism and political protest during this period, see S. J. Connolly, *Religion, Law and Power: The Making of Protestant Ireland, 1660–1760* (Oxford: Clarendon Press, 1992), 233–49.

15. This argument appears in Warren Montag's "Forum Response" to my review of his book in *Eighteenth-Century Fiction* 9 (1996): 102. The Forum exchange between Montag and myself continued over the next several issues of *ECF.*

16. *A Word to the Wise; or An Exhortation to the Roman Catholic Clergy of Ireland* (1749), in *The Works of George Berkeley,* eds. A. A. Luce and T. E. Jessop, 9 vols. (Edinburgh: Thomas Nelson and Sons, 1948–57), 6: 235, 248. Hereafter abbreviated *W* and cited parenthetically in the text by page number.

17. A fascinating reversal of this phobic response to the "savage" may be seen in the *literal* journey into the "heart of darkness" undertaken in 1903 by the Anglo-Irishman Roger Casement, sent as a British consul into the Congo's interior to investigate reports of the barbarous treatment of the natives by the rubber traders in King Leopold's employ, which resulted in his psychic and political identification with the brutalized blacks along with his discovery, and full acceptance, of his Irish identity: "In those lonely Congo forests where I found Leopold . . . I found also myself, the incorrigible Irishman." In the years immediately following, Casement devoted himself to the cause of eradicating slave labor in the Congo, becoming a prominent figure in the first international human rights movement of the twentieth century; later, as a committed Irish nationalist, he fought to liberate his own country from British rule. Casement was hanged for treason by the British on 3 August 1916, to the end affirming what he saw as the inextricable links between his role as Irish patriot and his exertions on behalf of the enslaved Africans. See Adam Hochschild, *King Leopold's Ghost* (Boston and New York: Houghton and Mifflin, 1998), 195–208; 267–68; 285–87; the quotation ("lonely Congo forests") appears on 267.

18. The letter of reply from the Roman Catholic clergy was appended to *A Word to the Wise* in the Dublin edition of 1750 and in most editions thereafter, including Berkeley's

Miscellany (1752). It is reprinted immediately following *A Word* in *Works of Berkeley*, 6: 248–49. The passages quoted appear on 248.

19. *Works of Berkeley*, 6: 248.

20. "A Letter from Dr. Swift to Mr. Pope," in *Prose Works*, 9: 33. Hereafter abbreviated *SP* and cited parenthetically in the text by volume and page number.

21. See Introduction, *Prose Works*, 9: xvi.

22. The second quotation is from *An Answer to a Paper called A Memorial* (1728), in *Prose Works*, 12: 19.

23. *Advice to the Freemen of Dublin* (1733), in *Prose Works*, 13: 82.

24. This comment appears in no. 6 of the *Intelligencer,* a periodical put out by Swift and Sheridan in 1728–29. See *The Intelligencer,* ed. James Woolley (Oxford: Clarendon Press, 1992), 86–87.

25. Joep Leerssen, *Mere Irish and Fior-Ghael: Studies in the Idea of Irish Nationality . . . Prior to the Nineteenth Century,* Critical Conditions: Field Day Essays and Monographs (Cork: Cork University Press, 1996), 311.

26. *Intelligencer* 19 (1728), in *Prose Works*, 12: 54.

27. See Introduction, *Prose Works*, 9: x.

28. *A Proposal for the Universal Use of Irish Manufacture* (1720), in *Prose Works*, 9: 19.

29. *Verses on the Death of Dr Swift*, 437–38, in *The Poems of Jonathan Swift*, ed. Harold Williams, 2nd ed., 3 vols. (Oxford: Clarendon Press, 1958), 2: 570, n. 4 ("The Peers of *Ireland*"). Subsequent quotations of Swift's poetry are taken from this edition.

30. This poem was originally published in no. 8 of the *Intelligencer;* see Woolley's edition (which includes Sheridan's Introduction to the poem), 103–14. Hereafter abbreviated *MM* and cited parenthetically in the text by line number. For additional background information on Tighe, see Woolley's prefatory comments, 101–103.

31. See Swift's account of the incident in *A Vindication of his Excellency John, Lord Carteret* (1730), in *Prose Works*, 12: 163.

32. Declan Kiberd, *Inventing Ireland: The Literature of the Modern Nation* (Cambridge: Harvard University Press, 1995), 9.

33. For a more extended discussion of this tract, see my essay, "Swift as Irish Historian," in *Walking Naboth's Vineyard: New Studies of Swift,* eds. Christopher Fox and Brenda Tooley (Notre Dame: University of Notre Dame Press, 1995), 64–66.

34. Swift defended the Irish Catholics' basic loyalty to the British Crown on a number of occasions, asserting, for example, that they had not "the least Design to depose or murder their King, much less to abolish Kingly Government" (*Queries Relating to the Sacramental Test* [1732], in *Prose Works*, 12: 257). He also firmly rejected the notion that the Catholics continued to pose a military threat to Protestant rule, declaring it "a gross imposition upon common Reason, to terrify us with their Strength" (*Queries*, 12: 258) and insisting that the Catholics had been "put out of all visible Possibility of hurting us" (*On Brotherly Love,* sermon preached in St. Patrick's Cathedral on 1 December, 1717, in *Prose Works*, 9: 172).

35. *Reasons Humbly Offered . . . ,* in *Prose Works*, 12: 287.

36. The Drapier's assertion that "the People here . . . unite as one Man: resolving they will have nothing to do with [Wood's] Ware" (*D*, 10: 57) was confirmed even by those opposed to his agitation against the coinage scheme. Archbishop Boulter, for example, was forced to admit to an English correspondent, the Duke of Newcastle, in a letter dated 19 January 1724, that "the people of every religion, country, and party here, are alike set against *Wood*'s halfpence" (*Letters to Several Ministers of State in England,* 7).

37. Thomas Bartlett, *The Fall and Rise of the Irish Nation: The Catholic Question, 1690–1830* (Dublin: Gill and Macmillan, 1992), 35–36.

38. William Molyneux, *The Case of Ireland's being bound by acts of parliament in England, stated* (Dublin, 1698), 19, 146, 106.

39. The Drapier attributes this specious view of a Catholic plot to "Rumours industriously spread" by "News-Mongers in *London*" that "the *Papists* in Ireland *have entered into an Association against* [Wood's] *coin*" (*D*, 10: 53). However, that these "Rumours" were also "home-grown" products is evident from Archbishop Boulter's comment to the Duke of Newcastle: "That there has been a great deal of art used to spread this infection [the agitation against Wood's patent], and that the Papists and jacobites have been very industrious in this affair for very bad ends, I find most of the men of sense here [in Ireland] will allow" (*Letters to Several Ministers of State in England*, 7–8).

40. *Letter to the Archbishop of Dublin concerning the Weavers* (written in 1729; first published in 1765), in *Prose Works*, 12: 71. Hereafter abbreviated *L* and cited parenthetically in the text by volume and page number.

41. See Introduction, *Prose Works*, 12: xvi–xvii.

42. See *The Humble Petition of the Footmen . . .* (1732), in *Prose Works*, 12: 235–37.

43. *Maxims Controlled in Ireland* (1729), in *Prose Works*, 12: 131. Hereafter abbreviated *M* and cited parenthetically in the text by volume and page number. This is but one of many instances in which Swift figures the debilitating effects of colonialism through images of bodily deformity and mutilation. Addressing a member of the English House of Commons, for example, Swift's persona declares, "If your little Finger be sore, and you think a Poultice made out of our [Ireland's] *Vitals* will give it any Ease, speak the Word, and it shall be done" (*A Letter . . . Concerning the Sacramental Test* [1709], in *Prose Works*, 2: 114); fifteen years later, the Drapier, while acknowledging the scarcity of money in Ireland, asserts that "Mr. *Wood*'s Remedy, would be, to cure a Scratch on the Finger by cutting off the Arm" (*D*, 10: 16). Swift's insistence on dramatizing how England's actions register in very concrete (at times graphic) terms on the Irishman's body anticipates the colonial analyses of Frantz Fanon, who describes the profound dislocations resulting from being "battered down" by racial stereotypes—including, as in the case of the Irish, cannibalism—by demanding to know, "What else could it be for me but an amputation, an excision, a hemorrhage that spattered my whole body with black blood?" Fanon similarly relates that "the crippled veteran of the Pacific war says to my brother, 'Resign yourself to your color the way I got used to my stump; we're both victims.'" *Black Skin, White Masks*, trans. Charles Lam Markmann (New York: Grove Press, 1967), 112; 140. (Originally published as *Peau Noire, Masques Blancs* in 1952.)

44. Seamus Deane, *Strange Country: Modernity and Nationhood in Irish Writing since 1790* (Oxford: Clarendon, 1997), 146. From a somewhat different perspective David Lloyd discusses the "unrepresentable" (and "unrepresentative") in Irish history in terms of popular oral culture such as street balladry as well as, more generally, those counter-hegemonic forces "resistant to the unifying drive of the ethical state." See *Anomalous States: Irish Writing and the Post-Colonial Moment* (Durham, N.C.: Duke University Press, 1993); the quotation appears on 9.

45. Swift to Dean Brandreth, 30 June 1732, in *The Correspondence of Jonathan Swift*, ed. Harold Williams, 5 vols. (Oxford: Clarendon Press, 1963–65), 4: 34.

46. See George Orwell, "Politics vs. Literature: An Examination of *Gulliver's Travels*," in *Shooting An Elephant and Other Essays* (New York: Harcourt, Brace & World, 1950 [1945]), 53–76; and Norman O. Brown, "The Excremental Vision," in *Life Against Death: The Psychoanalytical Meaning of History* (Middletown, Conn.: Wesleyan University Press, 1959), 179–201.

47. Aimé Césaire, *Discourse on Colonialism* (1955), trans. Joan Pinkham (New York: Monthly Review Press, 1972), 27, 18.

48. See the Introduction to *George Steiner: A Reader* (New York: Oxford University Press, 1984), 14.

49. These Berkeley quotations are taken from *A Proposal for the better supplying of*

Churches in Our Foreign Plantations (1725), in *The Works of Berkeley,* 7: 346. Also relevant in this regard is Berkeley's *Anniversary Sermon before the Society for the Propagation of the Gospel* (1731), which rejects as "an erroneous Notion" the idea that "being baptized is inconsistent with a State of Slavery" (in *Works* 7: 122). See Edwin S. Gaustad, *George Berkeley in America* (New Haven: Yale University Press, 1979), 91 ("Berkeley took a step"). David Berman makes some relevant comments in this connection in *George Berkeley: Idealism and the Man* (Oxford: Clarendon Press, 1994), 131–32.

50. Césaire, *Discourse on Colonialism,* 15, 29. Césaire is referring in his first remark to Renan's *La Réforme intellectuelle et morale.*

51. For a good introduction to the issues involved in the historical revisionist controversy regarding Irish history, as well as for some of the seminal essays in this controversy, see *Interpreting Irish History: The Debate on Historical Revisionism,* ed. Ciaran Brady (Dublin: Irish Academic Press, 1994). See also the argument against revisionism (particularly as exemplified by S. J. Connolly) in Emer Nolan, "Swift: The Patriot Game," *British Journal of Eighteenth-Century Studies* 21 (1998): 50–53.

52. Mary Daly, "The Operations of Famine Relief, 1845–47," in *The Great Irish Famine,* ed. Cathal Póirtéir (Dublin: Mercier Press, 1995), 123. Swift's own response to the famine of 1729 belies Daly's implication that the value judgments of later nationalist historians would have been alien to the way people looked at things in the earlier period. Swift tells a naïve proposal writer that "if our *Brethren* in England would contribute, upon this Emergency, out of the Million they gain from us every Year, they would do a Piece of *Justice* as well as *Charity,*" admonishing the proposer and his neighboring squires that if they do not act responsibly to prevent crop shortages they will "die with the Guilt of having driven away half the Inhabitants, and starving the rest" (*An Answer to a Paper called A Memorial* [1728], in *Prose Works,* 12: 22).

53. Césaire, *Discourse on Colonialism,* 24.

54. *Intelligencer* 19 (1728), in *Prose Works,* 12: 60.

55. Hill, *From Patriots to Unionists,* 8.

56. Connolly, *Religion, Law and Power,* 110.

57. Cited in Woolley, *The Intelligencer,* 170.

58. *A Short View of the State of Ireland* (1728), in *Prose Works,* 12: 12. Hereafter abbreviated *SV* and cited parenthetically in the text by volume and page number.

59. Woolley, *The Intelligencer,* 90; the quotations in parentheses occur on 89. It is worth keeping in mind that Swift's *A Short View of the State of Ireland* was itself reprinted in the *Intelligencer* no. 15, with an introduction by Sheridan; see Woolley, 173–81.

60. *An Answer to a Paper called A Memorial* (1728), in *Prose Works,* 12: 18–19.

Part V
Coda: Swift Today

Swift's Satiric Authority: Prospects from a Late Twentieth-Century Perspective

Kenneth Craven

I

LIKE THREE OF HIS CLASSICAL FOREBEARS, JONATHAN SWIFT HAS MADE the incredible leap for humanity from satiric author to satiric authority. But according to the *OED,* we immediately confront a millennium-old problem of definition. Since the twelfth century, the close French derivations of *autor* and *auctor* with added Latin complications have blurred the clear distinctions between author and authority. The former signifies the originator or creator of something; the latter has to do with power to influence and/or enforce behavior. Gods effortlessly play both roles, but humans who command aesthetic, moral, or legal supremacy in both categories must have earned or usurped that latter power in order to qualify. Within the eurocentric world, for example, the double mantle of preeminent satiric authority has been unhesitatingly conferred on Aristophanes, Horace, Juvenal, and the Renaissance writers Rabelais, Cervantes, and Shakespeare. True, a mere handful have that immense power to raise consciousness. Yet when we reach the debased modern world, their heir, Jonathan Swift has risen, almost by default, to this exalted state all by himself even as the genre has lost the aesthetic and moral power of his savage indignation.

In this now-limping genre, twentieth-century ironies and ambiguities abound. At some cost, Swift has maintained his satiric authority in both intellectual and popular circles. Encyclopedic entries on satire inevitably concentrate on *Gulliver's Travels.* Hardly an issue of the *Times Literary Supplement* appears without some incidental retentive reference to Swift as satiric authority against which some aspiring postmodern falls short. Swift studies also boast rich legacies of dedicated, meticulous canon preservation and keenly perceptive scholarship that Oxford, Yale, and the University of Chicago published widely by mid-century. Like Laurence Sterne, who evolves from the tradition of dark Irish humor, Swift also

269

shares a continuing dialogue through closet interest among fellow satirists. While immense literary energy has been exerted throughout the twentieth-century to preserve Swift as icon or exemplar, there is an uneasiness that esoterically, literary criticism has kept him under glass, while exoterically, Swift has been honored in the breach with media misappropriation of the satiric *Gulliver's Travels* as an entertaining and exotic period travel excursion for the popular culture and other juveniles. In this deferential discourse, nevertheless, he remains the once and future world-class image maker, wordsmith, satiric touchstone, and authority.

There is even a promising redirection to these intellectual and exoteric limitations. George A. Test rightly places satiric authority beyond literary criticism: "Literary forms have not been able to confine or define satire, nor can satire be restricted by or to any other medium. Satire for better or worse is beyond any medium in which it occurs."[1] The call has finally gone out for broadened cultural studies and cross-disciplinary approaches to Swift. It has most recently been heeded in Frank Boyle's *Swift as Nemesis,* which examines satire within historic political and social contexts. Ironically, Boyle quotes Edward Said, who lauds Swift for raising "profound questions about *current* critical responsibility." According to Said, Swift stands "so far outside the world of contemporary critical discourse" as to serve as our "best" critic.[2] At the very least, Said, Boyle, and this author have broadened the inquiry on Swift's satire to embrace both literary criticism and cultural studies.

The postmodern world at large is another matter. Swift's inclusive accommodation of the twentieth century among his legitimate targets stems from foreknowledge that his seventeenth century had set in motion new knowledge systems breeding truly fantastic expectations for the good life that would ultimately seduce and envelop the eurocentric world, high, low, and beyond. Autonomy for the twentieth-century reader means living the good life in a world of fantastic expectations aided, abetted and legalized by equally oblivious institutional authority and economically driven media. With tangible amelioration of the human condition since Swift, the issue is clearly joined: enjoying the present or raising consciousness. On one hand, the individual modern reader remains both the principal target and obliviously unimplicated in Swift's aesthetic, satiric, and moral supremacy. On the other, the power of satire, that is, its authority, hinges on the fundamental priority it accords human mortality over the good life: "It is better to go to the house of mourning, than to go to the house of feasting: for that is the end of all men" (*Eccl.* 7:2). Whether or not death is an expectation devoutly to be wished, giving precedence to any other priority or obsession like the good life violates the conditions implicit in the human situation. That we perforce must function in a universe of defeated expectation propels satire to identify self-deluded victims as fools and/or knaves and to qualify them for ridicule and indignation if they will not face that reality.

Heeded or not, satire can exert a direct impact in raising human consciousness. But consciousness itself is an interference that also must struggle for a hearing in an overloaded postmodern environment. The give-and-take of our daily lives requires infinite compromises between authority and autonomy. As we negotiate our routinized way, the ultimate realities of mortality and the human condition give way to pleasure-pain alternates, to the lures of increased autonomy, and to the impositions of institutional authority. When illusory pleasures and transient attractions obscure realities and pain, levels of consciousness atrophy, and satire becomes a dead issue. In contrast, satiric authority raises daily consciousness to attend to the narrow passage individual autonomy must negotiate between the cosmic joke—our absolute end—and institutional authority—the specific controls over our comings and goings. According to Alan Chalmers, Swift's satiric authority creates a narrow passage indeed for anyone else's individual autonomy: "Swift's severity of vision leaves little room between perishing and presuming."[3] Yet, in defense of Swift's world, supposed autonomous behavior encounters unsuspected obstacles at every turn, so we cannot presume too much. Daily occupations in a getting-and-spending postmodern world exact penalties on consciousness and its goal, autonomy: "We lay waste our powers." But satiric authority even in death will not be stilled in highlighting the primacy of the cosmic joke as the threshold to consciousness.

The cosmic joke deals with the natural and inevitable end of life and forms the height of satiric ridicule that logically begins with self before application to others. The epitaph of Swift's fellow Scriblerian John Gay celebrates this in-and-out affair with absolute truth: "Life's a joke and all things show it./I thought so once and now I know it." William Butler Yeats also encrypted our daily windchill factor on his epitaph: "Cast a cold eye/ On life, on death./ Horseman pass by!" Michael Seidel's 1979 *Satiric Inheritance: Rabelais to Sterne* fittingly ends with *Finnegans Wake*'s "'Tarara boom decay.' Joyce records the power, even the crazy joy, of degeneration."[4] Let everyone still above ground celebrate a rousing Irish wake of death and consciousness. The only alternative: waste with the endless decay of the immortal Struldbruggs.

Swift had reiterated this coda time and again: "Human Life is best understood by the wise man's Rule of *Regarding the End*."[5] "Books, like men their authors, have no more than one way of coming into the world, but there are ten thousand to go out of it and return no more" (*Tale* 36). Hamlet idly rummaging and ruminating in a graveyard satirically asks Yorick's skull: "Where be your gibes now?" (1.1.177). We all follow in the wake of Swift's and Ecclesiastes's absolute metaphor that "ALL Rivers go to the Sea, but none return from it."[6] Our grim terminus furnishes satiric authority with its unimpeachable universal mock. This authority's grim grin relegates the globe's antic species to the dust bin while reducing pride in the quality of life to humbling spiritual quietude. All consciousness raising begins with the specter of the cosmic joke.

II

What's left for clueless Prince Posterity eternally stalemated from his inheritance and stalked by the "inveterate Malice" of life's governor Saturn offering only "unavoidable Death"? (*Tale* 33). Should we simply follow Swift, Saturn's agent: a hard and testy taskmaster on himself and others? Fortuitously, satiric authority moves from the bitter truth of the cosmic joke to compensatory healing in a harsh world: its second priority.

After accepting the final blight nature places on all life, satirists and their fellow humans must attend to the slim pickings left for our autonomy-seeking natures. In the struggle between individual liberties and the power of the state, the balance falls to institutional authority. In the bargain, raising consciousness does not play well in either psychoanalysis or satiric authority in the twentieth century. Freud's *Civilization and Its Discontents* clearly distinguishes the state's purposes in every civilized society as inimical to, and more powerful than, the will and interests of the individuals within it. Seidel also notes the presence of this ceaseless conflict in the major narrative satires from Rabelais and Cervantes to Swift and Sterne. While different in literary execution, "each treats the complexities of individual and institutional sufficiency, possession, and perpetuation" (Seidel xii). By alternately propounding divine inevitability, human limitation, individual liberties *and* institutional power, Swift's satire comprehends all parties enmeshed in these contingencies and in the perpetual contention about the universally unequal distribution of property and human rights. Throughout this medley of conflicts, satiric authority also offers a sane nucleus, a balance wheel, a Nemesis, a *raisonneur,* an authorial voice. Immemorially rising from their own bile and contemporary limitations, satiric artists strive desperately to reach a true balance between autonomy and authority. While the artist has neither the power nor right to discipline, she has the creative power to raise consciousness.

Like Freud and his psychoanalytic heirs, no satiric authority can legitimately serve institutions before ministering to the individual, its second priority after confronting the cosmic joke. Both healing disciplines seek to afford liberty and function to a humbled and constrained individual autonomy. In sorting out the plurality of powerful authorities that impinge on autonomy, the satirist assumes two interacting medical roles: the preventive function of protecting human dignity and personal freedom and the healing or purging function by dramatizing extreme deviations at the borderlines. The coequal therapeutic alliance of the medical-psychiatric and literary humors traditions has been intertwined in Western society from Aristotle and Greek New Comedy through Roman Comedy, commedia dell'arte, the Elizabethan and French dramatists, Swift, Fielding, and Sterne to the nineteenth-century Russian novel of Pushkin, Dostoevsky, Tolstoy, and Gogol. Both therapies aim at sanguinity, a sound mind in a sound body, an Aristotelean balanced calm amid the unsettling mix of extreme human behaviors and the unforeseen. Plautus depends on Galen as well as Menander; Galen, in turn, on Aristotle's treatises and the golden mean. To find that golden balance between autonomy and authority, satirists from Roman Comedy to Jonson and Molière place the gyroscopic *raissonneur* at the center of their plays just as modern novelists introduce a digressionary interpretative voice speaking.

Satiric authority is a no-win position. Caught between the Scylla and Charbdyis of sure degeneration and impinging authorities, Swift must also find emotional strength and a theosophical position to confront the daily bombardment of myriad provocations. John Irwin Fischer's *On Swift's Poetry* sums up the rigors and ironies of Swift's own autonomous position in his last great poem: "In *The Legion Club* Swift exhibits a terrible paradox: he shows us that when called on to participate in a world that moves horror, pity, indignation, and contempt, good men like himself must be undone if they respond to what they see, and be undone if they do not."[7]

Equating satire, consciousness, and the will, Swift's readers and critics too see autonomy struck down at every turn. In the 1993 Rodino-Real collection on *Reading Swift,* a self-revisionary Richard Rodino redirects his discussion of the critical Babel surrounding *Gulliver's Travels* by newly allying Swift's works and intentions with St. Augustine's to trigger "regeneration of the individual will." He contends further that the reader's regenerated will must "begin with a certain humility about the manifold errors and lies of human knowledge, and the further recognition that all interpretation risks becoming a deathly struggle to defeat its other, to silence that which is different."[8] Satire, consciousness, and the individual will serve as bonded partners in the enterprise of psychic autonomy.

The wayward body like Freud's insistent id, hardly manageable by his balancing ego and authoritarian superego, institutes its own priorities. With bleak humor, Swift concentrates on his medieval notions of coordinated corruption of the flesh and society. As Chalmers observes, the body appears as a grotesque nightmare for the satirist, a far cry from Bakhtin's Rabelaisian carnival (Chalmers 78–86, *passim*). Swift's answer to the complaining fat man stifled in a filthy crowd to "bring your own guts to a compass" serves as Swiftian metaphor for physical autonomy in the modern world where one overbearing individual occupies the space of five (*Tale* 46).

If satiric authority raises consciousness and defines the limits of autonomy, it nonetheless courts and tilts with its natural ally and adversary, institutional authority. Institutional alliance becomes the third sphere of activity, that is, priority, for satiric authority after consciousness raising and autonomy regulating. Here power confronts power. We now apprehend what Brian Connery refers to as "the grids of power," "satire's relation to the law and its capacity to discipline and punish," its "implication within hegemonic discourse."[9] The potential conflict between two executive powers—that of the state and that of satire—has always created contention over who's in charge. State authority everywhere has depended on skillful manipulation by a normally generationally ensconced elite of three kaleidoscopically adjusted controls to maintain a stabilized reproductive society: myth, incentive, and terror. Satiric authority utilizes all three of these political and social controls, sometimes in alliance with the state, sometimes in opposition to it. Since the classical period, satirists have provided that critical executive expertise in one of three ways: either as official spokespersons within established or challenging priest systems or as isolated artists beyond the pale; the latter pronounce anathemas on existing or looming pontifical, yet reproductively dysfunctional hierarchies. Josef Stalin devoted the entire Nineteenth Party Congress in October 1952 to implementing a policy of official satire as an alternate to direct state terror and a spur to greater economic productivity among higher levels of the party *apparat* and state bureaucracy. The ironic reprieve of his death in March 1953 opened wide the satiric flood gates for press, stage, and narrative during the three-year *Khovanchina* interregnum before Nikita Krushchev shut them down decisively at the Second Writers Union Congress in December 1956.

The artistic genius Swift possessed of the satiric absolutes operated successfully in each of the three possible roles relative to the state: official spokesman, loyal opposition, incendiary independent. Having served faithfully and brilliantly as official priest of satire at the London hub for in-or-out Whigs and/or Tories as the case might be, Swift returned to Dublin to accept his marginally compensatory deanery award; in this setting, the Dean combined his satiric power with his knowledge of the ritual of governance, from which he derived the elitist rhetorical substance and style he assimilated into the scathing *A Modest Proposal.* That document—now globally pertinent—also patently exposed then the subtle but inhuman new economic demands by governmentally run mercantile systems requiring statistically high productivity and regulated orderly species reproduction—increase and multiply—among the benighted harvesters and processors of both raw and human materiel.

III

The three hundred years since Swift have actuarially delayed the cosmic joke and reconfigured individual autonomy and institutional authority. Thus each element of threefold satiric authority must be reassessed. The world now turns for countries, institutions, and individuals on sophisticated economic production. In the three-century interim since Swift began to write, institutional authority at all levels in the global society has subdivided into three definable classes—upper/middle/lower—and rewarded diversity within and among them for increased economic productivity. This single priority serves the universe as sacrosanct touchstone for all twentieth-century hegemonies. Institutions, good and bad, offer the prospect of membership at these three class levels, even as they raise the specter of bureaucratic insensitivity. Neither the grand cosmic joke nor the strict categorical imperatives Swift places on his own and our individual autonomy can possibly play well. Standards of virtue—the satirist's ultimate bottom line—have changed accordingly. Productivity, illusive and real, becomes the keystone of all postmodern institutional authority. The extreme economic determinant simultaneously realigns institutional power and individual autonomy. The traditional holistic societies have been replaced by individualistic ones featuring secularization, industrialization, and urbanization.

What now is virtuous? Self-reliance, a factor of economic productivity and a concommitant of autonomy, has become a staple virtue in the new world of moral pluralism.[10] The postmodern observes new ethical norms and associates his identity with standards set by a particular state, and, more recently, corporate authority. In Mary Margaret Mackenzie's paraphrase of Aristotle, authority depends on the natural structure of the state.[11] Within predetermined limits, autonomous agents capable of practical reasoning may exercise self-reflection and self-assessment leading to self-modification.[12] Autonomous agents may even hand over power to be better able to concentrate on those aspects of life for which they have better aptitudes.[13]

Old and new virtues in and out of Swift's classical and medieval lexicon intermix. Since creation, class reshuffling and ethnic striving have been facilitated by making virtue and vice, legitimacy and illegitimacy, reversible and interchangeable as circumstances warrant. Loyalty and conformity remain the principal virtues of the power elite, the ruling class. These socially stabilizing virtues still perpetuate the power of hierarchical feudalism in governance, religion, and industry. Since the Marian Exiles, the Puritan virtues of thrift, hard work, and self-help have created a powerful middle class in both free and closed societies. In the early seventeenth century, Ben Jonson had already satirized them via Zeal-of-the-Land

Busy; in the early nineteenth, Robert Burns satirized Holy Willie who wanted it all, here and hereafter. Solidarity and fraternity become the blue-collar virtues in urban societies. Peter Sellers posed for this role in *I'm Alright, Jack.*

We press good *fortuna* on an elite that extends increasingly to those of the middling sort. [Uninhibited by the platitudinous justifications of the economic developer in Swift's *A Modest Proposal,* most of us today comfortably enjoy the fruits of marginally compensated productive labor; we live in similar serene aloofness above third-world agonies and in blissful hedonistic kinship with Swift's lord projector; we sport logo sneakers provided by sweatshop laborers locked in poverty and exploited from their teeming births to their early deaths.] Heaven on earth with increasing medical and economic extensions has greater empirical validation than the allure of being absolute for death, humility, or anything else. Church, state, and art no longer provide the spiritual threshold or distracting lure of possible eternal salvation or threat of damnation; satiric authority no longer serves as a myth/incentive/terror-activating warning. The arcane great by-and-by seems less attractive than the mundane great buy-and-buy. Propaganda and information unattended by reason or knowledge promote serious, attainable fantasies and virtual reality that in another age would be grist for the satirist. The egoistic individual autonomy myth preferred over humble pie for all walks has been established beyond reasonable doubt by highly visible beautiful people, quality-of-life ads and the excesses promised lottery winners. Holy Willie be damned. We'll have it all now.

IV

While institutional authority has been seamlessly transferred to the corporate world, violence and fantasy have been conferred on its loyal ally, the pop culture. Understandably, in this environment geared to global economic productivity the journeyperson satirist enjoys only limited media access. On 1 March 1999, *The New York Times* published a New York University survey of thirty-six judges of the one hundred most outstanding and influential contributions of American journalism in the twentieth century.[14] The full-page list ran the gamut of TV documentaries, books, articles, accounts, reports, private journals, investigations, essays, editorials, and cartoons. From the results of the top ten, we can safely establish that the most extremely profitable economic productivity gains in this century can be awarded to genocide, nuclear delivery, and character assassination. Based on this self-incriminating, statistically valid assessment, we could modestly understate the latest twentieth-century variety of the species as "the most pernicious Race of little odious Vermin." In this flourishing, near-ideal world that Gulliver banked on, amusing innocuous satires on economics and McCarthy can be tolerated back in the media pack: Tom Wolfe (18, 24, 48), Herblock (39), Russell Baker (60) and Ben Hecht (62). According to the thirty-six judges, nothing satirically news-worthy vexed the world after 1979. It is pointless to look later or elsewhere for anything beyond good chuckles and comforting reassurance. Thank God for Tom Wolfe. On the Ides of March 1999, he proclaimed his satiric authority globally on CNN with *A Panegyrick upon the World:* "Since we have eliminated monsters like Nero and Caligula, we can all enjoy a comfortable 'cushion' of goodness in the next millennium." The grotesque and monstrous having been purged, why repair to Swift's low view of human nature? The world now inverts his statement of priorities: "The chief end I propose to myself in all my labors is to vex the world rather than divert it."

When the measure in all institutional alliances becomes economic pro-ductivity, the destructive byproducts multiply ironically. Institutional re-straints at one level simultaneously produce beneficiaries of material wel-fare and economic advancement at another. Thus, at the sacrificial expense of some poor souls, individual autonomy and all freedoms have widened immensely for others at the elite end. The extremes of egoist autonomy and corrupted authority burgeon and boomerang in both directions. Economic productivity at whomever's expense buys political license for the imposi-tion of controls and for egoist freedoms. Tyranny and permissiveness provide equal opportunity in either direction or both with role reversal entirely appropriate. With image creation for any one of these extreme roles offering big payoffs, revelatory satire has a particular difficulty in putting a word in edgewise.

When we move from the world of journalism to the world of serious fiction, alas, media-inspired, we find Ian McEwan's brilliant and ex-tremely popular satire *Amsterdam,* winner of the 1998 Booker Prize.[15] If satire wins the prestigious Booker Prize, can the genre really be enfeebled? McEwan easily trumps Freud's paradigm of the state inexorably inhibiting the individual will. The state authority of mere insensitive tyrants like Nero and Caligula, say, has been preempted in global society by a highly visible postmodern elite of political, economic, media, and cultural leaders. As they become media icons of egoistic individual autonomy these incestuous coteries dominate the longing psyches of vast majorities in postmodern societies in proportion as they celebrate with panache popular fantasies of sex, violence, wealth, and power. These icons have little incentive or knack for transferring this fabulous power to the cause of either an orderly or chained society, Freud's inference. McEwan describes them clinically as savage animals. But where is the injected sane character or satirist's voice representing the golden mean or consciousness, the sine qua non of the genre heretofore? Where is the positive prescription within a largely proscriptive text? The author succeeds brilliantly in exploiting the public voyeurism for scrubbed Yahoos and promoting an uninterrupted identification with these well-heeled leadership role models. *Amsterdam* is an exquisite confection of deceit, high-level power, mayhem, and murder by strategically well-connected beautiful males with no inkling of self-knowledge. These fleshed-out tabloid characters are tied together in postmortem knots by the untimely death of their mutually enjoyed, bed-trotting queen bee, Molly "philanders." There is a compensatory message for the best-seller and tabloid middling-sort of readers: those who can't have it all, nonetheless, through this read can hang out vicariously with the rich and famous.

Authenticity, not satire, is the criterion here. On 28 October 1998, London's *The Guardian* ran a front page news article on the McEwan satire winning the Booker Prize: "*Amsterdam* is the story of two men, a composer and a broadsheet newspaper editor, who become embroiled in controversy when the lover of both is photographed in compromising positions with the Foreign Secretary. Evidently, this year's chair of the judges, the former foreign secretary Lord Hurd, did not find the subject too close to the bone." Page two quotes the critic of *The Observer* as noting that McEwan is "too cool for actual satire" and *The Independent* critic as finding McEwan with a problem in a "novel with no sympathetic characters." No eyebrow need be raised that McEwan modeled one of his victims on Britain's former foreign secretary and that Lord Hurd who had filled that role and become the Booker chief judge should craftily endow the author and himself with infinitely more image enhancement and public visibility by voting for the book that is undisguisedly "close to the bone." Notoriety hardly injures fame. The author rubs shoulders with power. Fictional characters and real author compete for the prizes of economic, social, and political station. McEwan and his recognizable leadership caste deserve their rewards for high cultural performance and economic productivity.

McEwan strictly follows Molière who argued for "recognizable portraits of the contemporary world." Unlike with the French satirist, however, critics found no sympathetic character in McEwan. Even Molière in 1999 had to mimic McEwan: bring on the savages; dispense with any exemplary *raisonneur.* According to reviews of the 1999 Off Broadway production of *The Misanthrope,* our postmodern world produces trendy, unfunny, and lifeless types. So complained the Associated Press on 15 February, 1999. The *New York Times* headline followed suit the same day: "Molière's Savages Lose Out to Today's." Akin to McEwan's self-absorbed leaders, Molière's characters have been revamped to make our scene seem more odious than that of his seventeenth-century hypocrites.

In *Amsterdam* and the Molière adaptation, the satirist must yield his own prime time to the venerated autonomous savages without leaving scope for any currently recognizable *raisonneur,* the authoritative social prescription—the satirist's virtuous bottom line.

But the mindless contagion has become globally systemic. From the early eighteenth century of Kantemir to the present, Russia has served as a repository for Western satire with its native victims consistently drawn from Europeanized and corrupted nouveau riche. It would be difficult to differentiate McEwan's tabloid candidates and the revamped Molière characters from those caricatured in Gregory Belser's 1998 mock children's Technicolor comic-book lexicon, *New Russian Alphabet World of New Russia.* As he plows through the Russian alphabet with bad Russian and bad English, he surrounds his generic, mindless Boris with illustrations of glorified elitist perks in lurid cardinal colors: Reebok, Versace, Viagra, Playboy, Porsche, Nikon, Nissan, Rolex, mobile phone, Smith & Wesson, a $1,000 bill with Elizabeth II, roulette, and laptop.

Economic productivity, hedonistic oligarchical living, and property rights go hand-in-hand. Swift warned us of the world's major perpetrator of this three-pronged modernity, John Locke. We live among the discontinuities of the Janus philosophies of Locke, Swift's contemporary genius. In the past decade, the big gains in economic rights and self-determination globally have been matched by equal losses in political rights globally. Locke, the father of English colonialism and the natural law of property rights including slaveholdings, has also been the father of an opposing philosophy of human rights. The latter still provides an egalitarian facade for all private property claims: two incompatible rights that when linked have marched in Lockean step politically unopposed and militantly uncontrolled toward the American Civil War and toward subsequent recurring twentieth-century confrontations over strikingly similar economic hegemonies.

Capitalist and socialist economic systems come from the same watershed and both make exaggerated claims of higher economic productivity and GNP. They overlap in their claims of the relation of economic productivity to societal and personal well-being; they fulfill economic promises on the backs of the property poor—either at home or on some distant shore. As initial sponsor of these antithetical property and human rights, Locke attracted disciples on the right like the Bishop of Cork Peter Browne and the First Earl of Shaftesbury and on the left like the latter's grandson, the Third Earl, and John Toland. All are major objects of Swift's satire and especially Locke, recognized by Swift in his time as the catalytic genius for oligarchic utopia with slaves in the American colonies and ultimate dystopia of global oppression.

In setting up a philosophical conflict with Locke, Swift's satiric authority attracts a new generation of historians for his baldly laying out the conflicting institutional polarities of property and human rights in Locke's seventeenth-century treatises. Locke, a proponent of economic productivity, clearly propounds legal and philosophical doctrines that elitist property rights include entitlement to slaves and override human rights. Swift does not break us down into classes. Swift's Yahoos represent the entire human race as physically debauched slaves of their own making. But here, cultural studies and literary criticism on Swift go down separate paths.

Literary criticism glances tangentially at these historical-philosophical–power-grid issues. This literary criticism falls into two critical parts: ad hominem readings of Swift's works that find him caught between shores or measuring his works by a variety of theoretical and abstract twentieth-century principles. The 1993 Rodino-Real collection on *Reading Swift* illustrates the garden variety of both categories. The colonizer/colonized split, or as Robert Mahony records it, "the economic aspect of Swift's patriotism"[16] typifies one facet and a proliferating one of the ad hominem category. Swift is crowned with an "official position in the 'colonial enterprise.'" Alan Downie finds Swift alongside Locke on the property rights issue.[17] Wolfgang Zach expands on Swift's bifocal colonialism;[18] Ian Ross distinguishes between his Dublin colonial exile in contrast to the London hub.[19]

Rodino's "*Splendide Mendax*" essay typifies the theoretical category. He harks back to the hard and soft Swiftian schools on the fourth book of *Gulliver's Travels* promoted by James L. Clifford in mid-century in our Columbia graduate seminars and still a useful critical split. In keeping abreast of Stanley Fish, Mikhail Bakhtin, and Paul deMan, Rodino presents a dizzying array of plausible relative approaches to both Swift's and his character Gulliver's satires. Unlike the more comfortable Johnsonian industry and more like the Big and Little Endians, budding Swiftians have been encouraged since mid-century to burnish their careers by taking combative sides. These internecine academic wars read like Book One of *Gulliver's Travels,* while Swift's universal issues play out globally.

V

While the consciousness raising of all satire has run against the modern tide of economic productivity, hedonistic living, and the instincts of the popular culture, Swift's satiric authority has exerted a pivotal influence in rearranging twentieth-century knowledge and information systems globally. The past and present American Librarians of Congress lament the serious erosion of the knowledge base inundated by the tidal wave of information, humanistic learning being one of the casualties. Daniel J.

Boorstin correctly stated in 1979 what his successor James H. Billington reiterated in 1998: "In our ironic twentieth-century version of Gresham's law, information tends to drive knowledge out of circulation."[20] These displacements in the twentieth century have produced the most serious catastrophe of all: the concomitant loss of consciousness of individual autonomy within institutional authority.

Eurocentrism insists on knowledge systems requiring measurement. Hypotheses must forever stand the test of quantification. Numerical and probabilistic indices dominate an economically determined globe. Avoiding confrontation with its formidable epistemological challenger, the Eurocentric humanistic community has long rested on its classical and Judeo-Christian laurels.

The rise of the New Science or New Philosophy followed fifteenth-century European printing and consciously proclaimed its dominance over all other knowledge systems by the mid-seventeenth century with the formation of the Royal Society. The Royal Society and its spawn, the Newtonian synthesis, downgraded nonexperimental and nonutilitarian epistemologies that would not conform to their excluding and self-serving motto, *Nullius in Verba*. Having dramatically ameliorated the European human condition, all was serene in the New Science until a shocking October 1957 event of the Cold War. The Russian launching of *Sputnik One* had not only equaled and surpassed Western science as Peter the Great had hoped, but challenged the security of the seemingly invincible Western nuclear shield. *Sputnik* established the stark reality of this programmed epistemological imbalance in a world obsessed with diametrical economic hegemonies and a mutually ruinous cloak-and-dagger cold war, both dependent on pride-ridden, overly compensated scientific communities.

Excessive Western consternation led to exhaustive projects in learning, governance, and industry. Of these countless efforts, ironically for humanistic learning, Jonathan Swift's satiric authority produced the one viable rationale to recharge the West's military-industrial complex, to bring the scientific information explosion under control, and to create the first schools of information and computer science at MIT, Berkeley, Georgia Tech, and throughout the world. At this point, one might query how 250-year-old humanistic insights could redirect twentieth-century technology?

In the 1950s, I was on an intellectual bridge between these cold war cultures. Having served as a lowly instructor in English at West Virginia University until 1956, I had returned to Columbia to study at their Russian Institute to enhance a flagging career. Clearly, I could discern from this bridge, the West's consternation could best be addressed within the context of the intellectual history of both twentieth-century economic hegemonies—the doubly flawed and belligerent individual and collective—that harked back to the seventeenth century and the mad mandate of the Royal Society to appropriate all *scientia* and to eliminate words as impediments to pure reason. Meanwhile, Peter the Great's dream of Western style military power required words: a vernacular that bridged barriers to the European Enlightenment and *Aufklärung*. Old Church Slavonic would not do.

From my Columbia graduate school perch, I realized that the satirist had researched the *Sputnik*-sparked problem. Alternately, by concentrating on the word, the leading eighteenth-century Russian poet-scientist Mikhail V. Lomonosov had come up with his country's solution to the space race two hundred years earlier. This solution, which would have been patently obvious to Swift, had eluded the West. During Swift's formative years at Trinity College, Dublin, he had had intimate knowledge of the ostracizing quantitatively oriented experimental bias of the Dublin Philosophical Society initiated by the utilitarian statistician William Petty and the scientist Narcissus Marsh. Both had been indoctrinated in their earlier Oxford years through Hartlib's "Invisible College" and as charter members of the Royal Society.

Thus from the outset, Swift's satires underscored the conscious and damaging isolation of humanistic learning from all modern information systems. In the West despite Swift, *scientia* gradually became skewed toward the experimental, the empirical, the material, the measurable only, that is, the utilitarian sciences. State authority connected this myopic and skewed epistemology during the glacial transition from monarchical, oligarchical, and populist power toward economic productivity and the popular facade of ameliorating the human condition without violence. Knowledge of linguistics (including computer language), notational order, intellectual landmarks, historical continuity, institutional organization, human variables, mythic viability, and humane traditions, values, and ethics has each suffered discretely and cumulatively from this Western imbalance ever since Swift satirized the enthusiastic and ascendant projectors of knowledge that excluded *Verba*.

In stark contrast, Lomonosov in his person and in his cross-disciplinary contributions to mechanics and gaseous theories, reform of Russian literary language, history of Russia, and Russian grammar helped to shape the Russian Academy of Sciences from 1741 to 1765. His seminal contributions in all epistemologies illuminated the need in Russia for harmony and linkage among all learned disciplines, all knowledge systems. Perforce, linguistics—foreign and natural languages—became the necessary intellectual obsession of eighteenth-century Russia as it struggled to move beyond the straitjacket of Old Church Slavonic and acquire a literary and scientific vernacular to engage intellectually, politically, economically, and militarily in the Enlightenment and other emerging intellectual movements in the West.

Ordinarily, the powers that be would not ever have entertained my comparative logic on the *Sputnik* solution. In this rare instance of international crisis management, however, under long-term Federal grants from the U.S. Office of Education and the National Science Foundation, I codirected research and coauthored *Science Information Personnel* (Modern Language Association, 1961) with the university librarian, Leonard Cohan. It was this particular reoriented epistemological response to Sputnik that revolutionized the information profession in the Western world. Swift had directed us to the specific linguistic-literary-humanistic ignorance of cocksure scientific investigation in the West. To be sure, innovative scientific work was exploding in labs everywhere, but where was the universally accessible, organized documentation on these advances to expand new applications and to reduce needless redundancies worldwide? With the cooperation of leading American universities, Federal agencies, and the Fortune 500, we produced a document developing the first doctoral programs in systems analysis and information science, the first definition of the information cycle, and the enhanced professional status of all information specialists. Swift's satiric authority had achieved national consensus for new information systems.

Like its 1992 sequel, *Jonathan Swift and the Millennium of Madness,* this landmark document was reviewed extensively in scientific and professional journals throughout the world. "A substantial solution to handling . . . effectively the tremendous and continuous outpouring of scientific literature." "Anticipates more recognition of a more systematic and integrated approach to the organization of scientific information." "Information specialist . . . with knowledge in logic, language, intellectual operations, [and] appreciation of the role of recorded knowledge in the development of civilization."[21]

After celebrating these pragmatic benefits in reintroducing the word to Western science, it belatedly dawned on me that this comprehensive federally funded study would truly have angered Swift. With typical main chance zeal, we had empirically used Swift's profound understanding to develop further the New Science he abhorred. Already in Swift's mind, modern science had created an urban myth to accompany universal socioeconomic benefits that had displaced other critical human priorities. The grandees of science internationally had been given a real knowledge boost, while leaving Swift's uneconomic humanistic cause to languish further.

My 1992 book, *The Millennium of Madness,* serves as my eight-year apologia and penance to Swift for misusing his still powerful satiric authority.[22] One Swiftian author believes that my work "may come to be counted among the most original and significant works on Swift in the twentieth century. . . . As Swift seems to have relished representing the degradations that the Moderns were making their inheritance, Craven seems to relish the role of cataloguing the monstrous births that are the issue of modern times" (Boyle 23). Reviewers also acknowledge that I have made some amends: "Swift's uncanny foreknowledge that [democratic] governments tend toward a populace inundated by false information it cannot process, and leaders intent only upon power and the deceptions by which it is gained." "A subtler reading of Swift's perception of the madness of the moderns." "Craven approaches the *Tale* . . . as a *cri de coeur* by one of the first intellectuals to discern the horrific moral consequences of the circulation of unmanageable quantities of undigested information. [Swift's] particular fear is [the 'moderns'] intellectual self-sufficiency and independence, both of which lead men away from universal truths and towards the influence of power-structures."[23]

Satiric wisdom crieth in the streets, but few attend its warning. No postmodern satirist dares breathe uncouth savage indignation; meanwhile, political, economic and social power grows exponentially among global corporate, governmental, and well-cowed learned institutions; feeding the maw of popular culture for violence and fantasy becomes the chief global media message of this well-coordinated institutional control; the self-serving outpouring of global information further inundates knowledge and the verification time normally required heretofore. In this spiritual wilderness, governance, ideologies, and religions resort to the interwoven priorities of power, national enthusiasm, terror, and acquiescent conformity. Despite all its residual human truth and consciousness raising, Swift's satiric authority, caught in this maelstrom, retains few practitioners in literature and fewer in cultural studies. Yet Swift's early warning system about postmodern dystopia gives him vast untapped kinetic and potential power as a countervailing force on behalf of aesthetics and humane values.

NOTES

1. George A. Test, *Satire: Spirit and Art* (Tampa: University of South Florida Press, 1991), 11.

2. Frank Boyle, *Swift as Nemesis: Modernity and Its Satirist* (Stanford: Stanford University Press, 2000), 22.

3. Alan Chalmers, *Jonathan Swift and the Burden of the Future* (Newark: University of Delaware Press, 1995), 102.

4. Michael Seidel, *Satiric Inheritance Rabelais to Sterne* (Princeton: Princeton University Press, 1979), 265.

5. Jonathan Swift, *A Tale of a Tub, To Which is added The Battle of the Books and the Mechanical Operation of the Spirit,* ed. A. C. Guthkelch and D. Nichol Smith,. 2d ed. (Oxford: Clarendon Press, 1973), 145.

6. *The Prose Works of Jonathan Swift,* ed. Herbert Davis, 14 vols. (Oxford: Shakespeare Head Press, 1939–68), 1: 250.

7. John Irwin Fischer, *On Swift's Poetry* (Gainesville: University Press of Florida, 1978), 201.

8. Richard H. Rodino, "'Splendide Mendax': Authors, Characters, and Readers in Gulliver's Travels," in *Reading Swift: Papers from The Second Münster Symposium on Jonathan Swift,* eds. Richard H. Rodino and Hermann J. Real (München: Wilhelm Fink Verlag, 1993), 183.

9. Brian A. Connery and Kirk Combe, *Theorizing Satire: Essays in Literary Criticism* (New York: St. Martin's Press, 1995), 11.

10. S. Gosh-Dastidar, "Concepts of Individual Autonomy and Self-Responsibility," Oxford University, Ph.D. diss., 1984.

11. Mary Margaret MacKenzie, "Images of Authority," *Cambridge Philological Society Suppl.* 16 (1989): 168.

12. Alfred R.Mele, *Autonomous Agents* (Oxford: Oxford University Press, 1995), 252.

13. *Authority,* ed. Joseph Raz (Oxford: Blackwell, 1990), 90.

14. *New York Times,* 1 March 1999, sec. C, 1. Headline: "Journalism's Greatest Hits. The 100 best works of 20th-century American journalism according to 36 judges. List compiled by New York University's Journalism Department. Mitchell Stephens, departmental chair: 'You can see the 20th century understanding itself through its journalism.'"

15. Ian McEwan, *Amsterdam* (London: Jonathan Cape, 1998).

16. Robert Mahony, *Jonathan Swift: The Irish Identity* (New Haven: Yale University Press, 1995), 170, 173.

17. Alan Downie, "Swift and Locke's Two Treatises of Government," in *Swift: The Enigmatic Dean: Festschrift for Hermann Josef Real,* eds. Rudolf Freiburg, Arno Löffler, and Wolfgang Zach (Tübingen: Stauffenburg Verlag, 1998), 27–34.

18. Wolfgang Zach, "Jonathan Swift and Colonialism," *Reading Swift: Papers from the Second Münster Symposium on Jonathan Swift,* eds. Richard H. Rodino and Hermann J. Real (München: Wilhelm Fink Verlag, 1993), 91.

19. Ian Campbell Ross, "The Scriblerians and Swift in Ireland," *Reading Swift: Papers from the Second Münster Symposium on Jonathan Swift,* eds. Richard H. Rodino and Hermann J. Real (München: Wilhelm Fink Verlag, 1993), 81.

20. Gresham's Law: Knowledge or Information? Remarks at the White House Conference on Library and Information Services. Washington, November 1979. Washington, D.C.: Library of Congress, 1980.

21. George S. Bonn, *American Documentation* 13 (1962): 306; *Nature* 191 (1961): 452–53; I. M. Slade, *Journal of Documentation* 17 (1961): 246–48.

22. Kenneth Craven, *Jonathan Swift and the Millennium of Madness The Information Age in Swift's A Tale of a Tub* (Leiden: E.J. Brill, 1992).

23. Melvyn New, *The Scriblerian* 25 (1993): 20; Roy Porter, *Medical History* 37 (1993): 124; Andrew Carpenter, *Eighteenth-Century Ireland* 9 (1995): 141.

Select Bibliography

PRIMARY SOURCES

Addison, Joseph, *The Spectator.* 5 vols. Edited by Donald F. Bond. Oxford: Clarendon Press, 1979.

Barber, Mary. *Poems on Several Occasions.* London, 1735.

———. *The Poetry of Mary Barber 1690–1757.* Edited by Bernard Tucker. Edwin Mellen Press, 1992.

Bentley, Richard. *Dissertations upon the Epistles of Phalaris, Themistocles, Socrates, Euripides, and upon the Fables of Aesop.* Edited by Alexander Dyce. 3 vols. London: F. MacPherson, 1836.

———. *A Dissertation Upon the Epistles of Phalaris: With an answer to the objections of the Honourable Charles Boyle.* London: Printed by J. H. for Henry Mortlock and John Hartley, 1699.

———. *Remarks Upon a Late Discourse of Free-Thinking in a Letter to F. H. D. D. by Phileleutherus Lipsiensis* [Bentley]. London: Printed for John Morphew and E. Curll, 1713.

Berkeley, George. *A Word to the Wise; or An Exhortation to the Roman Catholic Clergy of Ireland* (1749). In *The Works of George Berkeley.* Edited by A. A. Luce and T. E. Jessop. 9 vols. Edinburgh: Thomas Nelson and Sons, 1948–57.

Blair, Hugh. *Lectures on Rhetoric and Belles Lettres.* [London, 1783.] Edited by Harold Harding. Carbondale and Edwardsville: Southern Illinois University Press, 1965.

Boswell, James. *Boswell's Journal of a Tour to the Hebrides.* Edited by F. A. Pottle and C. H. Bennett. New York: McGraw-Hill, 1962.

———. *Boswell's Life of Johnson.* Edited by G. B. Hill. Revised and enlarged by L. F. Powell. 2nd ed. 6 vols. Oxford: Clarendon Press, 1934–64.

———. *The Correspondence and Other Papers of James Boswell Relating to the Making of the Life of Johnson.* Edited by Marshall Waingrow. New York: McGraw-Hill, 1969.

Boulter, Hugh. *Letters Written by His Excellency Hugh Boulter to Several Ministers of State in England, and Some Others.* Dublin, 1770.

Boyle, Charles, Fourth Earl of Orrery. *Dr Bentley's Dissertations on the Epistles of Phalaris, and the Fables of Æsop Examin'd.* London: Printed for Thomas Bennet, 1698.

Boyle, John, Fifth Earl of Cork and Orrery. *The Orrery Papers.* Edited by the Countess of Cork and Orrery. 2 vols. London: Duckworth, 1903.

———. *Remarks on the Life and Writings of Dr. Jonathan Swift.* London, 1752 [1751].

———. *Remarks on the Life and Writings of Dr. Jonathan Swift.* Edited by João Fróes. Newark: University of Delaware Press; London: Associated University Presses, 2000.

Brewster, Sir Francis. *A discourse concerning Ireland and the different interests thereof: in answer to the Exaon and Barnstable petitions; shewing that if a law were enacted to prevent the exportation of woollen manufactures from Ireland to foreign parts, what the consequences would be for both England and Ireland.* London, 1698.

Brown, Thomas. *The Remains of Mr. Tho. Brown, serious and comical, in prose and verse.* London, 1720.

[Burnet, Thomas]. *Essays Divine, Moral and Political. Collected from the Works of J. S——t, D—— of St. P——k, and author of the Tale of a Tubb.* London, 1715.

A Catalogue of Pictures . . . of the Late Richard Mead, M. D. London, 1754.

The Churchman Armed Against the Errors of the Time. 3 vols. London: Society for the Distribution of Tracts in defence of the United Church of England and Ireland, 1814.

A Compendious Way of Teaching Antient and Modern Languages. London, 1728.

Cooper, Anthony Ashley, Third Earl of Shaftesbury. *Characteristics of Men, Manners, Opinions, Times.* Edited by Lawrence E. Klein. Cambridge: Cambridge University Press, 1999.

Delany, Mary Granville. *The Autobiography and Correspondence of Mary Granville, Mrs. Delany.* Edited by Lady Llanover. 6 vols. London: Richard Bentley, 1861.

Delany, Patrick. *Observations upon Lord Orrery's Remarks on the Life and Writings of Dr. Jonathan Swift.* London, 1754.

Dr. S——t's Real Diary; Being a True and Faithful Account of Himself. London, 1715.

Dunkin, William. "An Epistle to R——b—t N—g—t, Esq. with a Picture of Doctor Swift." *Select Poetical Works of the Late William Dunkin, D.D.* 2 vols. Dublin, 1769.

The Family Chaplain: Being a Complete Course of Sermons Upon the Festivals and Fasts . . . as Prescribed by the Book of Common Prayer. 2 vols. London, 1775.

Faulkner, George. *Prince of Dublin Printers: The Letters of George Faulkner.* Edited by Robert E. Ward. Lexington: University Press of Kentucky, 1972.

A Funeral Elegy on the Father of his Country, the Rev. Dr. Jonathan Swift. (Broadside.) Dublin, 1745.

Gay, John. *Trivia: or, The Art of Walking the Streets of London.* London, 1716.

Graevius, Joannes. *Callimachi Hymni, Epigrammata et Fragmenta, ex recensione Theodori J G F Graevii cum eiusdem Accedunt N. Frischlini, H. Stephani, B. Vulicanii, P. Voetii, A. T. F. Daceriae, R. Bentleii commentarius, et annotationes viri illustrissimi Ezechielis Spanhemii.* 2 vols., 1697.

Hawkesworth, John, LL.D. "An account of the Life of the Reverend Jonathan Swift, D.D., Dean St. Patrick's Dublin." In *The Works of Dr. Jonathan Swift, Dean of St. Patrick's Dublin.* London, 1755.

A Hue and Cry after Dean S——t; Occasion'd by A True and Exact Copy of Part of his Own Diary. London, 1714.

Jeffrey, Francis. "Jonathan Swift." *Edinburgh Review.* 27 September 1816. 1–58.

Johnson, Samuel. *Diaries, Prayers, and Annals.* Edited by E. L. McAdam. *The Yale Edition of the Works of Samuel Johnson.* New Haven: Yale University Press, 1958.

————. *Lives of the English Poets.* Edited by G. B. Hill. 3 vols. Oxford: Clarendon Press, 1905.

————. *The Letters of Samuel Johnson.* Edited by Bruce Redford. 5 vols. Princeton: Princeton University Press, 1992.

[King, William?] *A short account of Dr. Bentley's humanity and justice, to those authors who have written before him: with an honest vindication of Tho. Stanley, Esquire, and his notes on Callimachus: to which are added, some other observations on that poet: in a letter to the Honourable Charles Boyle, Esq. with a postscript, in relation to Dr. Bentley's late book against him: to which is added an appendix, by the bookseller wherein the doctor's mis-representations of all the matters of fact wherein he is concern'd, in his late book about Phalaris's Epistles, are modestly considered: with a letter from the Honourable Charles Boyle, Esq., on that subject.* London: Printed for Thomas Bennet,1699.

Lavater, John Caspar. *Essays on Physiognomy.* Translated by Henry Hudson. London, 1789–98.

Lipsius, Justus. *Somnium. Satyra Menippea.* In *Two Neo-Latin Menippean Satires.* Edited by C. Matheeussen and C. L. Heesakkers. Leiden: E.J. Brill, 1980.

Locke, John. *An Essay Concerning Human Understanding.* Edited by Peter H. Nidditch. Oxford: Clarendon Press, 1975.

Lowth, Robert. *A Short Introduction to English Grammar.* [London, 1762.] Rpt. Menston, England: Scolar Press, 1967.

Molyneaux, William. *The Case of Ireland's being bound by acts of parliament in England, stated.* Dublin, 1698.

Montagu, Lady Mary Wortley. *The Complete Letters of Lady Mary Wortley Montagu.* Edited by Robert Halsband. 3 vols. Oxford: Clarendon Press, 1967.

Oldmixon, John. *Reflections on Dr. Swift's Letter to Harley* (1712). In *Poetry and Language.* Edited by Louis Landa. Series 6; number 1. Ann Arbor, Mich.: The Augustan Reprint Society, 1948.

Pasquin, Anthony [John Williams]. *An Authentick History of the Professors of Painting, Sculpture & Architecture who have Practised in Ireland.* London, [1797].

Petty, Sir William. *The Economic Writings of Sir William Petty.* Edited by C. H. Hull Cambridge: Cambridge University Press, 1899.

Pilkington, Laetitia. *Memoirs of Laetitia Pilkington.* Edited by A. C. Elias, Jr. 2 vols. Athens and London: University of Georgia Press, 1997.

Pisani, Ugolino. *Repetitio Magistri Zanini Coqui.* In *Due commedie umanistiche pavesi.* Edited by Paolo Viti. Padua: Antenore, 1982.

Poliziano, Angelo. *Lamia: Praelectio in Priora Aristotelis Analytica.* Edited by Ari Wesseling. Leiden: E.J. Brill, 1986.

———. *Opera Omnia.* Reprint edition. Edited by Ida Maier. 3 vols. Turin: Bottega d'Erasmo, 1970–71.

Pond, Arthur. "Arthur Pond's Journal of Receipts and Expenses, 1734–1740." Edited by Louise Lippincott. *The Walpole Society* 54 (1988): 220–333.

Pope, Alexander. *The Correspondence of Alexander Pope.* Edited by George Sherburn. 5 vols. Oxford: Clarendon Press, 1956.

———. *Minor Poems.* Edited by Norman Ault and John Butt. *The Twickenham Edition of the Poems of Alexander Pope.* 10 vols. London: Methuen, 1964.

Richardson, Jonathan. *An Essay on the Theory of Painting.* London, 1725.

Swift, Deane. *An Essay upon the Life, Writings, and Character of Dr. Jonathan Swift.* London: Bathurst, 1755.

Swift, Jonathan. *Collected Poems of Jonathan Swift.* Edited by Joseph Horrell. 2 vols. London: Routledge and Kegan Paul, 1958.

———. *Jonathan Swift: The Complete Poems.* Edited by Pat Rogers. New Haven: Yale University Press, 1983.

———. *The Correspondence of Jonathan Swift.* Edited by F. Elrington Ball. 6 vols. London: G. Bell and Sons, 1910–14.

———. *The Correspondence of Jonathan Swift.* Edited by Harold Williams and revised by David Woolley. 5 vols. Oxford: Clarendon Press, 1963–72.

————. *Journal to Stella*. Edited by Harold Williams. 2 vols. Oxford: Clarendon Press, 1948.

————. *Journal to Stella,* Gloucester: Alan Sutton, 1984.

————. *The Poems of Jonathan Swift.* Edited by Harold Williams. 2nd ed. Oxford: Clarendon Press, 1958.

————. *The Prose Works of Jonathan Swift.* Edited by Herbert Davis et al. 14 vols. Oxford: Basil Blackwell, 1939–68.

————. *A Tale of a Tub and Other Works.* Edited by A. C. Guthkelch and D. Nichol Smith. 2nd ed. Oxford: Clarendon Press, 1958.

————. *The Works of Jonathan Swift.* Edited by George Faulkner. 8 vols. Octavo. Dublin, 1746.

————. *Works of Jonathan Swift.* 10 vols. Dublin, 1751.

————, and Thomas Sheridan. *The Intelligencer.* Edited by James D. Woolley. Oxford: Clarendon Press, 1992.

Temple, William. *An Essay upon the Ancient and Modern Learning.* In *Five Miscellaneous Essays by Sir William Temple.* Edited by Samuel Holt Monk. Ann Arbor: University of Michigan Press, 1963.

————. *Essay upon the present State and Settlement of Ireland, Select Letters to the Prince of Orange.* London: 1701.

————. *Miscellanea: the third part.* Published by Jonathan Swift. London: Printed for Benjamin Tooke, 1701.

Walpole, Horace. *The Works of Horatio Walpole, Earl of Orford.* 5 vols. London, 1798.

SECONDARY SOURCES

Adams, Robert Martin. "Jonathan Swift, Thomas Swift and the Authorship of *A Tale of a Tub.*" *Modern Philology* 64 (February 1967): 198–232.

Adorno, Theodor W. *Aesthetic Theory.* Edited by Gretel Adorno and Ralph Tiedemann. Translated by Robert Hullot-Kentor. Minneapolis: University of Minnesota Press, 1997.

Ahmad, Aijaz. *In Theory: Classes, Nations, Literatures.* London and New York: Verso, 1994.

Alcoff, Linda. "The Problem of Speaking for Others," in *Who Can Speak? Authority and Critical Identity.* Edited by Judith Roof and Robyn Weigman. Urbana and Chicago: University of Illinois Press, 1995.

Allen, Brian, ed. *Toward a Modern Art World: Studies in British Art I.* New Haven and London: Yale University Press for the Paul Mellon Center for Studies in British Art, 1995.

Ashcroft, Bill, Gareth Griffiths, and Helen Tiffin. *The Empire Writes Back: Theory and Practice in Post-Colonial Literatures.* London: Methuen, 1989.

Bakhtin, Mikhail. *The Dialogic Imagination.* Edited by Michael Holquist. Translated by Caryl Emerson and Michael Holquist. Austin: University of Texas Press, 1985.

————. *Problems of Dostoevsky's Poetics.* Edited and translated by Caryl Emerson. Minneapolis: University of Minnesota Press, 1984.

Balfour, A. J. "Biographical Introduction." *The Works of George Berkeley, D.D.* Edited by George Sampson. London: Bell, 1897.

Ball, F. Elrington. *Swift's Verse: An Essay.* London: John Murray, 1929.

Baron, Hans. "The *Querelle* of the Ancients and the Moderns as a Problem for Renaissance Scholarship." *Journal of the History of Ideas* 20 (1959): 3–22.

Barthes, Roland. *Mythologies.* Translated by Annette Lavers. New York: Hill and Wang, 1972; rpt. 1995.

Bartlett, Thomas. *The Fall and Rise of the Irish Nation: The Catholic Question, 1690–1830.* Dublin: Gill and Macmillan, 1992.

Beckett, J. C. *Protestant Dissent in Ireland: 1697–1780.* London: Faber and Faber, 1948.

Bender, John. "A New History of the Enlightenment?" In *The Profession of Eighteenth-Century Literature.* Edited by Leo Damrosch. Madison: University of Wisconsin Press, 1992.

Berman, David. *George Berkeley: Idealism and the Man.* Oxford: Clarendon Press, 1994.

Berwick, Donald. *The Reputation of Jonathan Swift 1781–1882.* New York: Haskell House, 1965.

Bhabha, Homi K. "The Other Question." *Screen* 24, 6 (1983): 18–36.

———. "Signs Taken for Wonders: Questions of Ambivalence and Authority under a Tree Outside Delhi, May 1817." In *'Race,' Writing, and Difference.* Edited by Henry Louis Gates, Jr. Chicago: University of Chicago Press, 1986.

Blanchard, W. Scott. *Scholars' Bedlam: Menippean Satire in the Renaissance.* Lewisburg, Pa., and London: Bucknell University Press, 1995.

Bloom, Harold. *The Anxiety of Influence: A Theory of Poetry.* Oxford: Oxford University Press, 1997.

Boyce, D. George. *Nationalism in Ireland.* 3rd ed. London and New York: Routledge, 1995 (1982).

Boyle, Frank. *Swift as Nemesis: Modernity and Its Satirist.* Stanford: Stanford University Press, 2000.

Brady, Ciaran, ed. *Interpreting Irish History: The Debate on Historical Revisionism.* Dublin: Irish Academic Press, 1994.

Brink, Charles Oscar. *English Classical Scholarship: Historical Reflections on Bentley, Porson, and Housman.* Cambridge: Oxford University Press, 1986.

Broadhead, Glen J. "Samuel Johnson and the Rhetoric of Conversation." *SEL: Studies in English Literature 1500–1900* 20, 3 (1980): 461–74.

Brown, Norman O. *Life Against Death: The Psychoanalytical Meaning of History.* 2nd ed. Hanover, N.H.: Wesleyan University Press, 1985.

Brownell, Morris R. *Samuel Johnson's Attitude to the Arts.* Oxford: Clarendon Press, 1989.

Burnett, John. *A History of the Cost of Living.* Harmondsworth: Penguin, 1969.

Caffrey, Paul. *John Comerford and the Portrait Miniature in Ireland, c. 1620–1850.* Dublin: Kilkenny Archaeological Society, 1999.

Castle, Terry. "Why the Houyhnhnms Don't Write." *Essays in Literature* 7, 1 (1980): 31–44.

Césaire, Aimé. *Discourse on Colonialism* (1955). Translated by Joan Pinkham. New York: Monthly Review Press, 1972.

Chalmers, Alan. *Jonathan Swift and the Burden of the Future.* Newark: University of Delaware Press, 1995.

Charney, Maurice. Introduction to *Bad Shakespeare.* Edited by Maurice Charney. Rutherford, N.J.: Fairleigh Dickinson University Press, 1988.

Cheng, Vincent. "Of Canons, Colonies, and Critics: The Ethics and Politics of Postcolonial Joyce Studies." *Cultural Critique* 35 (1996–97): 81–104.

Churchill, R. C. *He Served Human Liberty: An Essay on the Genius of Jonathan Swift.* London: Allen and Unwin, 1946.

Clark, John R. *Form and Frenzy in Swift's Tale of a Tub.* Ithaca: Cornell University Press, 1970.

Clements, Robert J. *Picta Poesis: Literary and Humanistic Theory in Renaissance Emblem Books.* Roma: Edizione di Storia e Letteratura, 1960.

Connally, S. J. *Religion, Law and Power: The Making of Protestant Ireland, 1660–1760.* Oxford: Clarendon Press, 1992.

Connery, Brian A. "Self-Representation and Memorials in the Late Poetry of Swift." *Aging and Gender in Literature.* Edited by Anne M. Wyatt-Brown and Janice Rossen. Charlottesville: University of Virginia Press, 1993. 141–63.

— and Kirk Combe. *Theorizing Satire: Essays in Literary Criticism.* New York: St. Martin's Press, 1995.

Corkery, Daniel. "Ourselves and Dean Swift: *Lives* by Stephen Gwynn." [Book review.] *Studies* 18 (1934): 203–18.

———. "The Nation that Was Not a Nation." *Studies* 23 (December 1934): 611–22.

Cotton, William. *Sir Joshua Reynolds's Notes and Observations on Pictures.* London, 1859.

Craven, Kenneth. *Jonathan Swift and the Millennium of Madness: The Information Age in Swift's A Tale of a Tub.* Leiden: E.J. Brill, 1992.

Crookshank, Anne, and the Knight of Glin. *The Painters of Ireland c. 1660–1920.* London: Barrie & Jenkins, 1979.

Crow, Nora. "Swift and the Woman Scholar." *Pope, Swift, and Women Writers.* Edited by Donald C. Mell. Newark: University of Delaware Press, 1996.

Crown, Patricia. "Portraits and Fancy Pictures by Gainsborough and Reynolds: Contrasting Images of Childhood." *British Journal for Eighteenth-Century Studies* 7 (1984): 159–67.

Curtin, Dermot. "Our Gaelic Democracy: Teaching the Lessons of Its History (with Special Reference to Swift)." *Catholic Bulletin* 23 (July 1933): 587–92.

Curtius, Ernst Robert. *European Literature and the Latin Middle Ages.* Translated by Willard Trask. Princeton: Princeton University Press, 1953.

Daly, Mary. "The Operations of Famine Relief, 1845–47." In *The Great Irish Famine.* Edited by Cathal Póirtéir. Dublin: Mercier Press, 1995.

Davies, Martin. "An Emperor without Clothes? Niccolò Niccoli under Attack." *Italia medioevale e umanistica* 31 (1988): 94–148.

Davis, Herbert. "The Augustan Art of Conversation." *Jonathan Swift: Essays on His Satire and Other Studies.* Oxford and New York: Oxford University Press, 1964.

———. "The Poetry of Jonathan Swift." *College English* 2 (1940): 102–15.

———. *Stella: A Gentlewoman of the Eighteenth Century.* New York: Macmillan, 1942.

———. "Swift's Character." In *Jonathan Swift 1667–1967: A Dublin Tercentenary Tribute.* Edited by Roger McHugh and Philip Edwards. Dublin: Dolmen Press, 1967. 1–23.

———. "Verses on the Death of Dr. Swift." *The Book Collector's Quarterly* 2 (March-May 1931): 57–73.

Deane, Seamus. Introduction to *Nationalism, Colonialism, and Literature* by Terry Eagleton, Fredric Jameson, and Edward Said. Minneapolis: University of Minnesota Press, 1990.

———. *Strange Country: Modernity and Nationhood in Irish Writing since 1790.* Oxford: Clarendon Press, 1997.

————. "Swift, Virtue, Travel and The Enlightenment." In *Walking Naboth's Vineyard: New Studies in Swift.* Edited by Christopher Fox and Brenda Tooley. Notre Dame: Notre Dame University Press, 1994.

de Man, Paul. "The Epistemology of Metaphor." In *Aesthetic Ideology.* Edited by Andrezej Warminski. Minneapolis: University of Minnesota Press, 1996.

DeMaria, Robert Jr. *Johnson's Dictionary and the Language of Learning.* Chapel Hill and London: University of North Carolina Press, 1986.

Doody, Margaret Anne. "Swift among the Women." *Critical Essays on Jonathan Swift.* Edited by Frank Palmeri. New York: G.K. Hall, 1993.

Downie, Alan. "Swift and Locke's Two Treatises of Government," in *Swift: The Enigmatic Dean: Festschrift for Hermann Josef Real.* Edited by Rudolf Freiburg, Arno Löffler, and Wolfgang Zach. Tübingen: Stauffenburg Verlag, 1998.

Eagleton, Terry. *The Ideology of the Aesthetic.* Oxford: Blackwell, 1990.

Ehrenpreis, Irwin. *Swift: The Man, His Works, and the Age.* 3 vols. Cambridge: Harvard University Press, 1962–83.

Elias, A. C., Jr. "Editing Minor Writers: The Case of Laetitia Pilkington and Mary Barber." *1650–1850: Ideas, Aesthetics, and Inquiries in the Early Modern Era* 3 (1997):129–47.

————. *Swift at Moor Park: Problems in Biography and Criticism.* Philadelphia: University of Pennsylvania Press, 1982.

Empson, William. *Some Versions of Pastoral.* Harmondsworth: Penguin 1995 [1950].

Fabricant, Carole. "Swift as Irish Historian," in *Walking Naboth's Vineyard: New Studies of Swift.* Edited by Christopher Fox and Brenda Tooley. Notre Dame: University of Notre Dame Press, 1995.

————. "Swift in His Own Time and in Ours: Some Reflections on Theory and Practice in the Profession." In *The Profession of Eighteenth-Century Literature.* Edited by Leo Damrosch. Madison: University of Wisconsin Press, 1992.

————. *Swift's Landscape.* Notre Dame: University of Notre Dame Press, 1982 [reissued 1995].

————. "Swift's Political Legacy: Re-membering the Past in Order to Imagine the Future." In *Locating Swift: Essays from Dublin on the 250th Anniversary of the Death of Jonathan Swift, 1667–1745.* Edited by Aileen Douglas, Patrick Kelly, and Ian Campbell Ross. Dublin: Four Courts, 1998.

Falkiner, Sir Frederick R. "The Portraits of Swift." In *The Prose Works of Jonathan Swift.* Edited by Temple Scott. 12 vols. London: George Bell and Sons, 1908.

Fanon, Frantz. *Black Skin, White Masks.* Translated by Charles Lam Markmann. New York: Grove Press, 1967.

Fischer, John Irwin. "The Government's Response to Swift's *An Epistle to a Lady.*" *Philological Quarterly* 65 (1986): 39–59.

————. *On Swift's Poetry.* Gainesville: University Press of Florida, 1978.

Fix, Stephen. "The Contexts and Motives of Johnson's Life of Milton." In *Domestick Privacies: Samuel Johnson and the Art of Biography.* Edited by David Wheeler. Lexington: University Press of Kentucky, 1987

Fletcher, Ernest. *Conversations with James Northcote.* London: Methuen, 1901.

Folkenflik, Robert. "Samuel Johnson and Art," *Samuel Johnson: Pictures and Words.* Los Angeles: William Andrews Clark Memorial Library, 1984.

Foot, Michael. "Round the Next Corner: The Pursuit of Jonathan Swift," in *Debts of Honour.* London: Picador, 1981.

Foskett, Daphne. *British Portrait Miniatures.* London: Spring Books, 1968.

————. *Dictionary of Miniature Painters.* London: Faber and Faber, 1972.

Foster, J. J. *A Dictionary of Painters of Miniatures 1526–1850.* Edited by Ethel M. Foster. London: Philip Allen, 1926.

Foster, R. F. *Modern Ireland, 1600–1972.* London and New York: Penguin, 1988.

Foucault, Michel. "Intellectuals and Power" (1972), in *Language, Counter-Memory, Practice: Selected Essays and Interviews by Michel Foucault.* Edited by Donald F. Bouchard. Ithaca: Cornell University Press, 1977.

————. *The Order of Things: An Archaeology of the Human Sciences.* New York: Pantheon, 1971.

Foxon, David F. *English Verse, 1701–1750: A Catalogue of Separately Printed Poems with Notes on Contemporary Collected Editions.* 2 vols. London: Cambridge University Press, 1975.

————. *Pope and the Early Eighteenth-Century Book Trade.* Revised and edited by James McLaverty. Oxford: Clarendon Press, 1991.

Freeman, A. Martin, ed. *Vanessa and Her Correspondence with Jonathan Swift.* London: Selwyn and Blount, 1921.

Freud, Sigmund. *Jokes and Their Relation to the Unconscious.* Translated by James Strachey. Harmondsworth: Penguin, 1991

Frye, Northrop. *Anatomy of Criticism.* Princeton: Princeton University Press, 1957.

Fussell, Paul. *Samuel Johnson and the Life of Writing.* New York: Harcourt Brace Jovanovich, 1971.

Garin, Eugenio. *La disputà delle arti nel Quattrocento.* Florence: Vallecchi, 1947.

Gaustad, Edwin S. *George Berkeley in America.* New Haven: Yale University Press, 1979.

Gibbons, Luke. *Transformations in Irish Culture.* Cork: Cork University Press, 1996.

Glendinning, Victoria. *Jonathan Swift.* London: Hutchinson, 1998.

Gold, Maxwell. *Swift's Marriage to Stella.* New York: Russell and Russell, 1967.

Graddol, David, and Joan Swann. *Gender Voices.* Oxford: Basil Blackwell, 1989.

Grafton, Anthony. *Joseph Scaliger: A Study in the History of Classical Scholarship.* 2 vols. Oxford: Clarendon Press and New York: Oxford University Press, 1983–.

Granger, James. *A Biographical History of England.* 5th ed. 6 vols. London, 1824.

Greenwood, David. *William King: Tory and Jacobite.* Oxford: Clarendon Press, 1969.

Gregory, Alyse. "Stella, Vanessa, and Swift." *Nineteenth-Century and After* 113 (June 1933): 755–64.

Griffin, Dustin. "Interpretation and Power: Swift's *Tale of a Tub.*" *The Eighteenth Century: Theory and Interpretation* 34 (1993):151–68.

Gumperz, John J. *Discourse Strategies.* Cambridge: Cambridge University Press, 1982.

Haraway, Donna. "The Promises of Monsters: A Regenerative Politics for Inappropriate/d Others." In *Cultural Studies.* Edited by Lawrence Grossberg, Cary Nelson, and Paula A. Treichler. New York and London: Routledge, 1992.

Hardy, Evelyn. *The Conjured Spirit: A Study in the Relationship of Swift, Stella, and Vanessa.* London: Hogarth Press, 1949.

Haydon, Benjamin. *The Diary of Benjamin Robert Haydon.* Edited by William B. Pope. 5 vols. Cambridge: Harvard University Press, 1960–64.

Hill, Jacqueline. *From Patriots to Unionists: Dublin Civic Politics and Irish Protestant Patriotism, 1660–1840.* Oxford: Clarendon Press, 1997.

Hilles, Frederick W. "Dr. Johnson on Swift's Last Years: Some Misconceptions and Distortions." *Philological Quarterly* 54 (1975): 370–79.

———. "The Making of the *Life of Pope*." In *New Light on Dr. Johnson: Essays on the Occasion of his 250th Birthday*. Edited by Frederick W. Hilles. New Haven: Yale University Press, 1959.

Johns, Adrian. *The Nature of the Book: Print and Knowledge in the Making*. Chicago: University of Chicago Press, 1998.

Joyce, James. "Ireland, Island of Saints and Sages" (1907), in *The Critical Writings of James Joyce*. Edited by Ellsworth Mason and Richard Ellmann. Ithaca: Cornell University Press, 1959.

Karian, Stephen. "Reading the Material Text of Swift's *Verses on the Death*." *SEL: Studies in English Literature* 41 (2001): 515–44.

Keilen, S. P. T. "Johnsonian Biography and the Swiftian Self." *Cambridge Quarterly* 23, 4 (1994): 324–47.

Kelley, Donald. *Foundations of Modern Historical Scholarship*. New York: Columbia University Press, 1970.

Kelly, Ann Cline. *Swift and the English Language*. Philadelphia: University of Pennsylvania Press, 1988.

———. "Swift's *Polite* Conversation: An Eschatological Vision." *Studies in Philology* 73 (1976): 204–24.

Kelly, Patrick. "The Irish Woollen Export Prohibition Act of 1699: Kearney Revisited." *Irish Economic and Social History* 7 (1980): 22–44.

Kennedy, Liam. "Modern Ireland: Post-Colonial Society or Post-Colonial Pretensions." *Irish Review* 13 (winter 1992/93): 107–21.

Kenney, E. J. *The Classical Text*. Berkeley: University of California Press, 1974.

Kiberd, Declan. *Inventing Ireland: The Literature of the Modern Nation*. Cambridge: Harvard University Press, 1995.

Korshin, Paul J. "Johnson and the Earl of Orrery." In *Eighteenth-Century Studies in Honor of Donald F. Hyde*. Edited by W. H. Bond. New York: The Grolier Club, 1970.

———. "Johnson and Swift: A Study in the Genesis of Literary Opinion." *Philological Quarterly* 48 (1969): 464–78.

Lacan, Jacques. *Écrits: A Selection*. Translated by Alan Sheridan. London: Routledge, 1977.

Lanza, Antonio. *Polemiche e berte letterarie nella Firenze del primo Quattrocento*. Rome: Bulzoni, 1972.

Le Brocquy, Sybil. *Cadenus*. Dublin: Dolmen Press, 1962.

———. *Swift's Most Valuable Friend*. Dublin: Dufour Editions, 1968.

Leerssen, Joep. *Mere Irish and Fíor-Ghael: Studies in the Idea of Irish Nationality, Its Development, and Literary Expression prior to the Nineteenth Century*. Critical Conditions: Field Day Essays and Monographs. Cork: Cork University Press, 1996.

LeFanu, William, ed. *A Catalogue of Books Belonging to Dr Jonathan Swift*. Cambridge: Cambridge University Library, 1988.

Le Harivel, Adrian, comp. *Illustrated Summary Catalogue of Drawings, Watercolours and Miniatures*. Dublin: National Gallery of Ireland, 1983.

———, and Michael Wynne, comp. *Illustrated Summary Catalogue of Paintings*. Dublin: National Gallery of Ireland, 1981.

Leslie, Charles Robert, and Tom Taylor. *The Life and Times of Sir Joshua Reynolds*. 2 vols. London, 1865.

Levine, Joseph. *The Battle of the Books: History and Literature in the Augustan Age.* Ithaca: Cornell University Press, 1991.

Liebert, Herman W. "Portraits of the Author: Lifetime Likenesses of Samuel Johnson." In *English Portraits of the Seventeenth and Eighteenth Centuries.* Los Angeles: William Andrews Clark Memorial Library, 1974.

Lillywhite, Bryant. *London Coffee Houses: A Reference Book of Coffee Houses of the Seventeenth, Eighteenth and Nineteenth Centuries.* London: George Allen and Unwin, 1963.

———. *London Signs: A Reference Book of London Signs from Earliest Times to about the Mid-Nineteenth Century.* London: George Allen and Unwin, 1972.

Lincoln, Bruce. *Authority: Construction and Corrosion.* Chicago and London: University of Chicago Press, 1994.

Lippincott, Louise. *Selling Art in Georgian London: The Rise of Arthur Pond.* New Haven: Yale University Press, 1983.

Lloyd, David. *Anomalous States: Irish Writing and the Post-Colonial Moment.* Durham, N.C.: Duke University Press, 1993.

Long, Basil S. *British Miniaturists.* London: Geoffrey Bles, 1920.

Longley, Edna. "Postcolonial *versus* European (and Post-Ukanian) Frameworks for Irish Literature." *Irish Review* 25 (winter/spring 1999–2000): 75–94.

Mahony, Robert. "The Irish Colonial Experience and Swift's Rhetorics of Perception in the 1720s." *Eighteenth-Century Life* 22, n.s.1 (February 1998): 63–75.

———. *Jonathan Swift: the Irish Identity.* New Haven: Yale University Press, 1995.

———. "Protestant Dependence and Consumption in Swift's Irish Writings," in *Political Ideas in Eighteenth-Century Ireland.* Edited by S. J. Connolly. Dublin: Four Courts Press, 2000.

Maner, Martin. "Johnson's Redaction of Hawkesworth's *Swift.*" *The Age of Johnson: A Scholarly Annual* 2 (1989): 311–34.

Marks, Arthur S. "Seeking an Enduring Image: Rupert Barber, Jonathan Swift, and the Profile Portrait." Ms. essay.

Marx, Karl. "The Eighteenth Brumaire of Louis Bonaparte," in *Marx: Later Political Writings.* Edited by and translated by Terrell Carver. Cambridge Texts in the History of Political Thought. Cambridge: Cambridge University Press, 1996.

Maxwell, Constantina. *Dublin under the Georges: 1714–1830.* London: Faber and Faber, n.d.

Mayhew, George P. *Rage or Raillery: The Swift Manuscripts at the Huntington Library.* San Marino, CA: The Huntington Library, 1967.

McKenzie, D. F. *Stationers' Company Apprentices 1701–1800.* Oxford: Oxford Bibliographical Society, 1978.

McLeod, John. *Beginning Postcolonialism.* Manchester: Manchester University Press, 2000.

Memmi, Albert. *The Colonizer and the Colonized [Portrait du Colonisé précédé du Portrait du Colonisateur,* 1957]. Translated by Howard Greenfeld. New York: Orion, 1965.

Mercier, Vivian. *The Irish Comic Tradition.* Oxford: Clarendon, 1962.

Mitchel, John. *The History of Ireland from the Treaty of Limerick to the Present Time.* Dublin: Duffy, 1869.

Mongia, Padmini, ed. *Contemporary Postcolonial Theory: A Reader.* London: Arnold, 1996.

Moran, D. P. "The Pale and the Gael." *New Ireland Review* 11, 4 (June 1899). Rpt. in *The Philosophy of Irish Ireland*. Dublin: Duffy, 1905.

Murry, John Middleton. *Jonathan Swift: A Critical Biography*. London: Jonathan Cape, 1954.

Myers, Jeffrey. "Autobiographical Reflections in Johnson's 'Life of Swift.'" *Discourse: A Review of the Liberal Arts* 8 (winter 1965): 37–48.

Nevinson, H. W. "Where Cruel Rage." In *Essays in Freedom and Rebellion*. New Haven: Yale University Press, 1921.

Nisard, Charles. *Les Gladiateurs de La République des Lettres aux XVe, XVIe, et XVIIe Siècles*. Reprint of the 1860 edition. Geneva: Slatkine Reprints, 1970.

Nokes, David. *Jonathan Swift, A Hypocrite Reversed*. Oxford: Oxford University Press, 1985.

Noon, Patrick J. "Miniatures on the Market," in *The English Miniature* by John Murdoch, Jim Murrell, Patrick J. Noon, and Roy Strong. New Haven and London: Yale University Press, 1981. 163–209.

Northcote, James. *The Life of Sir Joshua Reynolds*. 2nd ed. 2 vols. London, 1819.

O'Hegarty, P. S. "Jonathan Swift: Irishman." *The Bell* 10 (September 1945): 478–88.

Oliphant, Mrs. M. O. W. *Historical Characters of the Reign of Queen Anne*. New York: Century Company, 1894.

Orwell, George. "Politics vs. Literature: An Examination of *Gulliver's Travels*," In *Shooting An Elephant and Other Essays*. New York: Harcourt, Brace and World, 1950 [1945].

O'Sullivan, Seumas. "Jackel and Lion: A Note on Orrery's 'Remarks on Swift,'" in *The Rose and Bottle and Other Essays*. Dublin: Talbot Press, 1946.

O'Toole, Fintan. *A Traitor's Kiss: The Life of Richard Brinsley Sheridan, 1751–1816*. New York: Farrar, Straus and Giroux, 1998.

Parke, Catherine N. "Johnson and the Arts of Conversation," in *The Cambridge Companion to Samuel Johnson*. Edited by Greg Clingham. Cambridge: Cambridge University Press, 1997.

Paulson, Ronald. *The Fictions of Satire*. Baltimore: Johns Hopkins University Press, 1967.

———. "Swift, Stella, and Permanence." *ELH* 27 (1960): 298–314.

Payne, F. Anne. *Chaucer and Menippean Satire*. Madison: University of Wisconsin Press, 1981.

Penny, Nicholas, ed. *Reynolds*. New York: Abrams, 1986.

Peterson, Leland. "Swift's *Project:* A Religious and Political Satire." *PMLA* 82 (1967): 54–67.

Pfeiffer, Rudolf. *History of Classical Scholarship from 1300 to 1850*. Oxford: Clarendon Press, 1976.

Piper, David. *The Image of the Poet: British Poets and their Portraits*. Oxford: Clarendon Press, 1982.

Pollak, Ellen. "Swift Among the Feminists." *Critical Approaches to Teaching Swift*. Edited by Peter Schakel. New York: AMS Press, 1992.

Postle, Martin. *Angels & Urchins: The Fancy Picture in 18th-Century British Art*. Nottingham: Djanolgy Gallery, 1998.

———. *Sir Joshua Reynolds: The Subject Pictures*. Cambridge: Cambridge University Press, 1995.

Probyn, Clive. "Swift's *Verses on the Death of Dr. Swift:* The Notes." *Studies in Bibliography* 39 (1986): 47–61.

Quint, David. "Humanism and Modernity: A Reconsideration of Bruni's *Dialogues.*" *Renaissance Quarterly* 38 (1985): 423–45.

Quintana, Ricardo. *The Mind and Art of Jonathan Swift.* Oxford: Oxford University Press, 1936.

Reynolds, L. D., and N. G. Wilson. *Scribes and Scholars: A Guide to the Transmission of Greek and Latin Literature.* Oxford: Clarendon Press, 1974.

Richardson, Samuel. "Samuel Richardson on Swift." In *Swift: The Critical Heritage.* Edited by Kathleen Williams. London: Routledge and Kegan Paul, 1970.

Rodino, Richard H. "'*Splendide Mendax*': Authors, Characters, and Readers in *Gulliver's Travels.*" In *Reading Swift: Papers from the Second Münster Symposium on Jonathan Swift.* Edited by Richard H. Rodino and Hermann J. Real. München: Wilhelm Fink Verlag, 1993.

Ross, Angus. "*The Anatomy of Melancholy* and Swift." In *Swift and His Contexts.* Edited by John Irwin Fischer, Hermann J. Real, and James Woolley. New York: AMS Press, 1989.

Ross, Ian Campbell. "The Scriblerians and Swift in Ireland," in *Reading Swift: Papers from the Second Münster Symposium on Jonathan Swift.* Edited by Richard H. Rodino and Hermann J. Real. München: Wilhelm Fink Verlag, 1993.

Ross, J. C. "The Framing and Printing of the Motte Editions of *Gulliver's Travels.*" *Bibliographical Society of Australia and New Zealand Bulletin* 20, 1 (1996): 5–19.

Said, Edward. *Representations of the Intellectual.* 2nd ed. New York: Pantheon, 1996.

———. "Swift as Intellectual" and "Swift's Tory Anarchy." In *The World, the Text, and the Critic.* Cambridge: Harvard University Press, 1983.

Scaglione, Aldo. "The Humanist as Scholar and Politian's Concept of the Grammaticus." *Studies in the Renaissance* 8 (1961): 49–70.

Schakel, Peter J. "The Politics of Opposition in 'Verses on the Death of Dr. Swift.'" *Modern Language Quarterly* 35 (1974): 246–56.

Scouten, Arthur H. "The Earliest London Printings of 'Verses on the Death of Doctor Swift.'" *Studies in Bibliography* 15 (1962): 243–47.

———, and Robert D. Hume. "Pope and Swift: Text and Interpretation of Swift's Verses on His Death." *Philological Quarterly* 52 (1973): 205–31.

Seidel, Michael. *Satiric Inheritance: Rabelais to Sterne.* Princeton: Princeton University Press, 1979.

Shawe-Taylor, Desmond. *Genial Company: The Theme of Genius in Eighteenth-Century Portraiture.* Nottingham: Nottingham University Art Gallery, 1987.

Sibley, Gay. "*Satura* from Quintilian to Joe Bob Briggs: A New Look at an Old Word," in *Theorizing Satire.* Edited by Brian Connery and Kirk Combe. New York: St. Martin's Press, 1995.

Slepian, Barry. "The Ironic Intention of Swift's Verses on His Own Death." *Review of English Studies,* n.s., 14 (1963): 249–56.

Spivak, Gayatry Chakravarty. "Can the Subaltern Speak?," in *Marxism and the Interpretation of Culture.* Edited by Cary Nelson and Lawrence Grossberg. Urbana and Chicago: University of Illinois Press, 1988.

Stallybras, Peter, and Alon White. *The Politics and Poetics of Transgression.* Ithaca: Cornell University Press, 1986.

Starkman, Miriam. *Swift's Satire on Learning in A Tale of a Tub.* Princeton: Princeton University Press, 1950.

Stephen, Leslie. *Swift.* New York: 1898.

Stewart, Bruce. "'The Bitter Glass': Postcolonial Theory and Anglo-Irish Culture — A Case Study." *Irish Review* 25 (winter/spring 1999–2000): 27–50.

Steward, James C. *The New Child: British Art and the Origins of Modern Childhood 1730–1830.* Berkeley: University Art Museum, 1995.

Stone, Lawrence. *The Family, Sex, and Marriage in England 1500–1800.* New York: Harper and Row, 1977.

Strickland, Walter G. *A Dictionary of Irish Artists.* Dublin and London: Maunsel and Company, 1913

Taylor, Coley B. *Mark Twain's Margins on Thackeray's Swift.* New York: Gotham House, 1935.

Teerink, Herman. *A Bibliography of the Writings in Prose and Verse of Jonathan Swift, D.D.* The Hague: Martinus Nijhoff, 1937.

———. "Swift's *Verses on the Death of Doctor Swift.*" *Studies in Bibliography* 4 (1951): 183–88.

Test, George A. *Satire: Spirit and Art.* Tampa: University of South Florida Press, 1991.

Tinker, Chauncey Brewster. *The Wedgwood Medallion of Samuel Johnson.* Cambridge: Harvard University Press, 1926.

Trapp, J. B. "The Owl's Ivy and the Poet's Bays, an Inquiry into Poetic Garlands." *Journal of the Warburg and Courtauld Institutes* 21 (1958): 227–55.

Traugott, John. "*A Tale of A Tub.*" In *Focus: Swift.* Edited by C. J. Rawson. London: Sphere Books, 1971.

Treadwell, Michael. "London Trade Publishers 1675–1750." *The Library,* 6th ser., 4 (1982): 99–134.

———. "Observations on the Printing of Motte's Octavo Editions of *Gulliver's Travels,*" in *Reading Swift: Papers from the Third Münster Symposium on Jonathan Swift.* Edited by Hermann J. Real and Helgard Stöver-Leidig. München: Wilhelm Fink Verlag, 1998. 157–77.

Ugelow, Jenny. *Hogarth: A Life and World.* London: Faber and Faber, 1997.

Vander Meulen, David L. *Pope's Dunciad of 1728: A History and Facsimile.* Charlottesville: Published for the Bibliographical Society of the University of Virginia and the New York Public Library by the University Press of Virginia, 1991.

Vieth, David M. "The Mystery of Personal Identity: Swift's Verses on His Own Death," in *The Author in His Work: Essays on a Problem in Criticism.* Edited by Louis L. Martz and Aubrey Williams. New Haven: Yale University Press, 1978.

Vismara, Felice. *L'invettiva, arma preferita dagli umanisti: nelle lotte private, nelle polemiche letterarie, politiche e religiose.* Milan: Umberto Allegretti, 1900.

Waingrow, Marshall. "*Verses on the Death of Dr. Swift.*" *SEL: Studies in English Literature* 5 (1965): 513–18.

Ward, John C. "Johnson's Conversation." *SEL: Studies in English Literature* 12, 3 (1972): 519–33.

Warncke, Wayne. "Samuel Johnson on Swift: The *Life of Swift* and Johnson's Predecessors in Swiftian Biography." *Journal of British Studies* 7 (May 1968): 56–64.

Warner, Marina. *Joan of Arc: The Image of Female Heroism.* New York: Knopf, 1981.

Warren, Leland. "Turning Reality Round Together: Guides to Conversation in Eighteenth-Century England." *Eighteenth-Century Life* 8, 3 (1983): 65–87.

Waterhouse, Ellis. *Painting in Britain 1530–1790.* Harmondsworth: Penguin Books, 1978.

Webb, Sidney. *English Poor Law History.* London: Longman,1929.

Wendorf, Richard. *Sir Joshua Reynolds: The Painter in Society.* Cambridge: Harvard University Press, 1996.

Whelan, Kevin. *The Tree of Liberty: Radicalism, Catholicism and the Construction of Irish Identity.* Critical Conditions: Field Day Essays and Monologues. Notre Dame: University of Notre Dame Press, 1996.

White, Christopher. "Rembrandt's Influence on English Painting," in Christopher White, David Alexander, and Ellen D'Oench, *Rembrandt in Eighteenth Century England.* New Haven: Yale Center for British Art, 1983.

Whitley, William T. *Artists and their Friends in England.* 2 vols. London: Medici, 1928.

Wilde, William R. *The Closing Years of Dean Swift's Life.* 2nd ed. rev. Dublin: Hodges & Smith, 1849.

Williams, Harold. *Dean Swift's Library.* Cambridge: Cambridge University Press,1932.

———. "Swift's Early Biographers," in *Pope and His Contemporaries: Essays Presented to George Sherburn.* Edited by James L. Clifford and Louis A. Landa. New York: Oxford University Press, 1949.

Wilson, T. G. "A Hitherto Undescribed Death-Mask of Dean Swift." *Journal of the Royal Society of Antiquaries of Ireland* 81 (1951): 107–14.

———. "Swift's Death-Masks," *Review of English Literature* 3 (1962): 39–58.

Wimsatt, William Kurtz. *The Portraits of Alexander Pope.* New Haven and London: Yale University Press, 1965.

Wise, Thomas J. *The Ashley Library: A Catalogue of Printed Books, Manuscripts and Autograph Letters. Collected by Thomas J. Wise.* 11 vols. London: n.p., 1922–36.

Woods, Margaret L. "Swift, Stella, and Vanessa." *The Nineteenth Century and After* 74 (December 1913): 1230–47.

Woolley, James. "Autobiography in Swift's Verses on His Death," in *Contemporary Studies of Swift's Poetry.* Edited by John Irwin Fischer, Donald C. Mell, Jr., and David M. Vieth. Newark: University of Delaware Press, 1981. 112–22.

———. "Friends and Enemies in *Verses on the Death of Dr. Swift." Studies in Eighteenth-Century Culture* 8 (1979): 205–32.

Yeats, William Butler. "Introduction to *Words on the Window-Pane"* (1934), in *Fair Liberty Was All His Cry: A Tercentenary Tribute to Jonathan Swift.* Edited by Norman Jeffares. New York: St. Martin's Press, 1967.

Zach, Wolfgang. "Jonathan Swift and Colonialism," in *Reading Swift: Papers from the Second Münster Symposium on Jonathan Swift.* Edited by Richard H. Rodino and Hermann J. Real. München: Wilhelm Fink Verlag, 1993.

Zimmerman, Don H., and Candace West. "Sex Roles, Interruptions and Silences in Conversation," in *Language and Sex: Difference and Dominance.* Edited by Barrie Thorn and Nancy Henley. Rowley, Mass.: Newbury House, 1975.

Notes on Contributors

LOUISE BARNETT is professor of English at Rutgers University. In addition to her volume on Swift's verse, *Swift's Poetic Worlds* (University of Delaware Press, 1981), she has published frequent articles on women in and women reading Swift's work. She also writes on American and Native American literature and is the author of *Authority and Speech: Language, Society, and Self in the American Novel* (1993).

W. SCOTT BLANCHARD is an associate professor of English at College Misericordia in Pennsylvania. He has published a book on Menippean satire *(Scholars' Bedlam: Menippean Satire in the Renaissance* [Bucknell, Pa., 1995]) and articles in *The Journal of the History of Ideas, Renaissance Studies, Studies in Philology,* and *The Journal of Medieval and Renaissance Studies.* He is currently working on a study of early modern intellectuals and dissent.

BRIAN A. CONNERY is associate professor and chair of the Department of English at Oakland University. He writes frequently on Swift and coedited, with Kirk Combe, a previous collection, *Theorizing Satire: Essays in Literary Criticism* (1995).

KENNETH CRAVEN, a student of James L. Clifford, has worked in business and technology while pursuing his interest in the eighteenth century, especially the work of Laurence Sterne and Jonathan Swift. He codirected research and coauthored *Science Information Personnel* (1961) with university librarian Leonard Cohan. His *Jonathan Swift and the Millennium of Madness* was published in 1992.

DAVID DEEMING teaches eighteenth-century literature and twentieth-century literature and theory at Birkbeck College, London. He has recently completed a doctoral dissertation entitled *Swift, Ireland, and the Aesthetic Critique of Modernity* and is currently writing a book on Samuel Richardson.

CAROLE FABRICANT, professor of English at the University of California, Riverside, is the author of *Swift's Landscape,* (1982, reissued 1995). A former James L. Clifford Prize winner, she has published numerous articles on a variety of eighteenth-century topics, including a new historicist reading of *Gulliver's Travels* for the series, Case Studies in Contemporary Criticism (1995). Her edition of *Swift's Miscellaneous Prose* will be published by Penguin Classics. She teaches postcolonial studies, Irish literature, and autobiography, as well as Swift and eighteenth-century studies.

ROBERT FOLKENFLIK, professor of English University of California, Irivine, has edited Swift's *A Tale of a Tub* and *The Battle of the Books* and Tobias Smollett's *Sir Launcelot Greaves*. He has also published *Samuel Johnson, Biographer* and *The Culture of Autobiography: Constructions of Self-Representation* (1993). He has held National Endowment for the Humanities, Guggenheim Foundation, and Rockefeller Foundation (Bellagio) fellowships.

STEPHEN KARIAN is a Visiting Assistant Professor at Marquette University and is the author of several articles on Swift and eighteenth-century satire. He is also a coeditor of *Eighteenth-Century Contexts: Historical Inquiries in Honor of Phillip Harth.*

ANN CLINE KELLY is a professor at Howard University in Washington, D.C. She has published numerous articles on Swift and a book, *Swift and the English Language* (1988). Her second book, *Jonathan Swift and Popular Culture: Myth, Media, and the Man* was published in 2002.

ROBERT MAHONY is an associate professor of English at the Catholic University of America, and the founding director (1983–97) of the Center for Irish Studies at CUA. His books include *Jonathan Swift: The Irish Identity* (1995), and with Carole Fabricant he is editing a volume of Swift's Irish writings.

NICK RUSHWORTH graduated from the University of Sydney in 1988. He went to the University of California, Berkeley, to pursue a Ph.D. but dropped out and into journalism. He is now the senior researcher in the investigative unit of the "Sunday" program with the National Nine Television Network in Australia.

J. T. SCANLAN writes for both popular and scholarly publications, but most of his essays and reviews address in one way or another the eighteenth century, and particularly Samuel Johnson. He is currently making final changes to a comic-grim memoir on graduate school at the University of Michigan and Yale in the 1980s, *Terminal Degree: My Quest for a Ph.D.* He is also at work on a book on the relations between law and literature in eighteenth-century London, tentatively titled *A Spirit of Contradiction.* He teaches eighteenth-century literature at Providence College.

SEAN SHESGREEN teaches English at Northern Illinois University in Dekalb, Illinois. Author of *Criers and Hawkers of London,* he is currently completing a book-length history of the London Cries.

Index

academic satire, 59, 61, 62
Acheson, Lady Anne, 152, 161, 166
Acheson, Sir Arthur, 161
Addison, Joseph, 66, 143
Adorno, Theodor, 30, 34, 69
aesthetics, 30, 34
Agrippa, Cornelius: *De vanitate,* 66
Alcoff, Linda, 237
allegory, 27, 30
anatomy, 58–61, 62, 71n. 6
ancients and moderns, 25, 27, 43, 45, 46, 48–49, 51, 62, 63, 65–67, 153
Anglican Church, 30
anonymity, 54, 78, 171–74. *See also* Swift, Jonathan
Aodhagán, Ó Rathaille, 239
Apuleius, Lucius, 58
Arbuthnot, John, 79, 159–60
Aristophanes, 269
Arnold, Bruce, 11
authority: discursive, 161, 167, 269

Bakhtin, Mikhail, 14, 58, 153, 195, 210–11, 273
Balfour, Arthur James, 225
Bannerman, Alexander, 117
Barber, Constantine, 123, 124, 125, 133, 146n. 7
Barber, John, 124
Barber, Lucius, 123, 124
Barber, Mary, 122–25, 127, 133, 138, 143, 146n. 6
Barber, Rupert, Sr., 122, 123–24
Barber, Rupert, Jr., 16, 117–45
Barnett, Louise, 17
Barrow, Isaac, 159
Barry, Dr. Edward, 133
Barthes, Roland, 154–55
Bate, Walter Jackson, 100–101
Bathurst, Charles, 94
Beauclerk, Topham, 114
Beckett, J. C., 32

Bedlam, 28
beggars, 135, 136, 198–208, 249
Belser, Gregory, 279
Bentley, Richard, 14, 43, 45–54, 62, 63, 65; *Dissertation upon the Epistles of Phalaris,* 43, 48, 72nn. 18 and 21; *Epistolar ad Millium,* 14, 45; *Notes on Callimachus,* 14, 43, 46–47, 54
Berkeley, George, 18, 187, 188, 236, 242–45, 253, 258, 262n. 3
Berwick, Donald, 181
Bettesworth, Richard, 167
Bindon, Francis, 16, 120, 122, 129, 135, 137–138, 139, 140–43, 144, 145
Biographical History of England, 5th ed., 195
Blake, William, 61
Blanchard, W. Scott, 14
Bloom, Harold, 14, 25, 99
Bolingbroke, *See* St. John, Henry
book trade, 78, 79, 81, 82, 83–84, 85–86, 88, 92, 94
Boorstin, Daniel J., 280–81
Boswell, James, 99, 100, 159, 167, 181; *Journal of a Tour of the Hebrides,* 105, 181; *Life of Johnson,* 100, 167
Boyer, Abel, 151
Boyle, Charles, Fourth Earl of Orrery, 105
Boyle, Frank, 270
Boyle, John, Fifth Earl of Orrery, 89, 93, 102, 103, 104, 113, 117, 125, 132, 138, 140; *Remarks on . . . Swift,* 105–8, 118, 132–33, 145n. 2, 164–65, 169–70, 199
Brandreth, Dean, 256
Brewster, Sir Francis, 31, 34
Brown, Norman O., 36, 256
Browne, John, 259
Bruni, Leonard, 69, 73n. 23
Bryn Mawr College, 117
Buccleuch, Duke of, 137, 142
burlesque, 90, 96n. 15
Burlington, Richard Boyle, Earl of, 165–66

Burlington, Lady, 165–66
Burnet, Gilbert, Bishop of Salisbury, 172
Burns, Robert, 276
Burton, Richard, 143
Burton, Robert, 14, 57, 61, 70n. 1
Butler, Samuel, 87

Carolan, Turlough, 240
Caroline, Queen of England, 79
Carpenter, Andrew, 11
Carteret, John, Second Baron, 86, 89
Casement, Roger, 263n. 17
catachresis, 33
Catholics, Irish, 30, 197, 217–18, 220,
    221, 224, 225, 228, 231, 230–31, 235n.
    24, 237, 238, 242–45, 247, 250, 251,
    252–53, 263n. 14
Cervantes, Miguel de, 269
Césaire, Aimé, 256–57, 258–59, 261
Chalmers, Alan, 271, 273
Charney, Maurice, 102
Charteris, Francis, 79
Cheng, Vincent, 237–38
Chesterfield, Philip Dormer Stanhope, 4th
    Earl of, 127
Chetwode, Knightley, 171
children, 187, 194n. 30, 198, 202–208
Church of Ireland, 230, 236
Churchill, Charles, 143
Churchill, R. C., 226
Cibber, Colley, 80, 82
Cicero, Marcus Tullius: De Oratore, 67
Clarendon, Henry Hyde, 1st Earl of, 217
Clarges, Lady, 162
class, 160–62, 163, 164–65, 174, 187,
    195–96, 197–208
coffeehouses, 35
Cohan, Leonard, 283
colonialism, 3, 32, 33, 38, 218–23, 225,
    229–30, 239, 241, 246, 247, 259
Connally, S. J., 259
Connery, Brian A., 95n. 5, 184–85, 274
conversation, 159–75, 175n. 1, 176n. 7,
    192n. 12
Corkery, Daniel, 156–57, 225, 226
Craven, Kenneth, 19
Cromwell, Oliver, 217
Crow, Nora, 181
Crown, Patricia, 203
Curll, Edmund, 79–81, 84, 92
Curtin, Dermott, 157
Curtius, Ernst, 59

Daly, Mary, 258
Dante Alighieri, 49
Davenant, William, 143
Davies, Sir John, 219
Davis, Herbert, 77, 175n. 1, 185, 217, 254
Deane, Seamus, 224, 255
Declaratory Act (1720), 18, 229, 248, 249
Deeming, David, 13
Defoe, Daniel, 17, 191
Delany, Mary, 123, 125, 126, 127, 128,
    133, 138, 184
Delany, Patrick, 102, 103, 104, 113, 123,
    128, 138, 161, 199, 240; Observations
    Upon Lord Orrery's Remarks, 107–10,
    165, 169, 184, 199–200
Deleuze, Gilles, 238
de Man, Paul, 29
DeMaria, Robert Jr. 104, 114
Dingley, Rebecca, 161, 182, 184
dissenters, 30, 31, 32
Dr. Gregory's Legacy to His Daughters,
    158
Donnellan, Anne, 126, 127, 128
Downie, Alan, 280
Drayton, Michael, 143
Dublin, 90, 113, 122, 123, 164, 197–200,
    210, 211, 213n. 37, 249
Dublin College of Physicians, 123
Dublin Journal, 89, 126–27, 132, 140,
    244
Dublin Society, 126, 128
Duck, Stephen, 81, 82
Dysart, Lady, 128

Eagleton, Terry, 34
Ehrenpreis, Irvin, 12, 15, 26, 121, 123,
    139, 169, 175n. 1, 176n. 8, 185, 186–
    87, 188, 189
Ehrenpreis Institute, 15
Elias, A. C., 38n. 1, 121–22
emendation: conjectural, 45–48
Empson, William, 26
epistles of Phalaris, 105. See also Bentley;
    Temple
Erasmus, 14, 57, 62, 66, 70; Praise of
    Folly, 61

Fabricant, Carole, 13, 229
Falkiner, Sir Fredrick, 117, 135, 137, 138
Fanon, Frantz, 222
Faulkner, George, 85, 87, 88, 93, 94, 126–
    27, 132, 196, 201

Field Day Anthology of Irish Writing, 221
Field Day Theatre Company, 221
Fielding, Henry, 99, 140
Fiquet, Etienne, 117
Fischer, John Irwin, 273
Flaxman, John, 131
Folkenflik, Robert 16
Foot, Michael, 100, 226
Ford, Charles, 161, 177n. 9, 187
Forward, Toby, 237
Foster, Roy, 236
Foucault, Michel, 61
Foundling Hospital, 207
Freud, Sigmund, 36, 272
Fritsch, Christian Friedrich, 117, 126
Frye, Northrop, 58, 61, 71n. 8
funerary sculpture, 144
Fussell, Paul, 102

Gainsborough, Thomas, 206–8
Gaulstown, 151
Gay, John, 79, 123, 163, 164, 208–9, 271
George, James, 126
Germaine, Lady Betty, 124, 142, 184, 186
Gibbons, Luke, 221
Glendinning, Victoria, 117
Godolphin, Lady, 162
Graevius, Joannes, 46
Graham, Colin, 221, 222, 224, 227
Granger, James, 195
Grattan, Henry, 222, 225
Great Famine, 258
Greene, Valentine, 126
Gregory, Alyse, 188
Gunpowder Plot, 230

Habermas, Jurgen, 69
Hardy, Evelyn, 185, 191
Haraway, Donna, 237
Harley, Edward, Second Earl of Oxford,
    37, 86, 162, 163, 169, 173
Harris, Francis, 142
Hawkesworth, John, 102, 103, 104, 113;
    Account of the Life of . . . Swift, 110–
    11
Helsham, Dr. Richard, 124
Henley, John "Orator," 81, 82
Hesiod, 143
heteroglossia, 153
Hill, Dr. Edward, 135
Hill, Jack, 207
Hill, Jacqueline, 253

History of the Rebellion (Clarendon), 217,
    218
Hoare, William, 126
Hogarth, William, 140, 142–43, 206, 207;
    Rake's Progress, 82
Horace, 141–42, 269
Horkheimer, Max, 69
Hudson, Thomas, 126, 129, 210
Hume, Robert D., 77
Hyp Doctor, 82

ideology, 30, 36; of the aesthetic, 33
intellectuals, social function of, 62–63,
    68–70
International Society for Eighteenth-
    Century Studies, 11
invective, 59, 64, 68, 69
Ireland, 30–32, 198, 218–23, 250, 255–
    56, 259–61; Anglo-Irish elite, 30, 32–
    33, 223, 225, 228, 229, 230, 231, 232,
    236, 238, 240–41, 242–44, 248, 252,
    253, 262n. 23; divisions within, 30, 31,
    32, 33, 34–35, 220–21, 239, 240, 241,
    242–43, 247–48, 250, 251, 253; liter-
    ary tradition, 34, 38, 223, 237, 239; na-
    tionalism, 222, 223–24, 225, 231, 232,
    233, 237, 238, 248, 256, 262n. 9; par-
    liament, 84, 248, 250, 251, 254–55;
    Republic of, 223, 224
Irish studies, 18, 221–23, 224
Irish Woollen Export Prohibition Act, 31–
    32
Ivy Lane Club, 110

Jeffrey, Francis, 225, 231
Jennings, Sarah, Lady Marlborough, 162
Jervas, Charles, 16, 138
Joan of Arc, 154
Johns, Adrian, 78
Johnson, Esther, 12, 17,107, 161, 162,
    163, 166, 173, 177n. 10, 181–86, 188,
    190; last will of, 184, 192–93nn. 14
    and 17
Johnson, Samuel, 99–115, 210; *Adven-
    turer,* 110; "Bad Johnson," 102, 104;
    buried autobiography, 111–13, 114;
    bust of, 143; conversation of, 176n. 7;
    fear of death, 113; on *Gulliver's
    Travels,* 100; *Life of Cowley,* 99, 103;
    Life of Dryden, 103; *Life of Milton,*
    100, 103, 104, 106, 112, 113, 114; *Life
    of Swift,* 15–16, 100–115, 139, 167,

170, 177n. 11, 182; *Life of Waller,* 103;
*Lives of the Most Eminent English Po-
ets,* 101, 103, 111–12, 114; portrait of,
131; *Preface to Shakespeare,* 106;
Rambler, 104; Review of Soame
Jenyns's *Enquiry,* 106
Jonson, Ben, 143, 275
*Jonathan Swift and the Millennium of
Madness,* 283–84
Joyce, James, 238, 239, 271
Joyce, Myles, 239, 245
Juvenal, 269

Karian, Stephen, 15, 157n. 2
Keilen, S. P. T., 101
Kelly, Ann Cline, 15, 16, 167–68, 175n. 1
Kelly, Patrick, 30
Khan, Rahila, *See* Forward, Toby
Kiberd, Declan, 36, 250
King, William (Christ Church, Oxford),
46, 47
King, William (St. Mary Hall, Oxford),
93–94, 98n. 29
Knapton, George, 126
Kneller, Sir Godfrey, 130, 143
Korshin, Paul J., 101–2, 103, 110, 114
Kühenhumor, 59

Lacan, Jacques, 37
*Lady Pennington's Unfortunate Mother's
Advice,* 155
Lady's Pocket Library (1792), 155
Lambin, Denis, 44, 48
La Rochefoucauld, François, Duc de, 91
Lavater, J. C., 117
LeBrocquy, Sybil, 187
Leerssen, Joep, 247–48
LeFanu, Joseph, 117
LeFanu, William, 117, 125, 135
Lennox, Charlotte, 105
Levine, Joseph M., 39n. 5
Lillywhite, Bryant, 82
Lintot, Bernard, 79, 80, 81–84
Liotard, Jean-Étienne, 128
Lipsius, Jusus, 14, 66, 72n. 19; *Somnium,*
66, 67–68
Locke, John, 13, 27, 34, 37, 279–80
Lomonosov, Mikhail V., 282
London, 93
London Magazine, 129
Long, Anne, 184
Long, Basil, 135

Lowth, Robert, 156
Lucian, 58

MacGavran, Hugh, 240
MacNeill, J. G. Swift, 135
madness, 28, 108–9, 117, 171
Mahony, Robert, 12, 280
Malelas, John of Antioch, 45
Malone, Edmund, 102–3, 107, 111
Maner, Martin, 111
Marchi, Giuseppi, 210
Marcuse, Herbert, 69
Market Hill, 152, 161
Marlborough, Lady. *See* Jennings, Sarah
Marsh, Narcissus, 282
Marsh's Library, 11, 217
Marvell, Andrew: "The Garden," 143
Marx, Karl, 239
Mason, William, 202–3
Massarene, Lord, 126
McEwan, Ian: *Amsterdam,* 277–79
Mead, Dr. Richard, 122, 124, 125, 130–
31, 132–33, 138
McGee, Alexander, 184
Memmi, Albert, 272
Menippean satire, 14, 58
Menippus, 58
Mercier, Vivian, 37–38
Miller, Andrew, 140–42
Milton, John, 100
Mitchel, John, 222, 225
M'Loghlin, Bryan, 187, 194n. 30
mock epic, 26
modernity, 27–30, 34–35, 36
Molière, Jean Baptiste Poquelin, 278–79
Molyneux, William, 30, 252
Moor Park, 26, 33, 45
Moore, Thomas, 204
Moran, D. P., 225, 226
More, Hannah, 155
Moryson, Fynes, 219
Motte, Benjamin, 88, 93, 96–97n. 16,
98n. 31
Muenster Symposium on Jonathan Swift
(1989), 227
Myers, Jeffrey, 104, 112

Nacton House of Industry, 207
Nation, The, 225
National Gallery of Ireland, 120, 121,
122, 135, 136, 138, 141, 142
National Library of Ireland, 11

National Portrait Gallery of England, 130
natural rights, 252
neoclassical criticism, 57, 66
Nevinson, H. W., 226
New Orleans Museum of Art, 135, 137
Nokes, David, 115, 188
Nolleken, Joseph, 144
Noon, Patrick, 126
Northcote, James, 202, 204–5, 206
Nugent, Robert, 138

Ó Bruadair, Dàibhí, 239
O'Halloran, Sylvester, 240
Oldmixon, John 156
Oliphant, Margaret, 183
Ormonde, James Butler, second Duke of,
    162, 163
Orrery, Earl of. See Boyle, John
Orwell, George, 256

Parnell, Charles Stewart, 222, 225, 238
Pasquin, Anthony, 127
Penal laws, 30, 230, 238
Pendarves, Mary. See Delany, Mary
Penn, William, 162
Perlstein, Dr. Jacob, 133
persona, 249–50, 251
Peterborough, Charles Mordaunt, 3rd Earl,
    173, 228, 229
Petrarch, 143
Petronius, 58
Petty, William, 211, 235n. 24, 282
Phalaris, 45, 46
Pilkington, Laetitia, 87–88, 90, 165–66,
    167, 177n. 9, 190
Pilkington, Matthew, 88, 93
Pisani, Ugolino, 59, 71n. 4
Plautus, 141
poet laureateship, 143
politeness, 160
Poliziano, Angelo (Politian), 14, 59–60,
    61, 62, 65, 66, 67, 72nn. 18 and 19;
    Lamia, 66, 72n. 20
polyglossia, 59
Pond, Arthur, 122, 124–25, 127, 128,
    129, 130, 132, 135, 142
Pope, Alexander, 79, 81, 89–90, 92, 94,
    96–97n. 16, 124, 129, 130–31, 143,
    164, 245; Dunciad, 49, 52, 55n. 2, 81
Popish plot, 230
portraiture, 129; coin, 131–32; enamel,
    126; iconography of, 141–42, 143–44,

144n. 2; miniature, 126; posthumous,
    140, 144
postcolonial theory, 18–19, 218–25, 227–
    28, 229, 233; and Ireland, 218–25, 232,
    233, 259
Postle, Martin, 206
Poyning's Law, 248
Presbyterians, Irish, 31, 32, 230
print culture, 78, 93, 94
Prior, Matthew, 173
psychoanalysis, 36–37
public sphere, 15, 68–70, 73n. 23
Pyle, Thomas, 184

Queensbury, Catherine, Duchess of, 89
Quintana, Ricardo, 185
Quintilian: Institutio oratoria, 67

Rabelais, François,14, 26, 65, 70, 269
race, 219–20, 243, 258
railllery, 168–69, 176n. 8
Ravenet, S. F. 117, 146n. 3
Raymond, Anthony, 240
Reformation: English, 62, 220, 222
Reilly, Hugh, 240
Rembrandt, Harmenszoon van Rijn,129,
    130, 135
Rembrandt Group, 129, 135
Renaissance humanism, 58–70
representation, 18–19; political, in col-
    onial context, 236–40, 244–45, 246–
    47, 248, 249, 254–55, 257
revisionism, 221, 258
Reynolds, Sir Joshua, 17, 126, 201–8,
    210–211; Beggar Boy and his Sister,
    206; Boy with Cabbage Nets, 202; Chil-
    dren in the Woods, 204, 205; Child's
    Portrait in Different Views, 203; Count
    Hugolino and his Children, 202; For-
    tune Teller, 202; Infant Baptist, 212n.
    11; Infant Jupiter, 204; Infant Samuel,
    202; Iphigenia, 201; Master Crewe as
    Henry VIII, 203; Master Hare, 203;
    Piping Shepherd, 204; Puck, 204;
    Schoolboy, 202–3; Shepherd Boy, 203;
    Sleeping Girl, 204; Venus Chiding
    Cupid, 201
Richardson, Jonathan (Sr.), 129, 130–31,
    143
Richardson, Samuel, 99, 155
Rising of 1641, 217, 218, 230, 233n. 3,
    251

Rochefort, Deborah Staunton, 191
Rochefort family, 151–52
Rodino, Richard, 273, 280
Rogers, Charles, 129
Roscoe, Thomas, 155
Rose Tavern, 82–83
Ross, Ian, 280
Rothe House, 126
Roubiliac, Louis François, 144
Royal Society, 281
Rushworth, Nick, 14
Russell, John, R. A., 133, 124, 135
Russian Academy of Sciences, 282
Rymer, Thomas, 106

Said, Edward W., 62–63, 219, 224, 270
St. Patrick's Cathedral, 11, 123, 184
St. Werburgh's Street, 123
satire, 43, 257, 269–274, 277–78, 284; as
   medicine, 273
Scaliger, Joseph, 66, 67
Scanlan, J. T., 16
Schakel, Peter, 82–83
Science Information Personnel, 283
scholasticism, 65, 66
Scotland, 31
Scott, Sir Walter, 135, 155, 225
Scouten, Arthur H., 77
Seidel, Michael, 271, 272
Shakespeare, William, 269
Sherburn, Sir Edward, 46
Sheridan, Alicia, 117
Sheridan, Richard Brinsley, 132
Sheridan, Thomas (Sr.), 132, 161, 187,
   200, 247, 249, 262n. 3; Intelligencer
   No. 6, 260–61
Sheridan, Thomas (Jr.), 132, 133, 186,
   187
Shesgreen, Sean, 17–18
Sidney, Sir Philip, 143
Skelton, John, 143
Slaughter, Stephen, 138
slavery, 243, 258
Smyth, Dr. Edward, 126
Smythe, James Moore, 80, 81
Society for the Distribution of Tracts, 155
Southwell, Sir Robert, 33
Spencer, Gervase, 126
Spenser, Edmund, 49, 219
Spivak, Gayatri Chakravorty, 237, 238
Sputnik, 281
Stanley, Thomas, 46

Steiner, George, 257
Stella. See Johnson, Esther
Sterne, Laurence, 269–70
Stone, Lawrence, 211
Strickland, Walter G., 135
Stubbes, Phillip, 58, 61
Subaltern Studies Group, 222, 224
subalternism, 222–24, 230–31, 237
sublimation, 36–37, 256–58
Suffolk, Henrietta, Countess of, 79, 123,
   162
Swift, Deane, 103–4, 162, 167, 169–70
Swift, Godwin, 138
Swift, Jonathan: anonymity, 17, 51, 150,
   171–74; atheism (supposed), 155; authority, 16, 17, 77, 111, 115, 150, 154–
   55, 157, 160, 161, 163–67, 197–98,
   269–70; authority, lack of, 150–53,
   154; Battle of the Books, 25–27, 51,
   153; Bickerstaff Papers, 152; biography
   of, 12, 13, 15, 17, 99–115, 150; birthday poems to Stella, 181, 182, 190;
   bluntness, 163, 166; "Cadenus and Vanessa," 181; charity of, 200; and class,
   17, 123, 157, 161–62, 164, 195–201,
   247; "Clever Tom Clinch," 196; Complete College of Genteel and Ingenious
   Conversation, 159, 168; Conduct of the
   Allies, 151, 173; Contests and Dissensions, 172; conversation of, 123, 159–
   75, 175n. 1, 183–84, 191; "Description
   of a City Shower," 89, 196; "Description of an Irish Feast," 196, 240;
   "Description of the Morning," 196;
   Directions to Servants, 124, 196; Drapier Letters, 18, 84, 85, 123, 142, 144,
   161, 164, 231, 236, 241–42, 245–46,
   248, 251–54, 255; in Dublin, 164–65;
   "Epistle to a Lady," 89, 93; "An Epistle
   upon an Epistle," 123; Examiner, 153;
   as exemplary Christian, 155; fragmentariness in the writing, 14, 27, 34–35,
   41–43, 45, 48–50, 52–54, 150; feminist criticism of, 181–82, 183, 191,
   192n. 3; gaps in texts, 16, 17, 27, 160,
   166, 261; "Grand Question Debated,"
   152; Gulliver's Travels, 12–13, 100,
   144, 244, 270, 273, 274, 279; Hints towards an Essay on Conversation, 159,
   165, 168, 170; History of the Last Four
   Years, 93; hoaxes, 87, 94; "Holyhead
   Journal," 55n. 2; "Horace, Epistle 7.1,

Imitated," 151; "Humble Petition of the Footmen," 196, 254; and Ireland, 13–14, 18–19, 25–26, 30–31, 84, 113, 144, 153, 156, 198, 209–10, 217–19, 224–33, 236, 241–42, 245–61; and Irish Catholics, 156–57, 197, 217–18, 224, 225, 229, 231, 252–53, 264n. 34; and Irish nationalism, 156–57, 236; Jack and the Dane stories, 156–57, 226; "Journal of a Part of a Summer," 151–52; *Journal to Stella,* 162, 185, 189, 209; in Kilroot, 31; last will, 124; "The Legion Club," 250, 273; "Letter concerning the Weavers," 254–55; "Letter to a Very Young Lady," 155, 191; libels of, 152–53; "Life and Genuine Character of Doctor Swift," 86, 87–94, 96n. 15, 150–51, 152; in London, 162–63; "Mad Mullinix and Timothy," 249–50; marriage, secret, supposed, 107, 154, 185–86; *Maxims Controlled in Ireland,* 255; *Mechanical Operation of the Spirit,* 48; Menière's syndrome, 164; mental decline, supposed, 108–109, 110, 117, 138; miserliness, supposed, 200; "Mrs. Harris's Petition," 142, 152, 156, 254–55; *Modest Proposal,* 157, 161, 196, 198, 231, 246, 276; myth(s) of, 16, 79, 84, 150–57; "October Club," 173; "On Poetry: A Rapsody," 89, 93; "A Panegyric on the Dean," 152; paratext in writing, 14, 44, 54, 84; personality of, 150, 176n. 5, 177n. 11; and the poor, 157, 190, 195–201; portraits of, 16, 117–45; "Progress of Beauty," 196; *Project for the Advancement of Religion,* 153; *Proposal for Correcting . . . the English Tongue,* 37, 113–14, 157, 165; *Proposal for Giving Badges to the Beggars,* 197–98; *Proposal for the Universal Use of Irish Manufacture,* 85, 153, 218, 245, 248, 254; and Presbyterianism, 156; prose style, 156, 172, 201; pseudonymity, 150, 161, 174; *Public Spirit of the Whigs,* 84–85; publicity and public identity, 77, 78, 86, 87, 94, 150–57; raillery, 163, 168, 176n. 8; *Reasons for Repealing the Sacramental Test,* 250–51; reputation, 78, 79, 83, 100, 102, 151–52, 154; scatology, 28, 35, 156, 181; self-representation, 78–94, 151–52, 170–

71, 173, 185; and servants, 184, 201; "sexual anesthesia," supposed, 186; *Short View of the State of Ireland,* 259–60, 261; "Sid Hamet's Rod," 173; silences, 169–71, 172, 261; spectacles, reluctance to wear, 108–9; *Tale of a Tub,* 12, 13, 25–31, 32–38, 41–56, 57–58, 60, 62, 63, 64–70, 82, 152, 153, 156, 161, 256; at Trinity College, 25, 106; "Verses made for Women who cry Apples," 196–97; "Verses on the Death of Dr. Swift," 15, 77–94, 96n. 15, 135, 140, 144, 152, 160–61, 248; and women, 154, 155, 165–66, 174, 181–92, 199–200
Swift, William, 172
symposium (as literary form), 69

taste, 30
Temple, Sir Wiliam, 14, 25, 29, 37, 45, 46, 62, 65, 70, 105, 153, 176n. 8, 231; on ancients and moderns, 27; anti-Irish sentiments, 25, 33; dislike of satire, 26–27, 29; *Miscellanea,* the third part, 50
Temple of Fame, 143
Tenth International Congress on the Enlightenment, 11, 38
Test, George A., 270
Test Act, 30, 250–51, 238
Theobold, Lewis, 80
Thompson, William, 135, 136, 137
Thrale, Henry, 114
Thucydides, 228
Tickell, Thomas, 164
Tighe, Richard, 249–50
Tone, Theobald Wolfe, 225
Tooke, Benjamin, 50
Traugott, John, 25–26, 33
travesty, 90–92
Twain, Mark, 182

Ulster, 31
Ulster Museum, 126
University College Dublin, 11

Valla, Lorenzo, 62, 64; *Elegantiae,* 66
Vanhomrigh, Esther ("Vanessa"), 166, 181, 182, 184, 186–90
Venturo, David, 104
Vertue, George, 129, 135
Virgil, 143

Wade, George, 144
Walpole, Horace, 123, 203
Walpole, Sir Robert, 79, 81, 82, 228, 229, 251
Ward, James, 202
Waring, Jane, 190
Warncke, Wayne, 107
Warner, Marina, 154
Warwick, Earl of, 203
Waterhouse, Ellis, 125
Waters, Edward, 246
weavers, 164–65, 254–55
Weber, Max, 62, 69
West, Robert, 126
Whately, Solomon, 47
White, George, 201–2
Whiteway, Martha, 93, 138
Whitshead, Lord Chief Justice William, 84, 245
Whood, Isaac, 140
William III, 25

Williams, Harold, 103, 121, 144
Wilson, Benjamin, 117, 118, 129, 132, 140, 143
Wilson, Bridget, 126
wit, 25, 26, 28, 34–36, 168
Wolfe, Tom, 277
Wood, William, 84, 236, 251
Woods, Margaret, 183, 188
Woodworth, Mary K., 133
Woolley, James, 83
Woolston, Thomas, 81, 82
Worlidge, Thomas, 129
Wortley, Sir Francis, 143
Wotton, William, 43–44, 51, 54, 62, 65; *Observations upon the* Tale of a Tub, 43–44

Yeats, William Butler, 156, 271
Young Ireland, 225

Zach, Wolfgang, 227, 280
Zincke, Christian Friedrich, 126, 127